MW01073680

CHRISTIANITY AS A WAY OF LIFE

CHRISTIANITY AS A WAY OF LIFE

A Systematic Theology

KEVIN W. HECTOR

Yale

UNIVERSITY PRESS

New Haven & London

Published with assistance from the Louis Stern Memorial Fund.

Copyright © 2023 by Yale University.
All rights reserved.
This book may not be reproduced, in whole or in part, including
illustrations, in any form (beyond that copying permitted by
Sections 107 and 108 of the U.S. Copyright Law and except
by reviewers for the public press), without written permission
from the publishers.

Yale University Press books may be purchased in quantity for
educational, business, or promotional use. For information, please
e-mail sales.press@yale.edu (U.S. office) or sales@yaleup.co.uk
(U.K. office).

Set in Janson type by Integrated Publishing Solutions.
Printed in the United States of America.

Library of Congress Control Number: 2022949572
ISBN 978-0-300-24409-0 (hardcover : alk. paper)

A catalogue record for this book is available from the British Library.

10 9 8 7 6 5 4 3 2 1

To Simeon and Anastasia

Contents

Preface

My life is considerably easier because previous generations have passed their wisdom down to me. They have given me a fairly exhaustive guide, for instance, concerning which plants and animals are edible, just as they have provided all sorts of guidance about how to craft these things into safe, nutritious, and even tasty meals. Absent such guidance, I would surely get sick more often, go hungry more often, and have to spend far more time figuring out what in my environment is—and is not—food. (I do not eat lobster but I am astonished to think of the elaborate trial-and-error process that led to the conclusion that lobsters are edible only if one boils them alive.)

Previous generations have also passed down wisdom about plenty of things other than food: how to avoid conflict, for instance (by taking turns, getting in line, saying sorry, and so on); how to build and fix all sorts of structures (think here of online videos that explain how to do everything from unclogging a sink to building a picnic table); how to judge whether a given belief is true (in light of its epistemic credentials, along with other held-true beliefs that they have passed on); and so on. The influence of such wisdom is pervasive—so pervasive, in fact, that we hardly recognize just how much of our lives is guided by it.

This book makes the case that Christianity is a source of just such wisdom. More specifically, it aims to do two things: on the one hand, to offer a clear, understandable interpretation of Christianity, and, on the other, to highlight some of the wisdom that Christianity, so interpreted, has to offer about how to conduct one's life well in the face of success and failure, of risk and loss, of guilt and shame, of circumstances within and beyond one's control, and of loved ones and hard-to-love ones. One of this book's main arguments, in turn, is that Christianity conveys such wisdom not only through words and teachings, but especially through spiritual practices that train persons to conduct themselves well in these circumstances. I have much more to say about this in the first chapter and, indeed, the rest of the book, but readers should know that this is what I have in mind when I say that Christianity is a way of life.

Before proceeding, I need to offer a handful of clarifications, beginning with a word about this book's intended audience. One of my mentors, Jeffrey Stout, once told me that scholars should try to communicate their ideas in such a way that anyone who is willing to do the work can understand what they are saying; this meant, among other things, that we should strive to use ordinary language and examples to explain what we are saying, and that we should avoid unnecessarily technical vocabulary or unduly complicated points. I have tried to follow that advice here. My hope is that the ideas in this book will therefore be accessible, and perhaps even helpful, not only to scholars but to anyone who is interested in theology or wisdom. To be sure, there are plenty of instances where I do use technical vocabulary and make complicated points, just as there are instances where I fail to embody Stout's ideal, yet I remain hopeful that nonspecialists will readily grasp the book's main ideas. (That said, nonspecialists may want to skip the first chapter, or at least try not to get bogged down by some of its finer points.)

I also need to say a few words about context. It has become customary for authors to begin their books by mentioning a few facts about their social and historical location, though it is not always clear what, exactly, these admissions are meant to achieve. Very often, when white, male, cisgender, educated, Christian, middle-class Americans like me acknowledge these traits, they do so with a vague air of apology, as if to say that they are sorry the world will now have to absorb yet another book from the pen of an already overrepresented group. Then again, sometimes they name these traits and then simply move on, as if it sufficed merely to genuflect at the altar of context.

Needless to say, I find such approaches inadequate. I am indeed a white, male, cisgender, educated, Christian, middle-class American, and awareness of these facts has a significant bearing on the approach I take in this book (and, I hope, in life). Among other things, my social and historical location means that I am constantly tempted not to notice that my perspective is one among many, since so much of the world around me—intellectual and otherwise—has been designed with people like me in mind. In order to resist this temptation, then, I need to cultivate the discipline of considering, and taking seriously, perspectives other than my own; absent this, I will have a much harder time distinguishing between the way things *appear* to me, on the one hand, and the way they actually *are*, on the other. As Sandra Harding has pointed out, the more perspectives our views can account for, the less partial those views will be and, so, the more objective.[1] For each of the topics I treat in this book, therefore, I have tried to consider a broad array of different perspectives: Catholic, reformational, liberal, postliberal, liberation, and contextual, to name just a few of the relevant categories. In each case, my strategy is to try to do justice to both sides of traditionally opposed standpoints and, just so, to hold myself accountable to a maximally wide range of Christian perspectives. I say more about this approach in the first chapter. The point, for now, is that I observe this methodological constraint, in part, because I want to resist the temptation to identify my own, partial viewpoint with the way things are.

This methodological commitment raises a tricky question, however: how can I possibly do justice to all of the historical sources in which these perspectives are represented? After all, these sources can do their job only if they can push back, in all their specificity, against my own perspective, and they can exert this counterforce only if they are allowed to speak for themselves. It would appear, then, that my method requires me to take a properly historical approach to these sources, for it is only by attending to them in their original context that I can be sure that I am not imposing my viewpoint on them.

To see how this standard might be met, it will be helpful to consider a spectrum of approaches to historical sources. (For present purposes, I am focusing only on historical sources that purport to make an *argument*. The importance of this delimitation will become clear in due course.) On one approach, which might be termed *ventriloquizing*, one simply makes a text say what one wants it to say. Such an approach is obviously inadequate for my purposes, not least because a ventriloquized text is unable, in principle, to speak for itself. A second approach, then, is to *strip-mine* ideas and arguments from a text, that is, to treat them as abstract propositions whose goodness or badness swings free from their original context. This may be a defensible way of approaching a text, for insofar as a text purports to advance true or otherwise good ideas and arguments, it stands to reason that their truth is context independent. (The Pythagorean theorem may be a product of its historical context, but its truth-value is not.) Even if this is a defensible way of approaching historical texts, however, it is not a means of ensuring that they can push back against our viewpoint, for the simple reason that they are here situated in *our* context rather than in their own.

Insofar as we interpret an idea or argument in terms of its original context, by contrast, we are taking a *historical* approach to it. At a bare minimum, this means that one strives to understand ideas and arguments in light of the text in which they originally appeared, particularly in light of that text's overall argument or train of thought. This is the baseline of all historical interpretation, for when it comes to a text that makes an argument, the original argument itself is the context within which it must first be interpreted. I return to this point in a moment, but first I need to mention that, from here, one can move in the direction of ever more robust historical interpretation: one can thus understand ideas and arguments not only in terms of the text in which they originally appeared but also in light of an author's entire corpus, and then in light of the broader intellectual history by which the author was shaped and to which they contributed, and then in light of all the nonintellectual factors by which they were influenced. Again, though, the baseline of historical interpretation is met when one makes sense of ideas and arguments within the train of thought of the text in which they originally appeared, and this remains the prerequisite even if one then situates these ideas and arguments within broader historical contexts. To see why, consider how one would make sense of a particular move in a famous game of chess—the sixteenth game of the 1985 world championship, for instance. Even if one wanted to understand each of Garry Kasparov's moves in light of patterns from every game he had ever played, or in light of the history of chess, or in light of contemporaneous developments in Russian culture, the Soviet Union, and the Cold War, one would still have to understand those moves as moves *in this particular game*—as part of an unfolding strategy, as counters to Anatoly Karpov's moves, and so on. Assuming that one knows how chess works, a particular game provides all the context one needs in order to understand each of the moves made within it; it is, as it were, a complete context in its own right.[2] The moves within this particular game thus establish the baseline for any historical interpretation of those moves. I am suggesting something similar for the historical interpretation of ideas and arguments: insofar as these are moves within an overall argument, then the latter not only provides the context within which these ideas must be interpreted, it often (not always) provides an entire interpretive world within which these moves can be located.

For a theological example of all this, consider the Five Ways of Thomas Aquinas. (These are Thomas's five arguments for the existence of God.) Some people turn to these arguments solely for the sake of illustrating whatever larger point they already intend to make—to the effect, say, that Thomas fits God within the framework of human reason, or that he demonstrates the irrationality of atheism; on such an approach, it is obvious that Thomas's own ideas will not be allowed to speak for themselves. Others may be interested in the Five Ways taken by themselves and may thus lift them out of their original context in order to consider how the arguments work, how they might be improved, and so on; in that case, Thomas's arguments get to speak just insofar as they provide inspiration or resources for one's own thinking, since the historical context in which one situates them is decidedly one's own (rather than his). Still others may want to make sure they are letting Thomas's arguments speak for themselves, and thus focus on understanding not only the way these arguments themselves work but also the role they play within the larger argument of which they were originally a part. These people may therefore discover that, in the *Summa Theologiae*, the Five Ways are themselves part of Thomas's overall strategy for moving from talk about God's effects to talk about who God is "in Godself," and they may thus find that the Five Ways are not, in fact, meant to prove God's existence. By interpreting them in light of the overall argument in which they were originally situated, accordingly, one may discover that the Five Ways work much differently than one had assumed. At this point, note well that Thomas's arguments are understood in terms of *his* context, such that Thomas's own train of thought becomes a nonnegotiable factor in one's interpretation. At precisely this point, then, properly historical interpretation begins. From here, one can add several additional layers of historical context, including the wider context of Thomas's work and the broader social and intellectual context by which he was shaped; but notice that one can situate the Five Ways in these contexts only if one understands them in light of the larger argument in which they first appeared. (The fact that Thomas uses the Five Ways very differently in the context of his *Summa contra Gentiles* should help us see this point clearly.) Here again, then, the key idea is simply that if one wants to understand the ideas and arguments of a historical figure, one may and must interpret those ideas and arguments in light of the text in which they originally appeared.

That brings us back to the point with which we began: my own historical context may tempt me to take my perspective for granted and thus to draw generalizations directly from it. In order to resist this temptation, it is vital that I take a wide variety of other perspectives into account; that way, my own perspective can be kept from curving in on itself and, as a bonus, can be enriched by the insights and challenges brought by those perspectives. To take these into account as independent perspectives, however, and not just assimilate them to my own perspective, it is crucial that they be able to speak for themselves; this means, at the very least, that I must interpret their ideas and arguments in terms of their own context, which means, in turn, that I must understand them in light of their own trains of thought, animating concerns, and the like.

One further comment about context. I have received a lot of help in writing this book. I was given the opportunity to present some of this material in a variety of churches, including my own, and have always been given both a warm welcome and perceptive feedback. My colleagues and students at the University of Chicago have been an endless source of encouragement, insight, and supportive critique; I am particularly grateful to Liz Brocious, Olivia Bustion, Jason Cather, Ryan Coyne, Kristine Culp, Arnold Davidson, Michael Fishbane, Lisa Landoe Hedrick, Dwight Hopkins, Russell Johnson, Hannah Jones, Elsa Marty, Joseph Morrison, Willemien Otten, Mahala Rethlake, Rick Rosengarten, Izak Santana, William Schweiker, and Luke Soderstrom. I am similarly grateful for supportive colleagues outside Chicago, including Neil Arner, David DeCosimo, Paul DeHart, Tarick Elgendy, Keith Johnson, Terrence Johnson, Tamsin Jones, Mitch Kim, Charles Mathewes, Fred Simmons, Meghan Sullivan, Jonathan Tran, Daniel Treier, and Andrea White.

I had the chance to present versions of several chapters to keen, generous audiences; here I am particularly grateful for the hospitality of the Wheaton Department of Philosophy, especially James Gordon; of Fuller Seminary, especially Oliver Crisp, James Arcadi, and Jordan Wessling; of Georgetown, especially Terrence Johnson, Julia Lamm, and Michael Slater; of the Collegium Emmaus at the University of Fribourg, especially Christophe Chalamet, Walter Dürr, and Oliver Dürr; and of Yale Divinity School, especially Adam Eitel, Jennifer Herdt, Kathryn Tanner, and Linn Tonstad. The Yale Center for Faith and Culture—especially Matthew Croasmun, Janna Gonwa, Angela Gorrell, Ryan McAnnally-Linz, and Miroslav Volf—deserve special thanks for their endless encouragement of and thoughtful engagement with my work, not to mention a grant that provided me with some additional time to do it.

I am truly grateful, too, to Jennifer Banks, Heather Gold, Abbie Storch, and the entire editorial team at Yale University Press for their consummate professionalism, their commitment to making this book the best it can be, and for their willingness to take on (and root for) this project. I am likewise thankful for the Press's anonymous reviewers, each of whom was a model of careful, generous reading; their critiques and insights have made this book much better than it would otherwise be.

I am grateful, finally, to (and for) my family. Being married to Krista makes every day feel like a gift. She has also done more than anyone to broaden—and hold open—my perspective. Needless to say, this book, and everything else in my life, would be far worse without her constant presence.

That brings me to my two children, Simeon and Anastasia. When I began writing this book—and promised that I would dedicate it to them— they were little kids. Seeing them grow up over the past several years has been a blessing, especially because I genuinely admire the character they have each been cultivating over those years. The world is better because they are part of it, and my world immeasurably so. It feels like an honor to be their father, so it is likewise an honor to dedicate this book to them.

Sections of two chapters have appeared in print elsewhere: "Eternal Fulfillment? Some Thoughts on the Afterlife," *Journal of Religion* 101:1 (January 2021), 8–26, © 2021 by the University of Chicago; and "Kenosis as a Spiritual Practice," in *Kenosis: The Self-Emptying of Christ in Scripture and Theology*, edited by Paul Nimmo and Keith Johnson (Grand Rapids: Eerdmans, 2022), 309–22. I wrote both of these pieces with this book in mind, so I am grateful for permission to reproduce some of this material here.

As I developed models for understanding various topics in this book, I sometimes discovered that I had already worked out elements of such models elsewhere. I have therefore borrowed bits and pieces from previous work; such borrowings are identified as such in the footnotes.

CHRISTIANITY AS A WAY OF LIFE

CHAPTER ONE

The Good of Theology

D UE TO THEIR TRAINING, some people can perceive things that most of us would not. Many airport security personnel, for instance, have been trained to spot subtle, suspicious cues in a person's body language, just as copy editors have learned to notice all sorts of subtle grammatical and spelling mistakes, musicians to hear a lone discordant note in an orchestral performance, and chicken-sexers to detect whether a baby chick is male or female. In most of these cases, someone so trained cannot help but perceive these things; hence expert copy editors are likely to spot errors in someone's writing even when they would rather not, as when reading a note from a loved one.

Some persons have likewise been trained to *do* things that most people cannot: accomplished athletes and musicians belong in this category, of course, but so do knitters, cooks, carpenters, programmers, nurses, and anyone else who has mastered a particular skill. Within this group, some have trained themselves not only to do certain things but, when the moment arrives, to be almost incapable of *not* doing them. First responders, for example, as well as some especially virtuous persons, have trained themselves to help others even if it means putting themselves in serious danger, whereas habitual liars cannot help but lie if doing so might get them out of trouble, those accustomed to putting themselves ahead of others cannot help but do so, and so on. Some persons have thus been trained to *perceive* things in certain ways, some to *act* in certain ways, and some to be the sort of person who *cannot help* but perceive or act in certain ways.

Persons sometimes undergo such training for the sake of their liveli-hood, or because it was part of their upbringing, or for no reason at all. But there are some persons who undergo it precisely because they want to change the way they perceive and live in the world and, so, to become a different sort of person—the sort of person who cannot help but perceive and live this way. Insofar as they do so by engaging in a more or less uni-fied set of practices designed to bring about such a change, they adhere to what I would call *a way of life*.

In this book, I argue that we can understand Christianity as a way of life in just this sense, namely, a set of practices designed to transform one's way of perceiving and being in the world. I defend this claim by looking at three broad sets of practices, beginning with practices that aim to reorient persons to God; here I focus on imitation (both the garden-variety sort and the sort triggered by admiration), corporate singing, commensality, friendship, and working to become like-minded with others. The aim of such practices, simply stated, is to bring the lives of Christians more and more into conformity with their most fundamental commitment, namely, to devote themselves increasingly—intensively and extensively—to God.

I then turn to a set of practices designed to transform one's way of being in the world, such that one's relation to life circumstances would itself be oriented to God: here I consider prayer as a practice that trans-forms our relation to things we care about, primarily insofar as it positions us to experience their goodness and well-being as a gift; wonder as a prac-tice that trains us to appreciate the goodness of creatures in all their oth-erness; laughter as a practice that does not take the world as seriously as it takes itself, and that thereby undercuts the latter's would-be ultimacy; lament as a practice that enables persons to express their suffering and to "hold themselves together" in the face of it; and finally vocation as a practice that helps persons experience the particularities of their lives as good, and their lives themselves as hanging together in a potentially satisfying way.

Finally, I look at a series of practices that transform one's way of being with others—practices, that is, that cultivate an increasingly loving dispo-sition toward others (where "love" means that I care about others for their own sake, that I therefore have good reason to seek their good, and that I appreciate what is good about them). One way of cultivating love, accord-ingly, is through acts of beneficence—that is, acts wherein we seek others' good even if we do not yet do so on the basis of a caring, first-personal in-vestment in their well-being. The idea here—familiar to sports gamblers everywhere—is that by investing in another's good, we become more disposed to care about whether things turn out well for that person. By practicing beneficence, then, we may come increasingly to care about the well-being of others. Another such practice is "looking for the image of God," where this means that we strive to see others not as opponents or as instances of stereotypes or in a negative light but as having a particularity and integrity and goodness of their own. The relevant metaphor is the hermeneutical circle: we can make sense of a text's parts only by construing them in light of a whole, but we must continually reconsider our sense of the whole by attending carefully to the parts. "The image of God" here plays the role of "the whole" in light of which particular persons are understood, even as our notions of "the image" must be continually revised in light of those persons. A third love-cultivating practice is forgiveness, by which I mean the setting aside of our desire for vengeance upon a wrong-doer. (This is distinct, note well, from releasing persons from punishment, on the one hand, and not counting their wrongdoing against their character, on the other.) Forgiveness can play an important role in enabling us to love others, for if (a) benevolence is an essential ingredient in love and (b) a desire for vengeance means that we want bad things for someone, then it follows (c) that insofar as we desire vengeance upon someone, we cannot fully love that person; it would appear, then, (d) that in such a situation, love depends upon getting past our desire for vengeance, and forgiveness is a significant means of doing so.

So, then, three sets of practices: practices of being reoriented, of being in the world, and of being with others. Taken together, the aim of these practices is to transform not only one's way of perceiving and acting but one's very self. This is what I have in mind, in sum, when I claim that Christianity is *a way of life*. To understand *Christianity* as a way of life, however, we need to understand more than just these practices. We also need to situate these practices, and so understand them, in light of several other aspects of Christianity, particularly its ideas about the "old," sinful way of life by which persons have already been formed; what Jesus does to free persons from this old life; the putting to death of one's old, misoriented self; and the fulfillment—eternal life—to which Christianity's way of life orients one. To make sense of Christianity as a way of life thus turns out to require a systematic theology, albeit one of an unusual sort.

We can understand theology itself as a practice designed to transform our way of perceiving and being in the world, but in my academic context, at least, this would raise an obvious question: if theology is part of a specifically Christian way of life, does it have any place in a secular academic enterprise? This chapter addresses this question by considering the good of theology—the good at which it aims, and the good that it can contribute both to Christianity and to the secular academy. The strategy of this chapter, then, is to begin by observing theology in its native habitat, as it were, as part of a *way of life* that aims to bring persons' lives into greater conformity with their *devotion*. (These sections do double duty, since the categories "devotion" and "way of life" are central to the entire project.) This approach will position us to see two of the goods that theology might contribute to the life of faith and to the secular university, namely, *understanding* and *wisdom*.

Devotion

To get a sense of what theology looks like in its natural habitat, we begin with the concept of devotion. In the broadest sense of the term, devotion is a matter of setting something aside for the sake of, or dedicating it to, some purpose. We might say, accordingly, that certain lands have been devoted to public use, that a portion of my monthly paycheck is devoted to retirement savings, and that a dedicated server is devoted to certain computing functions. In each case, the phrase "devoted to" could be replaced, without loss of meaning, with the phrase "set aside for." Humans, too, can be devoted in this broad sense, as when a country devotes a certain number of soldiers to the protection of humanitarian aid, or when a corporation devotes a weekend of its employees' lives to "team building." Importantly for my purposes, however, there is also a narrower, more distinctively human sense of "devotion," where (a) that which is set aside is my very life or self (or a significant portion thereof), (b) I am the one who sets it aside, and (c) I set it aside for the sake of something I value. This is the notion of devotion that I want to get a grip on here.

Toward that end, it will be helpful to begin with the notion of *value*.[1] As I understand it, to value something is for that thing to matter or be important to us—and for us to take it to be worthy of so mattering—where such mattering means, in turn, that the thing occupies a particular place within our evaluative perspective, especially in connection with our emotion, motivation, reasoning, and perception.[2] So consider, first, that in valuing something, we render ourselves liable to certain *emotions* concerning that thing; hence, if I value the nonhuman environment, then I am liable to feel anger or sadness in the face of that which harms the environment, contempt for those who perpetrate such harms, guilt or shame insofar as I contribute harms of my own, and so on. Our emotions can thus be understood as felt evaluations or embodied appraisals of that which is going on around (and within) us, since, in valuing something, we come to have an emotional stake or investment in its well-being.

There is a similar connection between value and *motivation*, in the sense that valuing something gives us reason to do certain things and to leave other things undone. Again, if I value the nonhuman environment, this may give me reason to use public transportation, to reduce inefficiencies in my consumption of energy and consumer products, to donate money to environmental organizations, and the like. Hence, what we value can not only give shape to our emotions but also, by giving us reason to act in certain ways, shape our motivations and thus our actions. In some cases, too, what we value can give us reason not just to act in certain ways but to become a certain kind of *person* or cultivate a certain *character*; someone who values the nonhuman environment may thus have reason to work at becoming a simpler, less selfish sort of person, or one more attentive to the mundane realities of life. These two kinds of motivation can be mutually reinforcing, in the sense that acting in certain ways can shape our character over time, just as having a certain character will increase the likelihood that we will actually act according to our value-based reasons. Not all values shape our character in this way, however, nor even give us reason so to shape it; persons who value an annual family reunion, for example, will surely have reason to do certain things in connection with the reunion— make plans, research new games for everyone to play, buy food, and so on—but will have reason to cultivate a particular sort of character only if their character is currently at odds with their valuing of the reunion. Hence, persons who value reunions but whose disorganization perpetually gets in the way of their attendance at, or full enjoyment of, the reunion may thus have reason to work on their character, whereas someone who values reunions and whose character does not cause such problems would not have reason to do so. It would appear, then, that valuing *necessarily* gives us reason to do certain things (and leave others undone), and *may* give us reason to cultivate a certain character.

Valuing can also shape our *cognition*, in at least two senses. On the one hand, what we value can affect what is *salient* to us, with respect both to what we perceive and to what we pay attention to. With respect to the former, it is important to point out that at any given moment there are innumerable phenomena going on around (and within) us, such that perceiving any of them is necessarily a selective affair. Our values can play a role in such selection: so, for instance, someone who values the nonhuman environment may be intensely aware of certain sounds—the sound of a far-away leaf blower, say, or an idling engine—whereas most other persons would not even notice them. (In the same way, I used to be intensely aware of noise when my young children were sleeping, such that I could not help but notice every creak of the floor, every clink of silverware, every click of a door handle, and so on, whereas late-staying guests, for instance, usually—understandably!—did not.) Valuing can thereby play a role in rendering certain phenomena salient to us, and thus in shaping what we perceive. Values can likewise play a role in what we pay attention to, what we spend time thinking about, and, in short, what we take to be a worthwhile use of our limited cognitive resources. So, again, someone who values the non-human environment may think it is worthwhile to spend time learning about ice shelves, deforestation, species-specific migratory patterns, and the like, and to consider the most adequate solutions to problems connected with these topics, whereas someone who does not value the environment may think all of this would be a waste of their time. (For precisely this reason, teachers of introductory classes often spend time trying to convince students that their course content matters.) In this respect, too, our values can play a role in determining what is salient to us, such that, again, valuing turns out to have cognitive ramifications.

Valuing may also have ramifications for *theoretical reasoning* itself, though the connection here is looser than that with salience. As is well known, inferences are seldom strictly determined by evidence, premises, and the like, such that here, too, our values can make a cognitive difference. To take one obvious example, someone who values the nonhuman environment may be likelier to judge that certain data (and certain sources of data) are trustworthy and, on their basis, to infer that climate change is real, drastic, and so forth, whereas someone who values a carbon-intensive lifestyle may be less inclined to accept these data as trustworthy or as warranting a high degree of confidence in such inferences. In this respect, too, what we value can have an effect on cognition, though again there seems to be a stronger connection between valuing and salience—someone who values something should notice that which affects that thing—than between valuing and reasoning, since a person's values imply no comparable "should" with respect to theoretical inferences.

All of these points deserve further elaboration, but for now we can say, very roughly, that if we value something, this will (a) render us susceptible to certain emotions, (b) give us reason to act in certain ways and, perhaps, to cultivate a certain character, and (c) render certain phenomena salient to us and, perhaps, influence our reasoning.

These features of valuing will help us make sense of devotion, but three clarifications are in order. First, it is important to point out that believing that something is valuable is not a sufficient condition of actually valuing that thing; I believe that theoretical physics and get-out-the-vote efforts are worthy of being valued, for instance, but I myself do not value them. Second, although valuing is sometimes more or less equated with desire, this is a mistake. On the one hand, I can value something without desiring it: I may value justice, for instance, but not desire justice if, say, I am caught stealing, just as I can value someone's writing style (Kate Sonderregger's, for example) without *wanting* that style. On the other hand, I can desire something without valuing it: for example, I may still desire certain things even after I have renounced their value to me (think here of the desires of a recovering addict), or I may find myself wanting things I do not value simply because I am influenced by the desires of others, or I may want certain things that are not actually important to me (to see what is on TV, say, or to match all the socks in the laundry basket).

A third clarification, especially significant for our purposes, is that valuing should be distinguished from devotion, since the former is a necessary, but not sufficient, condition of the latter. On the one hand, I cannot be devoted to something that I do not value, at least not in the distinctively human sense of devotion. To be sure, someone might plausibly say something like "I no longer value the career for which I am training, but I've come too far to give up now, so I have no choice but to devote myself to my studies so I can finish my degree as soon as possible." It is conceivable, then, that persons could devote themselves to that which they do not value, but in this kind of case devotion is more akin to the military devoting troops to the protection of a convoy than like persons devoting their life to some purpose in the distinctively human sense of the term, since, again, a person's own valuing is a necessary condition of devotion in the latter sense. Crucially, though, it is not a sufficient condition, since persons are not necessarily devoted to everything that they value. I value local business and triennial family reunions, for example, but it would be a stretch to say that I am *devoted* to these things, for the simple reason that they do not play a very large role in my life: if family reunions give shape to my life only every three years, for instance, or if my commitment to local businesses makes a difference in my life only when I happen (as infrequently as possible) to go to the store, then even though I value these things, I would not say that I am devoted to them. We can arrive at the same point from a slightly different angle: if I value something but its value to me could easily be trumped by several things that I value more—if the value does not hold a certain *priority* among my values, in other words—then it would appear, once again, that although I value that thing, I am not devoted to it. To be sure, there may be cases where we are forced to choose between two or more objects of genuine devotion, in which case the mere fact of choosing one over the other would not indicate that we are not actually devoted to the latter; hence pastors may be devoted both to their family and to their ministry, and may thus have to choose, for instance, between attending a child's dance recital and officiating at a wedding. Having to make such choices does not imply a lack of devotion to either of the two objects. There are many other cases, however, in which our willingness to choose one value over another does indicate that we are not devoted to that value: so persons may genuinely value their relationships with particular friends, but if they regularly put their family, career, hobbies, and other relationships ahead of these relationships, they would surely not count as *devoted* friends, since the friendship would not then rank highly enough among their values. It would appear, therefore, that what matters in devotion is not just that I value something but that the value plays a particular kind of role in my life, namely, that it is significant in my life both *extensively* (that is, a significant portion of my life is actually oriented to that value) and *intensively* (that is, I prioritize that value or value it more highly than other things).

That brings us to a key component of devotion: to be devoted to something is not only to value that thing but also to set aside a significant portion of one's life for its sake, paradigmatically by *orienting* a significant portion of one's life to it.[3] If I am devoted to something, that is to say, my valuing of it will give shape to or put its stamp on my life. Hence, if someone is devoted to becoming an Olympic champion, they will plan their daily routines around practices and competitions; will spend time thinking about their sport and how to improve at it; will have reason to eat certain foods at certain times; will become attentive to certain phenomena that might otherwise go unnoticed, such as mild soreness in their little toe; and will be susceptible to feeling joy if they improve upon their personal best, guilt over a lapse in their dietary regimen, and so forth. To be devoted, accordingly, is not merely to value something but for that value to influence one's actions, emotions, perceptions, thoughts, and the like, and for that value thereby to impress itself on or give shape to one's life.

To be devoted is also to value that value's place among our values and, so, to value the value itself. Someone who is devoted to something will thus be susceptible to a range of emotions concerning not only the valued object but the person's very valuing of it; devoted teachers may thus worry about becoming less devoted to teaching ("burning out"), may feel contempt for teachers who are not similarly devoted, may feel guilty whenever they put something else ahead of teaching, and so on. Our devotion will similarly give us reason to do certain things related to our devotion itself: to surround ourselves with persons who reinforce that devotion, for instance, to pay careful attention to the state of our devotion, to cultivate the sort of character it would take to maintain that devotion over the long haul, and so on. In these ways, my devotion to a particular value will itself be something to which I am devoted, such that that value will be significant in my life not only extensively but intensively as well. (This is one reason devotion is almost always diachronically stable, since being intensely devoted to something seems to entail building up a kind of voluntary recalcitrance concerning its place in my life, which explains, in turn, why devotion likewise tends to have a "through thick or thin" quality.)

Much more could be said about devotion, but for present purposes this should suffice: roughly, to be devoted to something is (a) for my valuing of that thing to give shape and orientation to my emotions, motivations, and cognitions, and, therefore, to my life, and (b) for me to value this valuing itself, such that this, too, gives shape and orientation to my life. Ideally, then, the life of one who is devoted should be like a solar system in which everything orbits around and is held in place by the gravitational pull of a single sun.

This may be much more easily said than done, however, for in real life, the mere fact that persons have *decided* or *want* to devote their entire lives to something does not entail that their lives will *be* so devoted. For one thing, persons are not transparent to themselves, such that large swaths of their lives may escape their attention and thus escape their efforts to shape and orient them. More important, persons who so decide are usually not starting from scratch, so to speak, but have already been habituated into seeing, feeling, and doing things in ways that may be at odds with their devotion, and these habits can be extremely difficult to break—far too difficult, in most cases, to be broken merely by a decision. Basketball players who have bad shooting form, for instance, may sincerely want to change that form—indeed, it is not uncommon for them to pay trainers a lot of money to try to bring this about—but in many cases, it is too late: they have already become so accustomed to shooting in a particular way that their form has become all but inalterable. Likewise, at the beginning of every school year during my childhood, I earnestly resolved not to talk so much, but the resolution never ended up transforming my behavior, for the simple reason that I had already become the sort of kid who talked too much. In much the same way, persons who want to devote their entire lives to a particular value may already have been habituated into judging, feeling, and acting according to other values; if so, then if they want to bring their lives into conformity with their devotion, they will obviously have to transform these habits. That brings us to our next topic, "ways of life."

Ways of Life

By a *way of life*, I mean a constellation of practices designed to orient a person's life toward that which is taken to be ultimate—ultimately true, ultimately good, or ultimately important—especially where these practices are opposed to, and so meant to lift them out of, the taken-for-granted, misdirected ways of life that orient persons to half-truths and penultimate goods. Here I am building on insights from Pierre Hadot, who famously used this notion to interpret ancient philosophical schools; in Hadot's telling, these schools prescribed various spiritual exercises, chief among which was the practice of meditation on handy rules that would help persons to perceive the truth and act accordingly, so that, "just as by dint of repeated physical exercises athletes give new form and strength to their bodies, so the philosopher develops his strength of soul, modifies his inner climate, transforms his vision of the world, and, finally, transforms his entire being."[4] As Hadot sees it, then, a way of life is a set of spiritual practices designed to orient us to that which is really true, is really good, and really matters—and, since we have already been oriented otherwise by everyday life, to transform our lives themselves.

Hadot's account is helpful here, but before proceeding I should register one point where I differ from him: whereas Hadot tends to reserve the title "way of life" for spiritual practices intentionally undertaken for the sake of transforming our way of seeing and being in the world, I would apply it more liberally, since everyday, taken-for-granted life can likewise be understood in terms of practices that orient persons to that which is taken to be ultimately true and good; so, to take just one example, consumerism can be understood as a way of life in which practices of marketing, status conferral, conspicuous consumption, and the like habituate us to treating material goods as if they were what finally matters. As I use the term, accordingly, all ways of life are composed of practices that orient us to that which is taken to be true, good, or important, but not all are practiced for the sake of intentionally *transforming* our orientation.

To explain further what I mean by a way of life, it will be helpful to consider two examples, the first of which comes from *Sacred Attunement*, Michael Fishbane's important recent interpretation of Judaism.[5] Fishbane's account begins by claiming that everyday life—the taken-for-granted way that persons conduct their lives—involves going along with tried-and-true customs, and doing so because these customs give us a reassuring sense that the world is rooted in something dependable. There can be a danger in following such customs, however, for in addition to providing us with a secure, dependable way of coping with this world, they may also orient us to a this-worldly end, and, so, to a life oriented by worldly cares and worldly satisfactions.

Fishbane portrays Judaism, in turn, as a "covenant life" in which we receive all that is as a gift, bring our lives into conformity with such gift giving, and, just so, break out of the worldly horizon of everyday life. He claims, accordingly, that we must learn to no longer take the world around us for granted but to perceive it as a gift; this is accomplished, on Fishbane's account, by engaging in a set of reading practices that discipline our attention to the biblical text and, in consequence, discipline our way of attending to the wider world. More specifically, these practices train us to pay painstaking attention to the text's details; to see covenant-shaped patterns in these details; to probe beneath the text's surface in order to see its deeper truths; and, through reading, to become so attuned to the text that we become increasingly one with it. By learning to attend in these ways to the biblical text, Fishbane claims, we simultaneously learn to attend in these ways to the world around us; our attention is thus increasingly attuned to God even in the midst of everyday life, and we are thereby trained to perceive all that is as a gift and to hear in this a call to conform our lives to God's giving. The paradigmatic expression of such conformity is what Fishbane terms "radical kindness," or *hesed*, in which our lives manifest God's giving just to the extent that we entrust ourselves to it, embody this sort of giving in our relationship to others, and, in so doing, turn our back on the prudent, this-worldly calculations by which customary life is governed. On Fishbane's account, then, certain reading practices can transform our perception of the world, enabling us to see it more and more in light of God as giver, and this transformation should lead us not only to feel gratitude for this fact but also to embody such gift giving in the way we treat others. His account thus illustrates what I have been saying about ways of life, for as he sees it, Judaism is a set of spiritual practices designed to transform our ways of attending to and acting in the world and, just so, reorient us to what ultimately matters.

We see a similar pattern in Stephen Batchelor's influential interpretation of Buddhism, *Alone with Others*.[6] Like Fishbane, Batchelor begins with an account of our taken-for-granted, everyday way of life, which he terms the way of "having." His idea here, simply stated, is that we have a hard time facing the fact that we cannot ultimately hold on to that which we care about, so we pretend that this is not really true; we thus live as though everything is not finally impermanent and as though we could secure such permanence if only we kept a tight enough grip on things. As Batchelor sees it, then, our everyday lives are focused on securing that which we care about, and they are so focused because we cannot bear the fact that all things finally pass away.

That brings us to Buddhism, which Batchelor portrays as a way of life designed to help us face up to such impermanence. The key here is to transform our very perception of the world: through meditation, we come to an ever-broadening realization that nothing in the world—including us—is permanent and, positively, that this is because everything in the world is profoundly dependent on everything else. We should thus come to see the world as it is—impermanent and interdependent—which should free us, in turn, from the root cause of anxiety, for if we no longer have any illusions about self-sufficiency, about what could provide lasting satisfaction, and so forth, we will no longer feel anxious about the fact that the world may not conform to these illusions or feel distress when it fails to do so.

This transformation of perception should lead, in turn, to a transformed way of treating others. The first step in this transformation follows naturally from the foregoing, for the transformation of our perception applies to other persons, too: when it comes to other persons, this means learning to see the world from their perspective, which will lead us to see them, too, as interdependent with everything else, as lacking self-sufficiency, and therefore as anxious about their security. That brings us to Batchelor's second step: once we have perceived ourselves and others as bound together in a fabric of interdependence, we must be just as concerned for them as we are for ourselves; hence, we should perceive our interdependence with them as an opportunity to promote their flourishing. The final step, then, is to realize that the greatest need of others is to be relieved of their anxiety, such that the best thing we can do for them is to show them how they might be released from it; in this light, our own quest for peace takes on a different orientation, for we are now concerned not (only) with our own fulfillment but with achieving fulfillment precisely for the sake of sharing it with others. We become so freed from "having," in other words, and so concerned with the well-being of others, that we pursue the path of peace precisely for *their* sake.

Batchelor understands Buddhism, accordingly, as a set of practices designed to orient us to that which is ultimately true—namely, the impermanence and interrelatedness of all that is—by transforming our way of perceiving and being in the world, and, in turn, freeing us from a taken-for-granted orientation in which we try to resist impermanence by tightening our grip on the things that matter to us. Both Fishbane's and Batchelor's accounts thus nicely illustrate what I am calling intentionally transformative, comprehensive ways of life, in which spiritual practices transform our way of perceiving and being in the world so as to orient us to what is ultimately true, good, and important, while simultaneously freeing us from an everyday way of life that orients us to penultimate goods, half-truths, and trivialities.

With this account on board, we are now in position to see what theology looks like in its native habitat, since we can understand theology as just such a spiritual practice. To cut right to the chase, we might put the point this way: insofar as persons are devoted to something, they intend for their lives to be oriented by that devotion, and in so intending they obligate themselves to make judgments about the extent to which their lives actually are so oriented, what it would look like if they were, and so on, and the practice of making such judgments—especially when undertaken reflectively—is what theology looks like in its most basic form. This is what we see the apostle Paul doing, for instance, when he judges whether Christians can eat meat sacrificed to idols, or whether Gentile Christians must convert to Judaism; it is what Augustine is doing when he responds to parishioners' inquiries about, say, chastity, and when he tries to make sense of the church's relationship to pagan culture; it is what Thomas Aquinas is doing when he composes a manual to help his brothers see how all things, including themselves, proceed from and return to God; and it is what Rosemary Radford Ruether is doing when she assesses the extent to which Christianity supports, or is at least compatible with, the flourishing of women. Almost everyone would recognize these as instances of "theology," but they are of a piece with what laypersons do when they keep journals or reflect on what a passage of scripture means for their lives, when parents try to help their children think faithfully about how to handle schoolyard bullying, when citizens reflect on whether a particular government policy is consistent with their beliefs, when religiously minded teenagers try to discern their vocation, and so on. These are all instances of theology in the broad—and, I would argue, most basic—sense of the term, which denotes the practice of making judgments about how our beliefs, emotions, actions, and so on are and ought to be related to our devotion. So construed, theology is a practice that aims to bring our lives into greater conformity with our devotion, and thus qualifies as a spiritual practice of just the sort we have been discussing.

If this is even roughly correct, then it is plainly a mistake to say—as many of my colleagues in religious studies do say—that there is something inherently (and so worrisomely) "Christian" about the discipline of theology. For if I am right, then theology is a more or less natural outgrowth of, and indeed a natural ingredient in, all human devotion. The reason for this is simple: insofar as persons are devoted to something, they are committed to bringing their lives into line with that devotion; in most cases, persons so committed thereby obligate themselves to make judgments about the extent to which their lives are actually so aligned; and these judgments will often, if not always, take the reflective form characteristic of theology. There are exceptions, of course: if the object of my devotion were, say, a principle according to which "whatever is, is right," then my devotion would not thereby obligate me to make any judgments. But this is surely the exception; in most cases, devotion itself will obligate persons to make at least some reflective judgments, from which it follows that theology is not an inherently Christian discipline.

That brings me to a crucial point, however: namely, that theology, so understood, seems to be *exactly* the sort of thing that people in religious studies would want to distance their discipline from, for as they see it, the academic study of religion must be a critical, objective affair, rather than one that is in service of or otherwise devoted to religion; indeed, they would argue that religious studies is a properly academic discipline precisely insofar as it is independent of any such devotional aims. No wonder, then, that many of my colleagues in religious studies would worry about "theology," for on the account I have given of it thus far, it appears to be just what they have long accused it of being (and what their own discipline is duty bound to resist), namely, an expression of devotion, and ipso facto not an *academic* discipline. As they see it, therefore, the practice of theology has as much place in academic inquiry as the singing of hymns or the praying of prayers—which is to say, no place whatsoever.

I would make two points in response to this objection. First, not all theology is of the "devotional" sort I have been discussing thus far. Much theology, for instance—including mine—can be understood as a kind of second-order reflection on such first-order, devotional theologies; this is what Friedrich Schleiermacher has in mind when he claims that theology is "the discipline which systematizes the doctrine prevalent in a Christian Church at a given time" and that doctrines, in turn, are "accounts of the Christian pious disposition-states portrayed in speech."[7] We see something similar in postliberal theology, which, as Kathryn Tanner explains it, "does not appear to engage in Christian social practice in the full-blooded sense of, say, first-order theology where affirmations are made and life is actually experienced in Christian terms. In its capacity as a second-order exercise," rather, "academic theology seems merely to talk about such practices—about those affirmations, about that way of living."[8] Not all theology is of the first-order, devotional sort, accordingly, such that not all that goes by that name is straightforwardly liable to the objection we are considering.[9]

A second, more fundamental point is that what should really matter here, arguably, is not whether practitioners of a given discipline are personally invested in their subject matter but whether they produce epistemic goods that are recognizable as such even to those who are not so invested. The argument here, that is to say, is that the proper aim of academic inquiry is not to distance oneself from devotion but to produce epistemic goods such as knowledge and understanding; after all, someone who made up false accounts of various phenomena would not count as a scholar, irrespective of how thoroughgoingly devotionless these accounts were. Importantly, though, to count as a contribution to academic inquiry these epistemic goods must be recognizable as such even to the non-devoted, which is to say that one's arguments must be recognizable as valid even to them, one's methods recognizable as sound even to them, one's evidence recognizable as compelling even to them, and so on. Insofar as this is the case, scholars who are devoted to their subject matter may produce epistemic goods that are recognizable as such even to the non-devoted; their colleagues in religious studies might then think of them as *accidentally* devoted to that subject matter, since, from their standpoint, the epistemic goods that they produce swing free from that devotion. If so, then insofar as theology produces epistemic goods that are recognizable as such even to those who are not devoted to its subject matter, it counts as an academic discipline and should be recognized as such even within religious studies. In the next section, I argue that theology—and this book—produce just such a good, namely, *understanding*.

Understanding

"Understanding" may mean a variety of things, but as I use the term here, understanding is, roughly, a matter of perceiving a particular sort of pattern among phenomena. Consider some examples: I understand how an engine works insofar as I see how its parts interact to produce certain effects; I understand a story insofar as I see certain events as part of a plot; I understand why someone was elected to the presidency insofar as I see how various causes worked together to make that happen; I understand a person's behavior insofar as I have a sense of the character underlying it; I understand an argument insofar as I can see its would-be logical progression from one step to the next. In each case, to understand these phenomena is to see particular patterns among them; indeed, "work together," "plot," "causes," "character," and "logical progression" are each a name for a pattern that can help us relate phenomena to one another in an orderly way and, just so, make sense of them.

These are not the only sorts of things we understand, however; we also understand things like individual words and concepts. So what might it mean to understand a concept such as "indignation"? As I have argued elsewhere, to understand a concept is—at the very least—to see it as appropriate for application in certain circumstances and not others: in the case of indignation, it is applicable when one is bothered at having been disrespected or treated in a way that seems beneath one but not when one either is not bothered or is bothered by some other sort of circumstance.[10] (In many cases, we must also understand what follows from a concept's application—in the case of indignation, that it may now be permissible for a person to speak in an angry tone, to seek redress, and the like—but we will set this aside for now.) Here too, then, understanding turns out to be a matter of spotting a pattern, for we understand a concept like indignation only if we see a pattern in the circumstances in which it is rightly applied; indeed, the concept "indignation" is just a name for that pattern. Once armed with this concept, accordingly, we can use it to spot that pattern in various circumstances and thus make sense of them; hence if I observe someone responding to rude comments by turning around and walking away in a huff, I can understand that response by seeing it as an instance of a pattern named "indignation." In this kind of case, too, then, to understand something is to see it as following a pattern.

This is not to suggest that understanding is strictly identical with such pattern identification, however. For one thing, there are cases where understanding requires something more than that: if I say something like "I understand what you're going through right now," the implication is that not only have I identified a pattern of, say, grief in someone's feelings and behaviors, I myself have had this experience. It is important to note, then, that I am using the term "understanding" in the more bare-bones, pattern-identifying sense, and that this does not cover all of the term's relevant uses. It is also important to note—more important, for my purposes—that we can perceive a pattern among phenomena but still not understand them, since the pattern we identify may not actually explain anything; so, for instance, if the pattern a scientist identifies is simply that certain phenomena are correlated with others—rather than, say, causally related to them—then that pattern has not helped us understand those phenomena. Then again, even if we identify a pattern that actually does explain something, we may still not count it as understanding the phenomena in question, insofar as the features covered by the pattern are either peripheral to the overall phenomenon or too small a subset thereof. I may thus identify a pattern that actually explains certain voting trends in the 2016 election, but if that pattern makes sense only of a small subset of voters, or a small component of the overall trends, then it would be a mistake to think that I thereby understand the larger phenomena themselves. To count as understanding something, then, we must identify patterns that cover a significant range of significant phenomena and that actually explain these phenomena.[11]

This account explains why we often experience a satisfying sense of simplicity once we come to understand something: whereas a complex phenomenon had appeared to us as a confusing jumble—"I couldn't wrap my head around it"—once we have understood it, we see order among its various components and, so, no longer perceive them as hopelessly jumbled together. Think here of a technophobe who wants to install a new graphics card on a computer. Upon removing the computer's protective cover, the person is overwhelmed by a dizzying array of wires, colors, and shapes. Undeterred, they may consult various diagrams and DIY videos until they are able to differentiate some of the computer's main components—the microprocessor, the SSD, the fan, and so forth—and, eventually, figure out where a graphics card would go. At this point, the person no longer feels overwhelmed by what they see, since the computer now appears to them as a set of recognizable parts, rather than as a hodgepodge of colors and shapes. Something similar happens when a language learner begins to understand a language and when a game player understands a new game: as their understanding increases, the language or the game begins to "slow down," since they are no longer overwhelmed by its complexity. Again, because understanding enables us to see patterns among phenomena and, so, to bring the latter into orderly relationships with one another, it brings a kind of simplicity to that which might otherwise appear bewilderingly complicated.

This account also explains why we often try to explain things the way we do. An attorney may try to explain a case to the members of a jury, for instance, by drawing a diagram that helps them see the relationship among the case's key components, just as a philosophy teacher may try to explain a difficult text by outlining the steps of the author's argument, along with the logical transitions from one to the next, and a literature teacher may outline the major developments in a novel's plot in order to provide students with a framework for understanding it. But perhaps the most time-honored way of trying to explain something is to compare it with other—usually more familiar—phenomena that exhibit a similar pattern, in order thereby to help one's hearers perceive such a pattern in this case, too. So in my Introduction to Theology class, for instance, I once explained the difference between dualistic, eschatological, and apocalyptic approaches to suffering by comparing them to a few ways I tried to help my children handle scary scenes in a movie: sometimes I would remind them that it's just a movie, not real life; sometimes I would assure them that everything would turn out all right in the end; and sometimes I would simply tell them that the scary part would be over soon. In so doing, I hoped that my students would see that the three kinds of help I offered my children were relevantly similar to these three approaches to suffering, and that they would thus be able to see a familiar sort of pattern in each of these approaches.

Theologians have often used just this method to help their readers get a grip on difficult theological ideas. In *On the Incarnation of the Word*, accordingly, Athanasius tries to make sense of a perplexing supposition—that God redeems those who have violated God's law and who thus deserve condemnation—by appealing to a relevantly similar situation: "Suppose that a king founded a city," he writes, "and that the city is then taken over by bandits due to the carelessness of its inhabitants. The king will not by any means neglect it, but will avenge and reclaim it as his own work, having regard not to the carelessness of the inhabitants, but to what befits himself."[12] Athanasius thus portrays God's motivation in redeeming sinners as similar to a king's being motivated by his own honor, and thereby tries to help his readers make sense of an unfamiliar case in terms of a familiar one. We see something similar in one of the most famous arguments in the history of theology, namely, Anselm's answer to the difficult question of why God became human. To address this question, Anselm develops a model in which the guilt of sinners is likened to a debt that one cannot pay, and Jesus' death to the earning of an infinite treasury out of which that debt might be paid.[13] In these and countless other cases, theologians attempted to make sense of a complicated theological idea by relating its salient features to those of other phenomena, in order to enable readers to perceive a familiar pattern in those ideas and thus understand them.

That is what this book attempts to do. It does so, on the one hand, through the frequent use of illustrative examples; hence my frequent exhortations to "think here of," to "consider the following example," and so on. I err on the side of giving too many examples, rather than too few, since I would sooner annoy readers who already "get it" than leave any in the dark. On the other hand, and more important, the book does so by developing and deploying more extensive explanatory models. This is what I am doing with the category "ways of life," for instance, since that category enables us to perceive certain features of Christianity as relevantly similar to those of other phenomena—namely, those in which certain practices transform our way of seeing and being in the world—and thus enables us to understand Christianity as instantiating a set of familiar patterns. I try to do the same for the individual components of Christianity: to take just one example, I thus try to shed light on Christian practices of singing and eating together by looking at the role these practices often play in immigrant communities, particularly the way such practices provide people with some respite and a taste of home in a place that may not feel like home. Examples aside, my overall strategy is to relate Christianity to other phenomena in order to help us—Christian and non-Christian alike—see familiar patterns in it and, so, get a better understanding of it.

That brings us to a crucial issue. Thus far I have been talking about trying to understand Christianity, but "Christianity" includes vastly more than could be included in any single account. It would be more precise, then, to say that I am trying here to understand some of the things to which some Christians are committed: while I cannot get a grip on all of the ways that Christianity is practiced, much less everything that is included in each of those ways, I can—I hope—get a grip on some aspects of some of the ways that it is practiced. My ambitions for this project are modest, accordingly, though perhaps a bit less modest than this formulation would suggest, since I hope to provide an understanding not just of some things to which some Christians are committed but of several *significant* things to which a *significant* number of Christians are committed.

The commitments I have in mind—each of which is arguably, and in many cases uncontroversially, significant—include the following: that sin is a matter of living according to "the world" instead of the love of God; that sinfulness renders us beholden to the power of Sin and Death; that Jesus' entire life was an unbroken expression of devotion to God and others; that Jesus' death and resurrection defeated the power of Sin and Death; that, in repentance, we die to our old selves and rise to new life; that baptism enacts the church's—and God's own—recognition of this new self; that our death and new life free us from condemnation for sin; that life together should embody and orient us to the promised fulfillment of this new life; that, in prayer, we entrust our concerns to God and so should relate differently to them; that our will should be brought into conformity with the love manifest in Jesus; that eternal life consists in ever-abounding life shared with God and others; and that God is a triune communion and acts *ad extra* by repeating this communion. Few would disagree that these are significant commitments for those who hold them, and, indeed, are significant elements of what "Christianity" amounts to for these persons.

But is the number of persons who hold these commitments itself significant? Based on considerable evidence from scripture, the theological tradition, and the creeds, catechisms, and confessions affirmed by various churches, not to mention my own interactions with hundreds of Christians, it seems indisputably clear that a significant number of Christians do indeed hold each of these commitments. Beyond that, one way that I have tried to warrant this claim in what follows is by considering, and seeking to include, a wide range of viewpoints on each of the topics treated here and, in particular, to bring together traditions often perceived to be on opposite sides of a spectrum. I thus draw significantly from characteristically Catholic theologians as well as from Orthodox and Protestant theologians, just as I draw on a tradition usually set over against all three of these, namely liberalism, and on a tradition set against the latter, namely postliberalism—and then I draw on traditions often set in opposition to all of the above, namely "contextual" and liberation theologies. By bringing all of these viewpoints together, I hope to provide some warrant for the claim that a broad range of Christians hold these commitments, just as I hope to enrich my understanding of these commitments. (To be sure, there is a serious limitation in this approach, namely, that I am bound to focus on viewpoints that have caught on with a significant number of Christians, which could mean, in turn, that my approach will reproduce some of the exclusions characteristic of the Christian tradition. I have tried to counteract this tendency by drawing extensively from voices that would traditionally have been excluded, but some readers may worry whether I have gone far enough in this direction. I share this worry. Be that as it may, it is important to recall that my aim here is to understand Christianity rather than to recreate it, which means that some such limitations are to be expected.) I have also field-tested most of the ideas I develop here, both by soliciting feedback on them from a host of church leaders as well as laypersons, and by presenting them in—and eliciting responses from—several large lay conferences and adult-education classes. In light of all this, I would argue that there is good reason to think that the commitments on which I am focusing are indeed significant to a significant number of Christians, to such an extent that, taken together, they have a reasonable claim to represent "Christianity" for them. Nevertheless, I remain mindful of what James Cone had to say of his efforts to represent "Black Theology": "The real test of whether any given articulation of Black Theology is *black*," he claims, "depends upon whether the particular theology is consistent with what black people believe to be the basis of their struggle. Therefore we will have to wait and see how black people respond to what we say. Their response is the only test."[14] Like Cone, I too will have to wait and see whether (and to what extent) the people I am writing about can see themselves in what I am trying to say here.

Caveats aside, the book tries to explain a significant number of things to which a significant number of Christians are committed, and to do so in such a way that it realizes an epistemic good—understanding—that is recognizable as such even to those who are not devoted to Christianity. Naturally, the devoted and the non-devoted will disagree as to whether the resulting understanding extends only to Christians' commitments themselves or whether it reaches all the way out, so to speak, to that which those commitments are allegedly about—in other words, whether we end up understanding only the faith that believes, or if we also understand something about that *in which* it believes. As far as I am concerned, non-devoted readers should feel free to take my account solely as an explanation of Christian commitments themselves, just as devoted readers should feel free to take it as an account of that which is objectively the case (insofar as it squares with their commitments). Either way, my hope is that Christian and non-Christian alike can see this book as contributing to our realization of the epistemic good of understanding.

Some Christians may balk at this approach, but before considering their objections it is worth saying something, albeit briefly, about why we would *want* this epistemic good. What is so good about it? One rough-and-ready way of addressing this question is to see where understanding ranks among other such goods.[15] So it seems evident, first of all, that it is better to have *true beliefs* than merely to have beliefs, since true beliefs (about, say, which plants are suitable for eating) are much more likely to guide us successfully in our thinking and acting. Better still, though, to have beliefs that we *know* to be true, since we are then in position to distinguish, for ourselves, true from false beliefs, and thus to distinguish which of our beliefs we should rely on, how much we should rely on them, and so forth. Even better, though, is to *understand* what we know to be true. The simplest way to see why this would be so is to consider a case in which a person meets the minimum threshold to count as knowing something—a case, for instance, where I know that some belief is true but I count as knowing it simply because I heard a recognized expert sincerely assert it to be true; in such a case, even if I know that the belief is true, I may nevertheless not be able to make much sense of it or connect it to my other beliefs. So, for example, if an expert on cricket sincerely tells me that a player was just called for "LBW," I may take their word for it and thereby count as knowing that someone was called for this, but I may nevertheless have only the vaguest notion of how cricket is played, much less what this call means, why it is an infraction, what penalties it entails, and the like. If the expert then went on to explain these things to me, however, I would be able to see how it fits in a pattern and relate that pattern to other familiar phenomena, at which point I would be able to draw meaningful connections between this piece of information and others I possess; in sum, I would have advanced from merely *knowing* something to *understanding* it.

The latter is valuable, in turn, for at least two reasons: first and most obviously, because the more I understand a belief, the more I can meaningfully connect it with my other beliefs, and, in consequence, the more recognizable it is as my own belief. This is akin to the difference between making the correct moves in a board game because someone is telling me which moves to make and my understanding the game well enough to make these moves for myself. Second, if (a) true beliefs increase the prob-

ability that we will think and act successfully and (b) understanding involves relating beliefs meaningfully to our other beliefs, it follows (c) that
the more we understand a true belief, the more we will be able to use it
to guide our thinking and acting, and, so, the more we will increase the
probability of thinking and acting successfully. Someone who can drive
home from work successfully only by following the same route every day
is worse off, in this respect, than someone who can drive home successfully because they have a good understanding of the area's roads, since the
latter person will be successful in a far wider range of circumstances (where
these include, say, unexpected road closures). Understanding is a highly
valuable epistemic good, accordingly, because a belief is more recognizably our own to the extent that we can meaningfully connect it with our
other beliefs, and because such connections amplify a true belief's useful-
ness in guiding thought and action.

Insofar as this book helps us understand Christianity, therefore, it should
be recognizable, even by those not devoted to Christianity, as contributing
to the realization of a highly valuable epistemic good. At just this point,
however, some might worry that it is no longer recognizable as a good to
those who *are* so devoted, for if (a) God and God's works are categorically
unlike anything else and (b) understanding involves seeing a given phenomenon in light of certain familiar patterns, then it follows (c) that the
attempt to understand God is doomed to fail, since God cannot be seen in
light of familiar patterns—or, more to the point, that a God so seen is merely
an idol. This is what Karl Barth seems to have in mind when he asserts
that "God . . . is distinguished qualitatively from men and from everything
human, and must never be identified with anything which we name, or
experience, or conceive, or worship, as God."[16] In response to this worry,
it should first be pointed out that, as I have argued elsewhere, patterns
may change each time they are recognized in a new phenomenon, such
that recognizing familiar patterns in theology's subject matter need not be
thought to reduce that subject matter to something that would fit neatly
into a series with other phenomena; rather, a theological instantiation of
the pattern can be seen as fulfilling as well as judging the normative trajec-
tory implicit in other instances.[17] If so, then seeing God in light of familiar
patterns would not necessarily fit God into a uniform series with other
phenomena, which would mean, in turn, that the real issue is not whether
we should understand theology's subject matter in terms of various patterns but whether we do so in such a way that that subject matter is not

distorted. If so, then it is perfectly legitimate to criticize the explanations offered here insofar as they distort their subject matter but not simply insofar as they try to understand it.

This is related to a second response, which is to point out that a book's order of exposition—the order in which its claims are elaborated—does not necessarily correspond with the order in which its claims were initially developed or thought through. Think here, for instance, of the proofs commonly assigned as exercises in geometry classes, in which one starts with a conclusion and works one's way back to it, step-by-step, from various premises taken as given. In the completed proof, it may appear as though one started with given premises in order to see where they might logically lead, and that one's arrival at a particular conclusion was thus determined by those premises, whereas the opposite is in fact the case: in developing the proof, one actually began with that which now looks as though it came last, and one worked one's way back from there. Something similar can be said about the order in which this book treats various themes: although certain nontheological categories like "ways of life" may come first in the order of exposition, this does not entail that they came first in the actual development of my thinking; indeed, it would be nearer the truth to say that I proceeded by first reflecting on certain theological ideas and then working backward to consider a variety of candidate concepts and explanatory models that might help me make sense of those ideas. (The same could be said for my methodology itself.) Naturally, in theology as in geometry, we cannot choose concepts and models willy-nilly in order to work our way back to certain conclusions; to do the work required of them, these models must be independently defensible and independently intelligible. But contrary to one of the usual objections raised against the sort of approach taken here, the fact that I make use of independently intelligible models and categories does not, and should not be thought to, entail that these function as a sort of framework into which theology is then shoehorned, since I selected these categories and models precisely for the sake of doing justice to various theological commitments. This is not to suggest, of course, that the concepts, models, and methods chosen do not influence that which is understood in their light but to insist that the influence is not a one-way street and that, contrary to the optical illusion created by the order of exposition, the influence runs mainly in the opposite direction.

There are good reasons, then, not to accept these worries. There is also an important positive reason why devoted Christians—qua devoted

Christians—should value the sort of understanding on offer here. The reason goes something like this: if one is a devoted Christian, one will want to bring one's entire life into conformity with that devotion; to bring one's entire life into such conformity, one must see how various ideas, motivations, emotions, and the like should connect with that devotion; and understanding is a necessary (and sometimes sufficient) condition for making such connections for oneself. To see why this would be the case, recall that the more we understand a belief, the more we can use it to guide our thinking and acting; from this, it follows that the more devoted persons understand that to which they are devoted, the more they will be able to achieve that which they desire qua devoted, namely, to bring their life into conformity with that devotion. Understanding should be recognizable as a highly valuable epistemic good, accordingly, to those who are devoted to Christianity as well as to those who are not.

Understanding is not the most valuable epistemic good, however. After all, one can understand all sorts of things—even Christian things—but still be a fool. That brings us to a still-higher epistemic good, namely, *wisdom*.

Wisdom

There are at least two ways in which a person might be wise. On the one hand, a person might be wise in the sense of not being easily fooled—or, positively, of being reliably able to see what is true, even or especially in the face of potentially misleading factors (such as bias, illusion, small sample size, and "common sense"). We might call this sort of wisdom *discernment*, and it is the sort of wisdom that is counseled when we advise people not to judge a book by its cover or not to believe everything they hear. In addition to the habits of mind counseled by these maxims, discernment depends upon the storehouse of beliefs that we take to be true, since it is on their basis that we judge whether to accept other candidate beliefs; our beliefs thus dispose us to accept or reject other would-be beliefs, from which it follows that the goodness of these dispositions depends, in part, upon the extent to which our beliefs are actually true. On the other hand, there is also a kind of wisdom involved in knowing how to conduct oneself well in a variety of circumstances—or, more colloquially, how not to make a fool of oneself. We might call such wisdom *prudence* or *know-how*, and it is the sort of practical wisdom on offer when we tell people to think before they speak, to treat others the way they would want to be treated, and to measure twice before cutting. Roughly, then, whereas discernment is a matter of having dispositions that reliably track with the *truth*, practical wisdom is a matter of having dispositions that track with the *good*.

For present purposes we need to draw a further distinction, this time between two varieties of practical wisdom. On the one hand, there are *skill-based* varieties of practical wisdom, of the sort involved in knowing how to perform brain surgery, teach someone how to read, or design a building so that it will not collapse in an earthquake. On the other hand, there is the practical wisdom involved in, and necessary to, *living a good life*—knowing how to respond, for instance, to injustice, to tragedy, and to our own shortcomings, as well as to blessings and success and our own rectitude; knowing how to distinguish what is important from what is not, such that we will not get caught up in trivial matters; knowing what temptations we are liable to and how to handle them; and so on. In short, this is the sort of practical wisdom involved in having a vision of the good life and knowing how to orient ourselves toward that vision in a wide range of life circumstances. As this formulation should make clear, discernment is an important ingredient in the good life, such that a complete *practical* wisdom must include *theoretical* wisdom, too, though we can obviously be theoretically wise even if we are not practically so, just as we can be practically wise—if incompletely—even if we are not theoretically so.[18] (Hence the colloquial distinction between "book smarts" and "street smarts.") In the highest sort of wisdom, however, discernment is itself oriented to or set in service of the good life, such that it, too, becomes a kind of practical wisdom.

Insofar as a way of life is geared toward a vision of the good life, as most are, it will convey would-be wisdom precisely through its formative practices: it thus aims to cultivate discernment by transforming the way we perceive the world, and to teach us how to conduct ourselves well by transforming our way of being in the world. By exhibiting Christianity as a way of life, therefore, this book likewise exhibits it as trying to orient persons' lives toward wisdom and, in turn, as potentially contributing to our understanding—and achievement—of wisdom.[19] So, to take just one example from the chapters that follow, the practice of prayer can train us to entrust our concerns to God and, so, receive all goods as gifts for which we should feel grateful; over time, this practice can transform our emotional relationship to goods, not least by detaching us from our immediate investment in them, and thus free us to *enjoy* these goods without becoming unduly *bound* to them. This seems like a wise way of relating to goods, or so I will argue; for now, the point is that these practices aim not only to transform our way of perceiving and being in the world but also, in so doing, to teach us how to conduct our lives well.

That brings us to an obvious question, however: is the wisdom implicit in this way of life recognizable as such even to those who are not committed to it? To address this question, note, first, that the truly wise person will recognize wisdom wherever it can be found and thus in many would-be wisdoms. This is part of what it means, after all, to be discerning. That is not to say, however, that the wise person will recognize wisdom in *all* would-be wisdoms, since it is at least possible that some would-be wisdoms contain very little of the genuine article. Hence, in order to entitle myself to the claim that there is wisdom implicit in a Christian way of life—and that it would therefore be recognizable as such to a wise person—I will have to offer some reasons for thinking that this is plausible. Arguments to this effect are best defended after I have developed my account of Christianity, so I will hold off on offering them until we reach the final chapter.

For now, then, a promissory note will have to suffice: if Christianity has something to teach us about how to conduct our lives well, then this book may contribute something to the realization not only of understanding but also of the very highest epistemic good, namely, wisdom.[20]

Conclusion

With that, this chapter has completed its assigned work. To get an idea of what theology is and, importantly, what it might be good for, we began by considering the native soil, as it were, in which it grows. Toward that end, we looked first at *devotion* as intensive as well as extensive commitment to some value, and then at *ways of life* as a means by which to bring one's life into conformity with that commitment. From here, it was easy to see theology as contributing to such a way of life, insofar as theology is a practice of reflecting on what such conformity looks like and on the extent to which one's life exhibits such conformity. That brought us to an objection commonly raised against theology: if theology is indeed a practice connected with devotion, then it would appear that it is an inherently religious endeavor, which, as such, does not belong in a secular university. In response to this objection, I argued, first, that a candidate discipline—theology or otherwise—belongs in the university just in case it contributes to the realization of epistemic goods that are recognizable as such even to the nondevoted; and, second, that theology contributes to the realization of two such goods—indeed, the two most highly estimable epistemic goods—namely, *understanding* and *wisdom*. These are the goods to which this book aims to contribute and the standards by which it should therefore be judged: does it help us understand Christianity? And does it teach us something about how to live wisely? With those questions in mind, we now turn to my account of Christianity as a way of life, beginning with the way of life against which Christianity contrasts itself: namely, *the way of the world*.

CHAPTER TWO

The Way of the World

THE HEART OF THIS BOOK is an account of Christianity as a way of life, that is, an account of Christianity as a set of practices designed to transform our way of seeing and being in the world. By Christianity's own lights, however, we can understand it as such only against the background of the "old," sinful way of life by which all of us are formed and to which the Christian way of life is opposed—"the way of the world," as Teresa of Avila calls it.[1] The problem with this old way of life, as Christianity sees it, is twofold: on the one hand, it orients persons to "the world'" rather than to God and, on the other, it binds us to the power of sin. This sets the agenda, as it were, for the Christian way of life, for if it is going to transform our way of perceiving and being in the world, it will first have to free us from sin and from our old orientation. Before turning to this agenda, though, we first need to consider some of the ways in which persons experience this world—and they themselves— as *broken*, not least because such experiences often cultivate in us a desire for the sort of freedom and transformation that Christianity promises.

Worldliness

Not long ago, it was common for theologians to think about the doctrine of sin in terms of two main competitors: roughly, an Augustinian approach, focused on disordered love, and a Lutheran one, focused on misplaced trust.[2] Over the past half century, however, several theologians have argued, compellingly, that sin looks different for different people in different contexts, such that we need to have multiple approaches to the doctrine, rather than one or two boiled-down, homogenized ones. To my mind, these arguments represent an important advance in our theologies of sin, since the old approaches were often too narrow in scope and, therefore, offered up a distorted picture of "the human situation," as Valerie Saiving famously put it.

Something may also have been lost in the resulting proliferation of doctrines, however, namely, a sense of how various approaches to sin hang together. To be sure, this loss is much less important than what we have gained from this advance, but that does not entail that it is *un*important; after all, if we can see how various phenomena hang together, that usually means that we can understand them better, can more readily spot connections among them, and so on. The modest aim of this section, then, is to consider what—if anything—these doctrines have in common and, crucially, whether these points of commonality are significant to each. For if they do have something significant in common, we might then have a posteriori grounds for developing a unified—but not uniform—doctrine of sin. As it turns out, I argue that they do have something significant in common, namely, the view that sin is, in some fundamental sense, a matter of being oriented by and to "the world," and, so, a matter of treating the world, rather than God, as if it were ultimate. This is what I mean by "worldliness."

Before proceeding, three clarifications are in order. First, I am hardly alone in trying to discern what various accounts of sin might have in common.[3] The novelty of my contribution lies not so much in the attempt, accordingly, nor, certainly, in the superiority of my conclusions, but in the goodness of my (sometimes peculiar) analyses. That brings me to a second clarification: although I am trying here to develop a credibly a posteriori account of what certain doctrines have in common, I can do so only on the basis of an adequate interpretation of these doctrines. As a result, I have had to make significant interpretive choices along the way, and while I argue that these choices are themselves defensible, they are also what makes it possible for me to find commonality among these doctrines. The goodness of my overall argument depends, therefore, on the goodness of my interpretive choices, but I take this to be an unavoidable feature of human inquiry. If so, then readers can rightly object to my interpretations themselves, but not to the very fact that interpretation here goes all the way down, as it were.

And, third, lest readers be misled by the term "worldliness," it is important to note that these doctrines of sin are decidedly *not* anti-wordly or even other-worldly, for the key issue is not whether we value or are oriented by the world but whether we value and are oriented by it independently of our orientation to God; this is what Dorothy Day has in mind, for instance, when she claims, "In the eyes of God, any turning toward creatures to the exclusion of him is adultery."[4] The antidote to worldliness, accordingly, is not to oppose or flee the world but for our relationship to the world to be included in and oriented by our devotion to God. To be sure, there may be cases in which such reorientation would involve straightforward opposition to something (insofar as, say, someone's life was oriented by a hateful ideology), but there are others that would call not for opposition but for a shift in perspective (insofar as someone cares about some worthwhile cause, for instance, independently of God). It would be a serious misunderstanding, in any case, to think that the doctrine of sin that emerges here is necessarily anti- or other-worldly, for what matters is neither opposition to nor investment in the world but whether and to what extent such stances are themselves oriented to that which transcends the world. I say much more about all this in chapter 5; for now, the crucial point is simply that "worldliness" here concerns the way we relate to the natural and social world, rather than the goodness of those worlds in their own right. (As a gentle reminder of this distinction, in what follows I frequently put "the world" in quotation marks.)

Onward, then, to a consideration of some leading doctrines of sin, beginning with the highly influential approach that understands sin in terms of what we *love* or *desire*; this is what Thomas Aquinas has in mind, for instance, when he says that "every sin consists in the desire for some mutable good, for which man has an inordinate desire [*inordinate appetitur*], and the possession of which gives him inordinate pleasure."[5] To understand this approach, we first need to get a grip on the phrase "inordinate desire." In English, the phrase might seem to suggest that we desire and delight in mutable goods *too much* or *excessively*, from which it apparently follows that the antidote for sin would be to lessen our desire for and delight in them.[6] So understood, we might then think of this as a *quantitative* approach to sin. I may not only want good things for my children, for instance, but want them too much, and be too thrilled when they get them, too upset when they do not, and so forth; on this account, then, I would be less sinful precisely insofar as I desired these things less.

There is plainly something right about such an approach; we need only observe parents screaming unhingedly at their young child's soccer coach to realize that something can go wrong when we are overinvested in a loved one's flourishing. But it does not work as a general approach to sin, for not all sinfulness seems to be an instance of such overinvestment, and even in cases of apparent overinvestment, it would appear that overinvestment is not itself the problem. With respect to the former, think of cases in which someone cares not too *much* but too *little* about something: cases in which my heart is unmoved by the suffering of a neighbor, say, or the success of a loved one. Something has surely gone wrong in such cases, but it is not a matter of overinvestment in earthly goods; in consequence, it would appear that overinvestment is not a necessary condition of sin. Nor, apparently, is it a sufficient condition (or so I would argue). Consider: Is it wrong—sinfully so—when parents exult in the fact that their child's cancer has gone into remission? Is it wrong to rejoice unreservedly when a long-unemployed friend finally gets a fulfilling job? And are we ipso facto not sinning—or sinning less—insofar as we desire and delight in them less? If quantity were all that mattered, then insofar as we limited the amount of our desire, we would not be sinning, and insofar as we desired anything very much, we would be sinning. But it seems obvious that we can sin even if we limit our desire for earthly goods, and that boundless delight in such goods is not necessarily sinful. So it would appear that a merely quantitative approach cannot be right.

A better approach would be to think of such love as sinful not insofar as it is *excessive* but insofar as it is *disordered*—insofar, that is, as our love is out of place, improperly organized, or, in sum, not in the right order. This seems to be what Thomas actually meant, and it is clearly what Thomas's favorite precedent, Augustine, had in mind. To see what such an approach might look like, we can begin with a justly famous passage from the latter: "Supposing then we were exiles in a foreign land," Augustine writes, "and could only live happily in our own country, and that being unhappy in exile we longed to put an end to our unhappiness and to return to our own country, we would of course need land vehicles or sea-going vessels, which we would have to make use of in order to be able to reach our own country, where we could find true enjoyment. And then suppose we were delighted with the pleasures of the journey, and with the very experience of being conveyed in carriages or ships, and that we were converted to enjoying what we ought to have been using, and were unwilling to finish the journey quickly, and that being perversely captivated by such agreeable experiences we lost interest in our own country, where alone we could find real happiness."[7]

Augustine's point here is clear: these exiles should care about boats, carriages, and the like only insofar as these things can help them return to their homeland, not in their own right, for insofar as they do care about these things in their own right, they are treating a *means* to an end as if it were an *end in itself*. (Consider the difference between exiles who practice their boating skills in order to prepare themselves for the journey home, and ones who practice these skills solely because they want to win a local boat race.) The problem here, accordingly, is not that the exiles care *too much* about boats and carriages but that they care about them *for their own sake*, and thus orient their hearts to that which should be oriented to something else.

Augustine generalizes this point by means of his famous distinction between use and enjoyment: he thus defines *enjoyment* [*frui*] as "clinging to something lovingly for its own sake" and contrasts this with *use* [*uti*], which consists in "referring what has come your way to what your love aims at obtaining."[8] To begin with, then, "enjoyment" functions as a name for that which we care about as an end in itself, and "use" as a name for that which we care about for the sake of something else. Implicit in the distinction itself, however, is the idea that we can get it wrong: we can enjoy that which we should use, just as we can use that which we should enjoy. To take a mundane example, suppose that I love my family and that I care about certain things precisely because I love them: having enough money, for instance, or having time to spend with them. If the latter concerns are related in this way to the former, then my cares are more or less in the right order. But if, over time, I get caught up in earning money for its own sake, if my pursuit of money interferes with my relationship to my family, and so on, then my concern with money is obviously disordered, for in that case that which should be a means to an end has become an end in itself. (Think here of Walter White in *Breaking Bad*.) Even more obviously, if I become so consumed with making money that I treat my family as a means to that end—thinking of them, for instance, as props that I can use to impress clients—then my priorities are disordered or, as one says, "messed up."

From here, we can take two short steps to arrive at Augustine's more general account of sin. The first step is to note that the "ends" picked out by our love are that which give us reason to do certain things and to make certain plans—they are that around which our lives are organized, in other words. We see this most clearly in the lives of persons who are wholeheartedly devoted to a single project: if a woman wants wholeheartedly to be a concert cellist, for instance, this desire gives her a reason to do certain things (practice, watch videos of accomplished cellists, read up on particular pieces of music, and so on), to pay attention to certain things (the health of her fingers, the acoustics of a particular room, the judgment of an accomplished teacher), and to feel certain ways (upset if something happens to her favorite bow, worried about handling a tricky sequence of notes, delighted if a recital goes well, and so forth). The end she has set for herself can thus give shape to her entire life. People are not usually this single-minded about their life projects, of course, but the mechanism itself seems fairly typical, for even if persons are oriented to more than one end, those ends will give shape to their lives just insofar as they can be said to *lead* a life. Insofar as we are oriented to such ends, accordingly, they have a kind of practical ultimacy in our lives.[9]

That brings us to the second step: as Augustine sees it, we ought to treat God alone as an ultimate end and treat everything else—including not just money but also vocation, loved ones, and other earthly goods—as a means to that end. Note well, however, that his point is not that we should care only about God (and nothing else) but that we should care about other things only in view of our more basic concern for God, rather than as ends in themselves. Insofar as we do treat them as ends in themselves, on the other hand, we treat them as our ultimate aim and, just so, we sin. On Augustine's account, then, sin and rectitude alike are determined by the end we set for ourselves and the consequent ordering of our desires.

This idea seems straightforward enough, though a couple of points require further clarification. First, on the face of it, this account might seem to suggest that everything in the world—including other persons—should be used, that the world has no intrinsic value, and so on, such that Augustine would appear to be recommending an unduly utilitarian, even exploitative, attitude toward the world.[10] In response to this concern, it should be noted that valuing something for its own sake is not incompatible with valuing it for the sake of something else: because David loved Jonathan, for instance, he also loved his grandson, Mephibosheth—but he could love Mephibosheth for *Jonathan's* sake only if he loved him for his *own* sake; such is the nature of love, after all. It seems clear that our love for God should include such (relative) loving-for-its-own-sake, which means that Augustine's account need not entail a strictly utilitarian stance toward the world. Second, it is important to note that persons must not only *intend* to orient their life to God but *actually do so*. To see why we need such a clarification, picture a new employee who wants desperately to impress his boss, and who therefore orients his life toward trying to do so: working extra hours, writing unduly detailed reports, constantly asking what else he can do to help, and so on. And then imagine that his boss actually dislikes these things, since she thinks that they cultivate just the sort of unhealthy work environment that she has spent years trying to improve. In this sort of case, we might say that the employee's actions are subjectively, but not objectively, oriented toward impressing his boss, and that he is actually so oriented only if he is so in both senses. Likewise with our orientation to God: the mere fact that I genuinely want to orient my life to God does not entail that my life actually is so oriented, from which it follows that persons who want to orient their life to God must learn how to do so correctly.

On this sort of approach, then, sin is primarily a matter of treating anything other than God as an ultimate end, which is to say that sin is here a matter of orientation: we lead our lives, on this account, by orienting ourselves (and other would-be ends) to ends that are set by our love; insofar as that end is anything other than God—anything in the world—then we are sinful; we are not sinful, and are indeed righteous, insofar as we orient ourselves and everything else in our lives to God.

That brings us to a second major approach, according to which sin is a matter of *putting our faith in* or *trusting* anything other than God. The classic statement of this approach comes from Martin Luther: "A god," he writes, "is that to which we look for all good and in which we find refuge in every time of need. To have a god is nothing else than to trust and believe him with our whole heart. As I have often said, the trust and faith of the heart alone make both God and an idol. If your faith and trust are right, then your god is the true God. On the other hand, if your trust is false and wrong, then you have not the true God. For these two belong together, faith and God. That to which your heart clings and entrusts itself is, I say, really your God." He then offers a paradigmatic example of what such clinging-and-entrusting looks like: "Many a person thinks he has God and everything he needs," Luther observes, "when he has money and property; in them he trusts and of them he boasts so stubbornly and securely that he cares for no one. Surely such a man has a god—mammon by name, that is, money and possessions—on which he fixes his whole heart."[11] Broadly stated, then, the idea here is that sin is a matter of putting our trust in something other than God and, since we should put our trust in God alone, of treating the world (or something in it) as if it were god.

To get a firmer grip on this approach, we must first clarify what it means to put our trust in something. In general, we count as trusting something when (a) we are worried about whether something will come to pass, or at least are susceptible to worrying about it, and (b) we take some person, idea, institution, or the like as reliably reducing the probability that something bad will come to pass, or increasing the probability that something good will, and we thus depend upon or count on that person, idea, or institution. With respect to (a), it is important to point out that this condition can be met even if I am not actually worried, especially insofar as this is due to my being reassured that everything will turn out well. The only reason I am not worried about having enough food to eat, for instance, or about my children's safety, is because I take it for granted that we have enough food, that we live in a safe neighborhood, and so on. This condition is met, then, not only when we actually worry about something but also when we would be susceptible to worrying about it if we did not take its well-being for granted. This is obviously related to point (b), the upshot of which is that there are certain things—other persons, our own ability to control our fortunes, the reliability of our surroundings, and the like—that we count on in such a way that we either do not worry about certain things coming to pass or, if we do worry, that we can respond by telling ourselves, as it were, that, because of them, everything will turn out all right. Hence, it may never occur to me to worry about my vulnerability to bad luck or injustice, for instance, insofar as I take for granted the trustworthiness of my surroundings; then again, even if I do worry about my vulnerability to these things—worrying that a potential employer may have lost my application, or that I will be framed by a corrupt police officer, or that I will miss an important meeting because my alarm did not go off—I may reassure myself by reminding myself that, if all else fails, I can call a powerful ally, or find some way of avenging myself, or ask my parents for help, or find some other means of reassuring myself that everything will turn out well in the end. With this in mind, we can now summarize Luther's argument as follows: (a) our god is whatever either keeps us from worrying or provides us with reassurance when we do; (b) God alone should play this role; and (c) we are sinful insofar as anything else does.

Thus far, this account might seem to imply a strict either/or: *either* we trust in the world *or* we trust God, such that an increase in trust on the one side would automatically entail a corresponding decrease on the other, and vice versa. This is not the only way to understand this approach, however, and probably not the best way to do so, since such an understanding would mean, among other things, that we could trust only in God *or* medicine,

God *or* other people, God *or* the world's reliability, and so on. To be sure, some persons have thought this way—some mendicants, for instance, as well as persons who refuse all medical treatment. But most Christians seem not to think that we must necessarily choose between trusting God, on the one hand, and trusting medicine, trusting other persons, and the like, on the other. Importantly, Luther's account need not be construed as if it always required such choices, for the simple reason that our trust in such things can itself be an expression of trust in God and therefore not at odds with it. To see why not, suppose that at a concert I run into an old friend who promises to get me invited backstage. If a stage manager later brings me a special backstage pass, I would naturally see that as my friends keeping their promise and thus as vindicating my trust in them.[12] It would be odd, to say the least, if I refused the pass on the grounds that I intended to trust my friend instead; such refusal would indicate, among other things, that I failed to realize that a person can work indirectly—and not just directly—to fulfill their promises. In the same way, suppose a person trusts God for the healing of some sickness, and that they then take some medicine and get better: in such a case, they may experience their recovery as a vindication of their trust in God's provision and, so, experience their reliance upon medicine as fully compatible with their reliance upon God. Naturally, the two may be incompatible in certain cases, particularly insofar as one's trust in the world is not an expression of one's trust in God. The point here is simply that they are not necessarily incompatible, such that our trust in God does not entail that we cannot trust anything else.

That brings us to one further clarification: as I have explicated it thus far, it might appear that we could trust God, and so not sin, even if God were thereby treated simply as a means of securing other ends. To see what I mean here, consider first an innocuous example: witnesses against the mafia are worried about the safety of their children, and thus insist that the state deploy bodyguards to protect them. In that case, although the witnesses do trust the bodyguards, they do so only as a means to an independently valued end, namely, the safety of their children. There is nothing wrong with their doing so. Things are different when it comes to trusting God, however, since it is wrong to trust God only as a means to an end or, more broadly, to trust God only to a limited extent. Rather, as Luther puts it, we must trust God "with our whole heart," which means that we must entrust ourselves and our concerns wholly to God; we must therefore entrust not only our children's safety to God but our children themselves; trust not only that God will make our plans turn out well but entrust those plans themselves to God; and, in sum, not only trust God in the face of our concerns but so entrust them to God that we put them wholly in God's hands.

With that, we can now see that the Lutheran approach, too, turns on the question of our orientation, for insofar as we are concerned about something—insofar, that is, as we are invested in it—it will play a significant role in orienting our lives. (Recall here some of my claims concerning devotion.) Unlike the Augustinian approach, orientation here is less a matter of how our lives are organized and more a matter of immediately relating our concerns to some source of reassurance. Yet it is no less a matter of orienting our lives to that which we take to be ultimate, for, as Luther argues, whatever we entrust our concerns to is finally our god: if we cling tightly to our concerns and entrust them to our own control, then we are treating ourselves as god; if we entrust them to anything else in the world, then we treat that thing as god; and if we entrust them to God and so release them to God's safekeeping, then we treat God as god. Here again, then, sin and righteousness alike are a matter of our orientation.

A third approach to sin has gained prominence over the past half century, spurred, in part, by a sense that the preceding accounts fail to do justice to all the relevant instances of sin and, in particular, that they fail to do justice to important differences in the contexts of those to whom they are applied. Indeed, in a special sense, the would-be universality of these accounts itself came to be seen as a paradigmatic instance of a different sort of sin, namely, *the absolutization of a particular person or group.*

Unsurprisingly, contextual theologians were among the first to see such absolutization as the fundamental feature of sin. James Cone thus argues that an adequate account of sin must attend to the ideology of white supremacy or, in short, of "whiteness"; he claims, accordingly, that "the sin of whites is the definition of their existence in terms of whiteness," the purpose of which is to enable them "to play God in the realm of human affairs."[13] The characteristic sin of Black persons, by contrast, is acceptance of this would-be absolutization of whiteness, insofar as Black persons "let whites determine the shape of the future and what the limits are" and "have reinforced white values by letting whites define what is good and beautiful"—that is, insofar as they "desire to be white."[14] Rosemary Radford Ruether develops a similar approach to sin: she thus claims that sin "has to be seen both in the capacity to set up prideful, antagonistic relations to others *and* in the passivity of men and women who acquiesce to the group ego."[15] Here too, then, "the authentic, good self is identified with the favored center who dominates the cultural interpretation of humanness, and others are described in negative categories by contrast—this is the fundamental sin of the dominant group—while the dominated groups . . . internalize the dominant ideology, which shapes its own socialization."[16]

The idea here, then, might seem to go something like this: it is sinful either (a) for a particular group to take itself to be the measure of all things, or (b) for those measured by this group to accept that measure. (A similar formulation could be offered for individuals who take themselves to be the measure of all things, and for those who accept that measure.) Men, white persons, and others could then be said to sin, accordingly, precisely insofar as they judge others in light of their own norms—or their group's features treated as norms—just as other persons sin insofar as they have internalized these norms and thus judge themselves according to them.

This formulation of the problem would help us make sense of certain cases—the case of white supremacists and sexists, for instance—but not others, such that it falls short as a way of understanding the point that Cone and Ruether are making. The problem with this formulation, simply stated, is that it is not always wrong—much less sinful—to make judgments on the basis of our own norms, nor always wrong to accept the norms of another. With respect to the latter, there are all sorts of apparently non-sinful cases where we accept the norms of others: we do so every time we drive a car, for instance, or play a game, or use language, or file charges against a harasser. We cannot do these things without accepting others' norms, but, again, it is not obvious that we have thereby done anything sinful. With respect to the former, there likewise seem to be cases where we judge others in light of our own norms but do not thereby sin. It does not appear to be sinful, for example, or at least not necessarily so, if a software company assesses whether a prospective employee is fluent in the relevant computer languages, if a copy editor identifies errors in a manuscript, or, more seriously, if someone insists that cruelty and oppression are wrong. In such cases, the mere fact that persons or groups judge others in light of their own norms does not seem to entail that they have done anything sinful. Again, then, although there are some cases in which it is sinful to judge others in light of our own norms or to internalize the norms of others, it is not always so, such that we must look elsewhere for a formulation that does justice to all the relevant cases.

With these cases in mind, we might be tempted to say that the issue is not whether we judge others in light of our own norms but whether we judge them in light of *correct* norms: if the norm itself is a good one, on this formulation, then it is fine to judge others in light of it, whereas it is sinful to do so if not. Unfortunately, there are problems with this approach, too. On the one hand, the mere fact that persons use incorrect norms does not entail that they have thereby sinned: so, for instance, it would be embarrassing, but not necessarily sinful, if I were to correct another's pronunciation on the basis of my own mistaken perception of how a word should be pronounced; likewise if I used the wrong answer key to grade a set of quizzes, if I taught the wrong table etiquette to my children, and so on. In such cases, I may have made judgments on the basis of incorrect norms, but it would be a stretch to say that I have thereby done something sinful. By the same token, the mere fact that a person judges others in light of correct norms may not mean that they have not thereby sinned: if I judge another's grammar and pronunciation in light of correct norms, for instance, and, on this basis, decide that the person is stupid and unworthy of respect, then I may have sinned even though my norms are correct. To be sure, this case permits a different analysis, since it is possible to interpret it precisely as exemplifying the formulation in question—the problem here, on such an interpretation, just is that I have applied a bad norm to the effect that persons who speak incorrectly are "less" than me. I return to this point in a moment; for now, the implication is simply that using incorrect norms does not necessarily mean that we have sinned, and that using correct norms may not mean that we have not.

As the previous paragraph suggests, we may make some progress here insofar as we can get clearer on what makes these judgments not only wrong but sinfully so. In view of the preceding examples, one candidate suggests itself: what makes such a judgment sinful is not whether we judge others (and ourselves) in light of a particular group's norms but whether we thereby (a) see them (and ourselves) in a badly distorted way or (b) superordinate or subordinate them (and ourselves) on the basis of those judgments.

To get a clearer understanding what such distortion and super- and subordination look like, it will be helpful to consider the way harmful stereotypes and biases work. We can make sense of this in a few steps. The first step is to understand a general, seemingly innocuous feature of how human brains work, namely, that our brains are constantly making associations between various features of our environments and certain other features, such that they continually end up drawing a kind of quasi-inference from one to the other.[17] It is common, therefore, to associate a particular breed of dog with danger; to associate widened eyes with surprise; to associate certain professions—librarianship, for instance—with certain personal traits; and so forth. Human brains are apparently wired to make such associations, and thus they move more or less automatically from certain observed features to unobserved ones. (It is easy to see why this might be adaptively useful, since creatures who have to start from scratch every time they encounter certain circumstances will be much worse off, survival-wise, than those who immediately associate certain circumstances with danger, food, mating opportunities, and the like.)

From here, we can move quickly to a second step, which is taken when we apply this same associative mechanism to people; persons may thus associate certain observed features with membership in a particular group and associate that group with certain additional characteristics.[18] This is where harmful stereotypes may enter the picture. Persons may thus associate a given skin color, for instance, with diligence or laziness, athleticism or gracelessness, being hot-tempered or self-controlled, with honesty or deceitfulness, and so on; they may likewise associate a person's (apparent) sex with dominance or submissiveness, strength or weakness, rationality or emotionality, and so forth. By the same token, persons may also associate a given skin color or sex with certain jobs and certain social roles: some types of person are thus commonly associated with certain jobs in the sciences, for instance, or in manual labor, or with certain roles such as nurturer or provider. There are similar associations with age, social class, and so on, but the point is that this is how stereotypes generally work, namely, through the association of particular persons with certain larger groups and, so, with the traits one associates with those groups (and vice versa). (Here it is important to recall that people can apply stereotypes not only to others but to themselves as well, in virtue of their own associations with the groups to which they belong.)[19] Naturally, not all such associations are harmful: it is not clear how anyone would be harmed if I associated nurses with professional competence and conscientiousness, for instance, or if I associated certain accents with certain regions of the world. But many such associations are harmful. For one thing, they are harmful when we thereby associate a negative trait with certain persons—if we associate a particular accent not only with a particular region, for instance, but also with unintelligence, or if we associate skin color, sex, age, class markers, and the like with negative or subordinated traits such as those just mentioned.[20] (Such negative associations can also be indirect, of course, if, for instance, we associate a positive trait with a particular group, and the trait itself implies something negative about those who are not part of that group.) These negative associations are harmful, note well, even if they turn out to be true in particular instances, since (a) they may be true only because they reflect an oppressive history and, thus, reinforce that history, (b) they still harm others in the group by associating group membership with this trait, and, in any case, (c) it is still wrong to assume, in advance, that someone has certain negative traits, even if it turns out that they do.

Such associations can also be harmful even if the associated trait is positive: persons may thus feel that they are seriously distorted by being seen through the lens of these associations, for example, or, simply, not seen as individuals; members of certain groups attest to feeling this way, for instance, when persons automatically associate them with diligence or scientific aptitude. Positive associations can likewise be harmful insofar as they are embedded in a harmful history: so, while it may be positive, in itself, to associate dancing with certain groups, such associations are often embedded in a broader set of associations, the net effect of which has often been to associate certain people with entertainment, bodily intelligence (instead of "cognitive" intelligence), sheer physicality, and the like; against this background, it is not hard to see why this apparently positive association would turn out to be harmful. We could multiply examples—unfortunately—but the idea here is that people tend to associate certain traits with certain persons, and that some of these are harmful. The latter are what we customarily mean by terms like "bias," "prejudice," and "stereotypes."

A third step is obviously related to the second: people tend to associate evaluations—and not just traits—with particular groups. To be sure, the mere fact that a negative trait is associated with a group already carries with it an implicit evaluation of that group. But evaluative associations can also work more directly, as when persons associate group membership with a kind of ranking of relative worth: those in the upper class may thus look down on members of lower classes (and vice versa); professionals may think manual laborers are "beneath" them; those who speak English may automatically downgrade or ignore the views of those who do not; and so forth. Taken together, these evaluative associations, combined with the association of negative traits, can add up to a systematic set of snap judgments about persons. The logic of such judgments—which, I hasten to emphasize, I am *not* endorsing—goes something like this: persons who are members of a particular group are seen as having certain negative traits and as being "beneath" those in another group; the judgment that they are "beneath" is apparently justified by the negative traits associated with them; and these traits are more readily perceived as negative insofar as they are associated with a group that is "lesser" or "beneath." Automatic associations can thus reinforce one another and, accordingly, contribute to a systematic bias against certain groups.

That brings us to a fourth step, which is taken when persons are treated in accordance with such associations, or, in sum, when they are discriminated for or against on the basis of their group membership. Hence, persons who are associated with a group that is taken to be dangerous are often punished more harshly than members of other groups; persons associated with a group that is taken to be lazy or unintelligent are less likely to be taken seriously for jobs; persons from a group taken to be "lesser" are more likely to be redlined out of neighborhoods or otherwise marginalized. Persons are also often sanctioned when they "step out of line," that is, when their actions do not conform to the social roles associated with their group. Black basketball players who protest injustice are thus told that they should "shut up and dribble," for instance, and that, instead of complaining, they should "be grateful." Likewise, women are often punished—sometimes through violence, sometimes through social sanction—if they do not submit to men's wishes or otherwise conform to their taken-for-granted roles.[21] Such discriminatory treatment is a natural outgrowth of the sort of stereotypes we have been discussing. And once again, discrimination and stereotypes are often mutually reinforcing: insofar as stereotypes are taken to reflect "how things are," discriminatory treatment can be seen not as unjust but as natural; and insofar as discriminatory treatment succeeds in keeping a group beneath others, it can make the world look more and more like the stereotypes it invokes: women who have long been sanctioned for "stepping out of line," for example, may thus appear more submissive than men, and this discrimination-produced state of affairs can then be called upon as putative evidence that women are naturally submissive.[22] Here too, then, the interrelationship between stereotypes, evaluations, and discrimination is both mutually reinforcing and at least potentially systematic in scope. This is important to bear in mind, since the harmfulness of stereotypes and discrimination is linked both to power and to systematicity: if I happen to have an idiosyncratic bias against persons who drive a particular sort of car—Nissan Altimas, say—then my bias will harm these persons only in the unlikely event that I have power over them; at the other end of the spectrum, if my bias against a particular group is widely shared, enacted in discriminatory treatment, codified into law, and so on, then that bias will be maximally harmful to members of that group.

Brief as it is, this summary should help us get a clearer idea of what is so objectionable—and, according to Cone and Ruether, so fundamentally sinful—about white supremacy, patriarchy, and the like. Consider again the sinfulness of seeing persons (including ourselves) through a distorting lens. Naturally, not all distortions are harmful: if I mistakenly perceive a New Zealander as an Australian, for instance, it is unlikely to cause any real harm. But insofar as a distortion involves important aspects of people's identities, it may make it difficult for them to see themselves in others' views of them, to hold an accurate view of themselves, to navigate relationships in a healthy way, and so forth, and can therefore work to their serious detriment. (Think here of the lasting impact it can have on children if their parents see one of them as "the selfish one," "the stupid one," "the screwup," and so on.) Such views can thus be harmful. But what would it mean to say that they are *sinful?* One plausible answer—to my mind, the most plausible—is that such distortions are sinful insofar as they make it difficult for us to perceive others (and ourselves) as individuals who are loved by God and bear God's image: if God loves each person individually and if each bears God's image, then any view of persons that occludes this fact and makes it harder for them to live according to it is sinful. (I return to this point in chapter 6.)

We can say something similar about the sinfulness of superordinating or subordinating persons on the basis of a particular person's or group's norms. To be clear, the problem here is not simply a matter of using a particular group's standards to judge others, since there is nothing necessarily wrong with baseball umpires calling balls and strikes, teachers grading papers, magistrates deciding cases, and so forth, nor is it necessarily wrong for someone to believe that slavery, cruelty, misogyny, and the like are always wrong (even if some persons think, or have thought, otherwise). The problem, rather, is using such standards as the basis for judging persons *themselves*, usually in the form of judging their *worth*. Teachers would be doing something wrong, accordingly, if they not only graded students' papers but thereby drew conclusions about which students are, say, "losers" or a waste of time, just as it would be wrong to determine how much people matter, and how deserving they are of regard, on the basis of their skin color, gender, age, income, marital status, birthplace, pedigree, accent, height, body shape, attractiveness, fashionableness, and any number of other factors that people use to determine how people measure up. This should help us to see, in turn, why such judgments could be considered sinful, for whatever standard we use to judge others' worth is thereby treated as if it were absolute or ultimate, whereas, from a Christian point of view, God's standard alone should be treated as such. (To be clear, it would be sinful even if we tried to make such judgments on the basis of God's standards, since God's standard itself is, arguably, opposed to the idea that certain persons are worth either more or less than others; from this, it follows that if we use it to make such judgments, we are ipso facto not using God's standard.)

On this account, then, sinful distortion is a matter of seeing people (including ourselves) in such a way that it makes it hard to see God's image in them, and sinful superordination or subordination is a matter of judging others' worth in terms of a standard other than God's. As already mentioned, such distortion and super- or subordination usually reinforce one another, just as they usually reinforce and are reinforced by discriminatory treatment. As a result, this sort of sinfulness lends itself to a kind of systematicity or structuralness, which Oscar Romero characterizes as "the crystallization of individuals' sins into permanent structures that keep sin in being and make its force to be felt by the majority of the people."[23] This should help us to see, in turn, that sinfulness is obviously neither identical with nor reducible to the sinfulness of individual persons. For one thing— this bears repeating—these ways of seeing and treating others are often reinforced by sanctions (legal and otherwise), just as the latter are often rationalized by appeal to the former. For another, these ways of seeing and treating others also largely circulate under the radar of conscious thought, such that persons can both pick them up and pass them on without realizing it; individuals can thus function as mere junctions, so to speak, in the self-reproducing circuitry of discrimination. Indeed, we see this especially clearly when persons contribute to these patterns even when their so doing could not have been due to their own bias (and, so, not due to their own sinfulness). To see what I mean, suppose I hear someone trying to get into my neighbors' garage; that the person is on the other side of a tall fence, hidden from view; that I call out, firmly, "Can I help you?"; and that, coming around the corner, I then discover the person in question is a Black teen who had my neighbors' permission to get something out of their garage. In that case, it seems implausible to think that my actions were due to a sinful bias against Black teens, not least because I had no idea that I was addressing someone who was either Black or a teen—but my actions nevertheless carry on a pattern in which Black teens are unjustly associated with criminality and thus treated as such, which is to say that my actions carry on a sinful pattern irrespective of whether they are rooted in my own sinfulness. One of the things that this account of sinfulness helps us see, accordingly, is that sinfulness is irreducible to the sinfulness of individuals.

As with disordered love and misplaced trust, this account also helps us see that sinfulness is a matter of taking our bearings from something other than God, at precisely the point where we should be taking them from God: we should see persons as God sees them but we see them instead from a "worldly" standpoint; we should value persons as God does but we judge their value instead on the basis of a "worldly" standard. Insofar as we perceive and judge others in light of a worldly standard, we treat that standard as if it were ultimate and, just so, we are oriented by "the world" where we should be oriented by God.

With that, we can now say what should already be apparent, namely, what these three approaches have in common. The first approach focused on *disordered love*, wherein people's love directs them to an end other than God, and this end thus shapes and orients their lives. The second approach focused instead on *misplaced trust*, in the sense that persons entrust their concerns to someone—or something—other than God, and thus orient themselves to that thing. The third approach focused on *the absolutization of worldly standards*, wherein the concepts and norms of a particular person or group are treated as if they were the standard by which the worth of persons, groups, things, and the rest should be judged (and, indeed, seen); these standards thus give shape to one's perception, evaluation, and treatment of the world around one, which means, in turn, that one's way of seeing and being in the world is oriented by them. In all three cases, then, sinfulness is fundamentally a matter of being oriented by and to "the world," where we ought instead to be oriented by and to God.

It seems to me, therefore, that we do have a posteriori grounds for developing a unified (not uniform) account of sin. As I mentioned earlier, such unity can help us better understand particular varieties of sin and more readily identify connections among them. Here I will mention just one way in which that may be especially useful, namely, that it can make it easier for us to recognize the ways that different kinds of sinfulness can reinforce one another. So, for instance, one reason that white supremacy and patriarchy seem lately to be making a comeback is that many persons feel that their place in the world has become increasingly precarious; as a consequence, their absolutization of a particular group functions, in part, as a way of trying to restore a sense of reliability to their world. Misplaced trust and disordered love also reinforce each other: those who treat precarious goods as if they were ultimate ends render themselves especially vulnerable to that precariousness and, just so, drastically inflate their need for immediate security; giving in to one of these temptations thus increases the likelihood that we will give in to the other. It is not hard to think of additional examples, but my point, for now, is that seeing the unity among these varieties of sin should make it easier for us to spot them.

Supposing, then, that sinfulness is at least largely a matter of being oriented by and to "the world," where we ought to be oriented by and to God; insofar as we are so oriented, we treat the world as if it were ultimate. Just as persons can get so caught up in a game that they become forgetful of that which lies beyond it, so, here, persons get so caught up in the world that they forget that it is not ultimate. That brings us already to another view that a significant number of Christians have held concerning sinfulness, namely, that through our sinfulness, we have become bound to sin.

Bound to Sin

Again, in addition to claiming that humans are sinful insofar as we are oriented by and to "the world" where we should be oriented by and to God, Christians have traditionally claimed that we are bound to sin, in two respects: on the one hand, in the sense that we cannot help but be sinful and, on the other, in the sense that we have subjected ourselves to—and so become the bondservants of—the power of Sin. This section tries to make sense of both claims.

The suggestion that we cannot help but be sinful is common; this is what Teresa of Avila has in mind, for instance, when she maintains that "a soul in sin is without any power, but is like a person completely bound, tied, and blindfolded."[24] To be sure, there are broad differences concerning what this amounts to: it may mean, for instance, that everything we do (and leave undone) is sinful; or it may mean that our sinfulness leaves its stain on everything we do (and leave undone), even if the latter is not necessarily sinful; or that all persons are basically sinful and so necessarily sin, even if many of our actions are not themselves sinful. These differences are related to a second set of differences, concerning the reason people cannot help but be sinful. In this section, I consider two especially prominent responses to the latter question, one of which tries to understand our inability not to sin in terms of *habituation*, the other in terms of *inheritance*. As far as possible, I try to understand these accounts as complementary ways of explaining why, when it comes to sinfulness, it is always already too late for us: by the time we could choose not to be sinful, we have already been sinfully formed to such an extent that we cannot help but be sinful.[25]

To explain why this might be the case, it will be helpful to begin with a familiar source of constraint: namely, habit. A bit roughly, we might say that a particular way of thinking, acting, or reacting counts as a "habit" insofar as we have become so accustomed to thinking, acting, or reacting that way that we do so more or less automatically. So, for instance, I have a habit of checking my phone whenever I find myself waiting for more than a few seconds, of looking both ways before crossing the street, and of thinking that any news is going to be bad. In certain circumstances, then, I have become reliably disposed to do certain things, to think certain things, and to feel certain things, such that my doing, thinking, and feeling do not depend on any conscious decision on my part. (Notice that, as I use the term, a habit must be learned rather than innate; the fact that I automatically duck when something flies at my head is thus an instinct rather than a habit, whereas baseball hitters' equally automatic ability to distinguish balls and strikes, depending as it does on their having learned to do so, counts as a habit.)

With this idea in mind, it is easy to see how we might be constrained by our habits. We see a clear example of such constraint in cases where habit produces "weakness of will"—cases, that is, where we cannot help but think, feel, or do whatever we have been habituated into thinking, feeling, or doing, even though we earnestly want *not* to. Think here, again, of basketball players who genuinely want to change their shooting form but who cannot help but revert to their old form as soon as they are not consciously focusing on it—once they are taking a shot in an actual game, for instance. Or think of my own heartfelt desire, as a child, to talk less in school: every year, I ardently resolved to be less of a bigmouth, and every year, it was already too late for my resolve to make much of a difference; talkativeness was already too deeply ingrained in me. In cases like these, it is no longer simply up to us how we will act, think, and feel, insofar as our habits have already decisively shaped our acting, thinking, and feeling. We are not like Hercules standing at a crossroads, coolly deliberating about which road to take; we are more like Hercules barreling toward a crossroads at top speed, with enough momentum that it would be nearly impossible for him to turn from his present path, even if he wanted to.

This is the sort of account that Augustine uses, for instance, to make sense of his inability to turn away from his old life, in spite of the fact that he genuinely wanted to do so. He claims, accordingly, that "the law of sin is the violence of habit by which even the unwilling mind is dragged down and held, as it deserves to be, since by its own choice it slipped into the habit"; on Augustine's account, then, habit is the means by which our past weighs us down, maintains its grip on us, and keeps us in chains.[26] This explains, in turn, why he experienced himself as being divided against himself, since the one who wanted to devote his life to God was also the one who resisted this desire: "The self which willed to serve," he writes, "was identical with the self which was unwilling. It was I. I was neither wholly willing nor wholly unwilling. So I was in conflict with myself and was dissociated from myself. The dissociation came about against my will. Yet this was not a manifestation of the nature of an alien mind but the punishment suffered in my own mind."[27] As Augustine sees it, therefore, he is unable to leave his old life behind because "ingrained evil had more hold over me than unaccustomed good," or, more simply, because "my old loves held me back."[28] Habits might thus help us understand why persons are bound to their sinfulness, accordingly, since they offer us one way of explaining how our wills can be so constrained that we are no longer free to choose otherwise—even if we genuinely want to do so.

As an explanation of our inability not to sin, however, this sort of account faces an obvious objection: if we work at it, can't we resist the constraint imposed by habit? After all, the basketball player who focuses on shooting differently can often do so, at least temporarily, as can the big-mouthed kid who focuses on talking less. If so, then it seems like a stretch to say that habit imposes any sort of necessity or "bondage" upon us.

That brings us to two additional features of this account. On the one hand, theologians have pointed out that we are often *invested* in our bad habits, such that we may not want to resist them, or may in any case have a hard time bringing ourselves to do so.[29] To see what they have in mind, consider a case where certain habits are bound up with our sense of security—where we have a habit of trying to secure ourselves by imposing our will upon others, for instance, or by "othering" (and so dismissing) those who endure misfortune. In cases like these, to change our habits would also mean giving up one of the (perceived) bases of our security; it would be difficult to give up such habits, accordingly, not only because they are habits but also because we are attached to them.[30] The point is suitably general: insofar as my habits are bound up with things that matter to me, then these habits will matter to me, too; if so, then it will be even harder for me to bring myself to change them.[31]

On the other hand, some of our earlier considerations seem to suggest that "worldliness" is not a single bad habit or even a set of such habits but something more like a "super-habit," that is, a habit that is composed of several mutually reinforcing sub-habits and, crucially, that is irreducible to any one of them or, indeed, to several of them, insofar as the super-habit operates at the level of our more basic orientation to the world. If so, then even if we could change a handful of our sub-habits, our super-habit would itself remain intact.[32] Consider the example of people who have made a habit of healthy living. Such a habit is composed of countless sub-habits: getting a certain amount of sleep every night, eating only certain foods, maintaining a particular exercise routine, and so forth, and doing the things that are necessary to make sure these things happen—refraining from drinking coffee after noon, regularly buying fresh foods, carving out time for the gym, and so on. People following these healthy habits will likewise develop certain habits of seeing and feeling: they will perceive unexpected circumstances as an obstacle to their sleep or workout, for instance, and feel frustration or guilt when they fail to maintain their healthy habits. Obviously, insofar as these things have become habitual, we would find it difficult to change any one of them. And insofar as they are bound up with something that matters to us—insofar as we are invested in healthy living, in other words—it will be even more difficult to do so. But even if we were successful in changing some of these habits, it would not mean that we had thereby changed our super-habit, since it is not identical with any one of these sub-habits. To change the super-habit itself, we would need to change a more fundamental disposition that ranges over, but is not identical with, a wide variety of sub-habits, and while, in principle, this does not entail that super-habits cannot be changed, it does mean that it is extremely difficult to do so, that the changing of particular sub-habits may leave the super-habit untouched, and, again, that the difficulty is multiplied insofar as we are invested in it.

"Extremely difficult" is still distinct from "impossible," of course, which seems not to do justice to Christianity's widespread insistence that humans are somehow bound to their sinfulness—after all, if it were only "extremely difficult" to change our dispositions, then people could, in principle, free themselves from their sinfulness. This goes against the idea that humans are bound to sin in principle, and not merely accidentally. To address this objection, then, we turn from the idea of habituation to the idea that we humans somehow *inherit* our sinfulness.

One straightforward way of thinking about such inheritance would simply extend the habituation model, by recognizing that people's habits are formed not only by themselves but by the influence of others as well. We might think of this, in consequence, as a *social* inheritance of sin. This is what Albrecht Ritschl has in mind when he claims that "the cooperation of many individuals in certain forms of sin leads to a reinforcement of the same in common customs and principles, in standing immoralities, and even in evil institutions. Thus there develops an almost irresistible power of temptation for those who, with characters yet undeveloped, are so much exposed to evil example that they do not see through the network of enticements to evil. Accordingly, the kingdom of sin, or the (immoral, human) world is reinforced in every new generation."[33] The idea here, simply stated, is that, even from birth, humans are particularly susceptible to the influence of others, such that countless habits are formed in us long before we have any say in the matter. As young children, for instance, we learn countless words and concepts long before we could possibly choose which ones to learn, and it is only on the basis of these concepts that we will eventually be able to make judgments about them. More seriously, we likewise learn countless attitudes, countless ideas about how we should act, countless evaluations, and the like, and we do so, again, long before we are in position to make judgments about these things. Children thus pick up on their parents' attitudes toward vegetables, for example, as well as their attitude toward members of certain groups, just as they pick up on their parents' assessment of the child's own worth—hence some children are raised to think of themselves as the center of the world, while others are raised to think of themselves as worthless. Again, the idea here is simply that this same mechanism can explain how sinful habits are passed on to others and, crucially, how persons are habituated into a sinful orientation long before they could decide not to be. Hence, by extending the habituation model to include our habituation by others, this model could help us explain why all persons are bound to sin.

One might reasonably wonder, however, whether sinfulness still seems accidental on this approach, since it might appear that children could be free from sinfulness if, say, they were raised in isolation by particularly scrupulous parents. Naturally, one might doubt the possibility of such sin-free child-rearing, but the very idea helpfully presses us to consider a second way of thinking about the inheritance of sinfulness, according to which there is something about humanity's constitution that makes us sinful "by nature." Here some care is necessary, which is one reason I put "nature" in quotation marks. For if "sinful by nature" were to mean that human nature, *qua human*, is sinful, then it would follow, contrary to Christological tradition, that one could not simultaneously be sinless and fully human, just as it would mean that humans can be redeemed from sinfulness only by becoming something other than human. On the other hand, "sinful by nature" can simply mean not only that all humans are fundamentally sinful but that there is something inexorable about this, and that this inexorability is rooted in human nature in such a way that, barring some sort of supernatural intervention, every human will become sinful. I will be using the term in the latter sense here, for obvious reasons. If we were all sinful by nature, in this sense, then it would mean that, when we inherit our constitution as humans, we simultaneously inherit an inexorable drive toward sinfulness.

Here is one plausible way to think about what this might mean: Suppose that humans are self-orienting creatures, where this means that we orient ourselves by setting our hearts on certain things, putting our trust in certain things, and taking our bearings from certain things. This is part of our nature. And then suppose (a) that ordinary human development is such that we naturally orient ourselves by and to that which is around us, which is to say that we naturally set our hearts on things around us, put our trust in things around us, and take our bearings from things around us; (b) that we become so oriented long before we could orient ourselves to something that transcends these things; (c) that this orientation is reinforced though habituation and our social inheritance; and, finally, (d) that by the time we could orient ourselves to something beyond these things, we are already so oriented to them that our God-orientation would itself be oriented by our more fundamental "world"-orientation (rather than vice versa). Our world-orientation would thereby fix our horizon, in other words, and God would then be located within this horizon—the selfish person thus turns selfishly to God, the tribalist turns God into the god of a tribe, the money-obsessed person turns God into a good-luck charm, and so on. We hear an account along these lines from Friedrich Schleiermacher, who claims that "in each individual the flesh manifests itself as a reality before the spirit comes to be such, the result being that, as soon as the spirit enters the sphere of consciousness . . . resistance takes place"; on this account, then, "the strength of the resistance made by the flesh and manifested in the consciousness of sin is due to the advantage gained by the flesh during the prior time, though again, of course, in association with the corporate life upon which the amount of that advantage depends."[34]

Again, the idea here is simple enough: if humans are self-orienting by nature, and if their world-orientation gets a decisive head start over their possible God-orientation, then by the time they could so much as orient themselves toward God, it will be too late; they will already have oriented themselves to the world to such an extent that any subsequent God-orientation will itself be included in their world-orientation (such that God will be someone they call upon in the hopes of securing the worldly goods that they care about, for instance, or who validates their belief in their group's absoluteness). So small children thus learn what is good or bad, what matters, what is true, and other such things from their parents and other teachers, which is to say that they take their bearings from these people. When they feel afraid or insecure, they naturally turn to something nearby for reassurance—a blankie or a family member or a hiding place. They likewise set their hearts on things that are nearby: a toy, for instance, or a treat, or someone's attention. The point here is not that there is anything wrong with these things; the point, rather, is that they will inevitably become habituated into taking their bearings from that which is this-worldly, into putting their trust in that which is this-worldly, into setting their hearts on that which is this-worldly, and so, crucially, into the super-habit of being oriented by and to the world where they should be oriented by and to God. By the time they could orient themselves toward God, then, it is too late: they have already become so oriented toward the world that they will trust God as if God were a this-worldly source of security, set their hearts on God as if God were a this-worldly good, and take their bearings from God as if God were a this-worldly authority. We could thus say that we are world-oriented by nature—in the present sense of the term—but not in such a way that our *humanity itself* is considered sinful.

Taking everything together, then, appeals to habituation and to inheritance can help us understand one respect in which Christians have claimed that we are bound to sin, for on these accounts, by the time we could decide not to be sinful, it is already too late. This does not entail, of course, that we cannot resist particular sins and habits, only that we are, at bottom and on the whole, sinful.

That brings us to a second respect in which Christians have claimed we are bound to sin, namely, the sense in which we have become enslaved to "Sin," a cosmic power or tyrant that temporarily rules over this world.[35] Sin is here personified, in other words, as a power that reigns over this world, and humans are seen as falling under its jurisdiction and being subject to its authority or, to change the metaphor a bit, as its bondservants.[36] As Justo Gonzalez puts it, then, "The core of the human predicament is neither a debt to God nor a lack of spirituality but an enslavement to the powers of evil."[37]

There are two complementary ways of understanding this sort of bondage. The first explains it at a *collective* level. Just as ancient Israelites became the vassals of foreign powers such as the Babylonians, so, on this account, all of us became vassals of Sin when it conquered this world. This is the sort of thing that Luther has in mind when he claims, for instance, that "Sin, too, is a very powerful and cruel tyrant, dominating and ruling over the whole world, capturing and enslaving all men. In short, sin is a great and powerful god who devours the whole human race."[38] Basil of Caesarea likewise talks about "the enemy" making us "a slave to sin," just as James Cone talks about our being "enslaved by alien forces" and about "those powers which held man captive."[39] On this account, then, humanity is subjected to the power of Sin because Sin reigns over this world; everyone within this jurisdiction falls under its authority, from which it follows that everyone in the world is under its power.

Another version of the collective approach—fully compatible with the one just mentioned—finds its roots in the idea that all humans are "in Adam," in the sense that we are part of the family of which Adam is head. In the ancient world, at least, decisions for an entire family could be made by the head of that family, and the entire family would then be *bound* by those decisions; entire families could thus be sold into indentured servitude, for instance, just as entire families could apparently be converted to a particular religion.[40] On this account, then, if Adam pledged his troth to Sin instead of to God, and if this decision is binding not only on him but on his entire family as well, then it follows that his family—that is, all humanity—has been pledged to the power of Sin. Here too, then, humanity is subjected to sin *as a collective*: if (a) all humans are part of a single family, (b) the head of a family can make decisions that are binding on all members of that family, and (c) the head of the human family—Adam—subjected himself and his family to the reign of Sin, then it follows (d) that all humans have been subjected to that reign.

Mention of Adam's own subjection to the power of Sin brings us, quite naturally, to explanations of the *individual* character of such subjection. (These two sorts of explanation usually go hand in hand: the former are needed to explain the inescapability of Sin's reign, whereas the latter are needed to explain each individual's acceptance—even affirmation—of that reign.)

One straightforward way of understanding this would be to imagine that, by sinning, persons have taken a kind of vow to Sin, have pledged their binding allegiance to it, and have willingly sold themselves into servitude to it. Gregory of Nyssa depicts a mechanism of this sort, claiming that those who subject themselves to Sin become its slaves, in just the same way that "those who give up their own freedom for money are the slaves of those who bought them."[41] Gregory here echoes a common theme in the New Testament, as when Paul characterizes humanity as "sold under Sin" (Rom. 7:14).[42] Along these lines, Paul likewise asks, "Do you not know that if you present yourselves to anyone as obedient slaves, you are slaves of the one whom you obey, either of Sin, which leads to death, or of obedience, which leads to righteousness?" (Rom. 6:16). We hear something similar in the Gospel of John: "Everyone who practices sin is a slave to sin" (John 8:34). In each case, the idea is that we are slaves to and subjects of Sin precisely because we have put ourselves in that position. We might think of the mechanism here working in roughly the following manner: there is a life-and-death struggle—a war—being waged between God and Sin, and everyone must choose which side to be on; Sin reigns over this world, such that insofar as we treat this world as ultimate, we thereby side with Sin; persons who side with Sin place themselves under its authority— as one would place oneself under the authority of a military leader—such that they could then be said to be at Sin's service or under its dominion. To this, we need only add that the relevant taking of a side is akin to the taking of a binding, lifelong vow, such that one would remain in bondage to Sin *even if one later wanted to be free from its power;* this is roughly similar to the situation facing a British woman who, prior to the 1857 Matrimonial Causes Act, freely entered into a marriage but eventually wanted to get out of it: once she had taken her marital vows, there was no way for her to undo them. Once we have made such a vow, accordingly, there is no going back; it is binding for life. Hence, if we understand each person's sinfulness as a binding pledge of allegiance to the power of Sin, then we can get some sense of what Christians mean when they claim that we have all subjected ourselves to its reign.

We can explain this subjection further by considering some recent scholarship on Paul's understanding of "the Law."[43] As several scholars have pointed out, Paul seems to claim, quite provocatively, that the Law plays a key role in binding us to the power of Sin—indeed, he comes very close to saying that the Law *just is* the mechanism by which we are so bound. Paul thus asserts, for instance, that the Law "imprisoned all things under the power of Sin" (Gal. 3:22), that "the power of Sin is the Law" (1 Cor. 15:56), and that the Law can therefore be said to have "held us captive" (Rom. 7:6). It seems clear, then, that for Paul, the Law plays a decisive role in binding us to the power of Sin—indeed, in giving Sin its power over us. So how does this work?

Here is one way of thinking about it: the Law was given by God in order to maintain a moral order within the cosmos, where this means, at bottom, that it maintains the basic principle of justice—that people get what they deserve. As such, the Law could be regarded as the means by which God renders to each according to their works (Rom. 2:6) or of guaranteeing that each will receive their "wages" (Rom. 6:23). The Law would thus ensure a reward for those who are righteous and condemnation for those who are sinful, which seems to be the idea underlying passages which claim, for instance, that under the Law, "every transgression or disobedience received a just penalty" (Heb. 2:2), or that the Law keeps "a record that stands against us with its legal demands" (Col. 2:14). We find additional support for this idea from the Law's role in condemning persons to death; so Paul claims, for instance, that "the letter kills," and he equates the Law with "the ministry of death" and "the ministry of condemnation" (2 Cor. 3:6–9). He likewise claims—though without express reference to the Law—that "the wages of sin is death" (Romans 6:23), just as he connects sin, death, and the Law in his assertion that "the sting of death is sin, and the power of sin is the Law" (1 Cor. 15:56). With such ideas in view, the picture that emerges looks something like this: (a) the Law maintains order by ensuring that people get what they deserve; (b) if persons pledge their allegiance to the power of Sin, then Sin has a rightful claim over them, and the Law ensures that this claim is enforced; (c) if persons are sinful, they deserve condemnation unto death, and the Law ensures that they are so condemned.

To this, we need add only that there is a sense in which death itself thereby becomes a tool of Sin—the sense in which Paul can claim that "Sin exercised dominion in death" (Rom. 5:21). The idea here is straightforward enough: if the Law ensures that everyone who sins is liable to the death penalty, then it follows that Sin has the final word upon every sinful person's life, and the power of Sin thus exercises dominion over them. (An officer who is entitled—nay, bound—to shoot all deserters thereby maintains the military's dominion over them.) Condemnation would therefore have the ultimate word about each of us, which turns out to mean that *Sin* would have the final say about each of our lives. Death itself would thus have dominion over this age (see Rom. 5:17) and, just so, likewise become a power that is opposed to God's dominion. Assuming that whatever is opposed to God's dominion is ipso facto allied with the power of Sin, it follows, again, that death serves Sin.

On this approach, then, the Law is good insofar as it preserves moral order within the cosmos, but precisely in so doing, it gives Sin and Death their rightful power over us. (It turns out to be good in another sense, for, as we will see, God uses this death sentence precisely to free us from the power of Sin and Death.) This would explain what Paul means when he says that the Law serves Sin and Death, just as it would explain why our subjection to these powers can be broken only if our subjection to the Law is likewise broken. I return to the latter point in the next chapter.

For now, the main ideas are simply these: (a) that humans are bound to Sin insofar as we are part of a collective that has been handed over to Sin's dominion; (b) that we are bound to Sin insofar as we have made an irrevocable, lifelong vow to it; and (c) that we are bound to it insofar as the Law establishes its rightful claim over us, even unto Death.

Christians have traditionally claimed, then, not only that humans are oriented by and to the world but also that, as a consequence, we have become bound to sin, in the sense that we cannot help but be sinful, and in the sense that we have become bondservants of the power of Sin. To deal with our sinfulness, accordingly, humanity will need not only to be reoriented to God but also freed from our subjection to Sin. I turn to these issues in the next chapter. Before doing so, however, we need to analyze one additional feature of "the world," namely, people's sense that all is not right with it. We turn, therefore, to a consideration of *brokenness*.

Brokenness

"The way of the world" is marked not only by sinfulness but by a sense of brokenness as well, by which I mean a sense that this world is marked not only by beauty and goodness but also by wrongs and suffering. To explain what this means—and with an eye to what follows—I will here consider four paradigmatic ways that people experience such brokenness, two of which are directed at the world, and two at ourselves.

Let us begin with the experience of *tragedy*. As I use the word, an event counts as "tragic" when something importantly bad happens to something important to us. If something bad happens but it does not affect something important to us, then it will not matter to us in the way that tragedy does; hence, if something bad happens to something I do not care about—

if an old T-shirt gets a stain on it, for instance—I will not experience it as tragic. An event may thus be tragic in itself even if I do not experience it as such: it is tragic if a person loses a child, but if that person and child do not matter to me—if I do not even know about them—then I will not experience that event *as* tragic. By the same token, an event will seem tragic only if something *importantly* bad happens to something we care about. My children are important to me, and it would be bad if one of them fell off a bike and broke a finger, but I would hardly experience this as tragic, for the simple reason that breaking a finger is not (usually) bad enough to warrant that response. I would be more warranted in feeling that way if, say, their bicycles—an irreplaceable keepsake given to them by a now-deceased grandparent—were stolen, or if they fell and suffered more serious injuries. Again, the point is that an event counts as tragic only when something importantly bad happens to something we care about. To take just one example of what this looks like, consider Augustine's response to his friend's death: "He whom I had loved as if he would never die was dead," Augustine recounts. "So my life was to me a horror. I did not wish to live with only half of myself, and perhaps the only reason why I so feared death was that then the whole of my much loved friend would have died."[44] Augustine endured profound suffering precisely because his friend, who mattered so much to him, was now gone. Such is the nature of tragedy.

    If this is right, then, contrary to the dominant account, it follows that the concept "tragedy" should not be reserved for cases in which persons face a dilemma—cases, that is, in which we must choose between two things that we value, and in which we are therefore guaranteed to lose something of value. On the one hand, the mere fact that we face such a dilemma does not entail that we thereby experience tragedy: if the goods between which we must choose are fairly insignificant to us, for instance, then nothing tragic will follow from the choice. (It is not tragic, on my account, if students have to choose between two equally interesting courses or if parents have to choose which of their children should get the first turn on a merry-go-round.) On the other hand, persons can experience tragedy even in the absence of a dilemma: it was unspeakably tragic that a woman's young children were wrenched from her grip by the waters of Superstorm Sandy, irrespective of whether she had to choose between the two or to choose between them and some other good. It seems to me, then, that facing a dilemma is neither a necessary nor a sufficient condition of experiencing tragedy (as I am using that term). To be sure, there are cases in which persons endure tragedy precisely because they face such a dilemma; I am simply suggesting that these are not the only instances of tragedy, and that not every dilemma eventuates in tragedy.

One further qualification: an event counts as tragic when something importantly bad happens to something important to us, but only insofar as this is not the deserved consequence of our wrongdoing. If my house is repossessed because I got sick and lost my job, that is tragic; but if it is repossessed because I paid for it with funds that I knowingly embezzled, then it is not tragic, precisely because, in that case, I can be said to have brought this circumstance upon myself. (Naturally, if the ensuing badness is disproportionate to my wrongdoing, then it may still count as tragic even if my wrongdoing played some role in bringing it about.) There may be exceptions, of course: if my wrongdoing is long in the past, for instance, and I have in the meantime turned over a new leaf, then it might indeed count as tragic when my past catches up to me; if an elderly man committed a crime when he was a teenager, for example, but has since made restitution for his crime and turned his life around, then it might be tragic if he were sent to prison for it. Exceptions aside, the general principle is that something counts as tragic insofar as something importantly bad happens to something important to us, and this badness is not something that we have brought on ourselves. In such experiences, persons usually have a strong sense that something is wrong with the world, that things should not be this way—in short, that something is *broken*. This sense can lead persons, in turn, to a kind of protest against the world, or to a kind of resignation to it. I return to such experiences in chapter 5, when discussing the spiritual practice of lament.

That brings us to a closely related concept—namely, *injustice*—whose features require their own treatment. In the most basic sense, to experience injustice is for a particular sort of expectation to be unmet, namely, the expectation that we will be treated in accordance with our normative status or worth—in short, that others will *recognize* that status or worth.[45] So, for instance, if an applicant is not admitted to a particular school even though her credentials are better than the credentials of those who were admitted, she may experience this as an injustice; likewise if a person's conversational insights are routinely ignored while other, sometimes lesser, insights are taken up; if a person is addressed by her first name while others are addressed with titles and last names; or if store workers ignore certain persons or keep a suspicious eye on them. In cases like these, persons expect to be treated in a certain way—to be recognized as having the same worth as others who have been so recognized—and when they are not treated this way, they may experience this as an injustice.

In the cases just mentioned, one sees others being recognized as having a fairly particular status: the status of qualified applicant, say, or of full-fledged contributor to a conversation. But the status in question can also be the more basic status of being a person or a fellow human being. In response to unsanctioned police brutality, accordingly, many American activists have insisted that Black lives matter, precisely because such brutality seems to treat Black persons as if their lives did not matter and, so, does not recognize their worth as human beings. In the same way, if certain persons are prevented from getting an education or are deprived of their due process, they might likewise feel that their worth as a human being is not being recognized. This is the sort of worth at issue in the Second Vatican Council's *Gaudium et Spes*, to take just one important precedent: "Everyone must consider his every neighbor without exception," it urges, "as another self, taking into account first of all his life and the means necessary to living it with dignity, so as not to imitate the rich man who had no concern for the poor man Lazarus." The council thus classes as "infamies" "whatever violates the integrity of the human person, such as mutilation, torments inflicted on body or mind, attempts to coerce the will itself; whatever insults human dignity, such as subhuman living conditions, arbitrary imprisonment, deportation, slavery, prostitution, the selling of women and children; as well as disgraceful working conditions, where men are treated as mere tools for profit, rather than as free and responsible persons."[46] Here, again, the point is that persons should be treated in a way that befits their worth; insofar as they are not, they may—rightly—experience this as injustice.

One additional point: we characteristically respond to injustices with some sort of *righteous anger*, that is, a felt evaluation of a particular treatment *as a wrong done to our dignity*. Sometimes this felt evaluation takes the form of indignation (that is, the feeling that I have been treated in a way that does not befit my worth); other times, it takes the form of resentment, where my anger is directed not toward the treatment itself but toward the one(s) responsible for it. Either way, such feelings not only register the fact of injustice but also stand as a sort of protest against it: it is as if our feelings themselves were saying, "This is wrong. I should not be treated this way. I deserve better." Such feelings can thus bear witness to our worth and therefore help us resist the temptation to accept would-be diminutions of that worth; by doing so, they can likewise provide us with some of the impetus necessary to resist these diminutions not only internally but externally, too. Mary Daly thus observes that in the case of such diminutions, "rage is required as a positive creative force, making possible a breakthrough, encountering the blockages of inauthentic structures. It rises as a reaction to the shock of recognizing what has been lost—before it had even been discovered—one's own identity. Out of this shock can come intimations of what human being (as opposed to half being) can be."[47]

Here again, then, we have an experience of the fact that the world is not the way it should be—in this case, an experience of the fact that we are not being treated the way we should be. I return to these matters in chapter 6, when we consider the relationship between love and justice.[48]

Experiences of tragedy and injustice are two principal ways that we perceive that there is something wrong with the world. There are also two paradigmatic ways that we perceive that there is something wrong not with the world but with us, the first of which is the experience of *guilt*. In the most basic sense, to feel guilty is to feel bad about myself because of something that I have done. So, for example, I might feel bad about myself if I were to take money out of a lost wallet, or to talk badly about someone behind their back, or to act like a self-important jerk. In such cases, I feel bad about myself precisely because I have done something wrong. Naturally, I can also feel guilty about things I have left undone: I might thus feel bad about myself if I fail to speak up for someone who is being bullied or if I do not lend a hand when a neighbor is struggling to move a piece of furniture.[49]

There are a variety of ways that one can feel bad about oneself, so it is important to note that guilt is a matter of feeling bad about oneself insofar as one has failed to live up to certain norms. Not just any norms, of course: if I fail to live up to norms of good penmanship, for instance, I may feel slightly embarrassed, but I would not feel guilty; likewise, I may feel bad about myself for not winning an athletic contest but, again, I would not feel guilty about it. I feel guilty, rather, when I fail to live up to the norms by which I assess how good a person I am, morally speaking, or, in short, when I violate my *moral* norms. This way of putting things can help us make sense not only of cases where I have lied or cheated but also of cases where, say, I feel guilty about lacking the willpower to maintain a new diet. In both sorts of case, I would feel guilty precisely insofar as my behavior (or character) indicates that I am not living up to the standards by which I would judge a person's moral goodness—insofar, that is, as I am failing to live up to *my* moral norms, rather than moral norms per se. (From the opposite direction, if one violated an objective moral norm to the effect that, say, one should not be cruel to others but did not accept this as a norm by which to judge one's goodness as a person, then one would not feel guilty, though one would in fact *be* guilty.) To feel guilty, then, is to feel bad about oneself because one has failed to live up to one's moral norms. This is what Ritschl has in mind when he claims that "guilt, in the moral sense, expresses the disturbance of the proper relation between the moral law and freedom, which follows from the law-transgressing abuse of freedom, and as such is marked by the accompanying pain of the feeling of guilt. Guilt is thus that permanent contradiction between the objective and the subjective factor of the moral will which is produced by the abuse of freedom in non-fulfillment of the law, and the unworthiness of which is expressed for the moral subject in his consciousness of guilt."[50]

Note well that, on this account, guilt involves feeling bad about oneself rather than simply about what one has done, for in a case where I violated a moral norm but did not think that this reflected anything about my own morality, I would feel remorse rather than guilt. This explains, in turn, why guilt depends upon there being a connection between me and what I have done, and, in particular, of being morally, and not just causally, responsible for it; we often mark this distinction by appeal to the notion of "blameworthiness." Notice, too, that we can "feel guilty" even if we are not, at any given moment, actively feeling bad about ourselves, for we could still count as "feeling guilty" so long as we are liable to feel that way whenever our moral failings come to mind. Hence, if as an adult I were to say that I still feel guilty about a moment when, as a child, I was cruel to another child, this would mean that I am liable to feel bad about myself whenever I remember this moment, not that I have been feeling continuously bad ever since. (This is relevantly similar to the way that I can be said to enjoy my work even if I am not in a constant state of joyfulness about it, just as I can be said to be angry with someone for years even if I am not in a constant state of anger toward them.)

One's liability to feel bad about oneself for something one has done can also contribute to a more general liability to feel bad about oneself. The mechanism is straightforward enough: persons who are liable to feel guilty whenever they recall particular wrongdoings will also be increasingly liable to feel bad about themselves per se—that is, they will be liable to feel bad about themselves not only vis-à-vis particular wrongdoings but about themselves more generally. Very simply, they may begin to feel that they are bad persons, morally speaking. At this point, their guilt has begun to shade over into *moral shame*, which is a topic to which I turn in a moment.

To experience guilt, then, is to feel bad about oneself because one has done something that falls short of one's moral standards. People do not want to feel this way about themselves, of course, which is one reason we are tempted to make excuses for ourselves and to deceive ourselves about what we have actually done (and why).[51] This is not the only way to deal with guilt, however, and certainly not the best; I consider another approach, namely *forgiveness*, in subsequent chapters.

We can distinguish guilt from *shame*, though the two feelings obviously overlap at key points; after all, persons will often feel ashamed of their immoral acts or even over their immoral character. Not all shame is of the moral variety, however; persons can and do feel shame about all sorts of things that cannot plausibly be charged to their moral accounts—they may feel shame about their bodies, for instance, or about their family, or about any number of other things for which they are not responsible. In the most basic sense, we feel shame when we experience ourselves as failing to embody our ideals or values, in such a way or to such an extent that we experience our very selves as so failing. We might thus feel shame if we have cheated on our spouse, for instance, or lost face, or inadvertently hurt someone who matters to us, or come from a "bad" family, or had our privacy compromised, or if we take ourselves to be ugly or unsightly or deformed. In all these cases, there is some ideal that we fail to embody; insofar as the ideal matters to me, I identify with it, which explains why I would experience this failure as reflecting on my very self.[52] Simply stated, then, insofar as I fall significantly short of embodying this ideal, I experience my very self as falling short, and thus experience shame. As Dietrich Bonhoeffer claims, shame thus "give[s] unwitting witness to the fallen state of the ashamed."[53]

Such shame can move from the inside out, so to speak, or from the outside in: in a case where I feel bad about my character or my body or my background, I will feel shame if those things are exposed to the eyes of others; call this *inside-out* shame, for in such cases, my sense of shame is rooted primarily in my own self-evaluation and only secondarily in the way others see me. Indeed, even if others do not actually think there is anything wrong with me, I may still feel shameful in their eyes insofar as I project my self-evaluation into their perception of me. But shame can also move in the other direction: I may develop a sense of shame concerning some aspect of my character or body or background precisely because others treat those things as shameful; for obvious reasons, we can call this *outside-in* shame. If others act as though there is something wrong with me because I was raised in a working-class neighborhood, for instance, or because I have crooked teeth, or because I got a B in a class, then I may start to believe that there is something wrong with me and may therefore feel exposed insofar as others can see it. (In most cases, shame probably moves in both directions: insofar as I feel that there is something wrong with me, I perceive myself to be shameful in the eyes of others, and this perception reinforces my sense that there is something wrong with me; insofar as others treat me as if there is something wrong with me, I may start to feel that way, too, in which case I will be more likely to perceive myself as shameful in the eyes of others, which will, in turn, reinforce my sense that there is something wrong with me.)

That brings us to an important distinction, namely, that between *circumstantial* and *deep-seated* shame. As its name suggests, circumstantial shame is indexed to particular circumstances, in the sense that we may feel shame while those circumstances prevail, and maybe for a brief stretch afterward, but not much beyond that. If we feel shame during a short-lived illness, for instance, but our shame subsides once we return to health, we thus experience circumstantial shame. Deep-seated shame, by contrast, is attached more tightly to one's sense of oneself, such that one perceives there to be something shameful about oneself irrespective of one's circumstances. When this becomes part of one's self-conception, one may take this sense that something-is-wrong-with-me to be more or less definitive of one's identity. So, sadly, children who are treated as if they are worthless or unlovable may thus come to feel as if this is simply true of them—that, deep-down, they really are worthless or unlovable. Persons who have done something especially bad may likewise feel that their identity itself has been irrevocably stained, just as persons who feel deeply ashamed about a physical abnormality may come to feel that this is the defining feature of their existence. (On the latter point, consider Lucy Grealy, in *Autobiography of a Face:* "I was my face, I was ugliness.")[54] In cases like these, persons feel that there is something shameful, deep down, about their very self, and while they may thus be susceptible to intense feelings of shame when this is exposed by certain circumstances, their shame is not here reducible to such feelings. What characterizes this sort of shame, rather, is the way it shapes a person's self-conception—that is, the way it shapes the very framework that one uses to interpret oneself and things related to oneself: if one takes oneself to be fundamentally unlovable, one will then be disposed to see one's faults as more reflective of one's identity than one's strengths, to see the unloving actions of others as a response to one's unlovableness, and to see the loving actions of others either as mistaken—"You don't know the real me"—or as not actually loving. This is one of the reasons it can be so hard to change this sort of self-conception, since it filters out things that might otherwise call the self-conception into question.

We find a particularly moving description of these features of shame in Sally Rooney's recent novel *Normal People*, in which the narrator has this to say about a character named Marianne: "From a young age her life has been abnormal, she knows that. But so much is covered over in time now, the way leaves fall over a piece of earth, and eventually mingle with the soil. Things that happened to her then are buried in the earth of her body. She tries to be a good person. But deep down she knows that she is a bad person, corrupted, wrong, and all her efforts to be right, to have the right opinions, to say the right things, these efforts only disguise what is buried inside her, the evil part of herself."[55] This is what it looks like when shame has been written into a person's self-conception: they take there to be something fundamentally bad about themselves, and they interpret other aspects of their life in light of that fundamental badness.[56]

Deep-seated shame is thus a matter of feeling as though there is something fundamentally wrong with oneself or, indeed, that one is oneself fundamentally wrong. This, too, is a way that persons experience themselves as broken. I return to such brokenness in chapter 4.

In experiences of tragedy and injustice, we perceive that there is something broken about the world; in experiences of guilt and shame, we perceive that there is something broken about ourselves. Such feelings can lead persons to long for deliverance from this world, or at least for a remedy for its brokenness; in that case, it may prime persons to devote themselves to a God who promises to make all things right. Then again, it may also lead persons to self-deception or to doubling down on whatever this-worldly security they can find. Hence, even if a religious tradition offers a way of life that addresses this sort of brokenness, there is no reason to assume that persons will devote themselves to it.

Conclusion

The agenda for subsequent chapters has now been set: if sinfulness is primarily a matter of being oriented by and to the world where we ought to be oriented by and to God (through disordered love, misplaced trust, and the absolutization of worldly standards), and if we are bound to sin both because we cannot help but be sinful and because we are subjected to the power of Sin, then Christianity will have to explain how we could be freed from the power of Sin and reoriented to God. A step in that direction is sometimes taken when persons experience brokenness—injustice and tragedy in the world around them, guilt and shame in the world within them—for insofar as such experiences breed dissatisfaction with the world and, so, a longing for something beyond it, it can prime us to accept a message about a God who transcends this world, as well as a way of life that would orient us to that God. Christianity proclaims just such a message, to which we now turn.

CHAPTER THREE

Deliverance from Sin

THE PREVIOUS CHAPTER sketched an account of "the way of the world" according to which humans are sinful insofar as we are oriented by and to the world (where we should be oriented to God), and according to which we are bound to sin insofar as we cannot help but be sinful and are subjected to the power of Sin. This chapter (like, indeed, the rest of this book) considers an account of what it might take to be delivered from this predicament, beginning with some claims about the one whom Christians have traditionally held to play the central role in that deliverance: *Jesus*. In particular, I try here to make sense of two characteristically Christian ideas about Jesus, namely, that he inaugurates a new way of being in the world and that he breaks the power of Sin and Death. With these claims up and running, we can then turn to an account of how we are included in this new way of being and, in particular, how we share in Jesus' death and resurrection, by means of *repentance and new life*. Those who have embarked upon this new life will necessarily want to know what God thinks of them; Christianity meets this need through *practices of hearing God's judgment*—practices like baptism, confession and forgiveness, spiritual friendship, and the practice of learning to renarrate our life stories.

Before proceeding, a brief word about this chapter's use of biblical materials. Here as elsewhere, the aim is to understand Christianity, which may or may not coincide with a strictly historical understanding of the Bible. Many Christians are committed to historical accuracy, of course, and in any case historical scholarship can shed helpful light on Christian commitments and thus contribute to our goal of understanding Christianity. Indeed, with respect to Jesus' preaching, biblical scholarship has not only helped us understand what Jesus had to say but also helped us see that the center of his preaching was not ethics, per se, much less claims about his own divine nature, but the coming Kingdom of God.[1] Recent biblical scholarship has also shed valuable light on Paul's understanding of Jesus' death and resurrection; given that this can help us understand how we are freed from Sin, we should be glad to make use of it. Hence, although I am not trying to give a strictly historical reading of these texts, I have tried to listen carefully to those who do.

Jesus

We can get started by clarifying the norms implicit in Jesus' preaching; this will enable us to do two things: on the one hand, it will help us identify some of the norms by which a Christian way of life is constrained, and, on the other, it will provide us with a framework that helps us understand Jesus himself.[2] With this understanding on board, we can then turn to a consideration of how we are delivered from Sin.

We begin, accordingly, with some fairly basic facts about Jesus and his preaching. One of the most basic facts about him is that Jesus was a kind of end-times prophet, proclaiming that a new reign of God was about to dawn and that when it did, God would subject the world to judgment and fulfill God's promises. At the heart of Jesus' preaching, then, is a warning and an exhortation: "Prepare yourselves," he proclaims, "for the reign of God is at hand." He thus urges his hearers to ready themselves, in the same way that servants would get things ready for their master's return or homeowners would get ready if they knew that thieves were going to try to break into their houses.[3] A central aim of Jesus' preaching, therefore, is to tell people what they should do to prepare for God's coming reign and, in particular, what they must do to withstand the coming judgment; that is why Jesus likens those who heed his words to "a man building a house, who dug deeply and laid the foundation on rock; when a flood arose, the river burst against the house but could not shake it, because it had been well built" (Lk. 6:47–48). In the same way, he claims, those who heed his words will be well prepared for, and so be able to withstand, the coming judgment.

So how should they prepare? At bottom, Jesus' instructions are fairly simple: devote yourselves wholly to God; do what God commands, obey the will of God, and do so not only outwardly but with your whole self; or, in sum, "love the Lord your God with all your heart, and with all your soul, and with all your mind" (Mt. 22:37; see also Mk. 12:29–30, Lk. 10:27). About this command—to love God with all one's heart, soul, and mind—Jesus says, "Do this, and you will live" (Lk. 10:28). Again, then, the way to prepare for the coming judgment is to devote oneself wholeheartedly and unreservedly to God.

Jesus then adds two crucial details to this message. First, he tells his hearers that such devotion is at odds with storing up or setting one's heart on earthly riches. This is why Jesus insists that "no one can serve two masters; for a slave will either hate the one and love the other, or be devoted to the one and despise the other," and why he thus contends that "you cannot serve God and wealth" (Mt. 6:24; see also 6:21). This explains why he inveighs so uncompromisingly against the treasuring of monetary wealth (see Lk. 12:18–21), of power (Mt. 20:25–28), and of esteem (Mt. 6:1–18; Lk. 16:15). The idea here seems to be that by attaching themselves to earthly riches, persons attach themselves to the age that is about to pass away, which means, in turn, that they will not be able to withstand the coming judgment. Or, to come at the point from a slightly different angle, the idea is that insofar as we set our hearts on earthly goods, we not only fail to be fully devoted to God, we "cheat" on God (in the committed-relationship sense of "cheat"). In traditional marriages, at least, if a husband invests himself in a particular hobby such as painting, he would not necessarily count as being unfaithful to his spouse, whereas if he invests himself in a romantic relationship with another person, he would count as unfaithful. On Jesus' account, setting our hearts on earthly riches is more like the latter: "For where your treasure is," he says, "there your heart will be also" (Mt. 6:21).

From this, it follows that if we want to devote ourselves to God, we must leave all such riches behind (at the level of our investment in them, at least, if not necessarily at the level of actual renunciation, though this is a point of interpretive controversy). This is one of the most prominent themes in Jesus' preaching. We hear it in several of Jesus' parables: "The kingdom of heaven is like treasure hidden in a field, which someone found and hid; then in his joy he goes and sells all that he has and buys that field. Again, the kingdom of heaven is like a merchant in search of fine pearls; on finding one pearl of great value, he went and sold all that he had and bought it" (Mt. 13:44–45). We also hear it when Jesus tells people that they must hate father and mother for his sake, that they must deny themselves and take up their cross, and that whoever puts a hand to the plow and looks back is not fit for the kingdom of God (Lk. 14:26–27; Mt. 16:24–25; Lk. 9:59–62).[4] And we see it in the disciples' response to Jesus' calling: each of them leaves everything behind—boats, nets, fish, family—to follow him. This is one of the reasons that wholehearted devotion to God requires us to trust God, since it is hard to see how those who renounce all interest in earthly riches would be able to provide for their security and sustenance. Jesus thus reassures them: "Do not worry, saying 'what will we eat?' or 'what will we drink?' or 'what will we wear?' For it is the Gentiles who strive for all these things; and indeed your heavenly Father knows that you need all these things. But strive first for the kingdom of God and his righteousness, and all these things will be given to you as well" (Mt. 6:31–33).

That brings us back to a clarification I made earlier, namely, that Jesus calls people to renounce all investment in earthly riches, rather than to renounce all earthly goods per se (though these often amount to the same thing). Hence, when Zacchaeus gives away half of his possessions—not all—Jesus says to him, "Today salvation has come to this house, because he too is a son of Abraham" (Lk. 19:9). Arguably, then, Jesus' point is not that persons must become poor, per se, but that they must not set their hearts on earthly possessions. To be sure, if one's heart is not set on earthly possessions, it follows that one would be willing to become poor. But actual poverty is itself neither necessary nor sufficient for entrance into the kingdom of God, for poor persons may be just as likely as rich persons to set their hearts on earthly riches, just as those who have earthly possessions may not set their hearts on them.[5] (This is one way of understanding the moral Jesus draws from the parable of the shrewd manager: use wealth to make heavenly friends, as it were, so that when it is gone they will welcome us into their home [Lk. 16:9].)

So far, so good: to prepare ourselves for the coming reign of God, we must devote ourselves wholeheartedly to God, and so to devote ourselves, we must renounce our investment in earthly riches. Anyone familiar with the Gospels will recognize that something vital is missing from this summary, however, which brings us to a crucial detail in Jesus' preaching: to be devoted to God, and so to be prepared for the coming kingdom, we must also love others, especially those who are "least" by worldly standards. In his summaries of the Law, accordingly, Jesus tells his hearers not only to love God with all their hearts, souls, and minds but also to love their neighbors as themselves (Mt. 22:37–40; see also Mt. 7:12). I consider the meaning and scope of this commandment in chapter 6; for now, a placeholder will have to suffice: to love our neighbors as ourselves is to care about them for their own sake—to be first-personally invested in their well-being—and therefore to seek their good. The scope of this command, in turn, is maximally wide, applying not only to family members, tribe mates, and others whom we might naturally care about but even (especially) to enemies, foreigners, and those in need; Jesus is thus telling us, in Kazoh Kitamori's paraphrase, that "we must not limit ourselves to loving only those who are loveable."[6]

Again, I say more about this in chapter 6. For now, we need to consider how this second great commandment is related to the first: how is our love of *neighbor* connected to our love of *God?* A first answer is probably the most straightforward: if we are devoted to God, then we will want to do God's will; hence, if God loves all, then those who love God will want to love all, too. This seems to be what Jesus had in mind when he insisted that we must love even our enemies, since *God* shows love to all—righteous and unrighteous alike (Mt. 5:43–48). We can also understand this by analogy with David's love for Mephibosheth: because David loved Jonathan, he likewise loved the one whom Jonathan loved, namely, Mephibosheth; in loving Mephibosheth, then, he was expressing his love for Jonathan, too. In the same way, if we love God, we will likewise love the ones whom God loves, and our love for them will thus be an expression of our love for God.

A second answer is related to the first: God not only wills that we should love everyone, God identifies Godself with our neighbors in such a way that, in loving them, we are simultaneously loving God. The idea here, simply stated, is that when we love people, we become invested in them to such an extent that their well-being is included in our own well-being; if something goes well for them, accordingly, we experience it as good for us, and if something goes badly for them, we experience it as bad for us. Hence, if my children were mistreated, I would be upset not only on their behalf but first-personally as well, since love has tied my fortune to theirs. In the same way, if God loves people and is therefore invested in them to such an extent that their well-being is included in God's own, then it follows that if we do something good (or bad) for them, we are likewise doing something good (or bad) for God. I return to this point in chapter 6, but even with this rudimentary sketch in mind, it is no surprise that our neighbors—especially those who are "least"—would be considered a sacrament of God's presence, nor is it a surprise that Jesus told his followers that whatever they did for the least of these, they did for Jesus himself.[7]

Because love invests us in those we love, it follows that *we* are loved when-ever someone loves *them;* hence, because God is first-personally invested in our neighbors, we love *God* whenever we love them.

From these two answers, we can draw out a few key implications. First and most obviously, if we love God, then we will love others; to the extent that we do not love others, accordingly, we do not love God. (On this point, consider 1 John 4:20: "Those who say, 'I love God,' and hate their brothers or sisters, are liars; for those who do not love a brother or a sister, whom they have seen, cannot love God whom they have not seen." We hear some-thing similar from Teresa of Avila: "We cannot know whether or not we love God," she writes, "although there are strong indications for recogniz-ing that we do love him; but we can know whether we love our neighbor.")[8] The logic here goes something like this: to love others is to care about them; if I care about them, then what matters to them will matter to me; if someone else matters to them, accordingly, then that person will matter to me, too. Hence, if God loves others, then if we love God, we will love others, too. A second implication is a bit more subtle: if we show love for others, we may thereby show love for God, but not necessarily. To see why, suppose someone does something nice for my daughter: they write her an encouraging note when she is feeling downcast, for instance. Given my investment in her well-being, this note will promote my own well-being; in writing the note, then, its writer has done something good not only for my daughter but for me, too. That does not mean, however, that the writer has expressed *love* toward me; for that, they would need to have been doing something nice for her, at least in part, *because* they love me. If this is cor-rect, then people who do good for others can be said to do something good for God (whether they intend to or not), but they can be said thereby to express love for God only if their doing so is motivated, at least in part, by that love. One last implication: there is no reason to think that persons can love others only if they love God, though Christians have traditionally in-sisted that love for God does free us to love others more unconditionally and therefore more wholeheartedly. The idea here is that insofar as people are devoted to God, they will entrust themselves wholly to God, seek their good in and from God, and orient themselves by God's standards (rather than by worldly ones); in doing so, they will be freed from having to estab-lish and maintain their own security, from treating penultimate goods as if they were ultimate, and from the distorting influence of worldly standards. In consequence, they should likewise be freed to love others more uncon-ditionally, since they will not have to worry unduly about their security in so loving, nor will they be tempted to love others as if they were ultimately good, nor will they see them through a lens other than that of God's love. If this is right, then it follows that those who love God should be able to love others more unconditionally, but not that they alone can love others.

That brings us to one final clarification. As liberation theologians have argued, and as I have already mentioned, there is a sense in which God takes a special interest in the poor, the powerless, and the oppressed—in short, in "the least of these." Liberation theologians refer to this special interest as God's *preferential option for the poor*.[9] The idea here is not that God loves these persons more than others; the idea, rather, is that, precisely because God loves everyone, God is especially concerned with the well-being of those who are suffering and mistreated, in the same way that parents who love all their children will be especially concerned about the one who is not doing well, and in the same way that shepherds who love all their sheep will be especially concerned about the one that is lost. There is a sense, then, in which God is particularly invested in the well-being of the poor and the oppressed, which would explain why our love for them can be a clear act of love toward God. Insofar as these persons are in fact *least*, moreover, we cannot expect much of an earthly reward for loving them; in doing so, accordingly, we more clearly aim at a heavenly reward— that is, at that which God values rather than what the world does. (So Jesus: "If you love those who love you, what credit is that to you? For even sinners do the same. If you do good to those who do good to you, what credit is that to you? For even sinners do the same" [Lk. 6:32–33].) Hence, if God is especially invested in the least of these, then if we love God, we will want to invest ourselves in them, too.

Taking everything together, then, Jesus exhorts his hearers to devote themselves wholly to God, where this means that they must renounce worldly possessions and love others wholeheartedly (including especially those whom they have no reason to love). To prepare themselves for the coming judgment, in other words, they must turn away from the way of the world, since following the latter way involves setting one's heart on earthly goods, putting one's trust in the world, and accepting the world's assessment of persons.

We can now use this theological framework, drawn from Jesus' own preaching, to understand some of the theological claims often made about Jesus. The strategy will be to show how we can move from some claims about Jesus' life to claims about his nature, his significance, and his connection to God. (The argument here proceeds fairly quickly; this should suffice for our purposes, but I am well aware that each of the following claims deserves further elaboration.)

The first step is simply to see that Jesus himself is wholly devoted to God, in just the sense that he exhorted his listeners to be; this is what Karl Rahner has in mind when he claims that "the man Jesus exists in a unity of wills with the Father which permeates his whole reality totally and from the outset, in an 'obedience' from out of which he orients his whole human reality; he is someone who continually accepts himself from the Father and who in all of the dimensions of his existence has always given himself over to the Father."[10] On this account, everything in Jesus' life—his emotions, actions, beliefs, and so forth—is wholly oriented by, and so an expression of, this devotion. So his emotions—grief at the death of a friend, anger at the money changers, desire for friendship, compassion for the poor, and so forth—are all an expression of his devotion to God. Likewise his actions—healing, praying, preaching, going to a particular place, and so on—are an expression of this devotion. So too his beliefs—that God would keep God's promises, that God's reign would soon dawn, that God had sent Jesus to bring good news to the poor, and so forth. Simply stated, then, the idea here is that everything that Jesus thinks, does, and feels is an expression of his devotion to God; his entire life can thus be seen as a single act of devotion and, so, as a sort of "doing" or project. By a peculiar logic, moreover, even Jesus' sufferings—yea, even unto death—can be seen as an expression of devotion, and so as a kind of doing, for at least two reasons: first, because by his entrusting himself to God even in the midst of such suffering, his suffering is itself an act of devotion; and, second, insofar as his suffering is at the hands of those who oppose him in his mission, it has the character of defying such opposition, of remaining devoted even in the face of opposition, and, so, precisely, of expressing his faithfulness to his mission.[11] Julian of Norwich thus claims, of such suffering, that "he would count it all as nothing for love, for everything seems only little to him in comparison with his love."[12] Even here, then, every moment of Jesus' life expresses his devotion to God, and, just so, every moment is part of a single life project; we can thus see Jesus' life as marked by a kind of simplicity or "partlessness," since there is nothing in his life that is not included in, and an expression of, his devotion to God.

That brings us to a second step: if every moment of Jesus' life, as well as his life as a whole, is an act of devotion to God, then it follows that Jesus *is* what he *does*.[13] More precisely: what Jesus does—namely, devote himself wholly to God—is what is essential to or definitive of his identity, or, in short, what makes him who he is. To be clear, I am not here endorsing a general metaphysical claim to the effect that, say, every person's life is a kind of project, that such projects are thus definitive of a person's identity, and that the human kind of being is thus a kind of doing. I am suggesting, rather, that in a case where someone's entire life (as a whole and in each of its parts) is devoted to a single project, then it makes sense to say that that project is definitive of that person's identity. There are at least two ways in which we can see how this would work. On the one hand, consider someone who sacrifices (or rejects) every other life possibility for the sake of pursuing just one such possibility: a small-town teacher, for instance, who decides to remain in her job even when offered the opportunity of moving to a different area, taking up a different career, focusing her energies on something other than teaching (such as her family, or a hobby, or a cause), and so on; by repeatedly affirming this life possibility over alternative possibilities, she increasingly makes it the only possible shape that her life could have. And insofar as she does so because she is committed to this life—rather than, say, merely accustomed to or otherwise stuck in it—it follows that her life's shape is itself due to her commitment, and that that commitment is therefore definitive of her life.

On the other hand, consider someone who would stick with this life project even at the cost of suffering or even dying—someone who would rather die, in other words, than give up this life project; to the extent that a person is willing to sacrifice comfort and life itself for the sake of their commitment to that project, it follows that the life project is more essential to the person than even the most basic human needs and drives.[14] As Hegel thus argues—with a touch of overstatement—"it is solely the risking of life by which freedom is proved, through which it is proved that the essence of self-consciousness is not *being* (as facticity), not the *immediate* manner in which it emerges, nor its submergence in the dissemination of life, but rather that that which is merely present in it is nothing for it but a vanishing moment, that it is only pure *being-for-self*."[15] Overstatement aside, Hegel's point here is that persons are free only to the extent that they rise above merely given goals and life-determinations, that the desire to live is the most basic of these given determinations, and, therefore, that persons who would choose to determine their own life even at the expense of life itself thereby rise above mere givenness and, just so, are free. To this, we need only add the *content* of such self-determination: if persons would choose to devote themselves to some project even at the expense of life itself, it follows that their commitment to this particular project—rather than anything merely given to or about them—is what's essential to them. Either way, the idea here is that Jesus can be understood in just such terms: he devotes every moment of his life, and his life as a whole, to God; he sacrifices every other life possibility for the sake of this one (think here of the temptations in the wilderness); and he remains so devoted even at the cost of suffering and death. In just this sense, therefore, Jesus is what he does (and vice versa), and his person is his work (and vice versa): that which is essential to Jesus, that which wholly defines his life, is the doing of this life project. He is only as he does this.

That brings us to a third step: if Jesus always and only does God's will, it follows that his life perfectly reflects God's will. To understand this point, imagine a simple case in which someone whispers something in one person's ear, who then whispers it in the ear of another. If the mediator heard the original message correctly and wanted to pass it along faithfully, then the third person can rightly take the mediator's words as the originator's own. In the same way, if a person always and only imitates the actions of another person, then a third person would be able to discern what the first person was doing even if able to see only what the second person was doing. That is what Christians have claimed is true of Jesus, namely, that he always and only does what God does, says what God says, and so on, to such an extent that he is the perfect reflection of God and, therefore, that when we look at Jesus, we see God's own willing, acting, and speaking. As the Gospel of John puts it, Jesus came down from heaven not to do his own will but to do the will of him who sent him (John 6:38), such that "the Son can do nothing on his own, but only what he sees the Father doing" (John 5:19), from which it follows that "whoever has seen me [Jesus] has seen the Father" (John 14:9). To this, we can now add a bit of content: if Jesus devotes his entire life—even unto death—to bringing sinful humanity into communion with God, it follows that God's will is precisely that sinful humanity would be brought into communion with Godself, and that Jesus' life, death, and resurrection are the *enactment* and *fulfillment* of God's redeeming will. (I return to this point in a moment.)

A fourth step follows from the third: if God stands wholeheartedly behind this will and thus identifies with it in just the way that Jesus identifies with his devotion to God, then it follows that, in redeeming us, God is being faithful to Godself; this is one reason why Jon Sobrino can claim, for instance, that "God 'is' or 'exists' insofar as he creates community and human solidarity," and Kazoh Kitamori can insist, in response to the question "Is there anything deeper in the heart of God than his will for salvation?" that "the sheltering hand of God is his deepest and most essential nature."[16] We see evidence for this claim in the long history of God's covenant keeping: over and over again, God acts to redeem God's people even when they have turned from God, thereby forsaking any other way of being God. We also see evidence for it in the fact that God was willing to sacrifice God's beloved Son for the sake of this will; if God is willing to let God's own Son die for the sake of redeeming us, then redeeming us must be unsurpassably important to God. As with Jesus, then, we can say that this will (and its enactment) is definitive of who God is, to such an extent that God *is* only as God so *wills*.[17]

That already brings us to a fifth step. If Jesus is the enactment of God's will, and God wholly identifies with this will, then Jesus is the incarnation of God: at every moment, Jesus perfectly embodies God's will and, just so, embodies that which is definitive of God's identity, which means that at every moment and in his life as a whole, Jesus incarnates God.[18] Jesus is not only the embodiment of God's will, in other words, but also the embodiment of God's very self. (I say more about this point after considering a few additional steps.) Indeed, if God alone can redeem us from sin, and God redeems us precisely through the act in which Jesus has his being, then it follows that Jesus is himself the very act of God and, indeed, divine.[19] Again, I return to this point in a moment.

The sixth step hinges on the idea that, in doing these things, God does not change; if so, then God has eternally willed to redeem us and has eternally been doing that which God does when God redeems us.[20] A helpful way to make sense of this idea is to think of God's acts ad extra as a repetition of the act in which God eternally subsists. This might sound fairly complicated, but the idea is straightforward enough: whatever God does in the creaturely sphere has an antecedent in God's eternal way of being, such that, in doing the former, God is simply doing what God has always been doing, albeit in a different sphere. The theological move, accordingly, is to work backward from God's acts *ad extra* to an antecedent—and eternal—act *ad intra;* hence, if the Father begets a Son in order to redeem us, then the Father must eternally have been doing so; if this Son perfectly mirrors the Father in the creaturely sphere, this Son must eternally have been doing so; if the Father wholly identifies with this Son (and vice versa), then they must eternally so identify with each other; and if this Son sacrifices himself for the sake of drawing others into communion with the Father, then he must eternally have been sacrificing himself for the sake of that communion.[21] On this approach, then, we can say that the Father is eternally begetting a Son who is a perfect reflection of the Father and with whom the Father wholly identifies (and vice versa). What would it mean, though, to claim that the Son is eternally sacrificing himself? Here is one way to think about it: the Son eternally loves us and, so, identifies with us, to such an extent that he gives up any other way of being himself, and to such an extent that there are no lengths to which he will not go in order to redeem us. This "giving up" is an eternal prototype, as it were, of the sacrifice that he will make, in history, on our behalf. (Think here of parents who decided, long before their children were born, that they would give up anything for them. If one of their children got leukemia and needed a parent's bone marrow, the parent's giving it to the child would simply be the enactment of a determination made before the child was born.) If the Son is a perfect reflection of the Father, moreover, then it follows that the Father has eternally loved us and therefore identified with us, to such an extent that the Father, too, has given up any other way of being God, and to such an extent that there is no length to which he will not go in order to bring us into the communion that he shares with the Son. God has eternally willed, in other words, to be God-with-us and not otherwise, just as God has willed that we would be us-with-God.

An analogy may help. Imagine a clever inventor whose basement filled with water whenever it rained. Unsurprisingly, they decide to build a water pump, and they eventually refine their design to such an extent that the pump works perfectly: whenever it rains, the invention immediately pumps out the water and does so as efficiently as possible. The inventor is quite pleased with this outcome, until they see a news report about people's homes being destroyed by flooding. They are so moved by this report that they decide to take their pump on the road so that they can help these people— indeed, they so dedicate themselves to this mission that their entire life is now oriented around it. Notice that, in so doing, they do not have to change what they were already doing at home: the pump keeps doing what it had always been doing. The difference is simply that they now do these things not *at home* but *on the road*. We are saying something similar here about God: the Father has eternally begotten and been in communion with a Son, and this Son has eternally reflected and been in communion with the Father. Because they love us and in order to redeem us, Father and Son have decided to take this communion "on the road," to such an extent that they have given up the possibility of simply remaining at home with themselves. When God goes on the road, however, God does not have to change, since God can just keep doing what God has always done: the Father has eternally been begetting a Son and can thus beget a Son in our sphere without changing; the Son has eternally mirrored the Father and can thus mirror the Father in our sphere without changing; the Son has eternally given himself up for the sake of bringing us into communion with the Father and can thus give himself up for us in our sphere without changing. This is what it would mean, then, to say that God acts in history by repeating ad extra the eternal act in which God eternally subsists, and thus to say that God so acts without having to change.

So then: by understanding Jesus in light of the norms implicit in his preaching, we can move from his utter devotedness to God to an account of his incarnation of God's will and, indeed, of God's eternal being, and from there to an account of the eternal communion he shares with the Father. By tracing these steps, we can begin to make sense of some traditional claims about who Jesus is and who God is.

Before explaining how Jesus, so understood, plays a role in delivering us from sin, we need to address two questions that have loomed large within the theological tradition. First, in what respect is Jesus both fully divine and fully human? To oversimplify a bit, we can say that there are two main approaches to this issue. On the one hand, there is the approach that starts with the two natures, as it were, and then insists that Jesus has (or is) both of them: hence, if divinity is characterized by, say, immutability, omniscience, omnipotence, omnibenevolence, and other attributes, then these things must be true of Jesus; likewise, if humanity is characterized by finitude and dependence, then this must be true of Jesus, too.[22] The challenge for such an approach is to explain how these two sets of apparently incompatible traits could subsist in one person: how could Jesus be both omnipotent and finite, for instance? The most popular response to this challenge is simply to insist that the two natures are held together in and by the triune person—this is traditionally referred to as the hypostatic union—and explain this, in turn, by analogy to a piece of iron that, when heated up, takes on the properties of heat without losing any of its properties as iron.[23]

The alternative approach would be to say, simply, that Jesus is the eternal Son of God in the flesh, living a fully human life. As we have seen, the life of Jesus was a sort of doing, namely, the "doing" of wholehearted devotion to God. Such wholehearted devotion can be understood as a repetition ad extra of the doing in which the Son's eternal being subsists, from which it would follow that the Son need not change in order to live this human life; quite the contrary. This would mean, in turn, that the Son can remain fully divine when he becomes incarnate; he can likewise be fully human, since Jesus perfectly exemplifies that which a human life is supposed to be. On this approach, then, there is no problem of trying to explain how divine and human natures could hang together in Jesus, for the simple reason that this perfectly human life is literally the embodiment, the "coming down from heaven," of the eternal Son of God, in the very fulfillment of the act in which the Son eternally subsists.[24] As a rough analogy, imagine that I am a teacher who has one of my own children in class. If we suppose that to be a teacher is to care about whether each of my students is growing and learning and to act accordingly, and if we suppose further that being a parent means that I care about my child's well-being and act accordingly, then, in having my child in class, I can continue doing what I have always been doing: I will care about whether this student is growing and learning, and precisely in so doing, I will care about my child's well-being. I will not have to change what I have always been doing, in other words; I can thus be a parent and a teacher at one and the same time. Likewise, if the Son of God does not have to change what he has eternally been doing in order to become incarnate and live a human life for our sakes, then he can continue being who he has always been—fully divine—even as he becomes fully human. If we understand both natures in light of this fact, accordingly, there is no problem involved in figuring out how they could hang together.[25] Hence, although either answer would do the trick, this one fits much more neatly with the approach we have been following thus far.

That brings us to the second key question: what about the Spirit? I have more to say about the Spirit's work in the next chapter, but for present purposes we need to have at least some explanation of how the Spirit fits into this picture. Suppose, then, that the Spirit contributes at least the following three things to our redemption, as the theological tradition would claim: effective witness to what God has done in Christ; transformation of persons into the image of Christ; and uniting of Christians with God and one another.[26] Suppose, further, that the Spirit is wholly dedicated to the doing of these things—that is, that the Spirit is wholly dedicated to redeeming us and drawing us into communion with God. If we follow the same approach to the Spirit that we applied to the Father and Son, we can infer, first, that the Spirit is divine (because God alone can redeem, and the Spirit's being-in-act is a crucial part of God's redeeming act) and, second, that Father and Son identify with the Spirit in precisely the same way they identify with each other. We can likewise infer that the Spirit is eternally doing that which the Spirit does in redeeming us—that is, bearing witness, conforming to Christ, and creating unity. Here is one way of thinking about how that might work: (a) As is common when someone enjoys something incomparably good, Father and Son want to share their love and to allow others to appreciate it. (Think here of the excitement that people feel about sharing a favorite new artist with their friends or, upon seeing something beautiful, of wanting others to see it, too.) (b) The Spirit eternally witnesses the love of Father and Son and, in beholding something so incomparably good, delights in that goodness; the love of Father and Son is thus glorified precisely in its being witnessed by the Spirit. (c) The Spirit so delights in this love that the Spirit could properly be said to *love* that love and, so, to love those whose very being is bound up with it; by the same logic, Father and Son love the Spirit, whose very being is bound up with loving them. From this, it would follow that Father, Son, and Spirit share a communion of love. (d) There would also be a sense in which the Spirit eternally embodies this communion: as the one who witnesses the love of Father and Son, the Spirit reflects that love back to them, in such a way that, in beholding the Spirit, they perceive their love in the Spirit's perception of them. As the embodiment of their love, accordingly, it is entirely appropriate that the Spirit would be called "the bond of love"—not because the Spirit is the one who binds Father and Son together in love but because the Spirit is the very embodiment of this bond.[27] These themes are common throughout the theological tradition, but Teresa of Avila brings them together in a particularly striking passage: "Consider the great delight and great love the Father has in knowing his Son and the Son in knowing his Father," she writes, "and the enkindling love with which the Holy Spirit is joined with them; and how no one of them is able to be separate from this love and knowledge, because they are one. These sovereign persons know each other, love each other, and delight in each other."[28]

This is a very rough sketch, to be sure, but it should already help us see how the Spirit would act to redeem us precisely by repeating this eternal being-in-act ad extra. First off, the Spirit can bear effective witness to what Father and Son have done for us precisely by repeating the Spirit's eternal witness: just as the Spirit eternally beholds the love of Father and Son, so here the Spirit beholds their love in redeeming us and does so from within us—that is, in such a way that *we* can behold that love. This means, in turn, that the Spirit can transform us by repeating ad extra the natural consequence of such beholding, namely, the cultivation in us of a love for that love and, therefore, for Father and Son. The Spirit can thereby conform our lives to that of Jesus, whose life was nothing but an expression of such love. And finally, the Spirit can unite us with God inasmuch as the Spirit's own unity with Father and Son is now internal to us, as it were, and Father and Son love the Spirit's love in us; in the same way, the Spirit can unite us with other Christians as we behold and love that same love in them. Brevity notwithstanding, then, the bottom line is that we can understand the Spirit, too, as divine and as acting within history by repeating its eternal being-in-act.

From here, it is a short step to a model of the Trinity. Eternally in Godself, God subsists in an act of loving communion among Father, Son, and Spirit, and would so subsist even if God had not determined to create and redeem us. But God has determined to create us, redeem us, and draw us into the divine communion, and has thus determined that the divine act would eternally be oriented toward these acts: God will create us by repeating ad extra the Father's act of begetting a Son; God will become incarnate by repeating ad extra the Son's act of mirroring the Father; God will draw humanity into the divine communion through the Son's becoming human and thus including his humanity in that communion; God will bear effective witness to all this by repeating ad extra the Spirit's eternal glorification of their communion; and God will include us in that communion by repeating ad extra—in us—the Spirit's eternal act of loving Father and Son. God is eternally triune, accordingly, and acts ad extra by repeating the communion that God eternally enjoys within Godself.[29] As we will see in chapter 7, Christians traditionally maintain that participation in this communion is our highest good and the telos of our redemption.

That brings us back to the question of how we are delivered from sin. In the previous chapter, we considered two respects in which Christians have claimed that we are bound to sin: on the one hand, we are bound to sin because it has become second nature for us to be oriented by and to the world and, on the other, we are so bound because we have been subjected to the power of Sin. Christians are committed to the view that we are delivered from sin through Christ, which means that we must be delivered by him from our habitual world-orientation and from our subjection to Sin.

First, then, Christians believe that Jesus delivers us from our orientation by and to the world, and that he accomplishes this, in part, by orienting himself wholly by and to God and, just so, by not being bound by the sinful ways of the world. We see this plainly when Jesus declines to advocate for himself before Pilate, when he refuses to fight back against the authorities who had come to arrest him, and when he faces death: in each case, he could try to establish his security by looking to worldly powers and possibilities, but he opts instead to entrust his security to God. Jesus likewise refuses to treat worldly standards as if they were ultimate. This is why he insists, again and again, that the first shall be last and the last shall be first, and it is why he welcomes children and outcasts and is reviled as a friend of tax collectors and sinners. Jesus thus shows special favor to "the least of these" and, just so, rejects the world's value hierarchy. And finally, Jesus loves God with all his heart, mind, soul, and strength, and thus sets his heart wholly on God rather than the goods of this world. We see this when he refuses the temptations in the wilderness, for instance, and when he says that his food is to do God's will, and, in sum, when he sacrifices status, comfort, prosperity, and everything else for the sake of devoting himself to God. Here as elsewhere, then, Jesus orients his life to God rather than to this world. Hence, whereas the way of the world trains us to set our hearts on the goods of this world, to put our trust in the world, and to treat the world's standards as absolute, Jesus sets his heart on God alone, trusts God alone, and judges by God's standards alone. On this account, then, Jesus is so oriented to God that he is free from the sinful ways of this world; this is one of the things we need if we are ever going to be delivered from our bondage to sin. Naturally, the mere fact that *Jesus* is freed from the way of the world does not entail that *we* are; I spend the next several chapters explaining how the latter could come to be the case.

This is not the only thing we need in order to be delivered from sin, but before we proceed, it is worth mentioning that the sort of account just outlined has sometimes been termed a *recapitulative, ontological, Second Adam,* or even *Irenaean* model of deliverance.[30] The idea behind such models is simple: because humanity has gone wrong, what we need is a sort of do-over, that is, for one to live a human life in which one does *right* everything that we have done *wrong* and thus recreates the possibility of a life fully devoted to God. Think here of the movie *Groundhog Day:* Bill Murray's character keeps going through the same day until he gets it right and, in this way, undoes all of the bad things he had done the first time. He keeps recapitulating that day, in other words, in order to make it come out right. Very roughly, this is what Jesus does, though instead of a single day, he recapitulates an entire human life. Jesus himself is thus free from sinful-ness, and if we could somehow live that sort of life, we would be, too. Again, I spend the next several chapters considering how this might happen.

If we are going to be delivered from sin, then, we will need to be freed from our worldly orientations. This is a necessary, but not sufficient, con-dition of our being so delivered, for even if we were reoriented to God, we would still be subjected to the power of Sin; after all, Sin has a rightful claim to our lifelong subjection, irrespective of whether we have had second thoughts about it.

To address this problem, we turn to a second model of deliverance, commonly referred to as a *Christus Victor* model; we see an example of this model in James Cone, for instance, when he asserts that Jesus "is God himself coming into the very depths of human existence for the sole purpose of striking off the chains of slavery, thereby freeing man from ungodly principalities and powers that hinder his relationship with God."[31] Such models aim to explain how we are freed from the powers of Sin and Death, though they vary widely in respect of their explanations. The most famous versions appeal to the idea that humanity has sold itself into bondage to Satan, that God offered God's own Son as a ransom to free us from our bondage, and that Satan is finally defeated because he cannot hold on to God's Son; Satan thus loses his captives as well as the ransom.[32] This is a colorful, dramatic way of thinking about our deliverance from Sin; small wonder, then, that it became so popular. It is not the only way of thinking about our deliverance from the power of Sin, however; here I consider another approach, rooted in recent scholarship on Paul.[33]

To understand this approach, recall that we have been subjected to the power of Sin for the following reasons: on the one hand, because in our sinfulness we have pledged ourselves to Sin and thus given Sin a rightful claim over our lives; on the other hand, because the Law ensures that we get what we deserve, it follows that, as sinners, we are handed over to the dominion of Sin and sentenced to a death penalty, such that Death, too, holds power over us.

Paul claims that it is by Jesus' death and resurrection that we are delivered from both sorts of subjection. His reasoning here proceeds through roughly the following steps. First, Jesus himself is subjected to the power of Sin, whether that is because he is a member of the people whose head is Adam or because he enters into a world that is under Sin's rightful jurisdiction. However we understand it, the point is simply that Jesus, too, came under the reign of Sin.[34] Second, because Jesus has been subjected to the power of Sin, he is likewise subjected to the death sentence to which all under Sin are liable. In the crucifixion, accordingly, the power of Sin pronounces its final word on him, and the requirements of the Law are thus satisfied. That brings us to the crucial third step: Jesus is raised to new life after having been put to death; given that he has already satisfied the just requirements of the Law, it follows that he is no longer subject to the power of Sin or of Death. This is why Paul can claim, for instance, that "Christ, being raised from the dead, will never die again; death no longer has dominion over him. For the death he died, he died to Sin, once for all, but the life he lives, he lives to God" (Rom. 6:9–10). If Sin gets its power from the Law, and the Law has already given Sin everything to which it was entitled—condemnation unto death—then Sin no longer has any claim upon someone who has risen from the dead. That is the vital point. Consider an illustration: suppose that someone who has been sentenced to life in prison goes into cardiac arrest, their heart stops, and their brain functions cease, in consequence of which the relevant authorities declare the person legally dead. Then suppose that this person was not really dead and that they therefore "came back to life" (which is something that actually happened, apparently, in the not-too-distant past, even if it is difficult to imagine it happening today). Given that they had been declared legally dead, this person might argue that they should be released from prison immediately, since, legally speaking, they had fulfilled their sentence: a life sentence is complete, after all, once a prisoner has died. To be sure, a judge would never accept this argument, precisely because the person had not really died and, so, had not really completed their death sentence. But that is a key difference from Jesus, whom Christians insist was indeed dead, and who was *resurrected* rather than merely *resuscitated*. In Jesus' case, then, the life sentence has in fact been served—the death sentence has in fact been executed—which means that if *he* were to bring his case before a judge, the judge would have little choice but to recognize that his sentence had been completed. The Law has thus been satisfied, which means that if Jesus now lives again, his life is no longer subject to the Law, nor, in turn, to the powers of Sin and Death. For Paul, this is the key to explaining why it is precisely Jesus' death and resurrection that deliver him from the power of Sin.

In the next section, I consider how it is that we could be included in Jesus' death and resurrection and thus how we, too, could be freed from Sin and Death. For now, it is important to observe that Paul applies exactly this sort of account to our deliverance. This is what he seems to have in mind, at any rate, when he claims of himself that "through the law I died to the law, so that I might live to God" (Gal. 2:19); or, again, that "our old self was crucified with him in order that the body of sin might be destroyed, and we might no longer be enslaved to Sin. For whoever has died is freed from Sin" (Rom. 6:6–7). Paul thus understands *our* deliverance from the reign of Sin and Death in precisely the same terms he understands *Jesus' own* deliverance from this reign: if we, too, have died and risen to new life, it follows that we, too, have fulfilled our death sentence; this means, in turn, that the Law no longer gives Sin and Death a rightful claim over us and that we are therefore no longer subjected to them. Again, I explain how this works in the following section; for now, the vital point is that, for Paul, we are delivered from the power of Sin and Death precisely by dying and rising again, just as Jesus did.

Crucially, Paul claims that death and new life likewise free us from the lifelong vow we have made to Sin. Paul makes this point by analogy with marital vows: "Do you not know," he asks, "that the law is binding on a person only during that person's lifetime? Thus a married woman is bound by the law to her husband as long as he lives; but if her husband dies, she is discharged from the law concerning her husband. Accordingly, she will be called an adulteress if she lives with another man while her husband is alive. But if her husband dies, she is free from that law, and if she marries another man, she is not an adulteress" (Rom. 7:1–3). The idea here is that, in marriage, one makes a lifelong vow to one's spouse; that vow is binding upon one, accordingly, for as long as one (or one's spouse) lives. As long as that vow is in effect, one would be cheating on one's spouse if one were to get together with someone else. But if one's spouse dies, one would not be cheating, for in that case, one is no longer bound by one's lifelong vow— "till death do us part," after all. Paul takes a similar approach to the lifelong vow that we have made to Sin: if we have died, then we are no longer bound by our vow, from which it follows that the Law has been satisfied and that Sin no longer has a rightful claim to our allegiance. Hence, just as a person whose spouse has died is freed from their marital vows, so, Paul claims, "you have died to the law through the body of Christ, so that you may belong to another, to him who has been raised from the dead, in order that we may bear fruit for God" (Rom. 7:4). It turns out, then, that death and resurrection are the key here, too: we are freed from our lifelong pledge to Sin precisely because our lives have ended; hence, if we live after having died, it follows that we are no longer bound by that pledge.

Note well, then, that on this account the Law plays a role not only in making sure we get what we deserve and thus subjecting us to the power of Sin and Death, it also plays a role in freeing us from those powers. That is to say, although the Law does serve the power of Sin and Death, inas-

much as it gives them their power over us, the Law does so only penulti-
mately; ultimately, the Law still serves God's redemptive purposes, for in
executing a death sentence upon us, the Law serves finally to free us from
that to which it had bound us.

On this account, then, it is the death and resurrection of Jesus that
defeats the power of Sin and Death: because Sin and Death get their power
over us through the Law, and because the Law's requirements have been
satisfied by Jesus' death, it follows that when he rises to new life, the Law
no longer gives Sin and Death any purchase on him. This account thus
qualifies as a version of the Christus Victor model for understanding our
deliverance from Sin.

That brings us to one final point. It is a commonplace that there are
three prominent models within the Christian tradition for thinking about
such deliverance; we have already talked about two of these, namely, the
recapitulative and Christus Victor models.[35] The third prominent model is
penal substitution, according to which Jesus delivers us from sin by taking
our punishment upon himself; on this approach, God's justice is fully satisfied when Jesus bears our punishment, in virtue of which we are no longer liable to it. (This is akin to the moment in *A Tale of Two Cities* when
Sydney Carton goes to the gallows in place of Charles Darnay.) With some
qualification, we can see the model we have been considering as a version
of penal substitution, too; in dying on the cross, after all, Jesus is bearing
the condemnation that we sinners deserve. The key qualification is that
our account is not, strictly speaking, *substitutionary:* he does not bear this
condemnation so that we would not, but so that, by rising to new life, condemnation would not have the final word about us. We are delivered from
Sin, on this account, when we are united with Jesus and, so, when we too
die and rise to new life; hence, whereas substitutionary accounts often portray our deliverance from sin as occurring strictly outside ourselves, on the
present account we are delivered from Sin when we ourselves die and rise
again in union with Jesus. Again, I have more to say about this in the next
section. For now, I can simply add that our account could thereby address
some of the concerns often raised against penal substitution, to the effect
that it pictures God as a child abuser (meting out wrath upon his Son) and
Jesus as redemptive because he suffers on behalf of others; such concerns
have been raised by a wide range of theologians, including Delores Williams, Rita Nakashima Brock, Mary Daly, Rosemary Radford Ruether, and
Denny Weaver.[36] On our account, Jesus is condemned not by God but by

the power of Sin and Death, and his redeeming effects are attributable to his resurrection (not his death itself, much less his suffering) and to his singularly God-oriented way of life.

Christians traditionally claim that humans are bound to sin, both in the sense that we have become so oriented to the world that we cannot help but sin and in the sense that we have become subjected to the reign of Sin. Christians likewise claim that Jesus delivers us from sin in both respects. On the one hand, Jesus delivers us from sin by leading a life that is wholly oriented to God, thereby opening up the possibility that we, too, could be so oriented. And on the other hand, Jesus delivers us from Sin by rising to new life after having fulfilled the death sentence to which we are liable, thereby opening up the possibility that we, too, might be raised to new life after fulfilling our sentence. The next section tries to shed some light on how this might work.

This section began by considering the preaching of Jesus, in order to identify some of his central normative commitments and to develop a framework that we can use to understand some of the theological claims often made about him. On this basis, we tried to make sense of the claim that Jesus is wholly devoted to God and that his life therefore perfectly embodies God's will and is in fact the very act of God; that God definitively identifies with Jesus and the Spirit (and vice versa); and that Father, Son, and Spirit act in the creaturely sphere by repeating their eternal act ad extra. We then turned to the idea that Jesus delivers us from sin, in two respects: on the one hand, that his wholehearted devotion frees him from bondage to the way of the world and, on the other, that his death and resurrection free him from subjection to the power of Sin and Death. So far, so good, but the story is not yet complete; among other things, we still need to see how this new orientation might become ours, and how we might be included in Jesus' death and resurrection.

Repentance and New Life

Thus far, we have considered the idea that Jesus is wholeheartedly devoted to God and, so, free from a worldly orientation, and that he was raised to new life after death and, so, is free from the power of Sin. Taken together, these claims would explain how Jesus himself was free from bondage to sin but not how anyone else would be. To begin to address that question, let us turn to a consideration of the decisive transformation that persons must undergo—the very death of their old, "world"-attuned selves—if they are to follow Jesus in this new way of life. The New Testament as well as much of the theological tradition often talk as if this death-and-new-life occurs at the moment when a person comes to faith, repents, or, in sum, "converts," and as if "old" and "new" were therefore more or less synonymous with "pre-conversion" and "post-conversion." Many Christians do understand their lives in these terms. Countless other Christians never *came* to faith, however, because they were never *outside* it, yet presumably they, too, live lives marked by faith, repentance, and new life. This helps us see something that might otherwise be obscure, namely, that "old" and "new," here, refer not to periods in an individual's life but, for persons who have faith, to a world-orientation that no longer defines them (and is thus decidedly a thing of the past) and a God-orientation that now does define them (and thus marks their life as decidedly new).

To make sense of these ideas, it will be helpful to begin with some theological claims about "proclamation"—but to understand these claims, we need to recall some of the eschatological expectations that some early Christians had in mind when they encountered Jesus.[37] Speaking very broadly, in the Second Temple period, many Jewish persons were waiting for a Day of the Lord, a decisive turning point in history that would be marked by God's defeat of the hostile powers that ruled over Israel, by the outpouring of a new Spirit of righteousness, by the conversion of the Gentiles, and by the resurrection of the dead. Naturally, not everyone held such expectations, but it seems evident that many did, and, crucially for our purposes, that it was in terms of such expectations that many early Christians understood Jesus. To take one obvious example of this, for those who believed that Jesus rose from the dead, this seemed to mean that the Day of the Lord had indeed dawned, even if it was not entirely clear how to square this belief with the expectation that *all* the righteous dead would be raised on that day. Beyond this, the idea that the Day had dawned also found confirmation in their belief that the new Spirit of righteousness had been poured out at Pentecost, thus fulfilling the expectation that God would grant God's people a new heart. The expectation that God would defeat the hostile powers who ruled God's people was a bit trickier to account for, not least because Israel remained subject to Roman rule, but as we have seen, at least some Christians thought that this expectation was fulfilled in Jesus' defeat of Sin and Death.

That brings us to the fourth expectation, namely, the expectation that the Gentiles (or "peoples") would turn to the God of Israel. As Paul saw it, and as he eventually persuaded many in the early church, this expectation was being fulfilled in the fact that Gentiles, too, were receiving the end-times Spirit. Crucially for Paul's own theological development, moreover, he saw this fulfillment taking place precisely when the Gentiles believed the message that he proclaimed to them: they received the end-times Spirit and were thus "righteoused" because they had faith in the message about Christ, not because they first became Law-observant Jews. (This is arguably what Paul has in mind when he talks about being righteoused by faith rather than by works of the Law: whereas some of Paul's coreligionists thought of Law observance as a prerequisite for receiving the promised Spirit, Paul's experience with the Gentiles proved to him that this was not the case; the Gentiles received the Spirit simply because they believed the word about Christ. Hence, in Paul's knock-down argument against those who would insist that Gentile believers must convert to Judaism, he poses the following question: "The only thing I want to learn from you," he asks, "is this: did you receive the Spirit by doing the works of the law or by believing what you heard? . . . Well then, does God supply you with the Spirit and work miracles among you by your doing the works of the law, or by your believing what you heard?" [Gal. 3:2, 5]. This formulation parallels Paul's more famous statement in the Epistle's previous chapter, to the effect that "a person is righteoused not by the works of the law but through faith in Jesus Christ" [Gal. 2:16], though here works of the Law are contrasted with belief *in Jesus Christ* rather than in *what was heard*. It seems probable that, for Paul, belief in Christ and belief in what was heard amount to the same thing, which makes it probable that *being righteoused* and *receiving the Spirit* amount to the same thing, too. To be sure, this is a highly controversial interpretation of these passages, though there are no *un*controversial interpretations of them. But it is hardly outside of the Christian mainstream, as no less a theologian than Augustine identifies *justificationis* with God's law being written on our hearts, and equates both of these with the gift of the Spirit and with God's own righteousness.)[38]

Justification debates notwithstanding, the key point here is that, for Paul, a person receives the promised Spirit by believing in Christ, or, what comes to the same thing, believing the message about Christ. To receive this Spirit, for Paul, is equivalent to receiving a new heart and to becoming a new creation and, just so, to the dying of one's old self; if we want to understand what it means for us to die and rise to new life, therefore, we need to get a clearer sense of how we come to receive this Spirit. To do so, we can begin with Paul's emphasis on believing what we have heard.

To understand how "believing what was heard" could play such a vital role in our deliverance from sin, it will be helpful to unpack the idea that, when Christians proclaim the Gospel message, God speaks through them. This is a common claim in the theological tradition; on the Catholic side, accordingly, Hans Küng maintains that "Christ himself is at work in the word which is preached" and, so, that "through their witness the church must listen to the Lord himself, and allow him to speak in the midst of the church through their witness; he who hears them, hears the Lord."[39] Likewise on the Protestant side, John Calvin insists that God "deigns to consecrate to himself the mouths and tongues of men in order that his voice may resound in them," in consequence of which those listening should "hear the ministers speaking just as if he himself spoke."[40] These theologians, in turn, are echoing a common theme in the New Testament. Paul thus commends the Thessalonians, for instance, because "when you received the word of God that you heard from us, you accepted it not as a human word but as what it really is, God's word, which is at work in you believers"; or, again, Paul claims that "we are ambassadors for Christ, since *God is making his appeal through us,*" and that "*he* [God] called you through *our* proclamation of the good news."[41] The idea here is that Paul's words are somehow God's own, in such a way that God is speaking through those words—God is calling people through them, appealing to us through them, and so on.

We hear something similar in the Gospels, where Jesus charges his disciples with carrying on his ministry: "As the Father has sent me," he says, "so I send you," which explains why people's response to the apostles counts as their response to him: "Very truly, I tell you, whoever receives one whom I send receives me, and whoever receives me receives the one who sent me"; likewise, "Whoever listens to you listens to me, and whoever rejects you rejects me, and whoever rejects me rejects the one who sent me"; or, again, "Whoever welcomes you welcomes me, and whoever welcomes me welcomes the one who sent me."[42] Jesus' apostles are thus authorized to speak on his behalf, to such an extent that one's response to the apostles counts as one's response to Jesus himself—and because Jesus is in the same way authorized to speak on God's behalf, it follows that one's response to the apostles counts as one's response to God, too. Sometimes I send my daughter downstairs to tell my son that he needs to stop playing video games; if he ignores her or refuses to do what she says, that means he's ignoring or refusing me, since it is my message that she is conveying. In much the same way, if God has authorized certain persons to speak on God's behalf, then if we accept or reject their words, we are accepting or rejecting God's own word.

This is an important claim, so consider a few examples of how this sort of authorization might work.[43] Suppose my wife writes a thank-you note and I sign my name on the bottom; if so, her words become my own. (The same goes if I buy a thank-you card at the store and sign it; in that case, some anonymous writer's words become mine.) Or, if I have my teaching assistant grade exams, the grades count as mine (assuming that I think they're fair). Or, to take Paul's own example, in the old days (if not now), ambassadors had the authority to speak on behalf of their country. In each case, what matters is that someone stands behind the words of another and so makes them their own—which can happen either retrospectively (I see what you have said and so sign my name under your words) or prospectively (as when I authorize you to speak on my behalf). I might sign off on my TA's grades, accordingly, only after seeing them, whereas my wife can speak for me (and so sign up for things on my behalf) in advance, that is, apart from my giving any additional approval. The idea here is similar: when God authorizes someone to speak on God's behalf, God then stands behind that person's words in such a way that their words become God's own—God adopts them as God's own or "signs off" on them. More specifically, if God adopts our words as God's own, that means that God undertakes whatever commitments these words would generate; hence, if someone makes a promise in God's name, God is bound to keep that promise; if someone makes an assertion in God's name, God stands behind its veracity; if someone forgives someone in God's name, God releases them from their guilt; and so on. In this way, our speech acts can become God's own speech acts, which would explain why Paul can say that God is making his appeal through us, that the Thessalonians were right to hear Paul's word as God's own, that a person's response to Jesus' messengers counts as their response to Jesus himself, and so on.

Persons are authorized to speak on God's behalf, in turn, insofar as their words are faithful to God's own, where this turns out to mean that they faithfully pass on the message that has been passed on to them, which was passed on to those who passed it on, and so on, in a chain that can be thought to stretch back to Jesus' own apostles. This would explain why Paul is so keen to insist that he "received from the Lord what [he] also handed on to you" (1 Cor. 11:23). The key image here, obviously, is "handing on," which is literally what the word "tradition" means. So when I was young, my grandfather taught me how to play cards, and I taught my own children how to do so; once they have the hang of it, they can teach others—they can hand on what was handed on to them, in other words. Likewise, when

Luke Skywalker was young, he learned how to be a Jedi from Yoda; once he became a Jedi, he could teach Rey, and eventually she might be able to teach others. In much the same way, the apostles had to learn from Jesus what the good news was, but once they did, he sent them out to teach others; once others learned what it was, they could teach still others, and so on, in such a way that the calling and authorization to proclaim this news was passed on from person to person. Hence, in Letty Russell's nice formulation, "The means by which people participate in the traditioning is by sharing in the receiving and passing on of Christ."[44]

It is important to note, though, that this does not mean that those so authorized can or should lord this authority over others. (When I send my daughter to tell my son to stop playing video games, I will often add, "But don't act like you're his boss!") Quite the contrary, this message is best proclaimed when the proclaimers draw little attention to themselves. Paul thus writes, for instance, that Christ sent him "to proclaim the gospel, and not with eloquent wisdom, so that the cross of Christ might not be emptied of its power" (1 Cor. 1:17), and so that "your faith might rest not on human wisdom but on the power of God" (1 Cor. 2:5). He has the same thing in mind when he says that "we have this treasure in clay jars, so that it may be made clear that this extraordinary power belongs to God and does not come from us" (2 Cor. 4:7). Hence, those who would proclaim the Gospel must say, with John the Baptist, "He must increase; I must decrease" (John 3:30); after all, if people look at the pointing finger rather than at what it's pointing to (as my dog sometimes does), then the finger is not doing its job.[45]

Again, the basic point is that persons are called and authorized to speak God's own word, in such a way that their words count as God's own.[46] And this means, again, that our response to this word is our response not only to the person speaking but to God as well.

That brings us to a second point, namely, that the hearing of this message somehow has the power to transform us; this is one way of understanding what Paul has in mind when he claims that "faith"—the faith that is "unto righteousness"—"comes from what is heard, and what is heard comes through the word of Christ" (Rom. 10:17). Naturally, "hearing," here, cannot simply mean that the sound of certain words has reached a person's ears, nor even that they have merely understood what the words mean. If that were all it took, then a loudspeaker would serve as an all-effective instrument of mass conversion. On the contrary, the hearing at issue involves not just understanding what these words mean but *believing* them.

To understand the sort of believing involved here, we need to distinguish between what we might call "thin" beliefs and "thick" ones. Thin beliefs involve nothing more than assent to the truth of a proposition, along with a readiness to use this proposition in assessing whether other beliefs are true. Examples of such thin beliefs include the belief that a particular celebrity has adopted a puppy, that Microsoft released a new version of Excel overnight, or that the "cod" served at a local restaurant is really some other whitefish. Even if I believe these propositions to be true, they will have no impact on the rest of my life—apart, perhaps, from playing a small part in my assessment of other would-be truths. A belief is thick, by contrast, insofar as my belief in it would entail a more robust change in my life. Consider the following examples: "There's a fire; you need to get out right away"; "You should become a teacher"; "The boss will be back in town tomorrow." In cases like these, if I believe what someone is saying, I will not *only* believe it but do something about it, too: get out of the house, become a teacher, make sure my work is in order. Notice, though, that what determines whether a belief is thick or thin is not the belief itself but its connection with our other beliefs, values, and the like. Suppose someone tells me that there is a fire and I believe this. If I interpret it in light of my belief that the fire is safely contained within a science-lab sink, then even if I believe the person's message, I probably won't do much in response. By contrast, if I interpret it in light of the belief that the fire poses an imminent threat to something I hold dear—the lives of persons I love, for instance—then that message will prompt me to drop everything in response. Likewise, if someone tells me that I should become a teacher, but I do not think that the person either knows me very well or is a good judge of career paths, then I probably will not do much in response to their message; by contrast, if they know me well and they have wisdom about such things, then I will be likelier to consider changing my life in response to their words. The thickness or thinness of a given belief, accordingly, can vary depending on our collateral beliefs and values, just as its thickness can change as our collateral beliefs and values change.

Needless to say, Christians think that the message about Jesus calls for thick belief, which is why believing this message is usually characterized as *faith*. To see why, consider the content of this message: the new age has dawned; God is doing what God had long promised: the dead are being raised, the new righteousness is being conferred, the hostile powers are being defeated, and the Gentiles are being converted. To this, a further promise is added: if you believe that God has done this in Christ, then you will be included in the fulfillment of these promises. Again, to believe this message, in the relevant sense, is not merely to take it to be true; to believe *this* message is, roughly, to take it to be the fundamental truth about ourselves and the world. Believing it changes everything.[47]

It might be useful to summarize these points by considering a spectrum of beliefs, ranging from thin to thick. (a) At one end of the spectrum is mere belief: I believe that something is true, but this belief has little impact on my other beliefs or on my life itself. For me, for instance, the belief that Des Moines is the capital of Iowa is thin in just this sense. (b) Beliefs become relatively thicker insofar as they require some change either in my behavior or in my other beliefs. For example, if I believe that my university is going to fire faculty whose courses are unpopular, I may feel angry or anxious, just as I may resolve to offer more fashionable classes. (c) We get closer to the other end of the spectrum when we consider beliefs that require us to change our lives or belief system in some fundamental respect. So, for instance, if I watch a video of myself and come to believe that I am an obnoxious person, then insofar as I want not to be obnoxious, I will have to make some significant changes in the way I act. Likewise, if I came to believe that the Buddhist doctrine of dependent arising were true, I would have to change the way I perceive all the things I currently see as independent entities. (d) At the far end of the spectrum, we have beliefs whose truth we take to be absolutely fundamental, in the sense that everything else (including ourselves and the world around us) must be reappraised in their light. These are the sort of beliefs about which we would say, without exaggeration, "This changes everything." With respect to the far end of this spectrum—which is obviously the part that we are interested in here—consider an analogy. Imagine people living during World War II: their food is rationed, their children are fighting at the front, and their jobs have been shifted so as to support the war effort. The war influences not only the news they hear but also the news they seek out; they may now care very much about the daily weather reports from France, for instance. The war will thus shape the things they do each day, the things they think about, and the feelings to which they are liable (anger at the government or at another country, fear of loss, and so forth). Now suppose these people hear the news that the war is over. If they believe this news, it changes everything; the very thing that has defined their life for the past several years has come to an end, which means that the way they spent their time, the things they were concerned with, and the things that weighed on their mind are now oriented toward something in the past. Adjusting to

this news will surely take some time, and in the meantime they will probably experience some disorientation. They will surely have to remind
themselves, over and over, that the war is over. The point is not that this
news will change everything all at once, only that it changes everything *in
principle* and, so, that it has normative (if not yet actual) consequences for
all their beliefs, actions, emotions, and the like.

To believe the Gospel, for Christians, is to believe that it is fundamentally true in just this sense: if we take it to be true, it changes everything.
Drawing on the language of 2 Corinthians 5:17, Justo Gonzalez puts this
nicely: when one believes this news, "The old has passed away! Behold, the
new has come!"[48] If we believe this news, in other words, it follows that
whatever had previously defined our life is now in the past and that we will
now have to reappraise the way we act, the other things we believe, the
feelings to which we are liable, and so on. Again, just because we take this
belief to be fundamental does not mean that we have already reappraised
all our beliefs, intentions, and values in light of it, much less that we have
brought our entire existence into conformity with it. I return to this point
in a moment, when I consider repentance. The point, for now, is that if we
believe the Gospel, we will be committed to judging our entire lives—and,
indeed, *everything*—in its light.

This provides us with a way of understanding how persons come to
believe the Gospel—or, more precisely, how they come to understand their
coming to believe it. To be sure, people come to this belief for all sorts of
reasons: because they had an especially powerful experience, for instance,
such as seeing a blinding light or hearing a voice from heaven; because
they heard about it from someone they trust; because they were attracted
to the difference that this belief has made in someone's life; because they
were raised to believe it; because they "gave it a try" and then discovered
that the belief stuck; or for any number of other reasons. The key point,
for our purposes, is not how they initially came to believe the Gospel but
what happens once they do. Again, if we take this belief to be fundamental,
then we will judge everything else in its light—including the life we led
prior to arriving at this belief. We should thus come to see our past, along
with our circumstances, in light of this belief, which should give us a sense,
in turn, of how our past is retrospectively recognizable as preparing us for
this belief. I may thus view myself as finally "seeing the light" and therefore as being freed from all the lies I had believed about myself up to this
point, or I may see myself as always having longed for redemption from
my shame and guilt, or I may see my life to this point as getting me in a

position where I could finally take this step. There are countless ways that we might reinterpret our life in light of this belief; the point is simply that if we believe the Gospel to be the fundamental truth about ourselves and the world, we will reinterpret our past in its light. And, importantly, reinterpreting our past in this way will reinforce our sense that the Gospel is the fundamental truth, since our self-narrative will now be built around, and thus in support of, that sense.

From the perspective of people who believe this message, moreover, they will naturally see their believing of it as itself due to that which is fundamental, namely, God.[49] No wonder, then, that Christians have often explained their coming-to-belief in terms not only of their own way of arriving at this belief but also in terms of God's work of enabling them to believe it. The latter work, often characterized as the work of preparation and illumination, is customarily ascribed to the Holy Spirit. Notice, however, that what we have here is not necessarily two separate processes—the believer's own journey of coming to believe the Gospel, on the one hand, and the Spirit's work of enabling them to believe it, on the other—but two perspectives on the same process. Believers can thus talk about their coming to belief by recounting certain circumstances internal to their own lives, and they can talk about precisely these circumstances as the way that God was at work in their lives; as a result, they need not choose between a life-circumstances narrative, on the one hand, and a divine-work narrative, on the other.[50] On this approach, then, not only is the proclaimed word God's own speech, God works to enable us to hear that speech with faith.

To have faith, then, is not only to believe the Gospel but also to believe that it is the fundamental truth in the light of which everything else should be judged. This means, in turn, that the Christian life will have a peculiar shape, namely, that of working to bring our lives into conformity with this truth and, so, of working against aspects of our lives that are at odds with it. The name for this is *repentance*. Martin Luther famously insisted, accordingly, that "when our Lord and Master Jesus Christ said, 'Repent,' he willed the entire life of believers to be one of repentance," where to do this is to "'assume another mind and feeling, recover one's sense, make a transition from one state of mind to another, have a change of spirit'; so that those who hitherto have been aware of earthly matters may now know the spiritual. . . . By this recovery of one's sense," Luther concludes, "it happens that the sinner has a change of heart and hates his sin."[51] Karl Barth similarly asserts that in becoming devoted to Christ, a person "repents and renounces what he previously was and did, leaving his old way, abandoning himself as he was, boldly enterprising a completely new and different being and action, entering a new way," such that "it can never be a question of a routine continuation or repetition of what has hitherto been our customary practice. . . . Inevitably, the man who is called by Jesus renounces and turns away from himself as he was yesterday."[52] And finally Dietrich Bonhoeffer, with characteristic force of expression, contends that devotion to God necessarily involves "an endless manifold struggle of the spirit against the flesh," and that those who would so devote themselves are thus "called away and are supposed to 'step out' of their previous existence . . . former things are left behind; they are completely given up."[53] We could cite countless additional precedents, but the point is that repentance—turning against, and so away from, one's old way of life—is an essential component of the Christian life, which is exactly what we would expect if a person takes the Gospel to be the fundamental truth.

To understand what this might mean, we need to say a bit more about what repentance looks like—what it might look like, that is, for persons to turn against their old, sinful orientation. With respect to cognition, such repentance might mean becoming aware of, and renouncing, the self-deceptions and rationalizations that keep us from seeing ourselves clearly, so that we might then perceive the dissonance between what we trust and what we should trust, for instance, as well as between what we have set our hearts on and what we should set our hearts on, and might resist self-exonerating characterizations *of* that dissonance. One element of repentance, therefore, would be a renunciation of that which would cloud our ability to perceive ourselves and our circumstances clearly and truthfully. (Such truthful perception will turn out to include a crucial element of forgiveness, as we will see.) With respect to motivation, repentance gives us reason to act so as to turn against our old orientation—it would give us reason to avoid tempting situations, for instance, or to seek out persons who will hold us accountable for our actions, or to give an honest account of ourselves in, say, a journal. No surprise, then, that Christianity is teeming with these sorts of practices. Such turning away would also render us susceptible to certain felt evaluations: feeling guilt, regret, sadness, and the like in response to perceptions and cognitions of falling short (of the sort just discussed), and in response to perceptions and cognitions that themselves fall short; in response to actions and motivations, past and present, that deviate from our devotion to God; and in response to felt evaluations that are themselves a kind of holdover from our old ways—we may still feel jealous of another's success, or unduly anxious about our job security, or obsessed with procuring some shiny new good, but we may now have a negative felt evaluation *of* these felt evaluations and thus feel guilty or ashamed, say, for feeling jealous, anxious, or obsessively desirous. These feelings, in turn, may give us reason to do certain things or help us to see ourselves more clearly, which may give way to still further feelings, and so on, such that the cognitive, practical, and emotional components of repentance can be both mutually reinforcing and exponentially ramifying. The latter is crucial, since it means that repentance can spread fairly quickly—that is, can quickly come to range over an increasingly wide array of evaluative phenomena—such that one's determination to turn away from one's old ways can soon be instantiated in more and more concrete turning aways.

This is related to an even more crucial point: in the picture just sketched, persons not only turn against their old ways, they *take sides* with one element of their evaluative perspective—namely, their devotion to God—against other elements, and just so *stand behind* and *identify with* that element. We see this especially in the case of felt evaluations: if felt evaluations generally track with, and thus express, what we value, as I have already argued, then it follows that our felt evaluations can likewise express our valuation of some values (such as our orientation to God) over against other values (namely, those implicit in our old orientation). This is precisely what we see when persons experience negative felt evaluations in relation to their old cognition, action, and emotion (in relation, that is, to cognition, action, and emotion as oriented to other values) such that, again, these felt evaluations indicate that persons stand behind or side with this particular value in its contest with other values—and insofar as that which is basic to one's evaluative perspective is likewise basic to who one is as a self, this standing behind counts as *identifying* oneself *with* that value. Devotion to God will thus be registered not only—indeed, not primarily—in our decision to be so devoted but also in our felt evaluations as these side with this component of our evaluative perspective over against the rest.

Such emotional partisanship is therefore a vital—usually necessary—expression of a person's siding with devotion to God rather than with their old, "worldly" orientation, though it is important to note that if one's emotional expressions did not also cohere or find some resonance with cognitive and practical repentance, then the former would not count as the genuine article. This might seem untrue; it might seem that emotional partisanship alone would indicate which side a person was on, even in the absence of cognitive and practical repentance. But such emotions must be expressions of value, and if they are, the values they express must likewise have some practical and cognitive effects; absent such effects, it is hard to see how the emotions in question would be recognizable *as* expressions of value, let alone of a highly valued value.[54]

This brings us to two decisive points, the first of which is that, by means of repentance, one's life can be brought into conformity with one's devotion on an *evaluative* level, even if it is not yet so conformed on the *actual* level. Such evaluative conformity is relevantly similar to Kant's transcendental unity of apperception, for in both cases we achieve coherence within our evaluative perspective precisely by making *judgments* about how the contents of that perspective should relate to one another, rather than by making all of those contents actually fit neatly together.[55] Simply stated, insofar as we judge these contents on the basis of our devotion to God, it follows that our evaluative perspective hangs together—normatively, if not actually—on the basis of that devotion, which means, in turn, that our life can be oriented to God (evaluatively) even where it is not so oriented (actually). (Seeing one's life from the perspective of forgiveness adds a crucial dimension to this being-oriented-to-God-even-in-not-being-so-oriented, for one then perceives even one's misorientation in light of the Gospel and one thus remains oriented to God even in that misorientation. I return to this point below.)

A second, even more critical point is that, in siding with this element of one's evaluative perspective, *one becomes a new person*, for what finally matters about us, theologically speaking, is what we live or walk according to; hence, if a person whose life used to be oriented by and to the world now orients themselves to God, then theologically speaking they are no longer who they used to be. To see why this would be the case, it might be useful to consider a passably similar argument from Kant.[56] The argument proceeds through roughly the following steps. (a) Kant claims that one's nature as a person—one's nature, that is, as a moral agent—is determined by whatever it is that one uses as an ultimate basis for deciding among alternatives. (b) There can be only one such basis, since every decision a person makes must be made on some basis, and one's deciding among candidate bases must itself be so based, such that the branching tree of one's decisions must eventually terminate in a single, most fundamental basis; Kant calls this a person's "ground-axiom." (c) Ground-axioms come in only two flavors: a person's moral decisions must finally be based, Kant claims, either on pure respect for the moral law, or on some form of self-interest. (d) Kant thinks that self-interest is in fact the ground-axiom of all humans, such that we are all radically evil—evil right down to the roots—in our very nature as persons. (e) From this, it follows that if persons' ground-axioms were to change, such that they were now to base all of their decisions on respect for the moral law alone, this would mark a change in their very nature as persons; they would now be new persons, morally speaking, and their old nature would be put to an end. My argument differs from Kant's in important respects—for one, he thinks of personhood in terms of a more or less linear decision tree, whereas I think of it in terms of a fabric-like interweaving of emotions, cognitions, and motivations that constitute a more or less coherent evaluative perspective—but they share a key feature: both claim that what is fundamental to personhood is the way persons relate their decisions and other evaluative commitments to some most basic decision or evaluative commitment, from which it follows that if they were to renounce these basic decisions or commitments in favor of another— especially one radically opposed to the former—this would count as a change in their very nature, which is to say that they would thereby cease to be who they were, morally speaking, and become a new person. Less philosophically, we might simply think of someone who has turned their life around, and who might therefore inform persons from their past, "That's not who I am anymore." Insofar as one has indeed turned away from one's old ways, there is nothing hyperbolic about such statements—or so I am suggesting.

On the present account, then, to devote ourselves to God is to side with this devotion against our old ways, and so to side is simultaneously to put an end to our old self and to become a new person, theologically speaking. To take just one example from the theological tradition, this is precisely what we hear from Barth, who claims that "in the quarrel in which a man finds himself engaged in conversion—as he who is still wholly the old and already the new man—he has not fallen out with himself partially but totally, in the sense that the end and goal of the dispute is that he can no longer be the one he was and can be only the one he will be," such that this quarrel represents "the passing and death and definitive end and destruction of the one in favor of the development and life and exclusive, uncompromised, and inviolable existence of the other."[57] Again, the idea is simply that insofar as persons identify with *this* element in their evaluative perspective—insofar as they identify, that is, with their devotion to God— they stand against their old self and have become a new person, theologically speaking.

If so, then when we believe the Gospel and repent, our old selves are put to death and we become new creations. Not just any new creations, however. Again, the new self is constituted by the fact that we now identify with this element in our evaluative perspective in such a way that this element is now that which is most fundamental to our selfhood. Christians have traditionally regarded this "new thing" in us as God's Spirit and have equally regarded this Spirit as the Spirit of Christ or, indeed, as Christ in us. (Paul so equates them within the space of a couple verses: "But you are not in the flesh; you are in the Spirit, since the Spirit of God dwells in you. Anyone who does not have the Spirit of Christ does not belong to him. But if Christ is in you . . ." [Rom. 8:9–10].) By the same dual-perspective logic traced above, this would mean that our old selves have been put to death by—and only by—having this new Spirit, and it would likewise mean that our selves are recreated by—and only by—partaking in the life of Christ. From this perspective, accordingly, we can say that we are put to death and raised to new life only through our connection with Christ, since we would not have this new life (which puts to death the old) unless the Spirit of Christ were in us. I try to shed some light on this idea in the following chapter.

With this idea on board, we can now return to the issue with which we began. How are we included in Christ's deliverance from Sin? In the previous section, we noted that Christ, having been put to death, is freed from the power of Sin precisely because he has already endured the death sentence to which sin makes humanity liable; the Law has thus been satisfied, in other words, which means that Sin no longer has any rightful claim on him; the life he now lives, therefore, he lives apart from the Law and, so, no longer under the jurisdiction of Sin. We are now in position to see how this would be true of us, too, for if our old selves have likewise been put to death and indeed been put to death through union with Christ, then it stands to reason that we have likewise endured the death penalty to which we were liable and thus been freed from the power of Sin. As with Christ, then, so with us: if we have already been condemned unto death, then Sin and Death no longer have a hold on us; we are therefore free to live unto God.

Insofar as persons side with their devotion to God over against their orientation by and to the world, it follows (a) that they can be so devoted even if their entire life does not actually conform to that devotion, (b) that they have become new persons, theologically speaking, and (c) that they have thereby been freed from the power of Sin. So far, so good, but these claims raise a problem of their own: even if this is so, how could we know it to be true? For one thing, even such siding with and evaluative conformity will not be perfect. And for another, persons who have turned against their old self will surely be suspicious of the idea that they have turned decisively against that self, are truly a new person, are actually devoted to God, and so on. Just to the extent that they are devoted to God, moreover, they will necessarily want to know what *God* thinks of their devotion, which is, again, not something that they can simply tell themselves. From all of this, it follows that persons who have devoted themselves to God may not yet be able to perceive themselves as such—that is, they may not yet be *for*-themselves what they are *in*-themselves (to put the point in Hegel's idiom). To address this problem, accordingly, let us turn to our third topic: practices of hearing—and bearing witness to—God's judgment.

Practices of Hearing God's Judgment

Again, persons who take the Gospel message to be the fundamental truth and who thus devote themselves to God will necessarily want to know what God thinks of them. In this section, I consider several practices in which the church bears witness to God's judgment: the practice of baptism, the practice of confession and forgiveness, and the practice of friendship and self-narration.

We can understand *baptism* in terms of three claims: (a) that, in baptism, the church recognizes a person as having devoted themselves to God and as having repented of their old ways—the church recognizes that this is the case, and thus recognizes the person as "one of us"; (b) that the church's recognition represents God's own recognition of the person; and (c) that there is a sense in which baptism not only recognizes but also plays a role in constituting a person's death and new life, their adoption as God's child, and their forgiveness. The upshot of these points is that, in and through baptism, a person should now be for-themselves what they are in-themselves, precisely because they can now see themselves from God's perspective. To be devoted to God means, among other things, that one wants to see things from (and live according to) God's perspective, from which it follows that if God perceives one as a new, devoted self, then one's devotion should now include a recognition of oneself as such.[58]

The first step, then, is to understand baptism as the church's recognition of a person as "one of us," where the "us" in question is composed of those who have devoted themselves to God and thus turned against their old orientation. This step presupposes, of course, that they have indeed devoted themselves to God, which is why Luther insists, for instance, that "faith alone makes the person worthy to receive the salutary, divine water profitably," just as Schleiermacher claims that "one's being made a disciple [must] precede baptism."[59] (This helps explain the common—and ancient—role afforded to sponsors or witnesses within baptismal ceremonies, since they provide the church with some assurance that the persons being baptized have in fact devoted themselves to God, such that it would be appropriate for the church to recognize them as such.) It also presupposes that a person's devotion constitutes a kind of implicit petition to join the ranks of those who are similarly devoted. The logic here was undoubtedly clearer in the primitive church, for then it was plain that following Jesus' call to devote oneself wholly to God meant leaving everything behind and joining his band of followers (and vice versa), but the general idea still stands, which is why baptism can still be seen as "the mark by which we publicly confess that we wish to be reckoned God's people," as Calvin puts it.[60] Baptism can thus be seen as the church's response to this petition, as if, in baptism, the church were saying, "We recognize you as one of us—that is, as having devoted yourself to Christ and turned against your old ways." (This is almost exactly what many churches *do* say in baptism, at least according to the standard baptismal liturgies.) This would explain why baptism is commonly construed as a rite wherein a person is admitted to the church; thus Luther claims that it is baptism "through which we are first received into the Christian community"; Calvin, that "baptism is the sign of the initiation by which we are received into the society of the church"; Schleiermacher, that baptism is "the act of reception into the church"; Rahner, that baptism is "the sacrament of incorporation into the church"; and Küng, that "baptism is the basic sacrament of initiation, in which a new relationship is established between the candidate and the church."[61] Theological precedents notwithstanding, the first step is to see baptism as the church's act of recognizing one as having left one's old self behind in order to devote oneself to God, and, just so, its act of receiving persons into its ranks.

The second step is to see that the church here speaks on God's behalf—indeed, speaks God's own word to the one being baptized. This, too, is a common claim; to take just one example, Luther claims that a person being baptized must "see the difference in baptism between man who administers the sacrament and God who is its author. For man baptizes, and yet does not baptize. He baptizes in that he performs the work of immersing the person to be baptized; he does not baptize, because in so doing he acts not on his own authority but in God's stead. Hence we ought to receive baptism at human hands just as if Christ himself, indeed, God himself, were baptizing us with his own hands. For it is not man's baptism, but Christ's and God's baptism, which we receive by the hand of a man."[62] So then: if (a) we can understand baptism as the church's act of saying that someone has died and been raised to new life, and (b) we can understand this speech as God's own (according to the pattern described above), then it would follow (c) that, in baptism, persons hear not only what the church thinks of them but also what God thinks of them. Baptism could thus be understood as God's "ratification," "confirmation," or "sealing" of a person's faith, as Calvin likes to say.[63]

Crucially for our purposes, this would also mean that a person should now be *for*-themselves what they are *in*-themselves, namely, a self that is devoted to God, for if (a) God recognizes a person as such and (b) their devotion to God necessarily means that God's perspective is authoritative for them, it follows (c) that they can and must see themselves from God's perspective, such that (d) they can and must see themselves as devoted to God and thus as a new self. In baptism, then, God tells us that our old self has died and that we are a new creation, which enables—nay, requires—a devoted self to recognize themselves as such. (To be clear, I am not suggesting that God cannot confer such recognition apart from baptism; I am claiming, rather, that, when conducted with the appropriate authorization in the appropriate circumstances, baptism does confer God's recognition. This is the difference between saying that baptism is necessary for such conferral and saying that it is sufficient for it.)

That brings us to a third step, which draws out a handful of potential implications from the second.[64] One implication is that if one has indeed died to one's old self and been raised to new life, then one is forgiven (or, more precisely, one is no longer liable to condemnation for one's sins). The idea here, which should already sound familiar, is (a) that one is liable to condemnation precisely because the Law—in one sense of that term—makes sure that all people get what they deserve; (b) that death is a final pronouncement of this condemnation; from which it follows (c) that if one were to rise to new life after death, one would no longer be subject to condemnation, since one would then already have served one's just sentence under the Law; what is more, (d) if one has died, it also follows that one has fulfilled, and so been released from, whatever till-death-do-us-part vows one may have made, including one's lifelong pledge to the power of Sin. So then: if baptism tells us that we have died and risen to new life, and if a person who has died and risen to new life is no longer liable to condemnation for sin, then it follows that baptism tells us that we are no longer liable to condemnation for sin—or, in short, that we are forgiven.[65]

It makes sense, then, that when persons are worried about whether they are forgiven, the church has often encouraged them to look to their baptism for assurance.[66]

A second, more tenuous implication is connected to the first: there is a sense in which baptism not only recognizes but also brings it about that one has died and risen to new life. This is a tricky suggestion for me to make, not least because I have already claimed that one is dead and risen anew precisely when one repents and devotes oneself to God, such that it is not clear how I could now say that baptism plays some role in bringing about this state of affairs. But it is at least possible that baptism plays such a role *from the perspective of the person being baptized,* if not from the church's or God's perspective. To see what I mean here, consider cases where one has worked toward achieving a particular status but is not in position to recognize when one has achieved it: this is what it is like for many who work toward the status of "scholar," for instance, and, more seriously, it is what it was like for Luke Skywalker to work toward the status of Jedi.[67] In such cases, there is an important perspectival difference between those, on the one hand, who have already achieved this status and can thus recognize others as having achieved it as soon as the latter possess the relevant traits and, on the other, those among the latter who cannot yet recognize themselves as such, and whose self-recognition thus depends upon the recognition of others. So think of a case where a particular student has spent years developing the rigor, learnedness, and independence of mind that mark a scholar. From her vantage point, she might not be able to see herself as a scholar until a certain kind of event has occurred—the publication of an article in a peer-reviewed journal, for instance, or the conferral of the Ph.D. degree—such that she might therefore experience this event as the moment when she *became* a scholar. Established scholars, on the other hand, might see her as having developed these traits long before and recognize her work as scholarly—by accepting her article or conferring the doctoral degree—precisely because these things are *already* true of her. From their vantage point, then, such events recognize an already existing state of affairs, whereas from hers, they may seem to *establish* that state of affairs. Something similar might be true of baptism, at least in some cases: we can be recognized as new persons only if this is already true of us, but from the standpoint of the persons being baptized, they might experience such recognition as the moment that established them as such.

This brings us to a third possible implication. Drawing on the idea that a person who is raised to new life is simultaneously born anew as God's child, we can understand baptism as a kind of adoption ceremony; in that case, baptism would not merely report on an already-existing state of affairs but bring about a state of affairs as well.[68] To see what I am getting at here, consider some basic points about language: some words do things— so when a police officer says, "You are under arrest," someone is placed under arrest, or when a new mother says, "His name is Simeon," that becomes her son's name.[69] There are also doings that say things—so I might hold a finger to my lips to tell my kids to be quiet, or leave a jacket on a seat to let people know that the seat is taken, or baptize someone to let them know that they are "one of us." And finally, some of the doings that say something also do something—so I might shake your hand as a way of sealing a deal or making peace, or wave a white flag in order to surrender. I am suggesting that we can think of baptism, too, as an action that says something and, in so saying, does something: in baptism, God says something like, "Today I have adopted you as my beloved child," and in so saying, God thereby actually adopts one as God's child.[70] That would mean, among other things, that we could think of baptism along the lines of a swearing-in ceremony or the signing of adoption papers, where the doing brings about a new state of affairs, namely, that we are adopted as God's children and so share in the promised inheritance. To cite him yet again, this is what Calvin, for one, has to say: "In baptism, God . . . makes us his own by adoption."[71]

Some of these implications are admittedly tenuous, and I offer them here largely in an ecumenical spirit. The main point is less tenuous, namely, that in baptism the church—like God—recognizes persons as having left their old life behind and devoted themselves to God, such that they are now for-themselves what they are in-themselves; they can thus see themselves as a new person, as a devoted self, and just so can identify with their identity to God. They can thereby live more fully from God's perspective, which means that a higher level of devotion is now possible for them, since this fulfills one of the desires necessarily ingredient in devotion itself. Baptism can thus play a crucial role in helping persons perceive themselves as a new, devoted self.

That brings us to a second practice. Persons who accept the Gospel message as fundamentally true and thus devote themselves to God will surely feel guilty for certain things they have done and, indeed, for what they have made of their lives, just as they will feel guilty for whatever wrongs they continue to do. Naturally, they will want to know—indeed, feel compelled to know—how to deal with this guilt in light of that which is fundamentally true, which brings us to the practice of *confession and forgiveness*.

So, then, suppose that we feel bad about ourselves in light of our wrongdoing, or, in sum, that we feel guilty. The mere fact that we feel guilty does not mean that we *should* feel guilty; after all, there are times when we feel guilty not because we have committed an actual transgression but because, say, we have violated norms that are themselves wrong (to the effect that, for instance, a person should never say no to a request or take a day off work) or because we have an unduly accusatory conscience (such that we feel guilty about things we did not actually do or even consider doing). The antidote for guilt of this sort is not forgiveness—not directly, at least—but getting a correct perspective on it. Supposing, however, that we feel guilty for an actual transgression, then our guilt may lead us to feel that we deserve a negative evaluation of our moral character, and that others, too, including God, would now be right to feel that way about us.

That brings us to the practice of confessing our guilt and, in light of God's promise, seeking God's forgiveness.[72] The paradigmatic response to such confession is that God pronounces us forgiven—God declares, that is, that one's wrongdoing is no longer charged to one's moral account, as it were, because one is a new creation, such that a negative assessment attaches only to one's deed rather than to one's very self—and God makes this pronouncement through the mouth of a fellow believer. The latter point is a recurrent emphasis of Luther, for instance, who maintains that "confession consists of two parts. One is that we confess our sins. The other is that we receive absolution or forgiveness from the confessor as from God himself, by no means doubting but firmly believing that our sins are thereby forgiven before God in heaven."[73] The idea here, sometimes referred to as "the power of the keys," is straightforward enough: we confess our sin and desire for forgiveness to a fellow believer, whose pronouncement, spoken in God's name, counts as God's own pronouncement of forgiveness and should be heard as such. The underlying idea should be familiar enough, since we discussed it at length above: one person can speak for another, in such a way that the former's words count as the latter's own, insofar as the latter person appropriates that person's words and thus undertakes whatever commitments the person expresses. That is the idea here, too: believers are authorized to pronounce God's forgiveness, such that God binds Godself to this pronouncement and it counts as God's own actual pronouncement of forgiveness. In this way, God's forgiveness can be pronounced to us from without, by another, which is crucial, for otherwise—if it were a word spoken only by and to ourselves—its form would not match its content. (Think here of the CEO of a bank forgiving a person's sizable debt, and then consider the difference it makes if the CEO and the debtor are the same person. Or think of persons who are so mired in guilt that they could not possibly believe that they should not be condemned—could not believe it, that is, unless such a thing were pronounced to them from without.)

Before saying more about this, it is important to distinguish between two broad types of forgiveness. On the one hand, there is the sort of forgiveness that can be offered only by the person who has been wronged by us and, so, who may rightfully hold our wrongdoing against us. This is the sort of forgiveness on offer when we set aside our desire for vengeance against a wrongdoer. It is necessarily first-personal—"I forgive you"—and thus cannot be pronounced on another's behalf. On the other hand, there is the sort of forgiveness in which a person pronounces that a wrongdoer is not liable to a negative moral assessment. This sort of forgiveness is second-personal—"You are forgiven"—and can be pronounced by anyone with the requisite moral authority. To see the difference, suppose that I am caught spreading nasty rumors about a colleague. If so, I might sincerely apologize to my colleague in the hope that they will not hold my wrongdoing against me. No one else can pronounce me forgiven on their behalf; it is entirely up to them whether they continue to hold my wrongdoing against me. By itself, however, that does not mean that my wrongdoing continues to be held against me in the sense of counting against my moral standing; this point becomes clear if we imagine that my colleague is a petty, spiteful, vicious person. If someone with moral wisdom and authority observed that I was sincerely penitent and committed to making things right, this person may tell me that I am no longer rightly liable to a negative self-assessment—may tell me, in other words, that I should no longer feel guilty or, in short, that I am forgiven. The one who has been wronged is thus the only one who can first-personally forgive me, but I can be second-personally forgiven by anyone who has the requisite moral authority. I consider the former sort of forgiveness in chapter 6; for now, we are focusing solely on the latter.

So how should the second-personal variety of forgiveness, once pronounced, transform our feeling of guilt? First, if we hear God's pronouncement as authoritative, we should take God's evaluative perspective, rather than our own, to have the final word on our transgressions, and given (a) that God sees us from the perspective of grace, and (b) that seeing ourselves from this perspective means seeing ourselves as released from condemnation, it follows (c) that we should see ourselves as so released, and, thus, as no longer guilty. Teresa of Avila offers us a clear example of this: "Once while I was experiencing great distress over having offended God," she writes, "he said to me, 'All your sins are before me as though they were not.'"[74] Forgiveness of this sort entails that we should *no longer* feel guilty—not, to be clear, that we should *never have* felt guilty but that this particular occurrence of guilt should now be put behind us. Given that forgiveness is here entirely God's gift, it follows that the relief a person feels in being freed from guilt should simultaneously be experienced with gratitude.

Gratitude and an absence of guilt are not the only things one should feel, however, for the fact that we no longer feel guilty does not mean that we should no longer have any concern about our transgressions, nor that we should no longer have any negative evaluation of them. In light of forgiveness, we should feel not guilt but *regret* for our transgression, where regret means that we wish we had not done something (and so have a negative evaluation of our having done it), but this need not be coupled with a sense of deserving condemnation for it. The distinction matters: we can feel *regret* for a transgression without feeling *guilty* about it—as, for example, I wish I had not done countless bad things when I was a child, like impulsively throwing a bucket of sand into the open window of a passing car, but do not feel as if I ought to be condemned for doing those things—just as we can feel *guilt* without *regret*—so I might feel that I deserve condemnation if I cheat at poker in order to win thousands of dollars, but I might nevertheless not regret doing so; indeed, I might feel guilty but nevertheless be excited by the prospect of repeating the transgression. The idea here, then, is that persons who have been forgiven should continue to have a negative evaluation of their transgressions but that forgiveness should change this evaluation from guilt to regret, since the wrong no longer attaches to their moral character.

We get some idea of how this might work—and of why one might find the present suggestion plausible—in a key feature of my just-invoked example: the reason I do not feel guilty about something I did as a child is that I am not the same person I was then; there is enough distance between me and the person who did it that I am no longer liable for whatever negative evaluation my younger self might have deserved. The key here, obviously, is the notion that there can be significant "distance" between who I am now and what I did in the past. The passage of time can introduce such distance, as in the example, but, crucially, so can repentance and forgiveness: as we have seen, to repent and be forgiven is, among other things, for one's old self to be put to death and for one to be raised to new life, which means, in turn, that one's old, sinful self is no longer who one is, that

that self is decisively a thing of the past, and, in consequence, that there is a grave's worth of distance between one's sinful transgressions and who one is. To experience forgiveness, accordingly, is to see ourselves from this perspective—from God's evaluative perspective—and just so to be freed from the guilt we feel for those transgressions. Again, though, this does not mean that we should be freed from *all* negative feelings about such transgressions, since those who no longer feel that they deserve condemnation should nevertheless still regret having committed them, not least because some such evaluation plays an important role in guarding us against a recurrence of the transgression, in motivating us to change our ways, and in reminding us of our utter dependence upon grace.

I return to these points in a moment, but before doing so it is worth noting that the rudiments of this approach do show up in the work of at least one theologian, namely, Rudolf Bultmann, though he does not combine or elaborate them in quite the way I do. So, on the one hand, Bultmann repeatedly claims that forgiveness introduces distance between me and my old self and that it thus renders the latter a thing of the past; this is what he has in mind when he claims, for example, that, "by accepting me, God takes me to be a different person than I am; and if I (in faith) let go of what I am in myself, if I affirm God's judgment and understand myself in terms of him, then I really *am* a different person, namely, the one that he takes me to be."[75] On the other hand, Bultmann asserts that this distance puts us in a new relationship to our transgressions—not, note well, as if they had never happened but in that they lose their grip on us. He claims, accordingly, that when the Gospel is proclaimed to a person, it "announces to him the possibility of becoming free from his past. Such freedom does not mean, however, that he no longer has any past whatever. But he has won the power of free decision upon his past. *He may take it with him as that for which he has been forgiven.*"[76] Bultmann does not tell us what it means to "take it with one as that for which one has been forgiven," but it should be clear that this is what I have been trying to explain in terms of a distinction between guilt and regret.

Precedents notwithstanding, my point is that forgiveness introduces distance between who we are and what we have done, and that this distance should render us liable to feel regret, rather than guilt, over our transgressions. (To be clear, I am suggesting only that a person should be liable to such feelings when something calls a transgression to mind, not that the person should be in a constant state of occurrent regretfulness over them.)

This brings us to a tricky issue, however: what if one is forgiven, yet one's guilt does not change to regret? My earlier claims seem to imply that one should feel guilty about this—and if the latter guilt, once forgiven, does not change to regret, that one should feel guilty about this, too, and so on, such that a person who subscribed to the approach I have been tracing may end up locked in an endless spiral of guilt. Assuming, crucially, that they do not *want* to feel guilty, this is a serious concern, in response to which I would make two points. First, given the nature of emotions, we should expect that they will often take time to subside—they have a kind of momentum, after all, which is at least partly physiological in nature— such that we should not feel guilty if our guilt is not instantly transformed by forgiveness. Second, however, in genuinely recalcitrant cases it is vital to distinguish between instances, on the one hand, where a person contin- ues to feel guilty, at least in part, because they somehow *want* to feel guilty— instances where, say, a person feels so bad for what they did that they hold on to their guilt feelings precisely as a kind of self-condemnation—and instances, on the other hand, where one feels guilty but *wants* to let for- giveness free one from it. In the former case, persons *should* feel guilty about feeling guilty, so it does not count against the present account if they do. In the latter sort of case, by contrast, it is clear that persons regret feeling guilty—they wish they did not feel that way—such that they need not feel guilty for feeling guilty, nor must they seek forgiveness anew in order to arrive at this point, since, in this kind of case, their regret indicates (a) that they take God's evaluative perspective, rather than their own, as final and (b) that the recalcitrant guilt is not so much a transgression as something beyond their control, a carryover from their old self for which they have already been forgiven and from which they have already been distanced. In this sort of situation, what they need to hear is a word of comfort, spo- ken by a friend or counselor, rather than a new word of forgiveness. Here as elsewhere, the important thing may be simply to let persons know that they should not feel guilty and to treat them accordingly.

Tricky issues aside, let us suppose that in some cases, at least, forgive- ness can transform guilt into regret, especially if given enough time. This is important not only because it would free us from our sense of deserving condemnation but also because regret can itself play an important role in motivating us to change, for to regret something means not only to wish that we had not done it but also to want *not* to do it—and, because we have done it, to know that we may be tempted to do it again. To see what I mean, suppose that I lose my patience with my children and feel guilty about it, and that they then forgive me for my impatience and even pronounce God's own forgiveness over me; in that case, I might no longer feel guilt but would still feel regret. This would mean, on the one hand, that when I think about having lost my patience, I wish I had not done so and, on the other, that I want not to do so; I may therefore pray that God would give me this good, which prayer will, I hope, increase the likelihood that I will resist the temptation to lose my patience in the future, and make me see it as a gift if I do not give in to that temptation. And, again, in confessing our guilt and praying for forgiveness and transformation, we orient ourselves to God even in our not being oriented to God, and we can experience this orientation-in-not-being-oriented as due to God's forgiving love rather than to our orientation itself.

So far, so good, but one may still have a hard time experiencing the Gospel as fundamentally true of oneself—and thus have a hard time identifying with one's identity as a new creation—insofar as one continues to feel shame about oneself. Shame, recall, is a deep-seated sense that I fail, in some significant way, to embody a value with which I identify, in consequence of which I experience my very self as falling short. Because this sense is deep seated, one not only perceives this wrongness as fundamental to who one is but ends up perceiving other aspects of who one is as *surfaces*—not reflective of who one really is deep down; hence, even if one is outwardly very kind and thoughtful, for instance, one will not see this as reflective of who one actually is, since one knows that, deep down, one is in fact a terrible person. Indeed, by a strange sort of alchemy, one may take it that one is outwardly kind and thoughtful precisely because one knows what a terrible person one is, such that the former, too, is finally experienced as evidence of the latter. Unsurprisingly, people who feel this way about themselves may find it hard to believe that the Gospel message is fundamentally true of them, and even harder to *experience* this as true. Here, after all, we are dealing with competing fundamental truths, but one of these "truths" has the advantage of having long shaped a person's self-conception and thus having been written into other aspects of that self-conception.

The Christian tradition says surprisingly little about how a person might be redeemed from shame (by contrast with guilt), but it does offer some resources that might be helpful in thinking about such redemption. On the one hand, we find the practice of *spiritual friendship* (in Aelred of Rivaulx's nice phrase), particularly the sort of intimate friendship in which we trust another enough that we can let our guard down with them. Ambrose characterizes such a friend as, among other things, "someone to whom you can open your heart, someone with whom you can share your innermost feelings, and someone in whom you can confide the secrets of your heart."[77] Aelred likewise claims that "*a friend is the partner of your soul, to whose spirit you join and link your own and so unite yourself as to wish to become one from two, to whom you commit yourself as to another self,* from whom you conceal nothing, *from whom you fear nothing.*"[78] The point here is that one can trust a true friend not just with one's secrets but with one's very self, and that one can so trust them because the friend takes one's good as their "cause" and is therefore fundamentally an ally of one's self. Aelred thus characterizes a friend as "*the guardian of the soul* itself," which is precisely why "you may confidently entrust to the friend yourself and all that is yours."[79]

A friend is thus someone to whom I can entrust myself and, so, reveal myself. The friend is also someone whose opinion matters to me; as Aelred puts it, "The friend's counsel has great authority."[80] Aelred does not explain why a friend's opinion would matter so much to me, but it is not hard to imagine why: for one thing, they know me intimately; for another, given that they are allies of my good, I can count on the fact that their opinion will not be duplicitous or self-interested. And because I know them well, I should also have a good sense of how reliable their judgments tend to be; hence, if I know that they tend to offer wise counsel, then I have a dispositively strong reason for thinking that the counsel they are offering me is wise, too. More to Aelred's point, if I know that my friend—my *spiritual* friend—is reliable at perceiving things as God does, then it follows that this person is reliable at perceiving me, too, as God does—and because they are close to me, they can perceive who I am *deep down* as God does. They can thus bear witness to me of the way that God perceives me and of the fact that this perception, and not my shamefulness, is that which is fundamentally true about me. If their opinion carries weight with me, I may be able to perceive myself in their perception of me and, in so doing, come to perceive myself in God's perception of me.

Needless to say, though, even if I do trust my friend's judgment, I may still have a hard time accepting that judgment or experiencing it as true—and even if I could experience it as true, I may have a hard time seeing my whole self in its light (as opposed to seeing it as applicable only to a part of myself). We turn, then, to a related practice, which we can call the practice of *renarration*: the practice of renarrating our experiences in light of the Gospel, even as we may end up renarrating the Gospel in the process. We find a helpful example of how this practice works—and why it may be necessary—in *Lila,* Marilynne Robinson's brilliant novel. (I am tempted to call it a brilliant *theological* novel.) In the novel, Lila experiences shame for several reasons, including the fact that she was mistreated as a child, that she then lived as an outcast with the woman who helped her sneak out of that situation (and who has shame enough of her own), and that she worked in a brothel but was "too ugly" for the men. The net effect of all this, Lila confesses, is: "I got shame like a habit, the only thing I feel except when I'm alone."[81] Her path eventually crosses with that of the Rev. John Ames, a pastor who soon falls in love with her. Importantly for our purposes, Lila is unable to see herself in Ames's view of her, or, by extension, in God's view of her. We see an example of this in her response to being baptized. After Ames baptizes her, he informs Lila that she is a new creation: "I just washed you in the waters of regeneration," he tells her. "As far as I'm concerned, you're a newborn babe."[82] He insists upon this even when Lila reminds him of shameful facts about her past—about *her*. Ames thus sees Lila's shame, yet he does not see her as shameful; rather, he sees her as a new creation and thus bears witness to God's perspective on her. Lila still cannot see herself from this perspective, however, for the apparent reason that she thinks of baptism as saying that one is "clean and acceptable,"[83] yet she knows that she is *not* clean and acceptable; the following day, accordingly, she takes the extraordinary step of washing off her baptism.[84]

Spiritual friendship alone, therefore, is not enough to overcome her shame. For that, Lila needs to learn how to see her whole self, and so her entire past, in light of the Gospel; what she needs, then, is to renarrate her life in this light, though she can do so only by understanding the Gospel, too, in a new light. Crucially for our purposes, accordingly, the novel ends with a baptism that she can see herself in and therefore accept, precisely because she can now understand baptism first of all in terms of grace, and only secondarily in terms of being clean and acceptable. This is what allows Lila to grasp that "in eternity people's lives could be altogether what they were and had been, not just the worst things they ever did, or the best things either. So she decided that she should believe in it, or that she believed in it already."[85] And this allows her, in turn, to see her past as covered by grace and, just so, as taken up into her new identity: "There was no way to abandon guilt, no decent way to disown it." Lila knows this in her bones; it's one of the reasons why she could not accept her previous baptism. But now she knows something else in addition: "All the tangles and knots of bitterness and desperation and fear had to be pitied. No, better, grace had to fall over them."[86] The key, then, is not to try to leave the rest of one's identity behind ("you're a newborn babe"), but to see grace falling over one's entire life in such a way that "people's lives could be altogether what they were and had been." Lila can thus see her shamefulness in light of the Gospel, which means that even if she continues to feel shame for some aspects of her life, it is no longer basic to her self-understanding. Grace is.

Renarration can thus play an indispensable role in overcoming shame, for until one can see one's entire life in light of the Gospel, shame may continue to fundamentally shape one's identity. In Lila's case, the key was to renarrate her life in light of a more capacious sense of eternity and, so, to see her shame as covered by grace, though arriving at this point meant that she also had to renarrate her understanding of the Gospel. Others may renarrate their lives in other ways: they may now think that their old self-conception was in fact a lie, or they may think that that is who they *were* but not who they now *are*, or they may think that God has made something good out of their past and thereby redeemed it.[87] There are countless ways that persons can renarrate their lives in light of the Gospel; the point is simply that doing so can be vital in overcoming one's deep-seated sense of shame. Absent this, being told that one is a new creation would seem to confer a new identity merely in the sense that the witness protection program does.

Spiritual friendship and renarration can thus be mutually reinforcing means of addressing shame: a friend who knows me intimately can bear witness to God's perception of me, thereby inviting me to perceive myself in that perception, just as the practice of renarration can help me see my entire life in light of, and so as included in, the Gospel. Without renarration, I may still not be able to identify with my friend's perception of me, and without friendship, I may not feel like I can count on my would-be narrations.

If I take the Gospel to be the fundamental truth, then I will necessarily want to know what God thinks of me; Christianity tries to meet this need by providing what I am calling "practices of judgment." Baptism thus enacts God's own recognition of a person as a new creation and God's child; confession and forgiveness communicate God's judgment that we have been separated from our sin and freed from condemnation; and friendship and renarration convey God's view that, deep down, we are who God says we are. These practices are thus designed to help people perceive God's assessment of them and, crucially, to perceive themselves in light of that assessment. This is part of what it means to take the Gospel as telling us the fundamentally true story about ourselves.

Conclusion

This chapter began by considering who Jesus is and the role he plays in delivering persons from their bondage to sin. Jesus plays a crucial role in delivering us from sin, on this account, in two ways: on the one hand, he orients his entire life to God and thus rejects a "worldly" orientation and, on the other, his death and resurrection mean that Sin no longer has a rightful claim on him. We then turned to an account of what it would mean for us to participate in his death and resurrection and, so, be freed from Sin and Death. To begin with, Jesus' followers carry on his proclamation of God's new reign and, included in this, his calling of persons to live according to this reign and leave their old way behind. Those who follow Jesus are authorized to proclaim this call in his name, and, by a kind of transitive property, they speak his own word when they do so (just as an ambassador may speak for their president or a spouse may speak for their partner). The appropriate response to this call is faith, by which we mean a maximally thick sort of belief: "If this is true, it changes everything." For those who respond in faith, accordingly, their old self is put to death, and they rise to new life; to see why, consider that faith involves *repentance:* the renunciation of our worldly orientation in favor of devoting ourselves wholly to God, where this involves a commitment to seeing things, including ourselves, as Jesus did, being concerned as Jesus was, acting as Jesus did, and so on. For those who repent, this devotion is now fundamental to their evaluative perspective, in the sense that they stand behind or take sides with this component of their perspective over against its other components; in light of the account defended here, this means that they have become a new self, theologically speaking, and that their old self has passed away. In repentance, then, one's old self, identified with a worldly evaluative perspective, has been put to death, and one is raised to new life in Jesus; baptism enacts this putting-to-death and rising-to-life and, just so, enacts the community's recognition of a person as a new creation, as "one of us," which helps the person, in turn, to identify with their new self and experience it as what is fundamentally true of them. Moreover, by the logic outlined in the section on proclamation, the church's recognition of one counts as God's own, such that one can look to one's baptism to see God's perspective on one. In the same way, confession and forgiveness enable the community to pronounce God's own judgment upon our guilt, namely, that our guilt does not have the final word about us and, indeed, is part of our old, put-to-death self. Friendship and self-narration likewise bear witness to God's judgment—in this case, God's judgment concerning who we are deep down. As we learn to see ourselves in light of this judgment, we can be released from our deep-seated sense of shame.

Thus far, then, we have considered what Jesus did to bring about our deliverance from the power of Sin, as well as what it means for our old selves to be put to death, raised to new life, and, so, for that deliverance to be realized in our lives. In turn, those who have been so delivered will necessarily want to bring the rest of their lives into conformity with that which is fundamentally true of them. That brings us to the topic of the next three chapters, in which we consider a suite of practices designed to bring about just such conformity.

CHAPTER FOUR

Being Reoriented

THE PREVIOUS CHAPTER offered an account of how persons might be delivered from sin and thus become "new creations," that is, how their old, "worldly" selves could be put to death and then raised to new life. A crucial moment in this putting-to-death and raising-to-life is that one has faith: one takes the Gospel to be that which is fundamentally true, and it therefore becomes that which is fundamental within one's evaluative perspective. The fact that it is now fundamental in this respect does not mean, of course, that one's entire life is now aligned with it. But it does mean that one will necessarily want to transform one's life in order to bring it into such alignment, just as it means that one will take sides with this element of one's evaluative perspective over other elements. That brings us to the subject of this and the following two chapters, in which we consider a series of spiritual practices that aim to reorient one's life to God and thus to transform one's way of being in the world and of being with others. In this chapter, then, I consider three broad sets of practices that are designed to reorient us to God: *homemaking practices*, practices of *imitation*, and practices of *becoming one*.

Homemaking Practices

In one sense, to be "at home" is simply to be where one lives; this is what it would mean if one were to reply, "at home," to an inquiry concerning one's current location. Likewise if I were to instruct guests to make themselves at home: in that case, I would be inviting them to act as if they lived here and, so, to curl up on the couch or help themselves to a snack without having to ask. This is not the only sense in which one can be at home, however, which is why it would make perfect sense if someone were to say something like, "I have lived in this house for six months, but it still isn't home." We can thus feel at home—or not—where we live; by the same token, we can feel at home in our job or in certain relationships, just as we can feel at home using a particular tool or a language. In cases like these, to be "at home" refers not to the place where we live but to a kind of fit— an *ease* of fit—between ourselves and our surroundings. So, the more we "click" with other people, and the more we can be ourselves around them, the more we will feel at home with them; likewise, the more effortlessly we know our way around a place, the more fluent we are with a language, the more second nature a skill has become, the more we will be at home in these circumstances, precisely insofar as we experience an ease of fit be-tween ourselves and them. This is the sense of being at home that is rele-vant to this section.

Notice that there can be *levels* or *depths* of such being at home. There may be a significant difference, after all, between finding someone easy to talk with, on the one hand, and feeling that we can let our guard down and be ourselves with the person, on the other. There is a similar difference between being fluent in a language and it being "the first language of one's heart," as some multilingual persons would put it. And there is an impor-tant difference between feeling at home in our dwelling because we un-selfconsciously know our way around it, and feeling at home in it because it is "sedimented with meaning," as Iris Marion Young puts it. As Young explains, "Material things and spaces themselves become layered with meaning, as the material markers of events and relationships that make the narrative of a person or group."[1] The idea here is that as one customizes one's dwelling, it becomes more and more an extension of oneself and, in turn, one can feel more and more at home there. There need be nothing profound about such customizations, of course; I may install a sink a cou-ple of inches higher than standard simply because it means I won't have to bend down quite so far when I wash my face, just as I may have an artifact on my bookshelf that reminds me of a silly inside joke (a jar of pennies, for example, that someone inexplicably emblazoned with an official label: "68 pennies"). In such cases, my surroundings may thereby suit me, but only on a surface level. Other things are more significant: a jar of buttons that my young children and I spent hours playing with, for instance; a framed picture from my wedding; the chair I sat in when I wrote my first book; the bed I have slept in for the past twenty years; a wood carving that was given to me by a now-deceased loved one. Unlike a raised sink or a jar of pennies, the meanings attached to these artifacts make my dwelling feel more like home precisely because they create a fit between what *matters* to me and the things that surround me and, just so, between my surroundings and my deepest self.[2]

This helps us understand the way a home can both form and anchor one's identity. On the one hand, home can *form* our identity insofar as there is a give-and-take involved in creating a fit between ourselves and our surroundings. Being intimately at home with other people, for instance, usually requires not only that we can let our guard down with them and feel like ourselves in their presence but also that we adjust ourselves to them, so to speak—we take an increased interest in the things that matter to them, for example, and foreground aspects of ourselves that they appreciate. Similar adjustments are often required in order to be at home in a new job or a new town—we learn local customs, idioms, norms, and the like, and in the process we not only establish a fit between ourselves and our surroundings, we are thereby formed by the latter.

Home can also *anchor* my identity, for insofar as there is a place where I experience a sense of fit between my surroundings and myself—myself at some fundamental level—then this dwelling will reinforce my identity; this is one reason Young's "sedimentation of meaning" is so important, for insofar as I am surrounded by, say, mementos that reflect what matters most to me, as well as people who do the same, then my surroundings will be a standing reminder or reflection of who I am. Insofar as I am invested in these things and persons, and insofar as they thus have a kind of standing within my evaluative perspective, then being around them will strengthen my sense of self and help me remain true to it even when I am not around them. Think here, for instance, of a middle-schooler who has decided to forswear all the symbols of early teen status, and who accordingly wears only simple, homemade clothes, listens only to folk music, and spends their time reading novels and poetry instead of social media. While they are at school, at least, they may face significant pressure to fit in, and this may make it harder for them to remain true to themselves. If their family and close friends (along with the physical surroundings where they feel at home) reflect their true self back to them, however, then this may give them some of the strength they need to resist this pressure and to remain true to themselves in spite of it. Hence, home can also be a site of *resis-*

tance. bell hooks describes the home of her childhood as just such a site and her mother's homemaking, therefore, as a decidedly political act: "Politically," she writes, "our young mother, Rosa Bell, did not allow the white supremacist culture of domination to completely shape and control her psyche and her familial relationships. Working to create a homeplace that affirmed our beings, our blackness, our love for one another was necessary resistance."[3] Creating a home that affirms the dignity of Black persons is an act of resistance against a society that tells them that they are less valuable than white persons, just as being part of such a home can help Black persons resist those messages. By anchoring one's identity, accordingly, a home can be a site of resistance within a wider world that may stand in opposition to that identity.

By this same mechanism, home can also provide us with *respite.* Persons become drained when they constantly have to work to create and maintain a fit between themselves and their surroundings—cases where, say, they are speaking a language or practicing a skill that is not entirely second nature to them. Persons are likewise drained by spending time in surroundings where they must keep their guard up, where others do not perceive or value their fundamental identity, or where they must constantly put on a performance in order to be accepted. In such circumstances, if persons can spend some time in surroundings where they can simply be themselves, and in which they fit easily, it will provide them with a chance to rest—to take a break from the relentless effort it can take when they must work to create such a fit. For just this reason, many immigrants prize the time that they get to spend within immigrant communities, for within these communities they can speak their first language, eat familiar foods, practice traditional customs, and, in sum, simply *be* in a way that comes naturally to them.[4] Time spent within an immigrant community can thus provide persons with respite from the constant work of trying to fit in to a different culture, precisely because they experience an ease of fit within such a community—that is, precisely because they are at home there.

Thus far, then, I have suggested that we are at home in our surroundings just to the extent that we experience an ease of fit with them, and that home can thereby form and anchor our identity, just as it can provide us with respite and resistance in the face of surroundings where we do not fit. Mention of immigrant communities brings us to one additional class of cases, namely, those in which persons are away from their homeland but can nevertheless experience a taste of home when they practice its customs, speak its language, sing its songs, tell its stories, and get together with others from their homeland. These tastes of home can provide the sort of anchoring, resistance, and respite just mentioned, and they can also help persons remain true to their homeland; hence, insofar as the latter is something that they not only value but also want to continue valuing, such tastes will themselves be valuable to them. We hear a moving example of this from Soong-Chan Rah, who describes what the Korean immigrant church meant to his mother, Im Hee Rah: "Her work required her to converse in a language that was unfamiliar and difficult for her," he writes. "She worked nearly twenty hours a day, six days a week. . . . One day a week she could be part of a faith community that used her heart language instead of struggling with a language foreign to her in environments that took her out of her comfort zone. . . . The church is not only a haven where a familiar language is spoken, it is the haven where Korean culture and traditions are maintained. The Korean immigrant may be rejected by their neighbors and coworkers for their funny accents, strange customs, and smelly foods; but in the Korean immigrant church, this different behavior is accepted and promoted."[5] As Rah relates, his mother was exhausted not only by the long hours she had to work but also by constantly having to deal with, and try to fit into, a culture that did not feel like home (and that often told her, implicitly or explicitly, that it was not her home). No wonder, then, that the Korean immigrant church was so important to her, for there she could speak freely in the language of her heart, could share foods and memories and customs with people for whom they had the same meaning, could convey these meanings—and this identity—to her children, and could thus spend a few hours in a "haven" where she could enjoy an ease of fit between her surroundings and herself.

With that, we should already be able to see the relevance of this concept to theology, for Christians have traditionally understood themselves as away from home in precisely this sense. This is a common theme throughout the theological tradition; to take just one instance, consider a characteristic statement from Basil of Caesarea: "Sojourning," he writes, "means staying someplace as a temporary resident. It does not indicate living someplace permanently, but rather transitionally in the hope of migrating to a better place. Now a holy man lives this life transitionally and hastens to live the other life." He thus exhorts his hearers: "Do not forget your ancient homeland. Remember your nobility. Remember the homeland from which you were banished."[6] This is also a common theme throughout the New Testament; Heb. 11:13–14 thus characterizes Christians as exiles and strangers seeking a homeland, as do 1 Pet. 1:1, 1:17, and 2:11. The

New Testament likewise describes a Christian's true home as being with God; we hear something along these lines in 2 Cor. 5:1–9 (where Paul talks about being at home with the Lord), John 14 (where Jesus is said to prepare a place for us and where God and Jesus are said to make a home with us), and Rev. 21:3 (where the fulfillment of all things consists in God's dwelling with us, and us with God). The idea here, then, is that being with God is a Christian's true home, and that the present life is thus a kind of exile from that home. (Within the framework of this metaphor, "exile" or "sojourner" is preferable to "pilgrim," for pilgrims are usually persons who are making a journey *away* from home, whereas exiles and sojourners *are* away from home and thus experience themselves as such. The latter more precisely characterizes the Christian life.) It should not be surprising, then, that Christians have adopted several practices that are designed to form them such that (a) they would experience a fit between themselves and their true home; (b) their identity would be anchored by this fit and they could therefore better resist other would-be formations; and (c) they might experience a sustaining, respite-giving "taste of home" while they remain away from their true home. In this section, I want to suggest that this is a helpful way of understanding some of the things that Christians do when they get together with one another.

Usually once a week, Christians get together with other Christians. By itself, this can already be a sort of homemaking practice, insofar as these people "get" one another and are alike in the most fundamental respect, namely, their devotion to God. Insofar as they identify with one another, moreover, and are thus inclined to imitate one another's way of exhibiting such devotion, they will become increasingly adjusted to one another and, so, will experience more and more of a fit with one another. To surround oneself with other Christians, accordingly, is to be formed by them, and, one hopes, "to be trained in piety."[7] I consider how this works in the next section.

There are also particular things that Christians tend to do when they get together; they often collect an offering, for instance, and "pass the peace." They normally pray together, too, which is a topic I consider in the next chapter, just as they ordinarily hear (or preach) a sermon. We discussed proclamation in the last chapter, but it might be helpful to say a few more words on the topic here. If the Gospel is that which is fundamentally true— "If this is true, it changes everything"—then it follows that we should see our lives and circumstances in its light. This would explain why sermons usually take the form they do: if God's word is that which is fundamentally true, then we should bring our lives into conformity with it; sermons encourage us to take steps in that direction, whether by portraying us as figures in biblical narratives, by explaining how God's word applies to or makes sense of our lives, or simply by trying to make that fundamental truth come alive. Sermons thus aim to bring more and more of our lives into the light of the Gospel, and, so, to reorient us to God.

In addition to prayer and sermons, Christians also sing and eat together when they gather, and these, too, are practices designed to reorient them to God. These are the practices we need to get a better grip on in this section.

We can understand singing as an expression of our devotion to God, of course, but we can also understand it as a practice that attunes our hearts to God and thus orients us to God. The latter is what Augustine has in mind when he claims that "when the sacred words are chanted well, our souls are moved and are more religiously and with a warmer devotion kindled to piety than if they are not so sung," just as Thomas Aquinas does when he insists that "by praising him our devotion is aroused toward him. . . . And forasmuch as man, by praising God, ascends in his affections to God, by so much is he withdrawn from things opposed to God."[8] Such ideas are common throughout the Christian tradition: when Christians get together to sing, it is claimed, our hearts are kindled, our devotion aroused, and our souls moved toward God.

Augustine and Thomas also provide a rudimentary account of how such heart kindling is supposed to work, the central feature of which is the idea that particular sorts of music stir particular emotions. Augustine argues, accordingly, that "all the diverse emotions of our spirit have their various modes in voice and chant appropriate in each case, and are stirred by a mysterious inner kinship"; Thomas likewise asserts that "it is evident that the human soul is moved in various ways according to the melodies of sound."[9] To understand what they have in mind here, think about movie soundtracks: the ominous music that plays when the shark approaches the *Orca* in *Jaws*, for instance, or the mournful music that plays in *Titanic* when Rose realizes that Jack is dead, or the triumphant music that plays when the Rebel Alliance destroys the Death Star at the end of *Star Wars*. In each case, the score is meant to match a scene's emotional content and, so, either to evoke or to strengthen that emotion in the watcher. Augustine and Thomas are claiming something similar: music stirs various emotions in us, and the stirring of such emotions can kindle our hearts toward God.

Following some theorists of music, we can say a bit more about how such stirring of emotion might work.[10] On the one hand, music often moves us because we associate certain things with that music: so hearing the songs that we sang with old friends will often fill us with joy (and maybe a bit of nostalgia), just as we may be saddened upon hearing a song that was sung at a loved one's funeral. Through such associations, particular songs and pieces of music can become sedimented with meaning for us and thus evoke certain emotions in us when we hear them. On the other hand, music can also work more directly on our emotions, inasmuch as music's own "arc," as it were, can resonate with us in such a way that it causes or at least primes us to feel certain emotions. Sometimes sad music can make a person feel sad, accordingly, just as exciting music can make a person feel excited, tense music can make a person feel tense, and so on, or, again, it can simply make us more likely to feel sad or excited or tense about a particular circumstance. With respect to the latter, it might be helpful to think of something that we could perceive in a variety of different ways—the blank look on a person's face following a traffic accident, say; there are all sorts of things that might prime me to interpret people's expressions in a particular way, ranging from their reminding me of someone to my having just endured a painful trip to the dentist. Just as the latter will prime me to experience the person's expression as patient or angry, for instance, so, on the present account, music can prime me to experience certain circumstances in certain ways. To be sure, the mere fact that I am primed to experience something in a particular way does not mean that I will so experience it; after all, there may be other priming factors at work, and I may have reason *not* to experience things in accordance with my priming (if, say, the blank-looking person gives no other signs of being ill tempered). Hence, even if music does prime us to feel certain things in certain ways, this would not necessarily entail that we will do so.

With that in mind, we can return to Augustine's and Thomas's idea that particular sorts of music stir particular emotions and, crucially, that this plays a role in kindling our devotion to God. If music primes us to experience certain emotions, and if congregational singing combines music with lyrics that direct us to God, then we will be primed to experience such direction-to-God with certain emotions. (Naturally, congregants are directed to God not only by lyrics but also by the expectations they bring with them to church, the meanings with which their churchly surroundings have been sedimented, and the fact that they are singing with others—more on this in a moment.) Songs of praise and thanksgiving, accordingly, are typically accompanied by uplifting or "soaring" melodies (think here, for instance, of the music accompanying the lyric "Then sings my soul, my savior God to thee: How great Thou art, how great thou art!"), whereas songs of lament and contrition are accompanied by somber, sorrowful tunes (consider the tune of "Amazing Grace" or the one that accompanies these lyrics: "Nobody knows the trouble I've seen; nobody knows my sorrow. Nobody knows the trouble I've seen; glory, hallelujah"). In such cases, music can express—and, one hopes, evoke—an emotion that would be appropriate to the lyrics being sung, and can thus help one's heart to feel the appropriate emotion about whatever is being sung. Over time, week after week, such singing can thereby train one's heart to feel appropriate emotions toward God—can dispose one, in other words, to feel grateful toward God, to exalt God, to feel contrite before God, and to entrust one's sorrow to God. In that case, music would indeed kindle one's devotion to God.

So far, so good, but this account is missing a vital dimension, namely, the fact that Christians sing *together*, in one voice. As James Cone nicely puts it, "The spiritual is the community in rhythm," and something similar could be said of all congregational singing.[11] According to the theological tradition, there are at least two ways that this can contribute to one's spiritual formation. First, singing with others can form our hearts precisely because emotion can be infectious. On the one hand, emotion is infectious because we naturally tend to mimic the emotional states of those around us, particularly insofar as we identify with them. As I discuss in the next section, when we see "one of us" act or react in a particular way in particular circumstances, we are likely to act or react that way, too, and, over time, to become disposed to act or react in that way. Given that singing expresses one's emotions, accordingly, it follows that persons will be likelier to mimic the emotional expressions of others and thus become disposed to have those emotions, too. This seems to be just the sort of thing that Thomas had in view when he claimed that "the praise of the lips is also profitable to others by inciting their affections toward God," and Calvin when he argued that Christians should worship together so that "all men mutually, each from his brother, may receive the confession of faith and be invited and prompted by his example."[12] By singing with others, then, their emotional states may influence our own states (and vice versa), from which it follows that such singing can contribute to the shaping of our hearts. What is more, it seems that corporate singing influences not only our emotional states themselves but the *intensity* of those states, too. As is well known, people tend to feel happier if they are around others who share that happiness, angrier around others who share their anger, and so on. It stands to reason, therefore, that when we sing with others, we will not only share their emotional state of gratitude or contrition, for instance, but will experience this state more strongly than we otherwise might.[13] The more strongly we feel an emotion, in turn, the more it will dispose us to feel that way in relevantly similar circumstances, which means, again, that singing with others can play an influential role in shaping our hearts.

This is obviously related to a further claim, namely, that, by singing together, Christians become more attuned not only to God but to one another. The unity of their voices, in other words, can contribute to a unity of their hearts, and this can lead them not only to *be* but to *feel* more fundamentally united with one another. Hence, one of the key reasons for Christians to worship together, according to Calvin, is so that "with one common voice and, as it were, with the same mouth, we all glorify God together, worshiping him with one spirit and the same faith."[14] Bonhoeffer expresses a similar view: "Why do Christians sing when they are together? The reason is, quite simply, that in singing together it is possible for them to speak and pray the same Word at the same time—in other words, for the sake of uniting in the Word."[15] By singing together, then, Christians become disposed to share emotional states and to strengthen those states in one another; given this sharing and the fact that these emotional states express their most fundamental commitment, it follows that, by singing together, Christians should become more attuned to one another and more disposed to identify with one another.

Singing can thus play a vital role in forming a person's heart, anchoring their identity, and uniting them with others. It can thereby help create and maintain a fit between us and our true home—namely, being with God; can help us remain faithful exiles and, so, resist the temptation to become too at home here; can cultivate unity between ourselves and others so that we may experience a deeper sense of fit with them; and, in sum, can provide us with a taste of home even as we are in exile. As Howard Thurman puts it, then, when Christians sing together, "life is regarded as a pilgrimage, a sojourn, while the true home of the spirit is beyond the vicissitudes of life with God!"[16]

Christians also customarily share a meal when they are together, a meal that some call the Lord's Supper, others the Eucharist, and others Holy Communion. Whatever one calls it, the meal involves sharing bread and wine (or grape juice), usually accompanied by some words that recall the meal's spiritual significance. To be sure, there is considerable debate concerning that significance, though the disagreement tends to center on the question of whether Jesus is present in the meal and, if so, how. Here I focus instead on three ideas about which there is considerably greater agreement, namely, that it is a meal of *remembrance*, that it is a meal of *anticipation*, and that it is a meal of *unity*.

Let us begin with the idea that it is a meal of unity. This is a common theme throughout the Christian tradition; so Augustine exclaims of this meal, "O sacrament of faith! O sign of unity! O bond of love!"; Thomas, following Augustine, insists that "the Eucharist is the sacrament of ecclesiastical unity, which is brought about by many being *one in Christ*"; Bonhoeffer likewise claims that "the community of the holy Lord's Supper is above all the fulfillment of Christian community" and that "the life together of Christians under the Word has reached its fulfillment in the sacrament"; and the ecumenical document "Baptism, Eucharist, and Ministry" (BEM) maintains that "the sharing in one bread and the common cup in a given place demonstrates and effects the oneness of the sharers with Christ and with their fellow sharers at all times and places."[17] The idea here, then, is that this meal not only exemplifies the unity shared by Christians but somehow contributes to that unity as well.

To understand how this works, it is worth noting, first, that this seems to be true of *any* shared meal. Sociologists of eating have demonstrated, for instance, that persons who eat the same food are much likelier to trust one another and to cooperate with one another, even if those persons share no additional connections.[18] They have likewise demonstrated that persons— even strangers—pay more attention to each other when sharing a meal.[19] And they have advanced a compelling—if not definitive—argument in defense of the idea that meal sharing naturally evokes a sense of kinship among participants. The argument here is fairly complicated, but it goes something like this: (a) humans take about eighteen years to mature, during which time they need food to be provided for them; (b) this means, in turn, that we could not have evolved as we have if not for food sharing; (c) it stands to reason, then, that kinship ties (more specifically, pro-attitudes toward one's kin) lead to food sharing, which is in fact a universal phenomenon; and, finally, (d) the association between kinship pro-attitudes and food sharing means that the polarities can be reversed, so to speak, which would explain why food sharing can create (and not just follow from) such attitudes.[20] The upshot of these points is that sharing a meal can create a sense of fellowship or unity among those who partake in it. This alone would give us reason to think that the meal shared by Christians would do the same, which is just what many theologians have claimed: Karl Rahner thus argues that "man is closest to his loved ones when the fellowship of fidelity and love is embodied in the common sharing of bread and drink"; before him, G. W. F. Hegel maintained that "to eat and drink with someone is an act of union and is itself a felt union, not a conventional symbol. It runs counter to natural human feeling to drink a glass of wine with an enemy; the sense of community in this action would contradict the attitude of the parties to one another at other times"; from this, Hegel concludes that "the supper shared by Jesus and his disciples is in itself an act of friendship; but a still closer link is the solemn eating of the same bread, drinking from the same cup. This too is not a mere symbol of friendship, but an act, a feeling of friendship itself, of the spirit of love."[21]

The mere fact that Christians share a meal with one another can thus be thought to contribute to their sense of fellowship with one another. This sense should be reinforced, in turn, by certain distinctive features of this meal, particularly the fact that it represents our communion not only with other Christians but with Jesus as well (and, so, communion with others who are themselves in communion with Jesus). This is why BEM insists that "in the Eucharistic meal, in the eating and drinking of the bread and wine, Christ grants communion with himself," and it explains this communion in terms of our being invited to join with others at Christ's table, since "it is Christ who invites to the meal and who presides at it."[22] The idea here follows naturally from the preceding: if sharing a meal represents and effects fellowship among those who partake in it, then it stands to reason that, if someone invites others to share a meal with them, that meal represents and effects fellowship with that person. Hence, if Jesus invites us to share a meal with him (by the now-familiar mechanism by which his followers are authorized to speak on his behalf), then it follows that this meal represents and effects fellowship with him. To be sure, the mere fact that several persons share fellowship with a single person would not by itself entail that they share fellowship with one another; it is vital to add, therefore, that this fellowship is of fundamental importance to each of them and that it's of a particular sort—the fellowship to which Jesus invites us, after all, is characterized not merely by the sharing of meals but by wholehearted love and regard for one another. With all this in mind, it makes sense to say that sharing in *this* meal represents and effects fellowship with Jesus and with others.

That brings us to one additional sense in which this meal is supposed to cultivate unity, namely, that when the community celebrates this meal, its unity becomes tangible, capable of being beheld, and thus something that they can see and value *as such*. We hear a claim along these lines through-out the theological tradition; so, for instance, Augustine maintains that "people could not be gathered together under the name of any religion, whether true or false, if they were not bound together by some sharing of visible signs or sacraments," just as Hegel argues that, in this meal, "the unification is no longer felt but has become visible" or, a bit more Hege-lianly, that here "the spirit of Jesus, in which his disciples are one, has be-come a present object, a reality, for external feeling."[23] To see what these claims are driving at, consider an analogous example of what can happen when something is made explicit in this way. Think of a case, then, where we have a vague sense of admiration for another person, and where some-one else then names the person's praiseworthy traits—magnanimity, say, or guilelessness. Once named, we can see more clearly that which leads us to admire that person, just as we can now direct our admiration to that which is specifically admirable about the person. By making these traits explicit, accordingly, we can value them as such, which is something that we could otherwise do only vaguely (and perhaps confusedly). The argu-ment is that something similar can happen when the community gets to-gether to share this meal: something implicit in the community is made explicit and can thus be recognized and valued *as such*. Following our ear-lier claims, we might say that what is made explicit here is the communion that Christians share with Christ and one another, such that, in celebrating this meal, Christians can behold and, so, value this communion as such. Having done so, they can then see such communion as having already been implicit in the people gathered to share this meal and can thus see and value it in that light. Here too, then, sharing this meal is supposed to represent and effect unity among Christians—and, in this case, to effect unity *by* representing it.

The shared meal is thus understood as both representing and effect-ing unity among Christians and, so, as a meal of unity. It is also understood as a meal of remembrance and anticipation. This, too, is a common theme in the theological tradition, nicely summarized at the very beginning of BEM: "Christ commanded his disciples thus to remember and encounter him in this sacramental meal, as the continuing people of God, until his return"; in so doing, these meals simultaneously "proclaim and enact the nearness of the Kingdom."[24] Here there is an obvious echo of biblical pas-sages in which Jesus enjoins his followers to continue sharing this meal in memory of him, until they share it again with him at the eschatological feast. Those who are devoted to Jesus are thus supposed to continue sharing the meal that he ate with his followers, and they should do so as an act of remembrance and anticipation.

We can say a bit more about how this works—and how it would form us—if we focus on the fact that this meal represents a continuation of the meals that Jesus shared with his disciples. By all accounts, these meals were of the highest importance to them. Hence, if they were to continue sharing this meal once Jesus had been crucified—if they were to share it in his *absence*—the very act of doing so would be a powerful, and likely painful, reminder of the one whom they gathered around—and who was no longer there. By continuing to share this meal, then, they would not only have Jesus in mind but would remember the meals they shared with him, too, and would therefore both experience his absence and long to be with him again. As a rough analogy, consider the members of a family that maintains certain traditions: every Friday night they watch a movie and eat popcorn together; they go sledding together the first time it snows each winter; and they all watch the annual Home Run Derby together while eating foods that would usually be off-limits. Now consider what would happen if one of the children left for college: the remaining family members may still watch movies together, go sledding, and eat unhealthy food, but when they do so, they will be acutely aware that someone is missing. Carrying on these traditions in that person's absence will thus remind the remaining family members of that person and will surely make them wish that they could all be together again. My suggestion is that we can understand the shared meal along similar lines. Jesus' original disciples undoubtedly experienced it this way: they continued sharing meals with one another just as they had shared them with Jesus, but now he was gone. In breaking bread together and sharing a cup of wine, they would surely have missed being with him, and they surely would have longed to be with him again. Something similar should characterize the meal shared by Christians today: they are gathered to share a meal with someone who is absent (in one vital respect, at least), and, indeed, they are gathered precisely around the one who is most important to each of them—and who is not there. This fact should make them long to be with him, such that, in sharing the meal, they both remember him and look forward to being with him again.

There is another key sense in which this is supposed to be a meal of anticipation, of course, namely, that it is a sort of foretaste of the promised eschatological feast.[25] Here we return to the role of meals among immigrants and, especially, exiles: when persons who are away from home get together with others from there, they almost invariably share a meal composed of home cooking—composed, that is, of the sorts of foods they most associate with home. Such meals provide them with a literal and figurative taste of home, and this, in turn, can both sustain them amid the difficulties of being away from home and keep their hearts set on that home (however painful that may be). Christians are likewise supposed to be away from home; their true home is with Jesus in God's coming kingdom. If the shared meal is indeed an anticipation and a foretaste of the eschatological feast—presumably through being sedimented with the meaning of such a feast—then it should provide a taste of home that both sustains them amid difficulties and keeps their hearts set on their true home.[26]

Sharing this meal together should thus represent and effect unity among Christians; it should remind them of Jesus and make them long to be with him again; and, as a taste of home, it should help sustain them and keep their hearts set on their true home.

Thus far, I have tried to suggest some ways that singing and eating together might create unity among Christians (and so make them more at home with one another) and attune their hearts increasingly to God. These practices should thus help to create a fit between Christians and other Christians, on the one hand, and God, on the other, such that they might qualify as homemaking practices of the sort I discussed at the outset. To be sure, just about any devotional practice would probably meet these criteria and so qualify as such, but there is something special about these two practices. As several studies have demonstrated, music and food have a central place in almost all gatherings within immigrant communities, for the apparent reason that these are especially "sedimented with meaning" from home, such that, among other things, they convey a taste of home more strongly than just about anything else. My hunch is that food and music do the same—or ought to—for Christians, which is why I have brought them both under the rubric of homemaking practices.

One last point. Persons living in a land that is not their own—a land that does not feel like home—often report that it is exhausting. One is constantly having to speak a language that is not one's heart-language, to observe customs that are not one's own, and to have to *work* to fit in with one's surroundings. When such persons are able to get together with others from their homeland, accordingly, one of the things they often experience is, simply, *respite*, since, here, there is an ease of fit between themselves and their surroundings. They can speak their heart-language and practice their customs without even having to explain anything to anyone. While they are together, then, they can experience a bit of rest.

This should be true of Christians, too. They are living in a land that does not—or, by their own lights, *should* not—feel like home, a land where they constantly have to navigate language and customs that are not their own and, in sum, where they have to work to fit in with their surroundings, even as they have to work to *not* fit in with them. This, too, can be exhausting. When they get together with others who share a homeland with them, accordingly, and can enjoy tastes of home with them, this should likewise provide them with some much-needed respite: here, at least, there is an ease of fit with their surroundings, or at least a hint of it. If I am right about this, then we might arrive at what I would call a *practical* doctrine of the Sabbath, in which rest consists not so much in a cessation of work as in the respite experienced by exiles when they get together with others from their homeland to practice its customs, sing its songs, eat its foods, and speak its language.

By singing together, eating together, and spending time together, Christians can anchor themselves to a home away from home and, just so, become more and more oriented to that home. These practices can thus strengthen our commitment to that which is fundamental to us and play a role in reorienting our evaluative perspective, but taken by themselves, they would leave much of our everyday lives out of their orbit. To address this problem, I turn to a second set of practices, namely, practices of *imitation*.

Imitation

Imitation is one of the simplest, most basic ways that persons' lives are shaped, so it stands to reason that it would be one of the most basic ways that Christians' lives might become more and more oriented toward God. No surprise, then, that Paul would urge his fellow Christians to "be imitators of me, as I am of Christ" (1 Cor. 11:1; see also 4:16; Phil. 3:17; 1 Thess. 1:6; 2 Thess. 3:7), just as the author of Hebrews counsels readers to "remember your leaders . . . and imitate their faith" (Heb. 13:7; see also 6:12) and the author of 3 John tells readers, "Do not imitate what is evil but imitate what is good" (3 John 11). Within the theological tradition, this idea tends to be understood along roughly the following lines: Jesus perfectly embodies devotion to God; by imitating him, accordingly, and thus patterning my life after his, I likewise become devoted to God; others who imitate me—that is, who imitate whatever in my life is patterned after Jesus—will be simultaneously patterning themselves after him and will thus become more devoted to God, too; and so on. If I imitate the idiosyncratic way my doctoral adviser pronounces the word "epistemic," and if my students imitate the way I pronounce it, then the students are learning to pronounce it the way my adviser did; in the same way, as we imitate those who imitate Jesus, we can learn to live the way he did. Theologians often liken such imitation to reflections in a mirror: just as Jesus is the image of God, in the sense that his life perfectly reflects the very character of God, so others reflect God by reflecting Jesus' image; insofar as others reflect these reflections, they reflect that image, too; and so on. Hence, just as clean mirrors can endlessly reflect a particular image—think here of entering a hall of mirrors—so, on this account, Christians can endlessly reflect the image of God, precisely by imitating those who imitate him.

The claim of this section, simply stated, is that such imitation can be a spiritual practice, that is, something that Christians do and, in turn, that can play a vital role in reorienting their lives to God. To make sense of this claim, it will be helpful to distinguish between two broad sorts of imitation. On the one hand, there is the sort of imitation that we might term *emulation;* on the other, the sort we might term *mimicry.*

We begin with emulation, which is the sort of imitation that is triggered by admiration. I take it that this is what Paul has in mind in Philippians 3:17, for instance: "Brothers and sisters, join in imitating me," he writes, "and keep an eye on those who live according to the example you have in us." And I think it is what he has in mind when he says, just a few lines later, "Finally, beloved, whatever is true, whatever is honorable, whatever is just, whatever is pure, whatever is pleasing, whatever is commendable, if there is any excellence and if there is anything worthy of praise, think about these things, which you have also learned and received and heard and seen in me—practice these things" (Phil. 4:8–9). We hear something similar from theologians like Gregory of Nyssa: "In those deeds of virtue by which those living in the spirit are known, being alive and energetic and strong, look to this man as the model of your life. God has made him as a goal for our own lives. Let this one be for you the goal of the divine life as the fixed stars are for the pilots."[27] And we find a lovely example of this sort of emulation in Kelly Brown Douglas's *The Black Christ:* "My memories of my grandmother (whom my sisters, brother, and I affectionately called Mama) are still very vivid," writes Brown Douglas.

She was a hardworking woman who carried the burden of supporting herself and her family. She got up daily, even when she did not feel like it, to run an elevator in the local postoffice. She re-

turned home from work each evening to take care of my grandfather (her second husband) who suffered from multiple health
problems. The daily struggle to "make it" was not new to my grandmother; it had become her way of life since the death of her first
husband left her at the young age of eighteen with a small child
(my mother) to rear. The picture I have always had of Mama
Dorsey is of a poor, Black woman, without formal education,
doing what she could to make it with few material resources for
survival. I admired Mama because of her determination to survive.
Despite the enormous difficulties involved in trying to do so, she
never complained. She continued to smile and always made our
frequent visits with her very pleasant. I often wondered how she
did it. After watching her in church, seeing how she never failed
to get on her knees to pray before going to bed, and noticing her
Bible always opened to the twenty-third psalm, I had no doubt
that it was because of her faith in the God of Jesus Christ that she
could "keep going day in and day out."[28]

Brown Douglas looks up to her grandmother, accordingly, and in so doing,
her own faith is inspired and shaped by her—indeed, the rest of her book
can be seen as an attempt, among other things, to let this faith set the
standard for Brown Douglas's own faith in Jesus. Her admiration for her
grandmother thus spurs her to emulate the traits she admires in her, which
should already help us see how emulation can serve as a powerful spiritual
practice.

To get a better grip on how this works, it will be helpful to consider
the best recent account of emulation, namely, that developed by Linda
Zagzebski: "The model I am proposing," she writes, "starts with admiration of an exemplar, which leads to an imaginative ideal of oneself, which
in turn produces emulation of the exemplar's motives and acts. The moral
learner does the virtuous act from a virtuous motive because the learner is
emulating someone who does that act from that motive. With practice, the
agent becomes disposed to doing acts of that kind from motives of that
kind."[29] The idea here, simply stated, is that when we admire someone, we
imagine ourselves as having the sort of traits that that person has and acting in the ways that person acts, and that we thereby grow into our imag-
ined ideal self. Helpful as Zagzebski's overall account is, however, it is still
not entirely clear how admiration leads to emulation and, eventually, to
transformation; there are plenty of people, after all, who imagine that they

are like the persons they admire but who do not thereby become any more like those persons. Thankfully it is not hard to come up with a variety of plausible ways of explaining how such becoming-more-like would work. So, for instance, I may value a particular trait and thus want to embody that trait more fully; perhaps I currently embody it only in a narrow range of circumstances, say, or at the level of abstract commitment. In that case, if I observe someone whose life is more fully permeated by that trait, then I will have a clearer sense of what it looks like to embody this trait in a wide range of circumstances, and my valuing of the trait will therefore push me to realize this fuller embodiment in my own life. Think here of LeBron James playing on the 2008 Olympic basketball team with Kobe Bryant: Kobe was famously fanatical about hard work and preparation; he would get up to practice every day at 5 A.M., for instance, and gave maximum effort every second he was on the court—even if it was just an off-season practice. LeBron wanted to be the best, and hanging out with Kobe gave him a clearer idea of what that would take; as LeBron later put it, "I knew I had to be better because of Kobe Bryant."[30] Again, the point here is simply that when we are around people who embody traits that we value, that can give us a picture of what it looks like to embody those traits more fully and thus help us do so.

We see something similar in cases where we experience shame, guilt, or conviction when we are in the presence of someone who actually embodies traits that we say we value; this negative self-evaluation, too, can spur us to live up to our ideals. I have this experience when I am in the presence of a truly excellent teacher: I say that I care deeply about being a good teacher but then I see the lengths to which certain fellow teachers go to help each of their students, the care that they put into their syllabi, the meticulousness of their comments on student papers, and the way that they inspire their students to raise their game—in the presence of such teachers, I cannot help but recognize the extent to which I fall short of my ideal. Faced with this discrepancy, I can either admit to myself that I do not, in fact, care that much about being a good teacher or commit to closing the gap between what I value and my embodiment of that value. Here too, then, my admiration of someone can play a role in spurring me to grow into a particular trait.

There are also cases where admiration itself can play a role in disposing us to embody a trait. Suppose I have an intuitive sense that a woman I met is admirable: she is a thoroughly good and decent person. On this basis, I may then come to perceive certain of her traits as admirable and, so, as good to have; I may thus want to embody those traits, too. Notice, though, that the trait I want to embody, in such cases, is admirableness itself: I admire the trait of admirability, and thus commit myself to developing the traits that distinguish admirable persons. (This is importantly distinct, of course, from wanting to be admired, which may or may not track with being admirable.) Even the trait of admirableness can be something we admire and thus want to emulate—and in wanting to emulate it, we can become disposed to emulate other admirable traits.

There are plenty of other ways that admiration can spur us to embody particular traits, but these should give us an idea of how this sort of thing works (and, one hopes, *that* it works). No wonder, then, that Christians have often commended this practice, for if we admire certain aspects of a person's devotion to God—commitment to serving the least of these, fervency in prayer, faithful courage in the face of danger, and the like—then this might spur us to grow in those aspects, too. We can now go one step further: this is one of the reasons certain stories are often told within the Christian community, for when we hear stories about Joan of Arc and Mother Teresa and Martin Luther King and Maximilian Kolbe, we are encouraged to admire them and, just so, to grow in the traits that make them worthy of admiration. Whether we encounter them in person or in stories, the point is simply that when we admire certain characteristics of a person's devotion, it can play a role in pushing us to develop those same characteristics in our own devotion.

Before proceeding, two clarifications. First, note well that I can admire a trait without wanting to embody it; after all, I may admire someone's mastery of particular skateboarding tricks, but that does not mean that I will want to try them myself, much less master them. In addition to sheer admiration, then, we also need a first-personal valuing of that which we admire; otherwise, there is no reason to think that our admiration of some trait will have any impact on our own traits. Second, we need to address what we might call the Martha Stewart Problem: if we admire someone who seems to embody certain traits to a near-perfect degree, then even if we first-personally value those traits, our admiration might not spur us to grow in our embodiment of them for the simple reason that the person's near perfection seems to put those traits out of reach. In such cases, admiration may make us less likely to embody particular traits, rather than more. This problem helps us see two key aspects of emulation, namely, that the aim is to become *more* like the ones we admire, not *exactly* like them, and that the aim is for *us* to become more like them. When we try to emulate someone, our aim should not be to become identical with that person, but to embody certain traits more fully and to embody them in ways that fit with who we are. If we bear this in mind, then we may try to bring a bit more Martha Stewart into our lives, but we will not try to become Martha Stewart, and our admiration for her will therefore not create a barrier to our growth.

Emulation is thus a form of imitation that is triggered by admiration. *Mimicry*, by contrast, refers to the way that we more or less automatically imitate or mirror the people around us, particularly insofar as we identify with these people and therefore perceive them as "one of us." This is the sort of imitation that Solomon seems to have in mind when he says, "Whoever walks with the wise becomes wise, but the companion of fools will suffer harm" (Prov. 13:20), and it seems to be what Paul has in mind when he reminds the Corinthians that "bad company ruins good morals" (1 Cor. 15:33).

Friedrich Schleiermacher offers us a helpful model for thinking about how such imitation works.[31] On Schleiermacher's account, persons' lives are oriented by their dispositions or "attunement," and the attunement of each is shaped by the attunement of others (and vice versa). Schleiermacher explains how this works in terms of the following steps. (1) A person is disposed to respond in a certain way to some (internal or external) circumstance, and their outward gestures and behavior express this disposition to others.[32] (2) Insofar as others identify with this person—and perceive their behavior as "what one does"—they may imitate that person's response in similar circumstances. (3) If these other persons become reliably disposed to respond in this way, the response becomes their own attunement to these circumstances; still others may then identify their response as how "we" respond and imitate it, and so on; "a multifarious community of attunement" thus emerges in which each person is "both expresser and perceiver," both imitator and imitated.[33] (4) By means of this process, others' dispositions definitively shape an individual's own dispositions (and vice versa). Schleiermacher thus claims that, as a result of this process, an individual's attunement is modeled after that of others; the more alike our dispositions become, in turn, the more we will identify with one another, which will further increase the likelihood of our imitating one another, and so on. What he terms the "we-consciousness" is not only the condition of attunement's circulation, accordingly, it is also continually produced *by* that circulation: as Schleiermacher claims, it is precisely in virtue of this "ever-renewing circulation of self-consciousness" that one can come to "some determinate recognition of which individuals belong to a community and which do not."[34] On Schleiermacher's account, then, our outward expressions manifest our disposition toward some circumstance; these expressions are perceived by another as how "we" respond to such circumstances; this other person thus imitates that expression in similar circumstances until they have become reliably disposed to respond this way, at which point the response is an expression of their own disposition; others may then perceive the person's expression as how "we" respond, and so on. Particular ways of being attuned thus circulate through a community and become part of an individual's own attunement.

I explain how this applies to the Christian life presently, but first, it is worth pointing out that there is considerable independent warrant for this sort of model. Studies suggest, for instance, that what influences whether children eat their vegetables is not whether they are told to do so, nor whether their parents eat their own vegetables, but the look on their parents' faces when they eat vegetables; children's attitudes toward vegetables are thus shaped by their parents' attitudes, even if they are wholly unaware of the fact that these attitudes are being expressed. More generally, this sort of model finds support in the recent explosion of research on mirror neurons.[35] The idea behind such research, briefly stated, is that certain neurons in our brains are triggered when we see someone else performing a task, making a face, and so on, and that these neurons fire as if we ourselves were doing that thing, making that face, and so on. Our habits can thus be formed not only by our own actions, reactions, and the like, but also by the actions and reactions of those around us. Interestingly, researchers have found that these neurons fire only when we observe persons with whom we identify: if we recognize a person as "one of us," accordingly, then it is much more likely that their expressions will shape our own habits, whereas we are less likely to be shaped by those with whom we do not identify.

That brings us back to Schleiermacher's model, which he now uses to explain how Christians grow in Christlikeness. He does so by making two interrelated claims, one Christological, the other pneumatological. The pneumatological claim is that the Holy Spirit forms us primarily through such imitative practices, while the Christological claim is that this Spirit stretches back to the disciples' own imitation of Christ, such that these practices can be thought to carry on the Spirit of Christ and form *his* Spirit in us. To help us understand these claims, Schleiermacher points us to a critical moment in the life of the original disciples, when Christ not only recognized certain of their beliefs, actions, and reactions as faithfully imitating him but also recognized them as competent judges of what counts as such. Schleiermacher explains this process as proceeding through roughly the following steps. First, "in spending time together with Christ, the disciples' receptivity developed, and by perceiving what he held before them, a foundation was laid for their future effectiveness for the Kingdom of God."[36] Christ's activity had not yet become the disciples' own, however, for "at this point, what Christ expected of them was only practice in the sense of repeat-after-me, not practice in the sense of knowing how to carry on that practice, in consequence of which it was not yet their own free activity, because each expression still needed a particular prompting."[37] A crucial step in the disciples' development thus occurred when Jesus recognized their authority to bind and loose sin, since "the right binding and loosing of sin is essentially just an expression of a fully cultivated receptivity for what pertains to the Kingdom of God."[38] This is a decisive point, for once Christ had recognized some of his disciples as competent to judge what counts as imitating him, it follows that after he had departed, those who wanted to imitate him could learn how to do so by submitting to the judgment of those whom Christ recognized. One could learn to imitate Christ, in other words, by recognizing the judgment of those whom Christ recognized, in much the same way that they had learned to imitate Christ by recognizing Christ's own judgment. And once the latter would-be imitators were recognized as fellow recognizers, others could learn how to imitate Christ from them, too, and so on. A "multifarious community of attunement" thus emerges: those who have learned how to imitate Christ express that know-how through their gestures, words, actions, and judgments; if others imitate them in similar circumstances and eventually get the hang of doing so, then imitating Christ has become part of their own know-how; still others may then recognize the latter's expressions as imitating Christ, imitate those expressions, get the hang of doing so, and so on.[39] In this way, the Spirit of Christ is carried forward through a chain of imitation, and the practice of imitating him is passed along to those who never encountered him directly. This is what allows Schleiermacher to claim, finally, that "this effect of the community in bringing forth faith is simultaneously the effect of the personal perfection of Jesus himself."[40]

On this account, then, when we undertake a commitment to imitate Christ, we implicitly undertake certain further commitments: in order to learn how to imitate him, we must submit our beliefs, actions, reactions, and the like to Christ's judgment; hence, if Christ recognized his disciples' authority to judge what counts as imitating him, then our recognition of

Christ's authority commits us to recognizing theirs, too. And since they, in turn, recognized others as knowing how to imitate Jesus, and so on, it follows that in order to imitate Jesus, we must try to go on in the same way as those who have been recognized as knowing how do so; we must recognize the judgment, that is, of those who have been recognized by (those who have been recognized by . . .) Christ. (Readers familiar with the theological tradition should hear in this an echo of "apostolic succession.") In trying to imitate Christ, moreover, we not only recognize the authority of certain precedents, we also implicitly seek this same status for ourselves— and because our beliefs, actions, and reactions are being offered as a precedent for still others, it follows that we thereby undertake responsibility for getting these things right, thus rendering ourselves liable to—and, indeed, inviting—the assessment of those whose judgment we recognize.

Notice, then, that this is an essentially normative, objective practice. For although we not only learn to imitate Christ by imitating others, on this account, but also learn how to judge what counts as doing so by imitating them, we nevertheless intend thereby to do something correctly (or, better, faithfully), namely, imitate Christ. Imagine that I am an electrician's apprentice: I will watch the electrician run wires, test outlets, install appliances, and the like, and I will try to imitate what I see the electrician doing. My aim in so doing, however, is not to imitate them; my aim, rather, is to imitate them so as to learn what an electrician is supposed to do. In the same way, the aim of Christians is not simply to imitate other Christians but to imitate them so as to learn how to imitate Christ. Implicit in the practice of imitation, accordingly, is a normative commitment by means of which our imitation can be judged. Calvin's formulation of this point cannot be excelled: "The world is also, of its own accord, inclined to a misdirected imitation," he remarks, "and, after the manner of apes, strives to copy whatever they see done by persons of great influence. We see, however, how many evils have been introduced into the Church by this absurd desire of imitating all the actions of the saints, without exception. Let us, therefore, maintain so much the more carefully this doctrine of Paul—that we are to follow men, provided they take Christ as their grand model (*prototypon*), that the examples of the saints may not tend to lead us away from Christ, but rather direct us to him."[41]

At this point, the majority of Christians would probably turn to scripture as a standard with which to judge our would-be imitation of Christ. Scripture can function as such a standard, however, only if one can interpret it correctly, which some have thought raises a conundrum: if scripture can judge our imitation of Christ only if we interpret it correctly, then what standard should we use to judge our interpretations? There are plenty of plausible ways to answer this question, but one of the most compelling is to suggest that all of our interpretations can be judged by the standard of scripture, so long as we do not try to judge them all at the same time. A particular interpretation can be tested, that is, in light of other interpretations not then being tested; this interpretation can then be used as part of the standard with which to judge other interpretations, and so on, in such a way that the relevant testing proceeds piecemeal rather than all at once (as if we were starting from scratch).[42] Hence, as Wilfrid Sellars famously claimed of philosophy, we might say that biblical interpretation "is a self-correcting enterprise which can put *any* claim in jeopardy, though not *all* at once."[43]

One way that Christians are reoriented, then, is by emulating others who are devoted to God: by admiring someone so devoted, we can thereby become disposed to embody some of their traits. Christians are likewise formed by mimicry: insofar as we recognize other Christians as "one of us," we will be inclined to see what they do as what "we" do and, so, be inclined to do that, too. As we imitate others, accordingly, we can not only become more like them but in so becoming bring more and more of our lives into conformity with our devotion.

Becoming One

The previous section included some suggestions about the role that a sense of "we" can play in reorienting one's life to God. By thinking more clearly about what it means to become such a "we," we can make sense of some traditional claims about Christians being of one mind, being the body of Christ, and being in Christ, and we can also shed some additional light on the idea that unity is a spiritual practice in its own right.

To get a grip on these ideas, it will be helpful to begin with the notion of a "plural subject" or, in Dietrich Bonhoeffer's idiom, a "collective person."[44] Drawing on insights from Edith Stein and Georg Simmel, Bonhoeffer maintains that "where wills unite, a 'structure' is created—that is, a third entity, previously unknown, independent of being willed or not willed by the persons who are uniting"; once such a structure is up and running, he claims, a group "has its own center of activity that experiences love, compassion, shared joy, etc."[45] So structured, then, a group thereby becomes more than an aggregation of persons; it has its own agency *as a we*, which is what it would mean for a group to become a collective person or, a bit less controversially, a plural subject.

To understand these claims, consider a simple example: I am trying to put together a new bookshelf but am having trouble holding the boards in place while I drive the screws. I think to myself, "I wish I could sprout a couple more hands!" Now suppose I ask one of my family members to help me with the project. In that case, their hands literally become the additional hands that I had wished for. What is more, if they take as their goal the putting together of this bookshelf, they thus form with me a "we" for the sake of doing so; as such, they could then rightly say, "We are putting together this bookshelf," "We did the best we could," and the like, just as we can be held jointly accountable for the goodness of our work. In cases like these, we join together to become a single agent for the sake of tackling a project.

A group of persons can likewise constitute itself a single agent for the sake of thinking or reasoning about something. This is how I understand class discussions: if we want to make sense of a difficult text or idea, it will be helpful if we can draw on extra sets of cognitive hands, as it were, so that we can draw on additional sources of insight, test our hypotheses from a variety of perspectives, become aware of (and so resist) the partiality and limitations implicit in our own standpoint, and so on. In a good class discussion, accordingly, as in a good meeting, individual persons can join together to form a plural cognitive subject or, as I am inclined to say, to form a common mind. (A good class discussion should likewise improve one's own ability to think well, of course, in just the way that reading aloud can help children get better at reading "in their heads.") Naturally, this is a fairly ad hoc way of sharing a mind. Persons can also share a mind in a more robust sense. For one thing, people can be said to share a mind insofar as they come to agree with one another: after deliberating over some decision, they might thus check to make sure they are "of one mind" about it. More important, though, is that persons can also share a mind insofar as they are *like-minded*; think here of the way siblings and longtime friends "get" each other, to such an extent that they can finish each other's sentences, know exactly what the other is thinking or feeling in a particular circumstance, and excel at games that require participants to give their partner clues in order to get them to guess an answer. Or think of musicians and athletes who have played together for long enough that they are "on the same page" and can thus anticipate one another's moves; as a result, they can effectively act as a single unit, which basketball players often describe, quite fittingly, as "moving on a string." In cases like these, people not only join together for the sake of a common project, their individual agency is fine-tuned in such a way that it can mesh seamlessly with that of others; just so, members of a plural subject—a "we"—can come to share a characteristic way of seeing things, reacting to things, and doing things.

These claims about plural subjecthood can help us make sense of some traditional beliefs about the church. To get at these, we can start with the obvious fact that imitation should make us increasingly like-minded: in light of the foregoing, we have reason to believe that, insofar as Christians identify with one another, they will imitate one another and thus increasingly come to share a characteristic way of seeing things, doing things, and reacting to things; they should therefore "get" one another, be on the same page with one another, and, one hopes, even be able to move on a string. They should likewise be engaged in a common project—namely, the project of following Christ and bearing witness to the Gospel—but by itself, this would not entail that they have formed a plural subject in service of that project; after all, ten thousand fans cheering for a soccer team would form an aggregate rather than a plural subject or collective agent. Why would Christians be any different? On the one hand, the common project to which Christians are individually called—following Christ and bearing witness—inherently calls for, and should drive them toward, the formation of a plural subject. The reasoning here is straightforward enough: (a) Christians are called to bear witness to the Gospel not only by proclaiming it but also by embodying it; (b) the Gospel can be embodied only in a people who treat one another the way God treats us in Christ and who thus live according to God's standards rather than the world's; and (c) we can thus embody the Gospel, and so bear witness to it, only in concert with others, from which it follows that the common project of Christians should drive them to become a plural subject.[46] This is a project for which we need extra hands, in other words, both literally and figuratively. (This is one reason that the New Testament is riddled with "one another" passages.)

Christians are also driven to become a plural subject by the fact that they are called to love not only God but others, too; this is why Peter Phan insists, for instance, that "without being a communion, the church cannot fulfill its mission, since the church is . . . nothing more than the bond of communion between God and humanity and among humans themselves."[47] To love others means, among other things, that we are invested in their well-being; the well-being of Christians is largely a matter of following Christ well and bearing witness well; for Christians to love one another, accordingly, is for them to be invested in this project and to join forces with one another in pursuing it. Here too, then, the mutual love that Christians have for one another will push them to become a plural subject in service of a common project. By their own lights, therefore, Christians should come together to form a collective agent and become increasingly like-minded in pursuit of their common project, which is exactly what Schleiermacher had in mind when he talked about "the common bent found in all who constitute together a moral personality, to seek the advancement of this whole; and this is at the same time the characteristic love found in each for every other."[48]

With that, we are in position to understand the traditional idea that the church is the body of Christ—indeed, in some sense *is* Christ. Consider a few influential expressions of this idea: Augustine exhorts his readers to "give thanks not only that we have been made Christians, but that we have been made Christ. . . . For if he is the head, we are the members—a whole man, he and we. . . . The fullness of Christ, therefore, head and members. What does it mean, head and members? Christ and the church."[49] We hear similar claims throughout the tradition; Gregory the Great thus asserts that "our redeemer has shown himself to be one person with the holy church whom he has taken to himself"; Thomas Aquinas maintains that "head and members form as it were one and the same mystical person"; Joan of Arc contends that, "about Jesus Christ and the church, I simply know they're just one thing, and we shouldn't complicate the matter"; Elizabeth Johnson claims that "the whole Christ is a corporate personality, a relational reality"; and Karl Barth holds that the church "is the body of Jesus Christ which in the power of the Holy Spirit He as its Lord has personally called into existence and directs and sustains, so that in its existence it is the earthly-historical form and representation of His own."[50] Based on the foregoing, it is not hard to make sense of such claims: if the like-mindedness of Christians is shaped by their imitation of Christians who are themselves imitating Christ, then it follows that they are learning how to see, act, and react as Christ did and, in sum, that the mind of Christ is being formed in them, just as the Spirit of Christ is being passed on to and through them. (This would explain why, and on what basis, Paul declares that "we have the mind of Christ" [1 Cor. 2:16].) If so, then the collective agency of Christians likewise carries on the agency of Christ himself, which would explain why the church can be termed the body of Christ and, indeed, why it can be identified with Christ. To cite just one precedent, this seems to be what Schleiermacher is referring to when he claims that, in the church, there is a "common spontaneous activity which indwells all and in each is kept right by the influence of all, and prolongs the personal action of Christ."[51]

Fortunately for us, we have already considered one prominent example of what it would look like to carry on Christ's agency, namely, the church's authorization to speak in Christ's name and, just so, to speak Christ's own word. In light of the claims we have just been considering, we can now say that our authorization to speak on Christ's behalf is not merely a formal or external affair but a matter of being called to carry on Christ's agency and just so to speak on his behalf. To see why this matters, consider a different sort of example, in which I authorize someone to speak on my behalf so long as I trust that this person would faithfully relay my words, irrespective of the person's own attitude toward the message I meant to convey; this sort of authorization is formal or external, in the sense that it neither invokes nor depends upon any internal or material consonance between the one being authorized and the message they are authorized to relay. By contrast, if the would-be messenger has been decisively formed by their imitation of the message giver and is part of a plural subject dedicated to carrying on the agency of that message giver, then there would be an internal, material basis for authorizing them to deliver this message, for in that case, there is a real sense in which the message is the messenger's own. This is the sort of connection that Barth, for one, sees as characterizing Christ's relationship to the church's actions: "He wills to be specifically present with it, to dwell within it, and to speak and act by it, i.e., by its ministry . . . in the sense that He actually does these things, not in any external and contingent relationship, but in an intimate and necessary connection in which He is its Lord and it is the body inspired and directed by Him."[52] Insofar as the church is not just like-minded but Christ-minded, accordingly, it can carry on Christ's agency and thus speak on his behalf and serve as his hands and feet. Think again of a team where the players have played together for a long time, to such an extent that they move as one in service of a single project, know what each team member is thinking and what each will do in a given circumstance, and so forth. Now suppose that these players have been playing for a single coach this entire time and that their play embodies that coach's strategies; in that case, we might say not only that the players are like-minded but also that their like-mindedness is a faithful reflection of the coach's own mind and, indeed, that their play is an embodiment of that mind.[53] In the same way, the church should form a single subject that faithfully reflects Jesus' vision, that carries on his agency, and, as such, continues to embody Jesus himself in the world.

This idea faces an obvious objection, of course, namely, that the church falls far short of embodying Christ's agency in the world.[54] There is no gainsaying the truth of this objection. But it does not undercut the point we are considering, for two reasons. On the one hand, even if the church falls short of embodying Christ, it matters that the church remains committed to this project and, so, that when it falls short, it repents and seeks forgiveness, for this, too, is a way that it embodies Christ in the world. On the other hand, if a group of people did not embody Christ's agency to some significant extent, it would no longer be recognizable as a church or even as trying to be a church. Think here of an anthropologist who is trying to understand the game of soccer by watching a couple of bad teams play. If the teams are so completely inept that the anthropologist cannot distinguish between intention and error, then the anthropologist will not be able to figure out what sort of game these teams mean to be playing just by watching them—the teams do not sufficiently embody the game, in other words. In the same way, there is an important difference between embodying Christ's agency imperfectly and failing to embody that agency; if a church is so bad at bearing witness to Christ that it can no longer be said to embody his agency (albeit imperfectly), then it is fair to say that it would no longer merit the title of church.

If we assume that churches can embody Christ's agency, however imperfectly, then this account can help us understand what it means to say that we are "in Christ," and why being *in the church* is sometimes taken to be interchangeable with being *in Christ*. (So Bonhoeffer: "Being in Christ," he insists, "means being in the church.")[55] The logic here is straightforward enough: if the church is not only a plural subject but a plural subject that carries on and embodies Christ's own agency, then insofar as a person is part of this plural subject, it follows that they are included in Christ's agency; if it is further the case, as argued in the previous chapter, that Christ is what he does, then it follows that being included in Christ's agency is being included in Christ. It makes perfect sense, then, that Christians would sometimes equate being in the *church* with being in *Christ*.

This account can also help us identify some ways in which "becoming one" can itself be a spiritual practice. As we have already noted, oneness here includes a like-mindedness that is achieved by means of mutual influence and, in turn, is one of the primary ways in which the mind of Christ is formed in us; if so, then becoming one is obviously a formative practice of just the sort we have been considering. But this is not the only way in which oneness can form us. Crucially, because oneness with others is a structural feature of Christianity, our perspective should continually and necessarily be opened up to others and, just so, transformed. To see what this looks like, consider that being one with others means, among other things, that we will have to put up with them, just as they will have to put up with us; oneness will thus require us to practice grace, forbearance, and forgiveness toward others, which will thus train us to be more gracious, forbearing, and forgiving. Being one with others also means that we should see them as "one of us," and thus as would-be instances of what it looks like to follow Christ and bear God's image; being one with them should thus expand our vision of what each of these things can look like, just as it should expand our vision of what it might look like for us to follow Christ and bear God's image.[56] As we let others expand our vision of what it looks like to follow Christ and bear God's image, accordingly, the church can become "a place of appearing" for all—including us.[57]

Along these same lines, being one with others can also help us resist the temptation to identify God with our own perspective on God, to identify Jesus with our perspective on Jesus, to identify the Gospel with our perspective on the Gospel, and so on. Each of us is tempted to identify our perspective with the way things are, and if we are not compelled to take other perspectives seriously, we will have a hard time resisting that temptation; absent such compulsion, as Ludwig Wittgenstein famously put it, "I have no criterion of correctness. One would like to say: whatever is going to seem right to me is right. And that only means that here we can't talk about 'right.'"[58] We see plenty of examples of this temptation in real life—cases of multiracial churches where white people take their perspective for granted and thus impose it upon Black people (so Korie Edwards), or churches where nondisabled persons design their spaces and services for people like themselves and thus end up excluding persons with disabilities (so Mary McClintock Fulkerson).[59] We also see it in theology, as when theologians of each generation would read the Bible in order to find exactly the Jesus that they were looking for (so Albert Schweitzer).[60] Again, though, if we recognize others as "one of us" and thus feel compelled to achieve like-mindedness with them, then we should be better equipped to resist these temptations, since we should then be disposed to see others' perspectives as enjoying the same validity as our own; at the very least, this should mean that we now feel the need to provide some reasons for holding the views we hold (and thus no longer simply take them for granted).[61] Crucially, though, it should also mean that we come to perceive the partiality of our own views and viewpoints, and so turn to others in order to develop a broader, less partial, more objective way of seeing things. This is what Miguel De La Torre and Stacey Floyd-Thomas seem to have in mind, for instance, when they claim that "to read from the margins provides a 'double-consciousness' that can reveal what those blinded by their privileged status have missed."[62] It is hard for any of us to resist the temptation to identify our perspective with the truth but especially for those of us whose perspective is often so identified by society; luckily for us, insofar as we see others as both different and "one of us," their viewpoints can become a structural feature of our own, in consequence of which we can better resist this temptation and grow in our apprehension of the fullness of truth. Here again, then, being one with others can function as a spiritual practice.

Thus far, I have argued that we can understand what it means to be the body of Christ, to be in Christ, and so on, in terms of becoming a plural subject, and that so becoming is a spiritual practice, since it means we must bear with others and allow them to open up our perspective. This is not the only way that Christians become one with one another, however, nor the only way that becoming one can function as a spiritual practice. Another important way is through *spiritual friendship*. To understand how friendship could be a formative practice, it will be helpful to consider some of the characteristic marks of friendship. (Here I am building on some ideas considered in the last chapter.) One obvious candidate for such a mark is that friends tend to enjoy one another's company; as Aelred of Rievaulx remarks, "How delightful friends find their meetings together, the exchange of mutual interests, the exploration of every question, and the attainment of mutual agreement in everything."[63] Notice, however, that enjoying one another's company is not by itself a mark of friendship; after all, I may have a good time being around someone who tells funny stories, but that does not mean that I am friends with that person, and certainly not that we are close friends. What matters in close friendship is not simply whether I enjoy someone's company but whether that joy is rooted in, and thus an expression of, the things that we have in common—whether we are kindred spirits, as the saying goes.

To be close friends with someone, then, we must have certain things in common, one of which is the way we perceive and respond to (a wide array of) things; this is one of the reasons why friends usually experience themselves as being "on the same wavelength" with one another, since they will tend to find many of the same things funny, or offensive, or sad, or nostalgic, or cool, or whatever. This is part of what it means to "click" with someone. As Aelred puts it, "Spiritual friendship is begotten among the righteous by likeness of life, habits, and interests, that is, *by agreement in things human and divine, with good will and charity.*"[64] Notice that such agreement is usually *made* as well as *found*, so to speak: when people first become friends, they probably already agree on all sorts of things, but by spending time with each other, their friendship will cultivate all sorts of additional agreements. If so, then we can already see one of the ways that friendship can be a spiritual practice, for if friends tend to perceive and respond to things the same way, and if they are likewise devoted to God, then their friendship should help them bring their perceptions and responses into conformity with their devotion.

This is related to a second thing that close friends tend to have in common, namely, a shared commitment to things that matter to them; to whatever extent this is the case, close friends are thus *allies*. Naturally, I can be allies with people even if I loathe them, which is simply to say that allies need not be friends. But close friends do tend to be allies, since shared interests are part of the glue that holds two people together—part of the glue, that is, that moves people from the mere enjoyment of one another's company to true friendship. Tellingly, this is why friendships that lack shared interests are often characterized as lacking "depth." Robert Adams thus claims, in this connection, that "the friendships we regard as most perfect are characterized by a more profound alliance, a fuller sharing of interests, in which shared goals are valued for their own sake by both parties."[65] To be sure, there are countless interests that would do the trick to cement a friendship: close friends might share an interest in a particular sports team, for instance, or a particular genre of literature or television shows, or in partying. In order for it to count as a close *spiritual* friendship, however, the friends in the friendship must share an interest in at least three things, the first of which—obviously—is an interest in God and in devoting themselves to God; absent this, it would hardly count as a *spiritual* friendship. For it to count as a close friendship—spiritual or otherwise— they must likewise share an interest in each other and in the friendship itself. If the friendship itself were not important enough to be a priority to each of them, to such an extent that each of them could count on the other to care about the friendship, invest in it, and remain loyal to it, then it would not provide the sort of relational environment that enables them to open up their very selves to each other.[66] In the same way, if friends did not care about each other for their own sake, then they could not count on each other to look out for their well-being and so, once again, they would not be able to entrust themselves to that person.[67] Close spiritual friendship thus requires that friends share an interest, for its own sake, in God, in their friendship, and in each other.

In the context of close friendship, then, friends should be able to open themselves up to each other, since they can count on the fact that the other person will be there for them and will want nothing but the best for them. Thus Aelred: "By the law of charity," he writes, "we are ordered to welcome into the bosom of love not only our friends but also our enemies. But we call friends only those to whom we have no qualm about entrusting our heart and all its contents, while these friends are bound to us in turn by the same inviolable law of loyalty and trustworthiness."[68] I can entrust myself to my friend, accordingly, precisely because I am confident that they will not betray me or otherwise make me regret doing so, and I can have such confidence because I know that their character itself is trustworthy and that they are committed to my flourishing. If their character were not trustworthy, then even if they were committed to my flourishing, I would not be able to count on them; by the same token, even if they were trustworthy, I could not entrust myself to them unless they were committed to *me*, for in that case I might as well confide in a journal or a dog. Again, though, if their character is trustworthy and they are committed to me, then I can entrust my very self to them and let down my self-protective guard.

With that, the pieces are in place to see how close spiritual friendship can be transformative. If I know that another person will be there for me and that they want nothing but the best for me, then I can open up my very self to them and, just so, open myself up to the friendship's influence; if my friend and I share a devotion to God, then in opening myself up, I am likewise opening myself up to hearing more about God's perspective on me. More specifically, the fact that we share an evaluative perspective— that we are on the same wavelength—means that my friend's beliefs, actions, and feelings will shape my own, and that their perspective on me should shape my self-perspective; hence, insofar as their perspective is itself shaped by God's perspective, it follows that my self-perspective can thus be shaped by that perspective, too. Seeing myself in my friend's perspective can thus draw out certain traits in me: if my friend perceives me as a generous or loyal person, for instance, I may try to live up to that perception and, so, become a more generous, loyal person. My friend can likewise identify "the real me" with certain traits rather than others and can thus help me to identify with those traits: whereas I may see myself as fundamentally shameful or ugly or clumsy, my friend may see my defining traits as creativity and discernment and thoughtfulness; insofar as my friend's perspective matters to me (and mirror's God's own perspective), this may help me to perceive and experience my identity differently and, one hopes, more truthfully. My friend can also help me see what I need to work on but can do so without making it seem as if my sins and failings were the final word about me; hence, if a friend lets me know that I have a tendency to become prickly when someone talks down to me, for instance, or that I sometimes equate people's intelligence with their worth, then I should be able to face this criticism without catastrophizing ("I'm a horrible person! You think I'm a horrible person!"), or dismissal ("You're just saying that because you don't understand!"), or self-deception ("That can't be true; I'm a nice person!"), or withdrawal ("I can't be friends with someone who would say that to me!"). Quite the contrary: I should be able to face the criticism squarely, without evasion, because I know that it comes from someone who loves me and whom I can trust.[69] A close, spiritual friend can thus help me to grow into the person they (and God) perceive me to be, can help me identify with their (and God's) perception of me, and can help me recognize ways that I need to grow. Being friends with a person can thus be a spiritual practice.

There are at least two important respects, then, in which Christians can become one. On the one hand, they can become a plural subject that cultivates the mind of Christ in them and expands their vision of what it looks like to bear God's image and follow Christ. On the other hand, they can form close, spiritual friendships—friendships with persons who share a devotion to God, an evaluative perspective, and an investment in the friendship and one another. In both ways, as Christians become one with one another, they can be formed into the likeness of Christ and, just so, bring their lives into greater conformity to that which is fundamental to them.

Conclusion

If we take the Gospel to be that which is fundamentally true, then we will want to bring our entire lives into conformity with it. Small wonder, then, that Christianity abounds in, and sets so much store by, practices designed to bring about just such conformity. This chapter considered a few of these, beginning with *homemaking practices*. To be at home, we argued, was to experience an ease of fit between ourselves and our surroundings and, just so, to be formed and anchored by that fit. This is one of the reasons singing and eating together play such an important role in Christianity, since these are practices that cultivate and strengthen our fit with our eternal home, and thereby teach us to locate our citizenship in that home and anchor our identity there. We then turned to the practice of *imitation*, understood both as emulation and as mimicry. In both cases, being around others can help us to see what it looks like to orient our lives to God and to orient more and more of our lives that way. That brought us to practices of *becoming one*, wherein we are reoriented to God precisely through being made one with other Christians and with close spiritual friends. Taken together, practices like these are designed to orient more and more of one's life toward God and, in so doing, to bring more and more of one's life into conformity with that which is fundamental to one's identity. The next two chapters extend and, I hope, deepen this theme by giving more careful attention to two crucial places where our lives need such reorientation: in our relationship to the world around us and in our relationship to others.

CHAPTER FIVE

Being in the World

I N CHAPTER 3, WE CONSIDERED what it might mean for one's old, "worldly" self to pass away, and for a new, devoted self to emerge in its place. We saw what this might look like, at first, only under the guise of repentance, in which we side with one aspect of our evaluative perspective against other aspects and just so make that aspect fundamental to our identity. Insofar as devotion is fundamental to our evaluative perspective, however, we cannot remain satisfied with mere taking sides, for it is in the nature of devotion to want more and more of our lives to be oriented by it. A devoted self will therefore endeavor to bring their entire life into ever-greater conformity with that devotion. That brought us, in the previous chapter, to a set of practices designed to bring about such conformity: homemaking practices like singing and eating together, practices of imitation, and the practice of becoming one. This chapter continues that train of thought by turning to a set of practices designed to transform our way of being in the world: we thus consider *prayer and wonder* as practices that transform our experience of earthly goods; *vocation* as a practice that enables us to experience the particularities of our lives as good and our lives themselves as hanging together in a potentially satisfying way; and *laughter and lament* as practices that transform our experience of the would-be ultimacy of various life circumstances.

Prayer and Wonder

To make sense of prayer's transformation of our feelings about earthly goods, it will be helpful to begin by considering one such feeling, namely, joy (and cognate concepts like gladness and delight.) So, persons may experience joy when their favorite team wins a championship, for instance, or when their children are flourishing, or when they see their rivals suffer. In light of such examples, it might be tempting to say that persons experience joy when they feel some circumstance to be good, but this cannot be right, since the same could be said of an experience of mild pleasantness, for instance, or of amusement. It would appear, then, that joy is a matter of experiencing some circumstance not only as good but as a particular *kind* of good. What might this be?

One preeminent theologian of joy, Miroslav Volf, makes the interesting suggestion that, in joy, a person not only experiences some object as good but experiences this goodness as "un-owed."[1] There is something crucially right about this suggestion, and, indeed, this section can be seen as an attempt to discern just what this is. But there is also something slightly wrong with it, since there are plenty of cases where persons feel joy precisely in response to that which they have earned. My son experienced considerable joy, for instance, when, after much practice, he could finally play *Eine kleine Nachtmusik* on his school-issued recorder. And I suspect that most students experience joy when they finally graduate, yet that they nevertheless perceive the enjoyed good as something they have earned. In such cases, the object of joy is not experienced as un-owed, such that although I do think that there is something right about Volf's suggestion, I do not think that it can be included in a putatively general characterization of joy. More to the point, my worry is that characterizing joy's object as un-owed ends up baking into the *definition* of joy that which must be achieved by dint of spiritual *practice*. That is to say, it takes quite a bit of training to become the kind of person who feels joy only in response to genuine goods and who perceives such goods as gifts, and we do not get any closer to becoming such persons merely by writing these traits into our definitions.

With an eye to what follows, it is also worth noting that un-owed-ness is not only not a *necessary* condition of joy, neither is it a *sufficient* condition, since there are cases where the receipt of un-owed goods does not elicit joy: think here, for instance, of someone passing one a napkin before one knew one would need it, or a neighbor shoveling a few scoops of snow off one's sidewalk. I, for one, would experience such acts as a nice thing, and certainly as unowed, but they would not normally bring me joy. For that, they seem to be missing a key ingredient, which brings me to the conception of joy that I will be using here: simply stated, to feel joy in response to something is to experience it as a particular kind of good, namely, what we might term the *fulfilling* kind of good.[2] I say more about this in a moment. For now, I can illustrate what I mean here by considering what would have to be added to the napkin-passing and snow-shoveling examples in order for one to experience them with joy: I would be far more likely to experience joy if the napkin passing appeared to me as a token of thoughtfulness from someone important to me, for instance, or if the missing scoops of snow reminded me that I have new neighbors, such that after nine years of having to shovel my neighbor's walk as well as my own, I will no longer have to do so. In both cases, the added ingredient is a higher degree of concern or importance to me, such that being handed a napkin or having some snow shoveled would now *matter* to me: such concern or importance is a necessary condition, it seems to me, of experiencing some degree of joy in response to some circumstance. Very roughly, then, when I say that joy is an emotional response to some object as a fulfilling kind of good, this is the sort of thing I have in mind.

So far, so good, but this brings us to a problem: if I am right that joy involves an experience of fulfillment in response to certain circumstances, then it might seem to follow, a bit counterintuitively, that joy is *not* at present part of, or at least does not figure centrally in, a Christian way of life. The reason it might seem that way is simple: recall that the blessed, felicitous, or "good" life, as Jesus proclaimed it, is one in which devotion to God is all that matters, and Jesus portrays this devotion as opposed to all other loves; to set our hearts on earthly goods, accordingly, in such a way that we might find fulfillment in them, is apparently forbidden. Hence, if those who would conduct themselves according to Jesus' vision of the good life are supposed to set their hearts only on God and should therefore experience fulfillment and joy only in God, this seems to entail, again, that in the present life, joy is a temptation to be resisted.

I want to argue that this does not necessarily follow from Jesus' proclamation but that we should not arrive too quickly at this conclusion nor make it appear too easily achieved, for the contrary case—the case in which we can rightly experience fulfillment and joy in response to earthly goods— requires nothing less than a radical transformation of our hearts, since we can rightly experience joy in response to earthly goods, on the present ac-

count, only if we can (a) resist our natural disposition to seek fulfillment in
such goods and (b) expand the scope of our fulfillment in God to such an
extent that the latter can now include these goods, too. That brings us to
one of this chapter's central arguments, to the effect that prayer is a spiritual practice that can transform our emotional relationship to goods such
that our concern with them can be expressive of and included in our devotion to God.[3]

Let us turn, then, to a particular kind of prayer, namely, prayers of
petition concerning earthly goods. (By "earthly goods," note well, I mean
not only material goods like food, water, shelter, and the like but also goods
having to do with our relationships, our jobs, our plans, and so on.) The
idea here, simply stated, is that in petitionary prayer, we bring our concerns
about such goods before God, and that doing so can and should change
our relationship to them—it should, in Sarah Coakley's nice phrase, thus
result in an "ascetic transformation" of such concerns.[4]

My elaboration of this idea proceeds through four points, the first of
which is that in this sort of prayer we bring our concern for an earthly
good before God, and in so doing we subject that concern *to* God—paradigmatically by *entrusting* it to God. This is what Thomas Aquinas has in
mind when he claims that "prayer interprets our desires, as it were, before
God," and that one who prays thereby "subjects himself to him and . . .
confesses that he needs him as the author of his goods."[5] Closer to our own
day, Karl Rahner asserts that "the prayer of petition lifts earthly need and
earthly craving, earthly self-defense, into the light and the love of God."[6]
Many more examples could be adduced, but these should suffice to indicate an important theme in the Christian tradition, namely, that in prayer
we bring our concerns to God, and that we do so in order to seek God's
help, to entrust ourselves to God's provision, and so to surrender our concerns to God.

Taking this step can already have a transformative effect on our concerns, insofar as the mere act of making them explicit can make it easier
for us to judge them and thus recognize when a particular concern ought
to be revised or renounced. Augustine maintains, accordingly, that, "to us,
words are necessary, that by them we may be assisted in considering and
observing what we ask," just as Calvin insists that "it is very important for
us to call upon him . . . that there may enter our hearts no desire and no
wish at all of which we should be ashamed to make him a witness," and
Isaak Dorner, that "we must never engage in anything to a greater extent
than we can give expression to in prayer."[7] It is not uncommon for persons

to desire certain things that seem good and justified when we are simply desiring them or even entertaining these desires within our own minds, but that seem inappropriate as soon as we articulate them to others—at which point they begin to seem outlandish, say, or illegitimate. In the same way, when we articulate our concerns to God, some of these concerns will come to seem inappropriate, in which case we should revise or renounce them. (I say more about how this works in a moment.)

Not all concerns are of this sort, of course, which brings us to a second point, namely, that entrusting a concern to God should change our relationship to the object of that concern—paradigmatically by positioning us to perceive its well-being as depending upon God's goodness and, so, to receive it with gratitude. This theme, too, is well attested in the theological tradition, but here I will cite only Calvin, who claims, with admirable clarity, that when persons bring their concerns before God, "they profess themselves unworthy to obtain anything in their own name, so they obligate themselves to give thanks"; one important reason to pray, accordingly, is so that "we be prepared to receive his benefits with true gratitude of heart and thanksgiving, benefits that our prayer reminds us come from his hand."[8] The idea here, then, is that in entrusting our concerns to God, we acknowledge our dependence upon God's provision and thus put ourselves in position to feel gratitude if things go well for the object of our concern and, by parity of reasoning, to experience a kind of trustful resignation or even defiance if they do not. With respect to the former, suppose I ask someone to do me a favor by letting out my dog while I am out of town. If they do it, I should not only feel glad that my dog is being taken care of but also feel that this gladness is due to someone else's generosity and, so, experience that gladness with a sense of gratitude. (In most cases, to experience gladness and perceive this as due to someone else's generosity just is to experience gratitude—but not always, since we could feel gladness, perceive this as due to someone's generosity, yet perceive that person as a sucker, such that we would not feel grateful toward them.)

Trustful resignation, by contrast, is the kind of feeling a person would have if they were to trust that someone will keep their promise even in the face of momentary disappointments—say, if a trusted friend promises to get me a meeting with a public figure but several attempts to schedule that meeting fall through; in that case, I may surely feel disappointed, but if I still trust my friend, this disappointment will be tempered by continuing to see it in light of their promise and, just so, to sense that disappointment is not the final word. Trustful defiance, on the other hand, likewise perceives disappointment as not having the final word, but rather than resigning ourselves to it, here trust leads us to experience a sense of contrariness in face of it; think here of the self-trust that leads athletes to feel obduracy in the face of a loss or in the face of those who do not believe in them—a feeling that says, as it were, "you'll see." Either way, what matters is not whether one responds with resignation or defiance but whether these are an expression of trust in God (rather than, say, of defeatedness or mere self-assertion). We hear an example of such trustfulness in Julian of Norwich: "But sometimes it comes to our mind," she writes, "that we have prayed a long time, and still it seems to us that we do not have what we ask for. But we should not be too depressed on this account, for I am sure, according to our Lord's meaning, that either we are waiting for a better occasion, or more grace, or a better gift."[9] By entrusting our concerns to God, accordingly, we position ourselves—indeed *obligate* ourselves—to feel grateful when things go well, and trustfully resigned or defiant when they do not.

To get a firmer grip on how this might work, we need to recall some claims about concerns and their connection with emotions. Following much of the recent literature, I have argued that emotions are a kind of concern-based construal, an embodied appraisal, a perception of how things are going with what matters to us, or, in short, a felt evaluation.[10] Hence I am liable to feel angry if someone mistreats my children, and my so feeling is an expression of my concern for them and their well-being; likewise with my liability to worry about their future, to delight in their successes, to desire to spend time with them, and so on. In each case, I perceive certain circumstances not matter-of-factly but in terms of what matters to me; implicit in this perception, accordingly, is an *evaluation* in light of what is important to me—an implicit judgment, at the level of feeling, about how the circumstance relates to what I care about. (On the other hand, if I feel no anger when, say, strangers are mistreated, it indicates that I do not care about them or their well-being.) This should help us to see a key component of concern, namely, that concerns render us liable to emotions, and that emotions can thus be (and usually are) an expression of concern. To be concerned, then, is to care about something, to have an investment or a stake in how things go with it, such that we are susceptible to feeling certain emotions depending on how things go with the object of our concern.

Emotions should thus express, and so be in line with, what we care about, though for our purposes it is important to point out that they do not always do so. The clearest examples of this involve something analogous to weakness of will. Think, for example, of a man who had devoted his life to acquiring status symbols—fancy cars, clothes, friends, and so forth—but who has a midlife crisis and therefore resolves to devote himself only to that which is of lasting importance—helping those in need, investing in meaningful relationships, and so on. If the resolve is genuine, he will care about bringing his life into conformity with it and will thus render himself susceptible to certain felt evaluations in connection with that resolve—guilt insofar as his life does not reflect such conformity, worry that his resolve will fail, remorse about the way he had heretofore lived, and so forth. Yet in spite of this heartfelt resolve, many of his felt evaluations may still be calibrated to his old way of life, not least insofar as these had become second nature to him, such that his response to circumstances may still express his old commitments rather than those to which he has now devoted himself. He may experience felt evaluations, that is to say, that are at odds with what he now cares about and has devoted himself to. (He may be especially liable to such feelings when he is around others who care about status symbols—old friends, for instance.)

Again, though, insofar as this person cares about his devotion to that which is of lasting importance, he will be susceptible to felt evaluations concerning that devotion, which means, in turn, that he will be susceptible to felt evaluations *of* his felt evaluations: if he feels envious or unduly desirous of status symbols, he may therefore feel guilty or frustrated or sad about feeling this way. In turn, the latter evaluations should exert a kind of normative pressure on the former—saying, as it were, that these holdover evaluations do not represent the evaluative perspective in which he has invested himself, such that these evaluations ought to change—and, given our natural aversion not only to self-inconsistency but to negative felt evaluations as well, the latter can play a role in bringing this change about: if he feels bad every time he feels (or acts) this way, this feeling bad may operate, within his evaluative perspective, almost the way a shock collar works on an animal, by giving him a repeated, strong, negative reaction to that feeling and so, over time, training him not to feel that way. Such feelings about feelings can likewise alert us to, and so put us on guard against, certain temptations, and can thus position us to resist these temptations. To stick to our example, the man who has renounced his concern with status symbols may feel ashamed when certain old feelings surface, and this shame may alert him to the fact that he is still liable to such feelings and that he must therefore take care lest his newfound resolve should slacken; as a result, he may become concerned about facing a tempting situation—say, going to a party at an old friend's house—and therefore try to remind himself, again and again, of his new resolve, so as to render himself less susceptible to old felt evaluations. Examples aside, the point is that felt evaluations should cohere with our central commitments, and that this "should"—expressed in felt evaluations of our felt evaluations—can play a role in bringing them into line with those commitments.

That brings us to a third point about prayer. To devote oneself to God, in the present sense, is not only to commit oneself to orienting one's life to God but to *care* about this commitment, such that its importance to one is *itself* important to one. Prayer concerning earthly goods is an expression of this commitment, in that it brings our particular concerns before God and so integrates them—or at least *means* to integrate them—into our more basic concern to devote ourselves to God; if all goes well, our felt evaluations should then be aligned with that basic concern, such that we would feel not only gladness but also gratitude if something goes well, trustful resignation instead of worry if it does not, and so on. This is not magic, of course, such that prayer may not actually bring our felt evaluations into conformity with our devotion to God. Even in that case, though, they *should* be so conformed, which means that we can and should feel guilt, frustration, and the like insofar as they do not. The latter feelings should be the occasion for a different sort of prayer—confession—but they can also play an important role in realigning our felt evaluations by exerting normative pressure on them. Again, the idea here is (a) that guilt and the like can perceive—can be a felt evaluation of—a felt evaluation as wrong and (b) that feeling it as such can exert a kind of normative pressure on our disposition to feel that way, insofar as (i) we naturally want to maintain consistency within our evaluative perspective and (ii) we want to avoid negative evaluations of ourselves.

That brings us already to a fourth point, concerning prayer's role in transforming not just one's response to a particular object of concern but also one's very *disposition* to respond in certain ways. The idea here, very simply, is that each time we pray, we explicitly relate our concerns to God, and this has the effect of increasing the likelihood, over time, that our felt evaluations will actually so relate, especially when coupled with felt evaluations of those evaluations.[11] This is one way that theologians have tried to make sense of the biblical injunction to "pray without ceasing" (1 Thess. 5:17): by praying explicitly, in particular circumstances, we cultivate the habit of entrusting our concerns to God, and since prayer consists in precisely such entrusting of concerns, it follows that we pray without ceasing just insofar as we have cultivated this habit—insofar, that is, as we entrust all our concerns to God, whether we do so implicitly or explicitly.

As I have said, there is no guarantee that this will work, and even when it does work, the result will not encompass every aspect of our lives. But it is nevertheless plausible to think that prayer can change some of our dispositions to some extent, and this is important precisely because the *material* result of such changes is—or should be—that we become increasingly disposed to entrust all our concerns to God and thus to acknowledge *all* goods as God's *gifts*. To see how this might work, think of persons who have tried to make a list of everyone who has done something to help them: their list might begin with friends, parents, teachers, neighbors, ministers, coaches, counselors, mentors, coworkers, sponsors, and others who have played a significant role in shaping their lives; who then proceed to list less obvious candidates, such as the classmate who took their side against a bully, the secretary who took extra time to show them how to complete an important form, the librarian who helped them with a research project, and so on; and who then move to all the nameless persons—law enforcement officers, sanitation workers, farmers, builders, health-care workers, and the like—who have done something for them without their knowing it. As their list grows, they should think of more and more good things that their life would lack if not for such persons, in consequence of which they should feel increasingly grateful not only to each of them, but, more generally, for the goodness of their life itself. On the present account, prayer should have roughly the same effect: every time we entrust a good to God and, so, receive it with gratitude, we add to an ever-lengthening string of such experiences, the net effect of which should be to incline us to experience every good—and goodness itself—as a gift. As a result, prayer can dispose us to "recognize in God the author of our goods," as Thomas Aquinas puts it, or to see that "I have no good apart from you," in the words of the psalmist.[12] The idea, then, is that explicit prayers should increasingly dispose us to entrust our concerns to God and, in turn, dispose us to experience gratitude or trustful resignation depending on how things go with them, such that we would thus become disposed to perceive all goods—and goodness itself—as God's gifts.[13]

This account needs to be extended—and thereby expanded—in two key respects. First, if we are to experience all goods as God's gifts, then it is vital that we feel gratitude not only when we have been concerned about something, nor only when we feel glad about something, but even in response to good things that we would otherwise take for granted. That brings us to the practice of "blessing," in which we give thanks not in response to our feelings but simply in response to certain circumstances: so upon waking in the morning, for instance, or putting on clothes, lying down at night, eating a meal, or any number of other everyday occurrences, one blesses God and, just so, perceives these occurrences as an expression of God's goodness.[14] In Michael Fishbane's nice formulation, such blessings are thus "a detailed recitation of gratitude to the Lord for gifts of daily sustenance: the clothing of the body, the awakening of morning sight, the release from the bonds of sleep, the assumption of upright posture, the wherewithal of living, and the sense of determination and execution. Nothing is taken for granted; every thing is received as a gift flowing from the well of divine giving, and taking shape in the world."[15] By learning to recite certain blessings in certain circumstances, accordingly, we can get into the habit of giving thanks not only when we are feeling thankful, but, increasingly, whenever we have reason to give thanks, which would thus expand the range of goods that we experience as gifts.

The scope of one's gratitude is likewise expanded—exponentially—through prayer for others. Our treatment of such prayer can be relatively brief, since much of what needs to be said here has already been covered. Simply put, to pray for others is to bring *their* concerns before God, and in one variety of such prayers, we bring them before God *as our own* concerns. To be concerned first-personally with another's good, to be invested in it, and so to experience it from within our own evaluative perspective, is, obviously, part of what it means to love that person—such prayers for others are thus of the specifically *loving* variety. (I return to this point in the next chapter.) This is what Thomas Aquinas has in mind when he claims that "we ought to desire good things not only for ourselves but also for others," from which he infers that "to pray for another is an act of charity."[16] In some cases, we already love others—we are already first-personally concerned with and invested in their good—such that we are already susceptible to felt evaluations concerning how things go with what concerns them; following our earlier claims, we should bring these concerns before God, entrust them to God, experience gratitude if they go well, trustful resignation or defiance if they do not, and thus perceive the loved one's good, too, as a gift.

Prayer for others is not always an expression of felt love, however; sometimes it is simply an *act* of love, though one that should *cultivate* felt love. For there are cases where we might not be concerned with other people's

good, and even cases where we might want things to go badly for them—
if, say, we are angry with them, contemptuous of them, perceive them as a
"them" over against "us," and the like. In such cases, to pray for them is an
act of love: in spite of the fact that we want things to go badly for them, in
spite of the fact that we may feel that this is what they deserve, we nevertheless pray that God will provide for their good. As a result—and this is
the key point—we may thereby come to see their well-being from two
perspectives: our own and God's. Hence, we may still be liable to want
things to go badly for them—and so feel satisfaction when that happens,
irritation when it does not, and so on—but in praying for them, we open
up a second perspective, in which we perceive their well-being from the
standpoint of God's grace and love. In light of our devotion to God, the
latter perspective should exert a now-familiar kind of pressure on our felt
evaluations—we should feel guilty about delighting in others' misfortune
or resenting their flourishing—and this pressure, over time, should transform our felt evaluations regarding them. In consequence, prayer as an *act*
of love for others can play a decisive role in cultivating *felt* love for them—
that is, a state in which we have become first-personally invested in their
good or, as Kazoh Kitamori puts it, a state in which we have moved from
obligatory love to *willing* love.[17] Again, I have more to say about this in the
next chapter. For now, the point is that, even here, prayer for others positions us to experience their good as depending upon God's provision and,
so, can exponentially increase the range of goods that we are liable to perceive as gifts.

From all of this, three important implications follow. First, if we see all
goods as God's gifts—as ultimately due, that is, to God's grace—then the
connection between goods and desert will be loosened considerably, such
that we should no longer be tempted to see our goods as finally possessed
by or solely due to us. Privileged persons could thereby perceive, for instance, the extent to which their abundance is not finally a wage that they
have earned, a perception that would simultaneously undercut their temptation to look down on those who have less. This is related to a second
implication, namely, that prayer can lay the foundation for a theological
aesthetics, since it transforms not only a person's heart but, in so doing,
their way of perceiving the world, too. (I am using the term "aesthetics"
here in its original sense, as dealing with how things appear to us.)[18] The
idea, simply stated, is that prayer should make a difference in the way we
experience the world and the way it therefore appears to us, for if my account thus far is even roughly correct, it would follow that each and every

good—each breath, each meal, each touch of kindness, each meaningful day's work, each experience of beauty (traditional aesthetics, too), and so on—should be perceived as a gift of God, such that our perception of them should include a felt evaluation of gratitude. Our perception of that which is not good should change, too: every broken appliance, every condescending answer, every sickness, every worry, and so on should likewise be seen in light of our trust in God's provision, such that our perception of it should include a felt evaluation of trustful resignation or defiance. Prayer can thus enable us—and, over time, dispose us—to perceive good and bad circumstances alike in light of God's grace, which is why I say, again, that it lays the groundwork for a theological aesthetics.

That brings us already to a third implication, which is that prayer, so construed, can play a crucial role in what I would term a *practical doctrine of creation*—a doctrine of creation, that is, that focuses on the practices and dispositions that we must cultivate in order to treat the world—including ourselves—as the creation of a loving God. Whereas a *theoretical* doctrine of creation might focus on beliefs concerning the origin of the world, the relationship between providence and natural laws, and so forth, a practical doctrine focuses on whether we interact with the world as if everything depends upon God's goodness. To be sure, a practical doctrine of creation would have to include not only prayer but other practices as well—practices of stewardship and cultivation, for instance, in addition to practices of wonder. The claim here is simply that, in disposing us to treat all goods as God's gifts, petitionary prayer can dispose us to treat the world as creation, and that it can thus play a key role in developing a practical approach to that doctrine.

I have argued that prayer can change the way we perceive earthly goods, seeing them as depending ultimately upon God and so as gifts for which we should feel grateful insofar as we have them, and trustful resignation or defiance if we do not. Prayer can thus play a crucial role in transforming our felt evaluation of ourselves and our circumstances, such that, among other things, we would experience all goods as due to God's grace and would therefore experience gratitude precisely in our enjoyment of them. Joy can thus play a role in the good life, Christianly construed, but, again, it takes spiritual practice in order for it to do so.

I would argue, then, that prayer is an essential component of a Christian way of life. I return to this point in chapter 7, but I would also argue that a life that contains a practice like prayer—a practice, that is, that transforms our emotional relationship to goods, not least by detaching us from our immediate investment in them—will be a better one, all things considered, than a life that does not. Naturally, someone who adhered to a vision according to which the good life is a matter of feeling everything as intensely as possible, for instance, would not require prayerlike discipline, and should probably avoid such discipline; nothing I have said thus far would imply that adherence to such a vision is unwarranted. But for a wide range of plausible conceptions of the good life, prayerlike discipline *would* make for a better life. To see why, consider that most people are concerned with finite goods and that the goods with which we are concerned are fragile, seductive, and self-multiplying: these goods are *fragile* in the sense of being subject to the vicissitudes of history and sometimes threatened by hostile or indifferent forces, such that investment in these goods subjects us, too, to these vicissitudes and forces; they are *seductive* in that, to whatever degree we are invested in them, we are tempted to treat them as if they were that around which the world should be made to revolve, or, in short, as if they are not finite goods; and they are *self-multiplying* in the sense that investment in such goods itself ends up increasing the goods with which we are concerned—the goods that are the necessary conditions of the goods in which we are invested, the goods that are the concern of another person in whose flourishing we are invested, and so on—such that the fragilities and potential seductions to which we are exposed are likewise multiplied. It is not hard to see, then, why we would want to discipline our emotional relationship to such goods, which is one reason many conceptions of the good life include some such discipline, since these disciplines are meant to detach us from the objects of our concern, and in some cases reattach us to them, so as to loosen the grip of their fragility and seductiveness. If so, then it is plausible to think that the life of a person who practices such a discipline—prayer included—would be better, all things considered, than that of one who does not. It seems to me, then, that there is genuine practical wisdom implicit in Christianity's commitment to prayer, which is, again, a point to which we will return.

Thus far, then, I have argued that prayers concerning earthly goods should transform our felt evaluation of these goods, such that we should increasingly relate to *all* goods as God's gifts and thus integrate our concern with these goods into our devotion. Importantly, though, the world's goodness far outruns our concern with it; after all, creaturely goods are good in their own right and, so, in their otherness to our concerns. Hence, if this goodness, too, is God's gift, then a practical doctrine of creation should train us to receive it as such. That brings us to a spiritual practice—

the practice of *attention* and *wonder*—that is designed to help us notice and appreciate more of this goodness.

The notion of "attention" that I have in mind derives from Simone Weil, who characterizes it in the following terms: "Attention consists," Weil explains, "of suspending our thought, leaving it detached, empty, and ready to be penetrated by the object; it means holding in our minds, within reach of this thought, but on a lower level and in contact with it, the diverse knowledge we have acquired which we are forced to make use of. Our thought should be in relation to all particular and already formulated thoughts, as a man on a mountain who, as he looks forward, sees also below him, without actually looking at them, a great many forests and plains. Above all, our thought should be empty, waiting, not seeking anything, but ready to receive in its naked truth the object that is to penetrate it."[19] On Weil's account, then, we practice attention by letting go of our preconceptions in order to let ourselves be filled with the singular reality of a particular object. As Weil is quick to clarify, however, the letting go in question is a matter not of emptying one's mind of all concepts but of holding our concepts loosely, so to speak, by letting them be shaped and even selected by whatever it is that we are attending to. (Though Weil does not mention it, this procedure is relevantly similar to Friedrich Schleiermacher's "hermeneutical circle": in order to make sense of a text's parts, we must have some idea of the whole to which they contribute, but we must also continually revise our sense of the whole in light of those parts.)[20] At the most basic level, accordingly, to practice attention is to loosen the grip of our preconceptions in order to see a particular object in all its particularity and, so, to let our mind be filled with that object's peculiar reality.

To get a better sense of what Weil has in mind here, it might be helpful to consider the example of a poet like Marianne Moore.[21] Moore is justly famous for treating every creature as an entire world, filled with wonders; William Carlos Williams thus aptly remarked that, in reading her poems, "in looking at some apparently small object, one feels the swirl of great events."[22] We see a nice example of this in Moore's poem "The Jelly-Fish":

Visible, invisible
A fluctuating charm,
An amber-colored amethyst
Inhabits it; your arm
Approaches, and
It opens and

It closes;
You have meant
To catch it,
And it shrivels;
You abandon
Your intent—
It opens, and it
Closes and you
Reach for it—
The blue
Surrounding it
Grows cloudy, and
It floats away
From you.[23]

Moore is here making use of ordinary concepts, but she does so in such a way that these concepts are selected and refashioned for the sake of illuminating the singular reality of a singular encounter with a jellyfish. The poem is thus an act of attending to—and drawing our attention to—the particular reality of that jellyfish. The poem also intimates the elusiveness of this reality: as the reader reaches out to grasp the jellyfish, it pulls away; then, just when one has given up on catching it, the jellyfish gives another tantalizing glimpse of its splendor, thereby enticing one to reach for it again before it . . . floats away. Here as elsewhere, then, Moore's poetry attends to particular creatures *as* the particular creatures they are, and in so doing evinces a sort of wonder at them. It is as if each poem says, "I caught a glimpse of this creature, and it is a marvel—this very creature, in all its ordinariness, is so extraordinary that it stretches my descriptive capacities to their breaking point."

Poets are not the only ones who practice such attention, of course; we see something similar in photographers, who train themselves to pay exacting attention to light and color and every intricacy of detail within a visual field. In so doing, many also train themselves to perceive that which is extraordinary in ordinary, everyday life. To take just one example, this is exactly what Yasumi Toyoda's "Super Ordinary" project aims to do, namely, "notice more," as she likes to put it. One of the chief reasons that we do not notice more is that we have simply become used to seeing (and, so, not seeing) the things around us, which is why Toyoda's photography draws its material from the most anesthetizing, routinized aspect of her existence:

the daily commute. Many of her photographs themselves are striking, but the most important feature of her work, for our purposes, is her practice of giving herself little projects, instructing herself to be on the lookout for certain phenomena within her surroundings. She thus sets out, for instance, to photograph (and so notice!) instances of a particular color, such as yellow or mint green, or of seams and joints, or corners, or corrugation, or even peculiar objects like hoses or handpumps. By giving herself these assignments, she primes herself to notice these features within her surroundings; as a result, features that she would otherwise have hurried past are lit up with salience. She thus ends up noticing more and more of the things worth noticing in her daily life, which means, in turn, that she notices more and more of the richness and texture of her surroundings. (Think of what happens when she encounters a corner where yellow corrugated metal is joined to a flat, mint-green wall.) Once one begins to give oneself assignments like these, it quickly becomes evident that there is no end, in principle, to the assignments one *could* give oneself; we could thus be on the lookout for droplets or spidery cracks or circles or sun-faded colors or literally any number of other things, each of which would equally merit our notice. By giving ourselves the task of noticing certain phenomena, then, we train ourselves to notice how many phenomena are worth noticing, which is to say that noticing can beget noticing. Hence, whereas poetry can teach us to let our concepts be bent and chosen by particular objects, a photographic project like Yasumi Toyoda's can break the spell of routine and, with it, our routinized not-noticing of the world around us. And in helping us see more of the richness of that world, photography can thereby enable us to see more of its wonders; in this connection, Toyoda is fond of quoting the Hungarian photographer Brassaï: "If reality fails to fill us with wonder," Brassaï remarked, "it is because we have fallen into the habit of seeing it as ordinary."[24]

Examples aside, the idea here is that attention requires us to let go of the concepts and frameworks through which we ordinarily filter our surroundings, so that we can open ourselves to the richness and peculiarity of the world around us. In attending to an object, in other words, we try to empty ourselves of our preconceptions and predeterminations and then let ourselves be filled by the reality of the object itself.

With that, we can now consider a few ways in which such attention might count as a *spiritual* practice. First, as we have already seen, attention can open us up to wonder at our surroundings and, just so, train us not to take the world as a given but to experience more and more of it as creation. In our everyday lives, this is not how we experience our surround-ings; rather, we tend to experience the things around us either as part of our routine or as at our disposal and thus end up taking them for granted and reducing them to what they are *for us*.[25] We thereby fail to appreciate the richness and goodness of the world around us, just as we fail to wonder at the fact of its existence.[26] As Augustine insists, we should constantly be amazed at God's creative work, yet "his miracles, by which he governs the whole world and administers all creation, have lost their impressiveness by constant repetition, so that almost no one deigns to notice the wondrous and stupendous works of God in any grain of seed."[27] The fact that a grain of seed grows into a tree or flower or blade of grass is astonishing, as is the growth of each leaf and each branch on the tree. Yet we are so used to seeing trees and flowers and grass and clouds and water and countless other wonders that we seldom even notice them, much less stand in awe of the one who created them. Attention can be a spiritual practice, then, in-sofar as it trains us to notice more of the world around us and thus to ap-preciate more of its richness and wonder, for this is part of what it would mean to treat the world as created. Insofar as attention trains us to expe-rience the world in these ways, accordingly, it is part of what I have been calling a practical doctrine of creation—a doctrine of creation, that is, that focuses on the dispositions that one would have to cultivate in order to perceive the world as the creation of a loving God. After all, if one believes, with the angels in Isaiah 6:3, that the whole earth is filled with God's glory, then one must not only assent to the truth of that belief but actually *see* the world as so filled. The practice of wonder can help us do just that.

To be sure, the mere fact that we attend carefully to something does not mean that we will wonder at it; after all, sometimes the act of photo-graphing something is an attempt to domesticate it—we thus speak, tell-ingly, of using a camera to "capture" a moment. What must be added to mere attention, then, so that it will cultivate in us a sense of wonder and appre-ciation? Sometimes, nothing: we are simply stopped in our tracks by some phenomenon, taken by surprise, arrested by it. (I cannot help but react this way upon seeing deer, for instance, no matter how many times they cross my path.) In such cases, we cannot help but wonder; then our job is simply to linger in that wonder, to let it sink in, and, just so, to do justice to what-ever wondrous thing we have beheld. In most cases, however, we will spot that which is wondrous in the world around us only if we have put our-selves on the lookout for it. To see how this works, consider an instance where someone calls my attention to something by saying, "Oh, wow, look what's behind you." In that case, when I turn to look behind me, I will be primed to see something *as* wow-worthy. To be sure, I may zero in on something other than that which my interlocutor was calling to my attention: they may have been reacting in wonder to a brilliantly colored goldfinch, for instance, whereas I may so react to the shagbark hickory on which it is perched. The point is that if I am primed to perceive something wondrous— to perceive something *as* wondrous—then I will be much more likely to do so. The key to perceiving the world around us with a sense of wonder, then, is to prime ourselves to do so, which is to say that we will be much more likely to experience wonder if we are expecting to. This means, in turn, that wonder tends to beget wonder, for the more we are on the look-out for things that are wondrous, the more we will not only perceive things as wondrous but also be disposed to perceive them as such and, so, to treat the world not as a given but as creation.[28] By training us to notice more of the wonders around us, accordingly, attention can function as a spiritual practice.

That brings us to a second respect in which attention is a spiritual practice: the better we get at attending in this way to the world around us, the better we will get at contemplating God, both because we have gotten better at contemplating per se and because we are seeing more and more of God's glory. Weil makes the former point explicit in her theology of education: "The key to a Christian conception of studies," she writes, "is the realization that prayer consists of attention. It is the orientation of all the attention of which the soul is capable toward God. . . . Of course school exercises only develop a lower kind of attention. Nevertheless, they are extremely effective in increasing the power of attention that will be available at the time of prayer."[29] By disciplining our powers of attention, we become capable of attending more fully to objects, which means, in turn, that we become capable of attending more fully to God. As Sarah Coakley has pointed out, contemplative prayer requires considerable discipline, not least because we are so easily distracted. Coakley's own approach to distraction focuses on the practice of contemplative prayer itself, but it stands to reason that if we practice attention in our everyday lives, we will better be able to pay attention when we turn to God; after all, once we have learned to attend well to one thing, we have a better idea of what it looks like to do so and how to go about doing it, not to mention having an improved capacity for focusing our sustained attention on something. By getting better at attending to the world around us, accordingly, we can develop some skills and dispositions that will help us attend better to God. In attending to the world around us, we can also expect to see more and more of its beauty and, in turn, more and more of *God's* beauty. The logic here goes something like this: (a) the world around us is filled with beauty; (b) if God is infinitely beautiful, then the world's beauty must be an expression of God's own beauty;[30] (c) beauty is such that, as soon as we notice it, we want to linger on it and contemplate it; hence, (d) as we contemplate the beauty of the world around us, we are simultaneously contemplating God's beauty, whether we realize it or not. When I behold the sun setting over the ocean, lighting up the sky with bands of pink and purple, I cannot help but watch; I am transfixed; I want to take in as much of that moment as I can. The argument here is not simply that we should be similarly transfixed by the splendor of God, though that is surely true. Rather, the argument is that God's splendor is infinite and that all creaturely beauty is therefore a reflection of God's own beauty. In beholding the former, accordingly, our sense of the latter should be stretched and enriched such that we actually behold more and more of God's beauty; we might then begin to understand what it means to say, with Julian of Norwich, that "the fulness of joy is to contemplate God in everything."[31]

At this point, a question may occur to some readers: Does this account entail that poets and photographers and scientists and countless others are, in fact, putting into practice a doctrine of creation? To address this question, we need to emphasize a crucial point: in order to contribute to a practical doctrine of creation, what matters is not simply that we engage in practices of attention but that these practices cultivate (and are expressions of) particular *dispositions*, especially the disposition to *appreciate* or *wonder at* the world. There is a vital difference, after all, between a person who observes an ant colony simply in order to chart its various branches, circumstance-responsive changes, and so on, and someone who does these things with a sense of how interesting or impressive or mind-boggling or well designed or beautiful it is. Insofar as practices of attention cultivate and are expressions of the latter sensibilities, then they, too, dispose us to treat the world as God's creation, and just so contribute to what I am calling a practical doctrine of creation. And while I cannot do justice to the point here, I would argue that they can so contribute even if the persons practicing them do not realize that they are doing so. We could defend the point by appealing to an externalist account of reference, but for now I will simply offer an analogy.[32] Suppose a picture that my daughter has painted or a robot she has built is on display somewhere and that the people looking at it are admiring its use of light, marveling at its design, or whatever. Even if they mistakenly think the painting and robot were created by one of her teachers—or if they have no thought whatsoever about who created them—they are still appreciating and wondering at her creations, and their doing so redounds to her praise even if they themselves are not in position to realize it. And while it would surely be better if they knew who the creator was and so rightly directed their admiration to her, it does not change the fact that they are admiring *her creation* all the same. I would say the same of practices of attention: so long as they cultivate and are expressions of a sense of appreciation for and wonder at the world, they train us to treat the world as God's creation. Better still, of course, if their practitioners could not only treat but also recognize it as such, but these practices can contribute to a practical doctrine of creation even absent such recognition.

Prayer can thus train us to entrust our concerns to God and to receive all goods as God's gifts, just as attention can train us to wonder at and appreciate the world around us. In both ways, we can transform our relationship to the world and, just so, cultivate what I have been calling a practical doctrine of creation. So far, so good, but this account remains incomplete in two vital respects: on the one hand, how do we handle *bad* circumstances? And on the other, how do we not only respond to circumstances but *lead a life* in the midst of them?

Vocation

Our next step, then, is to consider what it would mean not only to respond to the world around us as creation but also to fashion a life within it. There is a proactive dimension to being in the world, after all, namely, the dimension in which a person can be said to lead a life. Within the Christian tradition, this dimension is understood primarily in terms of the concept of *vocation.*

In the simplest sense, vocation is a name for that which we have been called to do and to be; for Christians, it is a name for that which *God* has called us to do and to be, in such a way that our doing and being can thereby become an expression of devotion. (Christians also talk, at times, of groups and institutions having vocations, but the vocation of individuals is paradigmatic.) In his "Treatise on the Vocations," accordingly, William Perkins claims that "*a vocation or calling is a certain kind of life, ordered and imposed on man by God for the common good*"; Emil Brunner similarly maintains that "God never requires 'something in general,' he does not issue proclamations, nor does he set up any kind of program. He never issues commands into the air—with the idea that anyone may hear them who happens to feel like it! He tells me, or us, or you, as definite persons, to do some definite thing."[33] Again, the idea here is simply that God calls each of us to live our life in a particular way, and that this calling—this vocation—provides us with an answer to the question of how we should go about fashioning a life in the world.

We can get a clearer idea of what this looks like if we consider, first, the idea that, in calling us, God calls us to care for and cultivate particular goods; these goods can be the good of a certain "sphere," or of certain persons or relationships, or of certain created goods. (Note well that, on a Christian account, each of us is given *one* vocation—namely, to devote ourselves wholly to God—and *several* vocations, in the sense that we may be called to care for several goods precisely as an expression of that one vocation; hence, as Mother Teresa puts it, "The work that we are called to accomplish, is just a means to give concrete substance to our love for God."[34] Note, too, that there is a limit to the number of goods that a person can care for in this way, since caring takes time, energy, and prioritization. There are only so many things that one can prioritize, after all.) On the one hand, then, we may be called to look out for the goods at stake in a particular sphere: these spheres may be demarcated by a particular role, such as parent, teacher, electrician, citizen, and the like; or they may be delimited by a particular setting, such as a neighborhood, school, company, or other set of surroundings. However defined, the idea here is that each of us may be called to a particular domain or jurisdiction within which and for which we are responsible to answer God's call. As Karl Barth puts the point, when a person is given a vocation, "wherever and whatever it may be, he will always be confronted by the necessity of filling one specific sphere, of meeting its data and demands, of coming to terms with what is assigned to him in it, of being a man at this particular point."[35] On the other hand, we may also be called to care about certain persons and certain goods: a person might thus be called to love various friends, for instance, as well as to care for and cultivate natural, aesthetic, intellectual, and moral goods (think here of athletes, musicians, jurists, and activists). This is what Robert Adams claims in his celebrated essay on vocation: "My suggestion," Adams writes, "is that vocation is primarily a matter of *what goods are given to us to love*, and thus of *our part in God's all-embracing and perfect love*."[36] So then: sometimes God calls persons to care for the goods at stake in a particular sphere, and sometimes God calls persons to care for particular goods irrespective of where they show up: one conservationist may thus be called to look out for all the goods that reside in a particular forest, whereas another conservationist may be called to look out for a particular species of bird wherever it may be found. In the former case, the goods one cares for are determined by the sphere to which one is called, whereas in the latter, the sphere one is called to is determined by the goods one is called to care for. Either way, the point is simply that when God gives us a vocation, God is calling us to care for and cultivate specific goods.

Naturally, there may be instances when a person is called to care for a specific good as a one-time-only episode: if I drive past a family of strangers whose car has broken down, God may call me to stop and help them, but once I have done so, that may be the end of what I am called to do. In general, though, when Christians talk about vocations, they are talking about longer-term callings, which brings us to a second way that theologians have elaborated this notion: when God calls us to care for and cultivate particular goods, God likewise calls us to organize our lives around these goods. Indeed, this is part of what it looks like to answer God's calling, for we cannot care well for certain goods without a diachronically stable commitment to them and, so, a commitment to prioritizing them and becoming good at caring for them. Consider a simple example: suppose my daughter asks me to take care of her hermit crabs during a year when she studies abroad. If I am going to do the job she has entrusted to me, I will need to make sure I know how to care for the crabs—what to feed them and when, how to regulate their tank's temperature and humidity levels, what sort of shells need to be available, and the like. Such know-how is a necessary, but not sufficient, condition of doing the job; I will also have to make sure that the crabs are actually taken care of, which means that I will need to organize my schedule to ensure that they receive the care they require, just as I will need to take measures to counteract my native forgetfulness (by, say, setting alarms on my phone). So then: if I am going to do what my daughter has asked and thus take care of the things that she has entrusted to me, I will have to learn how to do so and make sure that I actually do so. Something similar could be said of most longer-term vocations, namely, that answering God's calling requires that we learn how to care well for the goods that God has entrusted to us, and that we organize our lives so as to ensure that these goods receive the care they deserve.

It is easy to see, then, how a vocation can give shape to our lives, for if we are called to care for certain goods, we will likewise be called to learn more about them and how to promote their well-being, just as we will be called to organize our lives in such a way that these goods will be well cared for; in being called to care for a particular good, accordingly, one is called to orient a significant portion of one's life toward that good. (Some of the goods that one may be called to cultivate are thus internal to one.) It is also easy to see, in turn, how the category of vocation could provide us with an answer to the question of what it means to lead a life: simply stated, if a vocation gives shape to my life, and if I identify with that vocation, then by pursuing that vocation, I give my life a shape with which I can identify. A bit more expansively: to identify with a vocation, not only must I perceive the goods I care for as valuable, it is *I* who must value them, to such an extent that I am first-personally invested in their well-being and, thus, to such an extent that my well-being is bound up with theirs. Insofar as this is the case, then in organizing my life around these goods, I am simultaneously giving my life a shape with which I can identify and, just so, directing my life toward an end that is recognizably mine.[37] This is one plausible way of thinking, then, about what it would mean to lead a life. If one pursues one's vocation as a response to God's calling, moreover, then it follows that, in orienting one's life toward that calling, one simultaneously orients one's life toward God. If everything goes as it should, accordingly, one need not choose between leading one's life and obeying God's will.

Vocation can thus give shape to one's life in such a way that one can identify with it, just as it can transform the leading of one's life into an act of devotion. Vocation can likewise imbue one's life with a sense of wholeness and value. With respect to wholeness, the idea should be straightforward enough: the more one's life is gathered up and directed toward one's vocation, the more one will experience one's life as hanging together as a single, unified act of will, and the more one will not simply endure or respond to circumstances but fashion a life within them. Think here of a mother who has been called to care for her son, and who therefore takes him on outings, provides nutritious meals, makes sure their home is safe, teaches him how to recite the alphabet and how to process his feelings, gives him opportunities for positive interactions with other kids, and, in sum, does what she can to promote her son's well-being. Just doing these things would occupy a significant portion of the mother's life. But if she wants to do these things, she will also have to do all sorts of other things: after all, if she wants to provide nutritious meals, she will have to learn some things about age-appropriate nutrition, shop for ingredients, and actually prepare the food, just as she will have to make sure she has a place to store and prepare the food, enough money to pay for it, and so on. Nor is that all; if she cares about her son, she will also spend time and energy worrying about his well-being, making plans to provide for it, and talking with her son about all of these things, not to mention countless others. These lists could go on, but the point is that when persons are called to care for a child, they are given a vocation that will absorb a significant portion of their life, and all the things that are included in this portion of their life will hang together as the doing of a single thing, namely, caring for their child. If we add to this the fact that caring for a child is, here, included in the larger vocation of devoting one's life to God, and if we add, further, that one's other vocations will be similarly included, then we can begin to see how vocation can imbue one's life with a sense of unity, of hanging together, and of being a single whole. As Albrecht Ritschl puts it, "The realization of the universal good within the special limited domain of our vocation, and in such a way that all extraordinary actions are regarded as essential from their analogy to our vocation, is the reason why the multiplicity of good works, in which action manifests itself, forms an inwardly limited unity, in other words, a whole."[38]

Vocation can likewise provide one with a sense of the value of one's life, for if one's life is a response to God's calling, then it is an act of serving God and, so, sacred. Imagine that I am a social studies teacher in a local high school, and then imagine that the Obamas had asked me to take a leave of absence so that I could teach their daughters during their time in the White House. If I had accepted, I would still be doing what I had always done but would now be doing it at the invitation of, and in service to, the First Family; as a result, I would surely feel that a special sort of dignity and worth had been conferred upon my work. Christian theologians have insisted that this is precisely the way we should feel when we are called to live our lives unto, and so in service of, God; Horace Bushnell thus claims that "God is girding every man for a place and a calling, in which, taking it from him, even though it be internally humble, he may be as consciously exalted as if he held the rule of a kingdom. The truth I propose then for your consideration is this—*That God has a definite life-plan for every human person, girding him, visibly or invisibly, for some exact thing, which it will be the true significance and glory of his life to have accomplished.*"[39] By experiencing our lives as a response to God's calling, accordingly, we can resist the temptation to judge their value by other, worldly standards, and can thus perceive their value irrespective of how they stack up by the light of those standards.

By the same token, if we experience our life as a response to God's calling, we can likewise come to terms with its limitations. The claim here, simply stated, is that if our life is oriented by and to God's calling, then we should be freed from the vague sense that we are somehow falling short insofar as we are not doing every single thing that needs to be done in the world, much less everything that would be worth doing. This is what we hear from Adams: "There are so many goods in the world that I could promote," Adams writes, "and so many needs in the world that I could try to meet. There is a danger that I will be either fragmented, going too many different ways; or crushed, seeing my obligations as unlimited; or immobilized by the clamor of competing claims. An idea of what is *my* task in the universe, and what things are *my* things to care for, may both impel me and free me to devote my attention to those things."[40] If I were part of a team that is planning a large fundraising banquet, I might constantly worry about all the things that have to be done and whether they are being done properly; hence, even if my role on the team were a small one—perhaps I am only in charge of providing centerpieces and gift bags for each table—I may have a hard time letting go of everything else involved in making the event a success. I may also have a hard time resigning myself to my limited role insofar as I think I am better suited than others to fill other, "bigger" roles. By contrast, if my role has been assigned to me by God, and if I wholly trust both God's wisdom and God's provision, then I should have a much easier time releasing the worry and the envy I might otherwise feel. That is not to say, of course, that I *will* find it easy to release my worry and envy; after all, emotions like worry and envy can be tenacious. But if I trust God, then I will feel these emotions in spite of this trust and, indeed, will feel them *as* in-spite-of-my-trust—that is, their in-spite-of-ness will be part of the emotional experience itself, and I will thus have an additional standpoint that I can occupy in relationship to them. In this context, then, "easier" does not mean "easy"; it just means "more possible" and, perhaps, "more likely."

Again, if we see what we do with our lives through the lens of vocation, it follows that we will see what we do as a would-be expression of our devotion to God; this means, in turn, that we should pursue our vocation always and only as an act of devotion, and that we cannot therefore pursue it as if it were ultimately important, nor as if the aim were to pursue our own success, aggrandizement, happiness, or the like. As William Law puts the point, "This is the only measure of our application to any worldly business, let it be what it will, where it will: it must have no more of our hands, our hearts, or our time than is consistent with a hearty, daily, careful preparation of ourselves for another life."[41] Suppose I am a hedge-fund manager who has been called to take good care of people's retirement funds. In that case, I will be sure to work at this vocation as unto the Lord and will thus make sure I am honest and fair in all my dealings, that I do not let this work absorb too much of my life or energy, that I do not become unduly focused on goods that are peripheral to my calling, and, in short, that I work at it only in such a way that it could express my devotion to God. The same could be said of any vocation.

Vocation is thus a matter of being called by God to care for particular goods, and persons so called can experience their life as an expression of their devotion, as hanging together, as having worth, and as having a shape that they can identify with. That brings us to an obvious question: how does one *discern* one's vocation?

One sort of answer to this question relies on the idea that our vocation can be discerned by appeal to an objective standard; on such an approach, we are called to do whatever it is that would contribute the most good to the world, for instance, or would earn us the most money or acclaim, or would enable us to ascend as high as possible on a hierarchy of vocations (with, say, monks or missionaries or activists at the top), or would make us happiest. These are recognizably *consequentialist* answers, in the sense that one is supposed to infer what one ought to do from certain predictable effects of doing it. Such answers are attractive not least because they provide us with a fairly straightforward response to the question of what we should do with our lives, but they are also liable to serious objections. For one thing, it seems evident that people are sometimes called to do things that make them unhappy, or less happy than they might otherwise be; if so, then it follows that happiness maximization is not a sure guide to vocation. More generally, though, this sort of approach has a hard time valuing our particularity: if all of us are called to do as much good as we can, or earn as much money as we can, or whatever, then it follows that the goodness of a person's vocation can likewise be judged by that standard and, so, that the goodness of the person's life can be thus judged, too; hence, if we think that there is something wrong with valuing lives in terms of a one-size-fits-all standard, or if we think there is value in a wide array of particular vocations, then we should probably resist this sort of approach.[42]

That brings us to an approach that might seem to remedy these problems, an approach according to which our calling is simply identical with whatever role history and culture have assigned to us. This approach has the merit of offering people a clear answer to the question of what they are called to do with their lives, and it has the further merit of valuing a max-

imally wide range of particular vocations. The problems with this approach
are obvious, however: if our calling is simply identical with whatever role
history has assigned to us, then our calling will likewise reproduce whatever injustices and other undue constraints have been written into that
role; those injustices and constraints would then be treated as if they were
God's will, and, given the points considered above, we would thus be called
to find our identity in a role defined by injustice and constraint. Small
wonder, then, that several theologians have rejected this sort of approach:
Karl Barth thus insists that "man can neither absolutize his own situation
nor rivet his fellows absolutely to theirs," just as Isaak Dorner maintains
that "class divisions, e.g., which *compel men to adopt particular vocations*, have
a mechanizing tendency and are immoral," and Emil Brunner contends
that such an approach "threatens to justify the status quo, and in so doing
to paralyze the moral will."[43] While it may make sense to suggest that God
calls people to care for certain goods in whatever role history has placed
them, this is distinct from suggesting that God calls them to that role itself. The dangers in the latter suggestion should be obvious.

Let us turn, then, to a third approach. Unlike the other approaches,
this one does not provide us with a clear, straightforward answer to the
question of what we are called to do with our lives. It aims, instead, to
provide some helpful, but not definitive, guidance for deriving such an
answer, and it does so by attending to the sort of *fit* that vocations usually
establish between a person and certain possibilities. We can think of this
approach, very roughly, as pulling together the answers to three questions:
What do we value? What do we have an aptitude for? And how can we use
our aptitudes to care for that which we value? These are the issues raised
by William Perkins, to take just one classic example: "Every man must
choose a fit calling to walk in," he writes; "that is, every calling must be
fitted to the man, and every man must be fitted to his calling. . . . Men of
years make choice of fit callings for themselves when they try, judge, and
examine themselves to what things they are apt and fit, and to what things
they are not. And every man must examine himself of two things: first,
touching his affection, secondly, touching his gifts. For his affection, he
must search out what mind he has to any calling, and in what calling he
desires most of all to glorify God. For his gifts he must examine for and to
what calling they are fittest. Having thus tried both his affection and gifts,
finding also the calling to which they tend with one consent, he may say,
that is his calling: because he likes it best, and is every way the fittest to it."[44]
On this sort of approach, then, we can get a sense of our calling by consid-

ering what we value and what we have an aptitude for: if I had aptitude for something but did not value it, then I would not care *about* whatever it is I would be caring *for*; on the other hand, if I valued something but lacked the aptitude to care for it, I would not be able to care *well* for it. If we assume, therefore, that when God calls us to care for something, God calls us actually to care for it and to do so well, then it makes sense that our values and aptitudes would provide us with some guidance as to our vocation. To be sure, there may be instances where we must develop the aptitudes necessary to caring for something, just as there may be instances where we must learn to value something; in such cases, we are called not only to care for some good but also to cultivate the traits necessary to do so. Sometimes vocation precedes the relevant traits, in other words, and sometimes it follows them. (I return to this point in the next chapter, under the rubric of "aspiration.")

This combination of value and aptitude can help me perceive a vocation as distinctively *mine*, for insofar as I identify with these values and can exercise my aptitudes in their service, it follows that what I am *doing* is an expression of who I take myself to *be*. As Barth points out, "Although man cannot simply read off God's command from what he has so far been and become on the basis of the creation and providence of God, yet in that which God wills of him according to his command, he will recognize himself as the one he has already been and become by the will of the same God. . . . Otherwise, how could his knowing and doing of what God will here and now have him know and do as this special thing be his own free obedience? How could he be obedient at all? How could there be free decision as distinct from mere occurrence?"[45] The idea here is that I can recognize some course of action as mine just insofar as it stands in some sort of continuity with my history—as the next step in my story, as it were— and that such continuity is established, in large measure, by the values I have come to hold and the abilities that I have developed. Such continuities may be recognizable only in retrospect, but in their absence it is hard to see how we could experience a vocation as ours.

As noted, this sort of approach does not provide us with a clear answer to the question of what we should do with our lives, which brings us to one additional bit of guidance it has to offer: in considering what we are to do, it can be helpful to seek the counsel of those who may have some relevant expertise. On the one hand, then, we should seek the advice of those who know us well. "Consult your friends," urges Horace Bushnell, "and especially those who are most in the teaching of God. They know your talents and personal qualifications better, in some respects, than you do yourself. Ask their judgment of you and of the spheres and works to which you are best adapted."[46] And, on the other, we should seek the advice of those who know well the vocation to which we may be called. Richard Baxter thus instructs his readers, "*Choose no calling (especially if it be of public consequence) without the advice of some judicious, faithful persons of that calling.* For they are best able to judge in their own profession."[47] This seems like straightforwardly sensible advice, for if others have a clear idea of what I value, of what I am capable of doing, and of what a particular vocation entails, it stands to reason that they may give me useful guidance in discerning whether that vocation is a good fit for me.[48]

That brings us to one final point. Suppose that one has discerned what one values and what one is good at, and suppose, further, that this leads one to pursue a vocation that would enable one to express these values and aptitudes by caring for certain goods. And now suppose that one cannot pursue this vocation, due to one's race or gender, for instance, or due to the fact that it is no longer possible to pursue it. In that case, one may experience vocational *injustice* or vocational *tragedy*, as when, for instance, a woman is not allowed to preach despite the fact that she wants to do so and would be good at it, or when a person cannot pursue a vocation because, say, it no longer exists (think here of elevator operators or telegraphers). Either way, it is possible that one may not be able to do some of the things that one is called to do. In the next chapter, I consider whether and how we may be called to do something to remedy such injustices and tragedies; for now, it is important that we at least register their existence.

Vocation is a matter of calling, specifically one's calling, by God, to care for particular goods. Even if there is no simple, straightforward equation that tells us what our vocation is, we do find some guidance in considering the relationship between our values and aptitudes, on the one hand, and our possibilities, on the other. By establishing a fit between the former and the latter, vocation can provide our lives with a sense of wholeness, orientation, and worth, just as it can enable us to lead our lives as an act of devotion; vocation can thus transform our way of being in the world.

Laughter and Lament

In the first section of this chapter, we considered the way that prayer trains us to entrust our concerns to God and experience all goods as God's gifts. As we noted at the time, however, not all circumstances are good; after all, scripture counsels us to give thanks *in* all circumstances but not *for* all circumstances. The Christian tradition offers us several practices that are designed to help us deal with such circumstances; to round out this chapter, then, let us consider two of these practices, namely, laughter and lament.

People laugh for all sorts of reasons: some laugh when they are nervous, for instance, or simply when they are feeling especially glad about something. They also laugh when they find something funny, which is the sort of case I want to consider here. In general, to find something funny is to take up a playful attitude toward it and thus to treat it as unserious; laughter is then an outward expression of such playfulness and, so, a way of signaling one's attitude to others.[49] (This is a necessary condition of funniness but surely not a sufficient one; after all, I can take up a playful attitude toward a game with my kids, but that would not mean that I thought there was anything funny about it. For our purposes, however, this condition is all we need.) Senses of humor vary widely, of course, which is why some people find pratfalls, flatulence, "dad jokes," puns, impressions, or practical jokes funny, and others do not. A sense of humor is thus relevantly similar to other aesthetic tastes: just as some people lack a taste for, say, Indian food or Post-Impressionist painting, so some people lack a taste for sarcasm or awkward humor. Importantly for our purposes, one of the things that people often find funny is *incongruity*; as Reinhold Niebuhr puts it, "We laugh at the juxtaposition of things which do not fit together."[50] Naturally, not all incongruities are funny; if I am at a funeral and hear someone talking badly about the deceased, I will perceive that as incongruous but probably not as funny; likewise if I hear the sound of email alerts during a hike in a remote forest or if I am enjoying a special moment with my family and one of my kids says, "Can we go now?" Again, not all incongruities are funny. But two broad sorts of incongruity often strike people as funny, and these are crucial for our purposes.

On the one hand, some people find it funny when there is an incongruity between how seriously some people take themselves and how seriously they should be taken. Hence we sometimes laugh at especially pretentious people, for instance, just as we may laugh at people who badly overestimate their talent or power. With respect to the latter, consider Barth's amusing description of someone who "thinks he sits on a high throne, but in reality he sits only on a child's stool, blowing his little trumpet, cracking his little whip, pointing with frightful seriousness his little finger, while all the time nothing happens that really matters."[51] In cases where people take themselves too seriously, we may be inclined to laugh at them (at least in our heads) or even to make fun of them, for the simple reason that there is something ridiculous about the way they are acting. Indeed, in such cases, we may laugh at them precisely because their being oh-so-serious seems like a sort of playing: just as children may play at being absolute monarchs and thus act as though they are everyone's boss, so it may seem that self-important people are playing the role of someone far more important than they really are. This may elicit a playful attitude from us, which may in turn be expressed either through laughter or through making light of them.

On the other hand, people sometimes find it funny when there is an incongruity between what they expect to happen and what actually occurs; this is why persons sometimes laugh when things go wrong. Think here of someone who has had a run of bad luck: they lost their job, their car broke down, and then, as they are walking home, a bus drives by and splashes water in their face. We may be tempted, in such circumstances, to give up—if everything is going wrong, what is the use of trying? If we respond in that way, then we have been defeated by our circumstances, at least temporarily treating them as if our fate were wholly in their hands. Interestingly, though, some persons respond to such circumstances precisely by laughing at the sheer absurdity of having so much bad luck—they respond, that is, as if their circumstances were playing a joke on them. By taking up a playful attitude toward these circumstances, we can not only relieve some of the distress they cause, we can also treat them as not absolutely serious and thus resist the sense of defeat to which they might otherwise incline us.

In examples like these, to laugh at something is to treat its would-be seriousness as incongruous and, therefore, to treat it as if it were not finally or ultimately serious. This should help us understand what Christian theologians have had to say about laughter as a spiritual practice. The key idea here is that Christians take God—and God alone—as ultimately serious, from which it follows that we can take up a less-than-serious attitude toward the would-be ultimacy of our circumstances, our peers, and even ourselves. This would explain Reinhold Niebuhr's contention that "the sense of humor is a byproduct of self-transcendence," as well as Dietrich Bonhoeffer's claim that "ultimate seriousness is never without a dose of humor."[52] This idea would likewise explain why the seriousness with which we take ourselves might seem incongruous to Christians and, so, why we might see this as funny; in Niebuhr's laconic formulation, "What is funny about us is precisely that we take ourselves too seriously."[53]

This account can also help us understand the role laughter can play in enabling people not to abandon hope when everything is going wrong.

Howard Thurman makes precisely this point in considering the importance of humor in the life of many Black people: "What is overlooked,"
Thurman explains, "is the fact that the basic laughter of the Negro is vital
and dynamic, leaping out of an elemental faith in life itself, which makes a
sense of ultimate defeat not only unrealistic but impossible." This is the
case, Thurman insists, because insofar as people can respond to their circumstances by laughing, "the contradictions of life are not in themselves
either final or ultimate."[54] Again, because laughing at our circumstances is
a way of treating them as not ultimate, it follows that if we can maintain a
sense of humor in the face of difficult situations, we can resist the would-be
finality of these situations. That is to say, if we can see the absurdity or ridic-
ulousness of our situation (and of the persons responsible for it), and if we
can therefore see the humor in them (or create humor in the midst of
them), then we can thereby take them a bit less seriously and thus relieve
some of their crushing weight. Consider one of many examples in Joseph
Heller's brilliant *Catch-22:* after a war-tormented soldier named Yossarian
confesses his belief that people are conspiring to kill him, it leads to the
following exchange:

> "No one's trying to kill you," Clevinger cried.
> "Then why are they shooting at me?" Yossarian asked.
> "They're shooting at *everyone*," Clevinger answered. "They're
>   trying to kill everyone."
> "And what difference does that make?"[55]

In normal circumstances, if countless people were looking to kill me, I
would have good reason to fret about a conspiracy; hence, by having Yossarian respond to wartime as he would respond to normal circumstances,
Heller exhibits one of the ridiculous aspects of the former. By seeing things
in this way, we can laugh at them and, just so, take them less seriously than
we otherwise might—not in the sense that we are here taking *death* less
seriously but are taking certain *rationalizations* of death less seriously.

When this taking-less-seriously is rooted in, and an expression of, an
elemental faith that God alone is ultimate, then laughter can function as a
spiritual practice: in the face of incongruities that arise when our expectations are subverted, or where people take themselves too seriously, or where
the world is simply absurd, we can laugh in response, and so take these
incongruities less seriously, precisely because we recognize God alone as
ultimately serious. Laughter can thus play a role in transforming our ex-

perience of the world, insofar as it disposes us to treat this world as penultimate rather than ultimate, and thereby enables us to take it with the
seriousness it deserves—no more, no less. Being able to laugh in the face
of difficult circumstances can also help people get through those circumstances and, indeed, remain oriented to God in the midst of them. Needless to say, however, laughter is not always an option for people; that brings
us to a related practice, namely, *lament*.

Lament is a way of responding to *suffering*, by which I mean an experience of distress in response to the perceived badness of some circumstance, where the acuteness, duration, or significance of this distress makes
it increasingly or intensely hard to bear. Persons who deal with long-term
physical pain may thus experience suffering, as may persons who have been
mistreated or persons who are grieving the untimely loss of a loved one.
Depending on how intense it is, how long it lasts, and how much it touches
that which is significant to us, suffering can be overwhelming, which is
why persons who endure suffering often wonder whether they will be able
to hold on in the face of it. Suffering can also be disorienting, in both one's
self-relationship and one's relationship to others, because it can seem all-
encompassing, can undermine that which one took to be stable and reliable, can isolate one from others, and, in sum, can short-circuit one's ability to make sense of one's life. We see an example of this sort of suffering
in Augustine's description of what he went through following the death of
his close friend: "Everything on which I set my gaze," Augustine confides,
"was death. My home town became a torture to me; my father's house a
strange world of unhappiness; all that I had shared with him was without
him transformed into a cruel torture. My eyes looked for him everywhere,
and he was not there." Augustine confesses, as a result of his suffering, "I had
become to myself a vast problem."[56] We hear the same sort of experience
described by Eric Cassell in his celebrated book *The Nature of Suffering
and the Goals of Medicine:* "Suffering occurs when an impending destruction of the person is perceived; it continues until the threat of disintegra-
tion has passed or until the integrity of the person can be restored in some
other manner. . . . Most generally, suffering can be defined as the state of
severe distress associated with events that threaten the intactness of the
person."[57] Notice, then, that what matters here is not pain, per se, but what
pain signifies to and for the person enduring it; hence, I may not experience any suffering if I feel pain in my lungs after completing an intense
workout, whereas I may experience suffering if I feel a sharp pain in my
knee, for in that case I may be distressed either by the overwhelmingness

of the pain itself or by the implication that I may no longer be able to do certain things that matter to me. Then again, a person can suffer even in the complete absence of physical pain; I may thus suffer if someone I love is in pain, for instance, or if I begin to experience signs of dementia-related memory loss, or if I feel certain emotions like guilt and shame. Again, then, suffering is a felt evaluation of some circumstance as bad, where this badness is experienced as threatening or compromising something that matters to me and, so, as potentially threatening or compromising my very self. This would explain why persons often experience suffering as threatening to tear them apart or "break" them, just as it explains why persons who suffer often characterize themselves as trying not to "lose it," trying to hold it together or, more simply, as trying to hold on.

That brings us to lament, by which I mean the act of bringing suffering to speech by crying out to God, usually with others. Psalm 13:1–4 is a paradigmatic example of such a lament:

> How long, o LORD? Will you forget me forever?
> How long will you hide your face from me?
> How long must I bear pain in my soul,
> And have sorrow in my heart all day long?
> How long shall my enemy be exalted over me?
> Consider and answer me, o LORD my God!
> Give light to my eyes, or I will sleep the sleep of death,
> And my enemy will say, "I have prevailed";
> My foes will rejoice because I am shaken.

It is evident here that David is suffering: there is pain in his soul, sorrow in his heart, and it would appear that he is doing his best to hold it together (as indicated by the repeated refrain "How long?"). In this suffering, David not only cries out but cries out *to God* and, just so, brings his suffering before God as a plea: how long, o LORD? As he does so, he gives language to his suffering and thus shares his experience with others and, in turn, provides an example—and a sort of script—that others can follow in order to cry out to God with him.

These elements—crying out to God, giving voice to our suffering, and joining our suffering with others—help us understand how lament can transform our experience of suffering and, in particular, how it can help us hold on and hold ourselves together as we endure it. First, bringing our suffering before God and crying out for God's help can help us to remember that God, and not suffering, has the final word on our existence; we can thus find some reassurance that suffering will not last forever. Think here of undergoing a medical procedure: if we know that the procedure will be intensely painful but that the pain will last for only thirty seconds, then we will find it much easier to endure that pain; by contrast, if we experience similarly intense pain but have no idea how long it will last, we will usually find that pain much more distressing. When we bring our suffering to God and thus perceive this suffering in light of God's love and provision, we may likewise perceive its duration as, finally, limited, and so as more endurable; as Calvin puts it in his commentary on 1 Pet. 1:6, "By saying, *though now for a season*, or, *a little while*, he supplied consolation; for the shortness of time, however hard evils may be, does not a little lessen them; and the duration of the present life is but a moment of time."[58] More generally, if we take it that God loves us and that nothing is more powerful than God's love for us, then it follows that that love is more powerful than suffering; this means, in turn, that suffering's power over us is finally limited and, so, less overwhelming than it might seem. By bringing our suffering to God, therefore, we can see it in light of God's love and power and can thus resist the message that suffering conveys to us, namely, that it has the final word on our existence. According to Howard Thurman, this is precisely what singing the spirituals has done for many Black people: in singing these songs, he explains, "what they discovered was that the bitter contradictions of life are not final and that hope was built into the fabric of the struggle. This meant to them that the intensity of the tragic passage in which they were pilgrims could not be separated from the God in whom their ultimate trust was placed."[59]

To see how this works, consider a very rough analogy: suppose I already know the ending of a movie that I am watching, even though I do not know the details of how the movie arrives at that ending. In that case, if I know that the movie ends with the triumph of a particular character, then even when things look bleak for that character during the movie, I will perceive that bleakness to be temporary. Christians take it that they know how this world's story ends, not least because the story's ending has already happened: in the resurrection of Jesus, the end of all things has already taken place, and in it we can already see God's ultimate triumph over every hostile power. Hence, although we may not know the details about how we will arrive at this ending, if we know how the story ends, this knowledge can help us perceive our suffering as temporary. By singing spirituals and otherwise lamenting our suffering, then, we may be able to see our suffering in light of God's love for us and, just so, as transitory, passing, and as not going to win. This reassurance can give people some of the strength they need in order to hang on in the midst of suffering.

This is related to a second point: as Christians lament, they bring their suffering into the context of that which is most important to them—that which is most fundamental to their very selves—and this, too, can help them hold themselves together. One way we see this is when persons perceive their suffering in light of their vocation—as that which must be overcome for the sake of remaining true to their vocation—and thus, finally, as secondary to their more ultimate purpose. Albrecht Ritschl maintains that this is exactly what we see in Jesus' response to suffering: on Ritschl's account, (a) Jesus experienced suffering as a temptation to forsake his vocation, since suffering naturally inclines one to pursue one's self-interest, whereas Jesus' vocation depended upon his setting aside that pursuit; and (b) he thus experienced suffering as a would-be obstacle to the accomplishment of his vocation, which we see most explicitly when Jesus' opponents threatened him with torture and execution; from this, it follows (c) that not giving up his vocation in the face of these threats meant that the threats, too, became occasions for faithfulness to his vocation and, just so, became part of the life he was leading.[60] This is what Ritschl has in mind, accordingly, when he claims that, "had he [Jesus] succumbed to one such temptation, it would have meant that, to preserve the tranquility of his individual existence, he had renounced his vocation. But, on the contrary, all the sufferings that befell him, and especially those he was ready to bring on himself by his appearance in Jerusalem, he steadfastly endured, without once proving untrue to his vocation, or failing to assert it. Therefore, these sufferings, which, by his enduring of them even unto death, he made morally his own, are manifestations of his loyalty to his vocation, and *for Christ himself* come into account solely from this point of view."[61] The key idea, more generally, is that if we endure suffering for the sake of remaining faithful to our vocation, then we have a purpose for enduring it, even if our suffering itself is purposeless. Think here of an aspiring violinist who breaks all their fingers in a freak accident: however painful and distressing this may be, and however purposeless the accident that caused it, the violinist will experience this suffering as something to deal with, and finally overcome, for the sake of reaching their goals, just as Christians may experience suffering as something that they need to deal with for the sake of remaining faithful to God. By bringing our suffering before God, accordingly, and therefore bringing it into connection with that which is most important to us, we may be able to perceive it in light of our vocation and thus experience it as something we have to endure for the sake of that vocation. This sense of purpose, too, can provide us with some of the strength we need in order to hang on.[62]

Bringing suffering into connection with that which is most important to us can also help us maintain (or restore) our fundamental sense of orientation, even in the face of profound disorientation. Paul Tillich characterizes this as a sort of faith "in spite of": "But it is the paradox of the belief in providence," he claims "that, just when the conditions of a situation are destroying the believer, the divine condition gives him a certainty which transcends the destruction."[63] We hear a moving example of such faith in Nicholas Wolterstorff's lament for his son, who died at the age of twenty-five: "I believe in God the Father Almighty," he writes, "maker of heaven and earth and resurrecter of Jesus Christ. I also believe that my son's life was cut off in its prime. I cannot fit these pieces together. I am at a loss."[64] Wolterstorff thus gives voice not only to his sense of loss but also to the *wrongness* of the loss, and his lament does not help him see his son's death as any less wrong; it remains a kind of surd in his relationship to God. That is not to suggest that his lament is wholly ineffectual, however, for precisely by lamenting it, that surd is itself now included in his relationship to God. This may not seem like much, but insofar as devotion to God is fundamental to one's identity, such inclusion may make a significant difference in one's ability to deal with suffering, for it may help one to feel that one's existence still hangs together even in the face of the loss, and, so, may help one not to be swamped by it.[65]

That brings us to a third point: by giving voice to our suffering, lament enables us to share our hearts with others (and vice versa), which can play a vital role in helping us endure it. As Thurman observes, this is one of the most important reasons Black people sing sorrow songs together, for doing so enables "a clear sharing by the members of the group with each other of the comfort and strength each found in his religious commitment."[66] So how does such lending of strength work? The simple fact that we are not alone in suffering does seem to make a difference, though it is worth noting that it is not the mere presence of others that matters, nor even "being seen" by them, for if they saw what I was going through but either did not care about it or delighted in it, their presence and "seeing" would not offer me much consolation. What seems to matter is not the mere presence of others but whether I am around others who see what I am going through *and are on my side* in it, for in that case I will know that I am not alone in bearing the suffering; they suffer it with me. This can give me strength, inasmuch as I now know that someone else is standing with me and has taken up my cause, as it were—the "cause," here, being my selfhood; I now know, in turn, that even if my suffering proves too much for me, it will not mean that my cause is lost, since someone else has joined me in fighting for it.[67] By analogy, think here of the last living speaker of a language. Once they die, the language will die with them; its survival rests entirely on their shoulders. Now imagine how heartened this person will be to discover that someone else speaks the language or to find someone else who is committed to learning it. In that case, their hope for the future no longer rests entirely on their own shoulders. Something similar can happen when others come alongside us in our suffering: our hope for the future no longer rests entirely on our own shoulders, for now we know that there are others who share our cause. This can help us resist the temptation to give up and can thus help us hold out against being overwhelmed by suffering. In so sharing, moreover, others can reinforce our commitment to this cause—can help us see that it does, indeed, matter—and this, too, can help us not give up on it.

Others can also help us endure in the face of suffering by "holding us in personhood," as Hilde Lindemann puts it.[68] According to Lindemann, such "holding" is a common, but usually unnoticed, feature of human existence; on her account, being a person is akin to being a scholar, in the sense that one becomes these things through becoming recognizable as such, both to oneself and to others. Importantly, just as others can hold one in the role of scholar even if one has come to doubt whether one merits the title, so others can hold one in the status of personhood even if one feels as though one is losing one's grip on that title. By the same token, others can hold us in the status of being *this* person, *this* self, and can thus help us hold on to our identity even if suffering compromises our own ability to do so. This may sound a bit esoteric, but again, it refers to a common feature of human existence. Consider a scholar who is undergoing a crisis of confidence because, say, their most recent book was panned by critics or they are experiencing an extended bout of writer's block; in these circumstances, they may find themselves wondering, "Maybe I was just kidding myself. Maybe I'm not really a scholar after all." If others continue to believe in them, and can thus reassure them that they are, in fact, a scholar, then the person may be able to hold on to that view of themselves even when it is extremely difficult for them to do so on their own. In the same way, even if suffering threatens to overwhelm one's sense of selfhood or personhood—

even if one feels that one is losing oneself, or that one is no longer oneself—others may nevertheless be in position to reassure one that one will get through this, that one will still be oneself once one does, and, more basically, that one remains a person and a self even if one does not feel as though that is true. Once again, then, insofar as lament enables us to share our suffering with others, it likewise enables others to help us hold on in the face of that suffering.

That brings us to a final, and fairly straightforward, point: to cry out to God in lament is to raise a protest against our suffering. Thomas Aquinas goes so far as to characterize suffering as an act of resistance; as he notes, if "the will . . . were not to resist, but to yield by consenting, the result would be not sorrow but pleasure."[69] The point is simple enough: to suffer in the face of some circumstance is to suffer *against* it, to endure it as that which should not be, and, so, as that which should be opposed. This is one of the reasons so many laments slide over into the genre of "spiritual complaint" (so Claus Westermann), and it also helps us see why it is so important that we support and stand alongside those who cry out in suffering, for insofar as we do so, we can help them resist the force of that which should not be—we can help them not only hold on, in other words, but also hold out against the forces of evil.

Lament may not remove the source of suffering, accordingly, though it certainly gives us a dispositive reason to try to do so (both individually and as a community). I return to this point in the next chapter. But by crying out to God in our suffering, we can bring our suffering into connection with God, with that which is fundamental to our selfhood, and with others. In so doing, lament can transform our experience of suffering, helping us to experience it as not having the final word about us and, so, helping us hold on in the face of that which might otherwise overwhelm us.

At first blush, it may seem surprising to pair laughter and lament; after all, they seem like polar-opposite reactions to one's circumstances. They share something essential in common, however, namely, that both can be practices that train us to perceive God alone—and not our circumstances—as ultimate. We do this when we laugh at the would-be ultimacy of the world around us (as well as ourselves), and we do it when we cry out to God in our suffering. (There can even be cases where we do both at the same time, since laughter and lament respond appropriately to different features of our circumstances.) Like prayer and wonder, then, laughter and lament can train us to respond to our circumstances in such a way that we are simultaneously responding to God.

Conclusion

If one wants to orient one's whole life—and not just a tiny fragment of it—to God, it stands to reason that one's way of being in the world will have to be so oriented. In this chapter, then, we considered a handful of practices that are designed to transform the way we relate to the world around us: prayer thus trains us to entrust all goods to God and receive them as gifts; wonder trains us to treat the otherness of creation *as* otherness and to appreciate it as such; vocation trains us to fashion our lives in response to God's calling and thus to draw more and more of our life into that calling; laughter trains us to take the would-be ultimacy of this world (and ourselves) lightly; and lament trains us to bring our suffering to God and thereby render it a bit more endurable. Taken together, these practices help us see what a new way of being in the world might look like—a way of treating the world as penultimate, as not speaking the final word, as filled with good gifts, as a place where we are called to care for certain goods, and, in sum, as God's creation. So far, so good, but one vital question remains: how are we supposed to relate to the other persons with whom we share this world? That brings us to the subject of the next chapter.

CHAPTER SIX

Being with Others

THE LAST TWO CHAPTERS discussed practices that reorient us toward God and that transform our relationship to various life circumstances. This chapter continues that train of thought by focusing on practices that aim to transform our relationship to a crucial subset of life circumstances, namely, our relationship to other persons. Toward that end, let us begin with an attempt to get clear on the nature of *love* and, in particular, of what we might call "Christian" love, then turn to some of the primary means by which such love might be *cultivated*, and, finally, consider the relationship between love, so understood, and *justice*.

Love

The agenda of this section is simple: on the one hand, we need to get clear on what we mean when we talk about "love," and, on the other, to consider what difference it makes—if any—to think about love from a "Christian" standpoint.

As I understand it, love is a particular way of valuing something for its own sake. To be sure, there are cases where I value things for their own sake but where it would seem odd to say that I love them: I value levelness when it comes to hanging a picture, for instance, but it would be a bit dramatic to say that I love levelness, for the simple reason that I do not value it all that much; the same could be said for my valuing brevity in meetings, correctness in pronunciation, and the like. This seems to suggest that love involves not only valuing something for its own sake but also valuing it a certain *amount*. That brings us to a first ingredient in love, namely, that to love something is to care about its well-being—for its own sake—to such an extent that one is deeply and first-personally invested in that well-being. This is what Thomas Aquinas has in mind, for instance, when he claims that, "in the love of friendship, the lover is in the beloved, inasmuch as he reckons what is good or evil to his friend, as being so to himself; and his friend's will as his own, so that it seems as though he felt the good or suffered the evil in the person of his friend."[1] We hear something similar in Bishop Butler's famous sermon on neighbor love, in which he contends that, "in the degree we love one another, his [our neighbor's] interest, his joys and sorrows, are our own . . . love of our neighbor would teach us thus to appropriate to ourselves his good and welfare; to consider ourselves as having a real share in his happiness."[2] The idea here is that to love something is to care about it so deeply that we experience its well-being as our own; in that case, we would feel gladness if things go well for it, sadness or anger if they do not, and so on, precisely as we would if these things were happening to ourselves. By caring about certain people, accordingly, their good becomes our own good—their good is good *for us*—their bad becomes our own bad, and we thereby come to identify with them. (This is one natural way of understanding what it means to love others *as oneself*, for insofar as another's good or bad is experienced as *my own* good or bad, I am first-personally invested in their well-being; I thereby identify with them and, just so, care about them "as myself." This is precisely how Bishop Butler understands these injunctions, to take just one example.)

Before we proceed, some clarifications are in order. First, to love others is, again, to be invested in their well-being, but it is important to note that we must be so invested for their sake, rather than our own. This is worth mentioning, since I can also care about another's well-being only for my own sake: so I may want my children to flourish just so it will reflect well on me, or the workers on my team to do well just so I can get a promotion. In such cases, the mere fact that I am invested in others' well-being does not mean that I love them, for the simple reason that I do not care about them for their own sake. Importantly, though, a peculiar kind of instrumentality can emerge when we care about others for their own sake, since caring about them means that we acquire a first-personal interest in things going well for them; caring about them for their sake can thus turn out to be equivalent to caring about them for my own sake, but only because the latter is included in the former. The point, in any event, is that the care that is an ingredient in love must be care for the loved one's sake.

The care involved in love must also be characterized by a certain degree of stability or lastingness. To see what I have in mind here, suppose I am watching a game and genuinely rooting for one of the teams; if so, then I will be first-personally invested in the team's success—but if my investment in it ends right after the game does, then I would not say that I love that team, since the care involved in love seems to involve a longer-term investment; by contrast, if I felt such investment every time I watched this team, then I would be more inclined to say that I love it. There may be no hard-and-fast rule about how lasting our care must be before it could qualify as love; the point is simply that some degree of lastingness seems to be a necessary ingredient in love.

This account of care leads us naturally to a second component of love, namely, *benevolence:* if we care about, and so necessarily desire, another's well-being, then we will have good reason to promote that well-being. Bishop Butler argues, accordingly, that when we care about others and are thus invested in them, this generates "an advocate within our own breasts, to take care of the interests of our fellow-creatures."[3] Thomas Aquinas draws the same inference: "When a man loves another with the love of friendship," Thomas writes, "he wills good to him, just as he wills good to himself; wherefore he apprehends him as his other self, insofar, to wit, as he wills good to him as to himself."[4] Again, the point is simply that, insofar as we are first-personally invested in others' well-being, we have reason to promote their well-being. This does not mean, of course, that we will always act on this reason; it might be, for instance, that we cannot actually do anything to promote their good, or that we have other, stronger reasons for doing something else. But caring about something does give us a dispositive reason to promote its good, which is what it means to say that benevolence is an essential component of love.

Consider an example: insofar as I care about the azaleas on the side of my house, I will want them to flourish, and insofar as I want them to flourish, I have reason to do things to make sure that they will; hence, if I notice that they look a little wilted, I have reason to water them; if I notice that they are crowded by some neighboring shrubs, I have reason to prune the shrubs; I likewise have reason to fertilize the soil, to read articles about azalea care, to add fresh mulch every spring, and so on. Naturally, the fact that I have such reasons does not by itself entail that I will actually do any of these things, since, again, I may have stronger reasons to do other things, just as I may be unable to do some of them; after all, if a loved one required urgent medical attention, then it would not make sense to spend a day caring instead for azaleas. But if it is in my power to do these things, yet I never do, it might cast doubt on whether I actually love the azaleas, since that would seem to indicate that my care-based reasons for acting are not very strong. As with azaleas, so with persons: if I care about them, then I have good reason to promote their well-being. And while that may not mean that I will always act on this reason—present circumstances may prevent it or I may have a more compelling reason to do something else—it would cast doubt on my supposed love for them if I could promote their good but never do.

To love other persons, then, is to care about them for their own sake and thus to have reason to promote their well-being. That brings us to one additional feature of what it means to value something for its own sake, which we can call *appreciation*. Very simply, to appreciate something is to see it as good and to be glad that it exists; so if I appreciate my friend's singing voice, I will not only perceive it as good but find gladness in it, too: I will be glad, for my friend, that they have this trait, just as I will be glad when that goodness is expressed.[5] Calvin thus insists, along these lines, that "we are bidden so to esteem and regard whatever gifts of God we see in other men that we may honor those men in whom they reside. For it would be great depravity on our part to deprive them of that honor which the Lord has bestowed upon them."[6] More recently, and more simply, Barbara Hilkert Andolsen claims that "love is the active affirmation of the goodness and beauty of the other."[7] The idea here is straightforward enough: if I love azaleas, I will not only care about and actively promote their flourishing, I will also delight in their goodness itself—the color and shape of their blooms, the sheen of their leaves, the hardiness of their branches, and so on. Likewise, if I love others, I will not only care about and actively promote their flourishing, I will also delight in that which is good about them—their sense of humor, their insights, their smile, their helpfulness, and so on.[8] This should help us to understand why appreciation is an important component of love, since it directs our valuing to "the thing itself," so to speak, and not just to its well-being.

This last point becomes even clearer when we observe that one of the goods we must appreciate is precisely the *integrity* of that which we love. To love something for its own sake, we must love it in its own right, which means, among other things, that if I love others, I must not only care about and seek their good, I must do so in such a way that I respect their dignity, which is why paternalism is a distortion—at best—of love. To take just one example, this is what Søren Kierkegaard has in mind when he claims that "to become one's own master, is the highest—and in love to help someone toward that, to become himself, free, independent, his own master, to help him stand alone—that is the greatest beneficence."[9] If I love others, then, I will want to promote their good, but if my love for them includes due respect for their integrity as persons, my promotion of their good must not violate their autonomy, their leading of their own life, and their own sense of what is good. Taking all this together, then, we can say that appreciation is an important component of love, for without it we might fail to value all the good things that persons have to contribute to the world, just as we might fail to value them as persons.

To love others thus means that we care about them, that we therefore have good reason to promote their good, and that we appreciate that which is good about them (including their integrity). Taken together, these mark off a particular way of valuing others for their own sake, the particular way we call "love."

Nothing I have said about love thus far is particularly Christian. To be sure, the sort of love I have described is distinct from some sorts of love that are further away from what Christians tend to mean by the term—erotic or romantic love, for instance. By itself, though, there is nothing Christian about our account. The agenda for the remainder of this section is thus fairly simple: we need to consider what, if anything, would qualify such love as Christian.

At the most basic level, love counts as Christian simply insofar as it is included in one's more fundamental love for God—insofar, that is, as love for others is itself an expression of one's devotion to God. Kierkegaard thus insists that "Christianity . . . makes every one of your relationships into a God-relationship," such that, even in loving others, God remains "the sole object of love."[10] And this is what Anders Nygren has in mind when he claims that "the Christian ethic is from first to last a religious ethic . . . inasmuch as the actual content of the ethical life is wholly determined by the religious relationship, by fellowship with God."[11] According to an old commonplace, bakers' work is Christian not because they put little crosses on everything they bake but because excellent baking is itself an act of devotion; likewise, if people's love for others is rooted in their devotion, then it is Christian—even if it looks much like non-Christian love—whereas if their love is not so rooted, then it is not. From this perspective, it is no accident that the commandment to love one's neighbor is second to the

commandment to love God with all one's heart, for the second commandment is supposed to follow from, and be included in, the first.

Based on claims we have already considered, it is not hard to see what
it might mean for one's love for others to be an expression of one's devotion. Recall the transitive property of love: if I care about someone, then
I will be inclined to care about what they care about; hence, if they care
about someone else, then I will be inclined to care about that other person, too, and my care for that person will itself be an expression of care for
the person I care about. We can say something similar of God: if I love
God, then I should love what God loves; hence, if God loves someone,
then I should love that person, too, and my love for that person will itself
be an expression of love for God. (Recall, too, that we can love someone
for the sake of another only if we love them for their own sake; otherwise,
we would not *love* them for another's sake.) Thomas Aquinas makes precisely this point: "When a man has friendship for a certain person, for his
sake he loves all belonging to him, be they children, servants, or connected
with him in any way. Indeed, so much do we love our friends, that for their
sake we love all who belong to them, even if they hurt or hate us; so that,
in this way, the friendship of charity extends even to our enemies, whom
we love out of charity in relation to God, to whom the friendship of charity is chiefly directed."[12] Hence, as Kierkegaard puts it, "It is thus as if God
were continually pointing away from himself, so to speak, and saying, 'If
you want to love me, then love the people you see; what you do for them,
you do for me.'"[13]

From this, it follows, first, that those who love God should love those
whom God loves, which means that if God loves everyone, then we should
love everyone, too—not only those we are close to, or those who are lovable, or those we would profit from loving, but *everyone*. Gustavo Gutierrez thus claims, in this regard, that "love for God is unavoidably expressed
through love of one's neighbor," which explains his insistence that "to love
one's brother, to love all persons, is a necessary and indispensable mediation of the love of God; it is to love God."[14] James Cone makes a similar
claim: "To accept God's act in Christ at the very core of one's existence,"
Cone maintains, "means a radical identification with all men. No one is
excluded. Every man necessarily becomes one's neighbor; his place in existence becomes ours, including the non-Christian."[15] The logic here is fairly
straightforward: if our love for God means that we should love those whom
God loves, and if God loves everyone, then we should love everyone.

If we suppose that those who love God should love those whom God loves, and that God's love is indeed universal, then it might seem to follow that we are obligated to love every one of the roughly seven and a half billion persons currently alive, and, indeed, every one of the one hundred billion persons who have ever lived, as well as everyone who ever will. It sometimes sounds as if this is what Kierkegaard means to say, as when he asserts, for instance, that "Christian love teaches us to love all people, unconditionally all."[16] But this seems implausible, not least because our love, as humans, is limited not only by selfishness, tribalism, favoritism, and the like but also by the brute fact of our finitude: if (a) love requires first-personal investment in others, and (b) human finitude means that there is only so much that any one of us can invest, it follows (c) that there is a limit to the number of others whom we can actually love. Think here of a rich person who invests one dollar in every stock on the New York Stock Exchange; this investment would not make a difference to any of these companies and, more to the point, the rich person would not thereby be significantly invested in any of them. As with stocks, so with other persons: if we were to try to love absolutely every person, we would end up investing a vanishingly small amount—virtually nothing—in any of them.

Small wonder, then, that Kierkegaard talks elsewhere not of loving each and every person in the entire world but of loving those who are "nearest" (which is how he understands the word "neighbor"); we hear something similar from Kazoh Kitamori, who maintains that "'neighbor' is a concept applicable to anyone at hand."[17] This seems more promising, but here we face a problem from the opposite direction: the mere fact that we love those who are nearest does not mean that we are loving as God loves, for if those nearest to us include only our kin, our tribe, our favorites, and so forth, then our love for those nearest to us will not look very much like God's does.

That brings us to a different account, according to which our love mirrors God's not because it actually includes every single person in its scope but because it is *disposed* to include everyone. We find a nice formulation of this account by Bishop Butler, who reasons that, "as man is so much limited in his capacity, as so small a part of the creation comes under his notice and influence, and as we are not used to consider things in so general a way; it is not to be thought of, that the universe should be the object of benevolence to such creatures as we are. Thus in the precept of our Savior, 'Be ye perfect even as your Father which is in heaven is perfect,' the perfection of the divine goodness is proposed to our imitation as it is promiscuous, and extends to the evil as well as the good; not as it is absolutely universal, imitation of it in this respect being plainly beyond us."[18] On this account, then, our love mirrors God's not because it actually includes everyone but because our hearts are disposed to love everyone; we should thus be disposed to love not only those who are lovable or who are naturally dear to us but the unlovable and the "strange," too. In the parable of the good Samaritan, this seems to be Jesus' own answer to the problem, for when a lawyer asks Jesus who his neighbor is—when he asks, that is, which persons he is bound to love—Jesus replies not by specifying the scope of his obligations but by pointing to the traits that would lead someone to be a neighbor to others. Parables notwithstanding, the idea is that our love can be universal not only if we actually love every single person in the world but if we are disposed to love all others; the latter, unlike the former, is a kind of universality that can be approximated by finite human beings.[19]

Thus far, then, I have claimed that love is Christian insofar as it is an expression of love for God, that it is such an expression if we love those whom God loves, and that we love those whom God loves insofar as we are disposed to love everyone. That brings us to a crucial clarification: to love others as God does also means that we *take sides* as God does, especially with the poor, the oppressed, the suffering, and the mistreated. Such taking sides should not be thought incompatible with the universality of love; after all, parents can simultaneously love all their children and yet be especially concerned with the well-being of one of them if they are hurt or sick.[20] Likewise—and more to the point—parents can simultaneously love all their children and yet, if one of their children is being mistreated by another one, they should surely stick up for the mistreated one. It would be perverse to suggest that parents' equal love for all their children entailed that they could not side with or otherwise take a special interest in a child who is suffering. (Needless to say, it would be vastly more perverse to suggest that parents should side with an abusive child over an abused child.) Just so, Christian theologians have insisted that God's universal love does not preclude but positively requires exactly such taking of sides: to give just one influential example, Gustavo Gutierrez maintains, for instance, that "the universality of Christian love is, I repeat, incompatible with the exclusion of any persons, but it is not incompatible with a preferential option for the poorest and most oppressed"; from this, it follows that "to preach the universal love of the Father is inevitably to go against all injustice, privilege, oppression, or narrow nationalism."[21] Just as parents are especially concerned when one of their children suffers or is mistreated, and just as they will be

especially invested in alleviating that child's suffering or rectifying mistreatment, so God is especially concerned with the poor and the oppressed.
To love others as God does, accordingly, we must likewise become disposed to take sides as God does.

Putting everything together, then, to love others is to value them for
their own sake, where this means that we care about their well-being, have
good reason to promote that well-being, and appreciate that which is good
about them. Such love is Christian when it is an expression of love for God,
and it is such an expression when our love for God disposes us to love
those whom God loves (namely, everyone) and to share God's preferential
option for those who are poor and oppressed.

This account raises an important question, namely, how persons can
cultivate a loving disposition toward others. Before turning to this question, however, we need to address a concern often aired about Christian
accounts of love. To see what this is, consider the fact that theologians have
often insisted that Christian love includes—or maybe just is—*self-sacrifice:*
so Luther claims, for instance, that a Christian "lives only for others and
not for himself";[22] Kierkegaard, that "love is a giving of oneself";[23] and
Nygren, that Christian love "is a love that gives itself away, that sacrifices
itself, even to the uttermost."[24] Claims like these seem to suggest that self-
sacrifice—pouring ourselves out for the sake of others—is a characteristic
feature of Christian love, such that one mark of "good Christians" would
be that they consistently put others' needs, desires, and interests ahead of
their own.

The putative generality of such claims has been subjected to serious
critique, especially (but not only) by feminist theologians. Their objection,
note well, is not to the idea that persons should sometimes put others'
needs, desires, and interests ahead of their own but that this is always and
everywhere what persons are supposed to do. They concede, accordingly,
that persons who always put themselves ahead of others probably do need
to be reminded that love may require self-sacrifice. But some persons—
often women, though of course not always and not only—are in danger of
making too much self-sacrifice for the sake of too many others. As feminist
theologians like Valerie Saiving, Barbara Andolsen, and Ada Maria Isasi-
Díaz have argued, claims about the need for self-sacrifice often take for
granted a characteristically upper-class, male perspective, and this, they
maintain, explains the approach's one-sided emphasis. When one's audience
is prone to selfishness, this emphasis makes sense. But not everyone is upper-
class, male, or prone to selfishness; other persons may be prone not to self-

ishness but to self-abnegation, in which case an emphasis on self-sacrifice may reinforce the sort of unjust social arrangements that require some persons to set themselves aside for the sake of others, just as it may encourage some persons to neglect or even lose their sense of self. Mary Daly thus points out that women have "hardly been helped by an ethic which reinforces the abject female situation," and Andolsen maintains that "women have too often found in practice that Christian self-sacrifice means the sacrifice of women for the sake of men."[25] Again, then, the concern is not with the idea that love sometimes requires self-sacrifice; the concern, rather, is that Christian love is sometimes *equated* with self-sacrifice, to such an extent that persons may feel that they are doing something wrong if they are not constantly giving themselves away.[26]

This is a serious concern. To address it, we need an account of vocation and an account of self-love. We considered vocation in chapter 5; there I claimed, among other things, that persons are called to love *particular* goods, which means that there are limits to the things and persons that a person is obligated to care for. That means, in turn, that persons are not obligated to pour themselves out for others per se, but simply to love those whom God has called them to love; I return to this point below. It also means that what matters, finally, is not whether I come first or others come first, but whether *God* comes first; sometimes this will entail putting others first, and other times it will entail putting oneself first.[27] This is related to the idea that one is called to love not only others but oneself as well. To see why one would be thus called, consider a simple pair of conditionals: if I love God, then I should love those whom God loves; if God loves me, then I should love myself. By itself, this already seems to suggest that I should care about myself (and not just others), that I have reason to promote my own well-being, and that I should appreciate—and even take pride in—that which is good about myself. This is something that womanist theologians like Delores Williams and Karen Baker-Fletcher have rightly stressed, often echoing Alice Walker's insistence that Black women must "*love themselves*. Regardless."[28] If these claims are correct, then it follows that loving God does not entail that one should simply neglect or negate oneself, though, again, there may be cases where one is indeed called to love others sacrificially.

Putting everything together, we can say that love involves care, benevolence, and appreciation, and that love is Christian when it is an expression of our love for God and, so, an expression of God's love for people. As such an expression, Christian love must apply not only to our friends or kin, nor only to those who are lovable, but to everyone, especially the "least of these." Naturally, this does not entail that we can or should actually love every single person as God does, but it does mean that we should be disposed to love people.

Cultivating Love

Supposing, then, that we should become disposed to mirror God's love for others. How would we go about becoming so disposed? Some think that we cannot, and that it therefore makes no sense to command someone to love others: Kant thus claims, for instance, that the sort of love we have been talking about "cannot be commanded, for no one has the power to love someone simply on command." From this, he concludes that when we are commanded to love our neighbors, this can involve only "practical love," that is, the duty to promote their well-being.[29] It is easy to see why Kant would think this: even if my life depended on it, I probably could not bring myself to obey a command to care about, appreciate, and want what's best for, say, mosquitoes. There is plainly a sense, then, in which this sort of love is not voluntary; I cannot simply decide to love certain things, which would seem to imply that I cannot simply obey a command to do so.

This is not the whole story, however. While we cannot simply decide to love something, we can grow to love it, and this growing-to-love is, to some extent, up to us. Agnes Callard talks about such growing-to-love under the heading of *aspiration*, in which we value a value that we do not yet have and thus try to cultivate that value by doing things that would help us develop it.[30] Suppose, for example, that I want to value the music that my children value: if so, I may spend time listening to it, talking with them about what they like about it, and trying to hear what is good about it.[31] If I already have negative associations with this music, or a distorted perception of it, then obviously I will have to work on ridding myself of these things. And I will have to get past whatever is not good about the music—clichés and lazy rhyme choices, for instance—not by pretending that these things are actually good but by resisting the urge to treat them as if they were sufficient reason to draw negative conclusions about the music as a whole. The point of all this, again, is to cultivate a value: in this case, my valuing of the music that my kids value. Hence, while musical taste may not be immediately and directly responsive to a command, it can be cultivated in response to one.

We can try a similar approach to cultivating our love for others and, in particular, to becoming the sort of persons who love others as God does. Within the Christian tradition, we find three sets of practices specifically designed to cultivate such love: the practice of beneficence, the practice of looking for the image of God in others, and the practice of forgiveness.

One way we can cultivate love for others, then, is to show them *beneficence*, that is, to invest in their well-being even if we do not yet care about them in the first-personal sense. The mechanism here is familiar enough: even if I do not care about certain persons, if I make an investment in their well-being, I now have a rooting interest in that well-being; my interest in their well-being can then dispose me to root not only for their well-being but for the persons themselves, at which point I have become invested in them (and not only in their well-being). We see this when someone drafts a player for a fantasy sports team, for instance, and ends up forming a disposition to root for that player even after the season is over; we also see it when unaffiliated voters put a political candidate's sign in their yard and then end up voting for that candidate. It makes sense, then, that when Therese of Lisieux wanted to cultivate love for a difficult person, she employed precisely this strategy: "There is one sister who has the knack of rubbing me the wrong way at every turn; her tricks of manner, her tricks of speech, her character, strike me as unlovable. . . . God must love her dearly, so I wasn't going to let this natural antipathy get the better of me. I reminded myself that charity isn't a matter of fine sentiments; it means doing things. So I determined to treat this sister as if she were the person I loved best in the world."[32] By seeking others' benefit, then, I can become invested in their well-being; by becoming invested in their well-being, I may become invested in them—in the persons themselves—and thus move from a beneficent attitude toward them to a benevolent one.

There is an obvious problem with this approach, however, namely, the problem of paternalism: if I seek to benefit others without respecting their dignity as persons, then I may grow in my sense of my own munificence but not in my love for the persons themselves. I would also be wronging the recipients of my beneficence, since persons deserve to be treated *as* persons. Hence, although beneficence can play a helpful role in cultivating in us an investment in others, we need to make sure we invest in others in such a way that their otherness, and they themselves, are appreciated and respected.

To meet this need, let us turn to a set of practices that cultivate love for others by *looking for the image of God in them*. Here Calvin's dictum is often cited: "There is but one way in which to achieve what is not merely difficult," he claims, "but utterly against human nature: to love those who hate us, to repay their evil deeds with benefits, to return blessings for reproaches. It is that we remember not to consider men's evil intention but to *look upon the image of God in them*, which cancels and effaces their transgressions, and with its beauty and dignity allures us to love and embrace them."[33] Many theologians have defended a view along these lines, but as it turns out, "looking for the image of God" can refer to several different practices. For one thing, looking for the image can mean, simply, that we see others as God's political representatives, so to speak, in the sense that our response to them would count as our response to God. The idea here is straightforward enough: our treatment of political representatives often counts as our treatment of those they represent, such that honoring ambassadors may count as honoring the countries they represent, just as attacking a battleship may count as attacking the country it represents. In the same way, if "bearing God's image" means that humans function as God's political representatives, as it were, then our treatment of others would count as our treatment of God. Basil of Caesarea has something like this in mind when he suggests that the devil "acted like an angry man who throws rocks at the emperor's image because he cannot throw them at the emperor himself."[34] Seeing others as God's representatives in this way would certainly encourage us to treat them well, or at least not treat them badly. But it is not clear how it would help us cultivate *love* for them, not least because we might treat them well (or not badly) simply for instrumental reasons, rather than for their own sake; after all, I might honor an emissary only so that things would go well for me or because I value the one they represent, but neither of those things need have anything to do with the emissary themselves.

That brings us to a different approach to this idea, in which our response to others counts as our response to God precisely because God *loves* them: if God loves them, then God is first-personally invested in their well-being; if God is first-personally invested in their well-being, then if I promote their well-being, I do something not only for them but for God, too. What's more, if I love God, then, by the now-familiar transitive property of love, I will want to love those whom God loves, such that my love for them can be an expression of my love for God (as David's love for Mephibosheth was an expression of his love for Jonathan). Our love for others can thus count as love for God, which can help us understand such claims as the following, from Gustavo Gutierrez: "Love for God," Gutierrez maintains, "is unavoidably expressed *through* love of one's neighbor. . . .

To love one's brother, to love all persons, is a necessary and indispensable mediation of the love of God; it is to love God"; Gutierrez concludes, then, that "an act of love toward them is an act of love toward God."[35] So then: if we love God, and God loves others, then we have reason to love them, too, and our treatment of them will count as our treatment of God. We can thus see them as representing God and, just so, as bearing God's image; our love for God therefore gives us reason to love others and to cultivate love for them—and, crucially, because God loves them for their own sake and in their own right, it gives us reason to love them that way.

To explain how we would cultivate such love, let us turn to a third sense in which we might look for the image of God in others, namely, the sense in which "the image of God" serves as a lens through which to see and interpret them. To understand how this works—and why it matters— we can begin by considering some ways that concepts can make it *harder* to love others. For one thing, using the wrong concepts can make it much harder to love others as the particular person each is. Recall here the "hermeneutical circle": as we read a novel or an essay, we can make sense of its parts only if we have some idea of the whole to which they contribute, yet we must be ready to revise our idea of the whole as we continue to encounter new parts. (This is one reason plot twists can be so interesting, since they force us to revise our sense of the whole and therefore to reinterpret all the preceding parts.) If I am unwilling to revise my idea of the whole, however, then I will have to force the parts to fit into my preconceptions and, so, not be responsive to their particularity; except in cases where nothing unexpected happens—as when a story conforms perfectly with the most well-worn clichés—this will invariably lead to misreadings. Likewise, if I have a sufficiently bad idea of what a novel is about or of what an essay is arguing, I will have a much harder time understanding its parts, and in many cases will simply end up misunderstanding them; this is one reason "standard readings" of certain texts can be so recalcitrant, even where they are demonstrably wrong.

As with texts, so with persons: we can understand what others are saying and doing only in light of a "sense of the whole," where this includes some idea of what kind of person they are, what sort of activity they are engaged in, what narrative arc their life is following, and the like. (I see a car driving fast and cutting off other cars on the highway. I interpret the driver as a reckless, self-important jerk. Needless to say, if I later discover that the driver was racing to the hospital, I would need to revise my interpretation.) If my idea of the whole is sufficiently off-base, or if my use of that idea is unresponsive to a person's particularity, then I will find it nearly impossible to see that person accurately and thus to love them in their own right. As Kierkegaard puts it, "When it is a duty in loving to love the people we see, *then in loving the actual individual person it is important that one does not substitute an imaginary idea of how we think or could wish that this person should be.* The person who does this does not love the person he sees but again something unseen, his own idea or something similar."[36] If we see people in light of concepts we associate with certain groups, accordingly, and if these concepts are either distorting or unresponsive to their particularity, then we will have a hard time (at best) getting to know them as they are and, so, loving them in their own right. (Suppose I see a man wearing fancy clothes and so assume that he is a rich person, and I associate "rich person" with snobbiness, insensitivity to the plight of others, being entitled, and so on. If these associations make it harder for me to see the ways he does not fit with my concept of him, then my concept gets in the way of seeing him for who he is.) By seeing others in light of distorting or reductive concepts, accordingly, I fail to do justice to their particularity and thus fail to love them in that particularity.

Bad concepts can thus make it harder for us to love others *in their own right*; they can also make it harder for us to *love* them in their own right. If I perceive certain persons in light of the concept "competitor," for instance, I may experience their good as at odds with mine and, so, not want them to get that good; depending on how significant that good is, this may mean that I cannot desire their well-being and thus cannot fully love them. (Basil characterizes this as "envy," which he defines as "distress caused by your neighbor's prosperity.")[37] If I am competing with opponents in checkers, then I will not want their pieces to jump mine, but this is an insignificant good in their lives; hence, my not wanting them to have it will not necessarily get in the way of my being invested in their well-being. By contrast, if I am competing for a scarce but important resource, such as a job or a would-be romantic partner, then I will not want my competitors to have a significant good and will therefore not want them to flourish in this respect. Seeing someone as a competitor can thus make it harder for me to love that person, precisely insofar as it makes it harder for me to desire the person's good.

By the same token, if the concepts I apply to others include a negative evaluation, then I may have a hard time appreciating that which is good about them or caring about their good and, in turn, have a harder time loving them. In some cases, this is a particularly pernicious instance of distortion, as when one sees others in light of a negatively biased preconception. If one associates negative concepts like "lazy," "stupid," and "self-important" with certain people—whether directly or by way of associating these concepts with a group concept that one applies to them—then one will be less sympathetic toward them, less likely to appreciate that which is good about them, less likely to want good things for them, and more likely to see their misfortune as deserved (and therefore not as something one should care about trying to avert). Howard Thurman provides a stark example of this: "When the Southern white person says, 'I understand the Negro,'" Thurman writes, "what he really means is that he has a knowledge of the Negro within the limitations of the boundaries which the white man has set up. The kind of Negro he understands has no existence except in his own mind."[38] Again, what we see in such cases is a particular form of distortion, in which we fail to see others for themselves because we see them only in light of mistaken preconceptions, and these preconceptions are such that we see these persons in a negative light. Needless to say, insofar as this is the case, we will not be able to love them in their own right.

This is not the only way that negative evaluations can make it harder to love others, however, for even correctly applied negative concepts can get in the way of loving them. If a certain person habitually lies, for instance, I may correctly apply the negative concept "liar" to them. But if I take the additional step of *identifying* them with this negative concept— seeing them as nothing but a liar or otherwise seeing "liar" as definitive of their identity—then I will find it vastly more difficult to want good things for them or to appreciate that which is good about them. This is what Jean Hampton characterizes as "moral hatred": "I may feel anger toward my attackers and call them 'evil' or 'wicked,'" Hampton writes, "because I am unable to comprehend why they should have done what they did to me unless they had lost to some significant degree the decency which normally is part of our humanity. Thus I see *them* as 'bad.' Not just their actions or their character traits but their entire nature as persons takes on an evil cast. . . . How could one hate the sin but not the sinner in this case?"[39] Hence, even if the negative concept we apply to people is accurate, it can make it harder to love them insofar as we identify them with that concept, for if we see them as fundamentally or exhaustively bad, we will not be able to see anything good about them or want good things for them.

Negative and distorting concepts can thus make it harder for us to love others, just as, by these same mechanisms, good concepts can help us to love them—and, in turn, serve as an effective remedy for negative and distorting ones.[40] That brings us back to Christianity's favorite candidate for such a good concept: the image of God. "Image of God" here refers to the idea that each of us *resembles* or *reflects* God. This is roughly what "image" means in a phrase like "spit and image" (or "spitting image," depending on one's linguistic scruples): to say that a child is the spit and image of their parents is to say that the child looks or acts very much like them; likewise here, the idea is that humans bear the image of God insofar as they look or act like God. To look for the image of God in this sense is thus to believe, with Kierkegaard, that "in each individual there continually glimmers that essential other, which is common to all, the eternal resemblance, the likeness."[41] Just as bad concepts can make it harder for us to see others with loving eyes, so this concept—the image of God—can help us to see others in the best possible light. The idea, then, is that if this concept plays the hermeneutical role of "the whole" in light of which we understand others, it will help us to love them.[42]

To be sure, there is more than one way of thinking about how humanity bears a resemblance to God. Some theologians have claimed that we reflect God's image insofar as we are rational; others, insofar as we are inherently relational; still others, insofar as we exercise dominion over the world. The mere fact that particular people are rational, relational, or in charge does not, however, mean that they resemble God; after all, CEOs who exploit their employees in order to maximize profits exhibit all three traits but do not thereby resemble God. What is missing here, arguably, is a resemblance to God's *character*: to bear God's image is not simply to reflect certain formal traits such as rationality, relationality, or dominion but to embody God's material traits, such as wisdom, justice, love, mercy, and the like. There is a reason traditional accounts have focused on formal rather than material traits, however, namely, the fact that we are sinful and so, apparently, have lost our material likeness to God.[43] In response to this objection, it is important to note that, on the present account, our resemblance to God is understood primarily as a matter of what we were created for and what we hope to be restored to, and that, just so, this resemblance is not completely vitiated, since (a) sin is not powerful enough to defeat the God in whom Christians hope and (b) eschatological fulfillment must stand in some recognizable continuity with our present reality (as I argue at length in the next chapter). Absent such qualifications, an account of human nature would reflect a Manichaean, rather than a Christian, theological sensibility.

Supposing, then, that we bear the image of God by bearing some resemblance to God's character; if so, what would it mean to look for that image in others? Here is one way of thinking about it. If God is infinitely good, then there are infinitely many ways that God's goodness can and should be reflected; this is one way of understanding what it would mean for all creation to be filled with God's glory. For God's infinite goodness to come to expression in and through finite creatures, then, each of them must express that goodness in their own, unique way—not only because they reflect this goodness in response to unique circumstances but also because they do so in a way that bears the stamp of their individuality, for again, God's infinite goodness can and should be infinitely expressed. We see a version of this approach in Schleiermacher, who maintains that each of us becomes a microcosm of the Infinite by gathering up and expressing the goodness expressed by others and, in turn, by adding our own contribution to the stockpile of goodness that others can gather up and express, in such a way that the plenitude of God's goodness comes to ever-fuller expression.[44] I say more about what this looks like in the next chapter; for now, the upshot is straightforward: on this account, to look for the image of God in others is to be on the lookout for the way that they can and do reflect God's infinite goodness. More specifically, it is to be on the lookout for the ways that they are *meant* to reflect God's infinite goodness, and thus to be disposed to appreciate whatever goodness their lives reflect and see this as a clue, as it were, to the goodness that could come to expression in their lives. We thereby cultivate a sort of proleptic vision, which is similar to something we often observe in parents and teachers: good parents and teachers are constantly on the lookout for evidence of goodness in a child, whether this be the goodness of kindness or of artistic talent or of intelligence. Once they spot evidence of it, they are likely not only to see it as a hint of the goodness this child might someday embody but also to encourage the child to do so. Not only that, but by seeing children in this way, parents and teachers can help them to see themselves this way and, in turn, to start patterning their lives after this vision. Proleptic vision can thus become a self-fulfilling prophecy, in other words.[45] Teresa of Avila nicely captures this line of thought, claiming that Christians must "look to see if there is something to love in the soul. And if there isn't anything lovable, but they see some beginning and readiness so that if they love this soul and dig in this mine they will find gold, their labor causes them no pain."[46]

If we assume, then, that all persons are made to reflect the image of God, then we should be on the lookout for the ways in which they do so. At the very least, this means that we can never simply identify persons with whatever is worst about them, much less be on the lookout for that which is worst about them, for no matter how bad they may be, we can still reasonably hope that they will reflect God's image as they were intended to. This is one reason for holding, with Bryan Stevenson, that "each of us is more than the worst thing we've ever done."[47] Think here, again, of the hermeneutical circle: if I am watching a movie in which I know there is a Big Twist, I will assume that characters may not be what they initially seem, for the simple reason that they may turn out very differently once the twist has been revealed. We can do something similar when we encounter people in real life: if I know that the people around me are meant to bear the image of God, then irrespective of how awful they may seem, I should hold off on making any final judgments about them, since I know that they may turn out very differently in the end. Negatively, then, looking for the image of God in others means that we should resist the urge to identify people with that which is worst about them.

One way of resisting this urge, in turn, is to practice what Kierkegaard calls "mitigating explanation": "It is always the explanation that makes something what it now becomes," he writes. "The fact or the facts are basic, but the explanation is the decisive factor." Kierkegaard points out, accordingly, that "it is always in my power, if I am one who loves, to choose the most lenient explanation. If, then, this more lenient or mitigating explanation explains what others light-mindedly, harshly, hardheartedly, enviously, maliciously, in short, unlovingly explain summarily as guilt, if the mitigating explanation explains this in another way, it removes now one and now another guilt and in this way reduces the multitude of sins or hides it."[48] The idea here is straightforward enough: when I observe others, I not only ascertain facts about what they are doing but also interpret those facts in light of larger narratives and evaluative frameworks. Suppose, then, that I discover that certain students have plagiarized significant parts of a research paper. I might interpret this so that it reflects very badly on their character ("These students are cheaters, plain and simple!") or less badly ("These students would never have done this if they weren't under so much pressure right now"); I can likewise interpret their plagiarism as intentional or accidental, deceptive or foolish, or in any number of other ways. Naturally, whatever interpretation I choose will have to do justice to the facts; there are limits, accordingly, to interpretive leniency. The point here is simply that we are (and must be) constantly interpreting what others are doing, and that we can do so in terms of harsher, more condemnatory frameworks, or in light of more sympathetic, understanding frameworks. By trying to interpret others in light of a sympathetic sort of framework, we resist the urge to see them in the worst possible light as well as the urge to identify them with that which is worst about them.

More positively, to look for the image of God in others means, first, that we should be *primed* to see it in them and therefore primed not only to see good things in them but also to see these as glimpses of who they might be.[49] To understand how this works, consider a few examples. If we read an article published in a "good" journal by a "good" scholar, then we will be more inclined to see the article itself as good and, so, to see its ideas and arguments as good ones. (This is one reason journals anonymize the review process, since the so-called halo effect can increase the likelihood of false positives.) Likewise, if I hear a song being played by someone whom I take to have especially good taste, I will be inclined to perceive it as a good song and thus to appreciate particular things about it. In the same way, if certain people seem intelligent, I will be more likely to take what they are saying to be intelligent, just as I will be more likely to assume that their apparently unintelligent statements are to be explained as jokes or as mis-interpretations on my part. The point here, more generally, is that if we assume that someone has such-and-such trait, we will be inclined to per-ceive the person's words, actions, and other traits as manifestations of that trait. Something similar happens when we strongly associate certain traits with one another, such that we assume that someone who has one trait has certain others: we might therefore assume that someone who has a fancy British accent is classy and clever, and we might further assume that some-one who is classy and clever is a good person; these assumptions, too, will lead us to see someone's words and actions as evidencing those traits. These points should seem familiar, since we considered them in chapter 2. Their upshot for the present discussion is that if we assume that people bear the image of God, and especially if this is the most fundamental assumption we make about them, then we will be much more likely to see their words, actions, and other traits as would-be manifestations of that image and we will therefore be much more likely to appreciate that which is good about them and to see it as part of the larger goodness they are meant to embody in the world. We will be primed, accordingly, to catch glimpses of people's creativity or fortitude or gentleness, for instance, or of their being good with kids or animals or words. Again, insofar as we assume that all persons bear the image of God—insofar as we assume that this is their most basic, and therefore salient, feature—then we will be disposed to perceive them as such, and will therefore be disposed to see the ways they reflect God's goodness.[50]

The more we practice looking at others in this way, then, the more we will become disposed to see them as reflecting God's goodness; we will likewise become more skillful and resourceful at doing so. Kierkegaard offers us the striking metaphor here of a hunter who has become adept at tracking his prey: "Because with each year he gains experience, becomes more and more inventive, overcomes more and more difficulties, so that he, the old experienced hunter, now knows how to track the game when no one else knows how, now discerns signs that no one else understands how to use, now has worked out a more ingenious way to set his snares, so he is always fairly sure of success in having a good hunt even when all others are unsuccessful."[51] We are thus invited to imagine a hunter who has learned, over time, to spot a broken twig here, a half-eaten leaf there, and who therefore knows where and when a particular animal has passed through, just as we can imagine the hunter knowing that if, say, he places a fresh carcass upwind from a particular spot and then waits, the animal will come into the open. With every successful hunt, the expert hunter's repertoire grows, thereby making it more likely that future hunts will be successful. In the same way, our repertoire should grow every time we succeed in catching a glimpse of God's image in others, for every time we spot an example of what it looks like to embody that image, it gives us more to work with when we look for that image in others still. And because there is no end, in principle, to the ways that God's infinite goodness can and should be expressed, it follows that there is no limit, in principle, to the stock of examples that we can use in order to help us spot that image in an unfamiliar case. Hence, each time I see people embodying the image of God in their own way—bringing God's infinite goodness to expression in their individuality, with their own "proprietary blend"—it should enable me to spot other embodiments, which should enable me to spot still others, and so on, in an endless honing and enrichment of my ability to perceive God's image. Once again, then, unlike other categories that we might use in order to make sense of others, the category "image of God" should continually open us up to, rather than close us off from, the particular reality of others.

By the self-fulfilling mechanism discussed earlier, moreover, the more we see others as embodying the image of God, the more likely they will be to embody it—and the more they embody it, the more likely we will be to see it. Here is an important disanalogy from hunting: whereas a hunter's quarry should become less likely to conform to the hunter's perception of it (if, say, the quarry knows that it is being tracked), other persons are likely to grow into the good, image-bearing traits that we see in them, not least insofar as our perception of them enables them to perceive these *as* good traits. Think here of the difference it can make when a strong-willed girl is valued precisely for her strong will and can thus experience this aspect of herself not as evidence that she is "difficult" but as part of what it means for her to embody God's image; instead of doing her best to suppress this aspect of her personality, she may now learn to harness it and draw on it as a way of standing up for people or becoming more resolute in the face of various temptations, and she may thus intentionally use this trait to reflect God's image in the world. By seeing others as God's image, accordingly, we can help them embody that image and, in turn, render God's image in them more visible to themselves and others. "To themselves" is crucial, for we often find it difficult to spot the image of God not only in others but in ourselves as well. By looking for the image of God in others, therefore, we can help them see it in themselves. We can thus help one another to meet Karen Baker-Fletcher's exhortation: "Surely if we are created in the likeness of God," she urges, "we can love ourselves as we are scripturally challenged to do. If that likeness of God is within us, surely we can find God in ourselves, realizing empowerment and our full potential as we learn to love God and ourselves."[52]

Thus far, it might sound as if looking for God's image is a more or less solitary endeavor; surely that is what the hunter metaphor would encourage us to think. To round out this account, then, it is important to mention the church's role in training us to perceive others in this way. The idea here is simple: in the church, we are surrounded by people who have devoted themselves to God, who are thereby bringing their lives more and more into conformity to that devotion, and, so, whose lives should more and more overtly reflect God's image; by learning to spot the image of God in these more overt cases, we should become more disposed and better able to spot it in more difficult ones. Just as teachers of logic help students identify logical fallacies by using clear-cut, tailor-made examples before asking them to spot examples in the wild, so Christians are surrounded, in church, by people who should offer fairly clear-cut, tailor-made examples of God's image; these examples should give Christians plenty of practice in spotting that image and should therefore help them spot it more easily in the persons they encounter outside church. Needless to say, Christians should also be surrounded, in church, by persons who see others this way, which should likewise have a formative influence on them; to understand how this works, it should suffice to recall our discussion of imitation in chapter 4. The church should likewise train Christians not only to perceive others in a particular way but also to *care* about them, for if Christians are called to love one another as themselves, then they will likewise love those whom others love and thereby enlarge the circle of those whom they care about.[53]

Looking for God's image can thus dispose us to appreciate the goodness in others and provide us with more and more resources with which to do so; it can likewise help us resist the urge to see others in light of negative or distorting concepts. If we also see others as God's representatives, then we should be increasingly disposed both to care about them and to see them in the best possible light. Looking for God's image can thus help us to love others, but a serious problem remains: what if they have wronged us or someone else we care about?

Even if we see others in the best possible light, we may still find it difficult to love them insofar as we are holding something against them. If I feel that certain people have wronged me or someone I care about, then I may want to get even with them or, more generally, I may want bad things to happen to them, in which case I will have a hard time wanting *good* things for them. Feelings of resentment, anger, and hatred can thus get in the way of our ability to love others.

Forgiveness is, among other things, the practice of setting aside such feelings.[54] (I say more about how this works, and what it amounts to, presently.) As such, it would appear tailor-made to help us love others in the face of their wrongdoing. We should not be too quick, though, to assume that these feelings ought to be set aside; after all, resentment, anger, and even hatred give expression to the belief that we ought not to be mistreated, that we have been wronged, and that justice matters. Howard Thurman explains: "As they [the disinherited] look out upon their world, they recognize at once that they are the victims of a system of denial of the rights and privileges that are theirs, by virtue both of their being human and of their citizenship. Their acute problem is to deal with the estimate that their environment places upon them; for the environment, through its power-controlling and prestige-bearing representatives, has announced to them that they do not rate anything other than that which is being visited upon them. If they accept this judgment, then the grounds of their self-estimate is destroyed, and their acquiescence becomes an endorsement of the judgment of the environment. . . . If they reject the judgment, hatred may serve as a device for rebuilding, step by perilous step, the foundation for individual significance; so that from within the intensity of their necessity they declare their right to exist, despite the judgment of the environment."[55] Thurman's point here is that when persons are wronged, it can feel as if the wrongdoer (and others) are saying that they do not deserve to be treated justly; in such a case, hatred and other vindictive passions make a counterstatement to the effect that their dignity as persons should be respected and that they do *not* deserve to be treated this way. Absent such emotional responses, persons might find it harder to resist the message implicit in their mistreatment, just as wrongdoers, too, might find it harder to resist that message.

If forgiveness involves setting aside these feelings, then the crucial question is how we can forgive without thereby condoning the wrong that has been done.[56] To address this issue, it is important to note, first, that setting aside our vengeful feelings toward wrongdoers is distinct from releasing them from punishment.[57] Thomas Aquinas makes precisely this point in his commentary on Colossians 3:13: "One forgives an injury," Thomas explains, "when he does not hold a grudge [*rancorem*] against the person who did it to him, and does not injure him in return [*nec malum contra ipsum procurat*]. Still, when punishment is necessary, the person committing the injury must be punished."[58] The distinction here is straightforward enough: on the one hand, we can hold on to our hatred for persons even if we release them from punishment, as when our hatred runs so deep that we want nothing further to do with them and thus refuse even to press charges against them, for instance, or when we do not press charges because we are scared that the wrongdoers will retaliate against us if we do. On the other hand, and more important for the present point, I can let go of my hatred for persons but still want them to be punished for what they did; we saw a striking example of this from several of the people whose loved ones were murdered at Emanuel African Methodist Episcopal Church in Charleston in June 2015: during a sentencing hearing, Bethane Middleton-Brown (sister of the Rev. Depayne Middleton-Doctor) told the unrepentant murderer, "I wanted to hate you, but my faith tells me no. I wanted to remain angry and bitter, but my view of life won't let me"; likewise, Dan Simmons Jr. (son of the Rev. Daniel Simmons Sr.) told the murderer, "I forgive you. I know that you don't understand that, but God requires me to forgive you. I forgive you."[59] Many others expressed similar sentiments. If we take their statements at face value, we can conclude that they have, in fact, renounced the hatred and vengefulness they might have felt toward the murderer. But this obviously does not entail that they think he ought to go unpunished; they are saying these things *at a sentencing hearing*, after all. Again, then, the fact that people set aside their hatred or resentment does not mean that they think wrongdoers should go unpunished. Hence, if punishment can express that what someone did was wrong, then forgiveness does not by itself entail that I am condoning that wrong-doing, for in that case, my vindictive passions are not the only thing saying that it was wrong.[60]

It is also useful, in this context, to observe a distinction between re-sentment and hatred, on the one hand, and indignation, on the other: resentment and hatred respond to mistreatment by saying, as it were, "You have wronged me (or others), and I am holding it against you"; whereas indignation says, "I (or others) should not be treated this way."[61] In both cases, we react to mistreatment *as* mistreatment and thus experience it as wrong. In the case of resentment, however, our reaction condemns the wrongdoer; in indignation, by contrast, it condemns the wrong itself. Re-sponding to mistreatment with indignation rather than resentment is thus one way of doing what Augustine famously enjoined, namely, showing love for persons but hatred for sin.[62] And it opens up the possibility that persons who forgive—and thus set aside their vengeful desires—can still oppose, and so not condone, wrongdoing.

Christianity can supply some additional resources for addressing this issue, but to see what these are, we need to get a clearer picture of what forgiveness involves. Crucially, we do not count as having forgiven some-one merely because we no longer have vengeful feelings toward them, for our vengefulness could simply have run out of steam. To count as having forgiven, accordingly, we must *set aside* these feelings, which is to say that forgiveness must be an *act* rather than something that simply happens; to say that forgiveness must be an act, in turn, entails that it must be done for a reason.[63] Not just any reason, however: if we were to set aside our vengefulness solely for our own sake—solely for the sake of our health, for instance—then our so setting it aside would not count as forgiveness (at least not in the Christian sense). Rather, for it to count as forgiveness, we have to set aside our vengefulness for a *moral* or *other-regarding* reason and must throw our evaluative weight behind this reason, so to speak, by giving it a certain priority among our normative commitments and thus treating that reason as more basic than our desire for vengeance. With respect to setting aside our desire for vengeance, notice that, on the present account, forgiveness neither means nor requires that we no longer have any venge-ful desires; it means, rather, that these desires have been subordinated to an other-regarding reason and, so, been put in their place. With respect to forgiveness, consider some suitably other-regarding reasons for setting aside our desire for vengeance: if I value my relationship with the wrong-doer, for instance, then I may have good reason to set aside my desire for vengeance; likewise, if I know that I, too, am a wrongdoer, and I thus feel compassion for other wrongdoers, then I may set aside my desire for vengeance. If we were to throw our moral weight behind a reason like this and thus de-prioritize our desire for vengeance, then we would count as forgiving a wrongdoer. On the present account, that is what it means to forgive someone.

That brings us to some specifically Christian reasons for forgiving others. If we love God, then we will want to love those whom God loves (for their own sakes); in that case, our desire to love them might give us reason to set aside our desire for vengeance. As Marilyn McCord Adams puts it, for the Christian, "his/her love of God will bring a dedication to learning, as nearly as possible, to seeing as God sees and loving as God loves, or at least as God wants and enables one to see and love."[64] On Adams's account, seeking to love as God loves is precisely what enables us to forgive others. Then again, if I know how much I have been (and need to be) forgiven, then I may feel compassion toward other wrongdoers and thus have reason to treat them the way I would want to be treated—with forgiveness. We hear something along these lines from Bonhoeffer, among many others: "When God was merciful to us," he writes, "we learned to be merciful with one another. When we received forgiveness instead of judgment, we too were made ready to forgive each other. What God did for us, we then owed to others. The more we received, the more we were able to give. . . . Thus God taught us to encounter one another as God has encountered us in Christ."[65] So then: forgiveness is setting aside our desire for vengeance in view of an other-regarding reason, and Christianity supplies several such reasons, including (a) the desire to love others because God loves them and (b) the desire to offer others the grace and compassion that we know we ourselves need.

We see an example of such forgiveness during the Montgomery Bus Boycott. Just when it seemed that the Montgomery Improvement Association was about to find vindication in the courts—after six long months of walking, carpooling, and organizing—the M.I.A.'s recording secretary, the Rev. U. J. Fields, publicly accused the movement's leaders of embezzling funds. It turns out that the Rev. Mr. Fields leveled this charge because he was upset about the fact that he had not been reelected to his position, but that did not change the fact that such a charge could seriously compromise the boycott's credibility and threaten its hard-won progress. The M.I.A.'s leaders had good reason to be angry, accordingly. Yet they responded not with hatred or retaliation but with an exhortation to forgiveness. At the movement's next meeting, therefore, the Rev. Dr. Martin Luther King Jr. first implored everyone present to take a compassionate perspective on Rev. Fields: "We are all aware of the weaknesses of human nature," he reminded them. "We have all made mistakes along the way of life, and we have all had moments when our emotions overpowered us." By reminding them of their own failings, Dr. King was trying to soften their hearts toward the Rev. Mr. Fields, and he was also giving them a reason to forgive him, namely, the recognition that we all need grace. With that reason in view, Dr. King called them to set aside whatever vengefulness they may have been feeling toward the Rev. Mr. Fields: "Now some of us are here this evening to stone one of our brothers because he has made a mistake," Dr. King remarked. "But let him who is without sin cast the first stone." He then concluded by invoking the parable of the prodigal son: "Will we be like the unforgiving elder brother, or will we, in the spirit of Christ, follow the example of the loving and forgiving father?"[66] The Rev. Mr. Fields then addressed the members of the gathering, and, when he finished, was met with warm applause—apparently they were, indeed, willing to forgive him. To be sure, members of the movement had good reason to be angry with the Rev. Mr. Fields, but if Dr. King's account is to be believed, they forgave him because they recognized that we should give others the grace that each of us requires—the grace that God has freely given each of us. This episode thus nicely exemplifies the sort of forgiveness we have been discussing, in which persons set aside their vengeful feelings for the sake of an other-regarding reason.

With that, we can return to the issue of condonation. Those who forgive for Christian reasons can still seek non-vengeful punishment for a wrongdoing and can remain indignant about it, as can those who forgive for non-Christian reasons. But Christians have two additional resources with which to resist condonation. On the one hand, their sense of moral worth should be rooted in, and so safeguarded by, God's recognition of that worth. This is the sort of thing James Cone has in mind, for instance, when he claims that "the oppressed know that they have a *somebodiness* that is guaranteed by God who alone is the ultimate sovereign of the universe."[67] We hear something similar from Marilyn McCord Adams: "For each created person," she writes, "the primary source of meaning and satisfaction will be found in his/her intimate personal relationship with God. This relationship will also be the context in which a created person can be best convinced of his/her worth, because it is the place where God's love for the individual is most vividly and intimately experienced."[68] Persons whose sense of moral worth is guaranteed by God are thus in position to experience demeanment *as* demeanment and so to feel appropriately indignant in response. They are likewise safeguarded from the temptation to condone such treatment *to themselves*, for the simple reason that they know it to be at odds with their transcendent worth. Because their worth is guaranteed by God, then, they need not resort to "vengeful passions" in order to secure their sense of self-worth. (If I were the best golfer alive, I would not feel the need to defend myself against the blustering trash talk of the course duffer.)

On the other hand, Christians should trust that God will vindicate them and, accordingly, that they do not have to vindicate themselves (or be vindictive). This brings us to the realm of some biblical claims to the effect that believers should leave vengeance to God. To be sure, such claims may seem to suggest that we should not, in fact, set aside our desire for vengeance but rather entertain the grandest of revenge fantasies—as if I were to say, by analogy, "I'm not going to get back at you, but only because I want to let my martial-artist cousin do it for me." This is not the only way to understand these claims, however. On another plausible understanding, God's vengeance differs from ours in this crucial respect, that whereas our getting even involves wanting bad things for others, God's does not. Thomas Aquinas draws precisely this distinction: "In the matter of vengeance," he writes, "we must consider the mind of the avenger. For if his intention is directed chiefly to the evil of the person on whom he takes vengeance and rests there, then his vengeance is altogether unlawful: because to take pleasure in another's evil belongs to hatred, which is contrary to the charity whereby we are bound to love all men. . . . If, however, the avenger's intention be directed chiefly to some good, to be obtained by means of the punishment of the person who has sinned (for instance that the sinner may amend, or at least be restrained and others not disturbed, that justice may be upheld, and God honored), then vengeance may be lawful, provided other due circumstances be observed."[69] Imagine a case where someone fouled me during a basketball game: if I know that the referee will enforce the rules and that my cause will therefore be vindicated, I do not have to take vengeance into my own hands. In the same way, if we trust that God will vindicate our cause, then we can set aside our own desire for vengeance without thereby condoning wrongdoing. Because Christians can look to God both for their worth and for their vindication, they can set aside their vindictive passions without thereby condoning wrongdoing.

Christians have good reasons to forgive, then, and they have faith-specific resources that enable them to do so without thereby condoning wrongs. This leaves us with an important question: under what circumstances should a Christian forgive? More precisely, under what circumstances *may* we forgive, and under what circumstances *must* we? With respect to the question of when it is permissible to forgive, many have suggested that we may forgive wrongdoers only if they are sincerely repentant for the wrongs they have done, for otherwise, the thinking goes, we will be condoning what they have done, letting them off the hook too cheaply, and re-victimizing ourselves.[70] There is at least one obvious instance where sincere repentance would seem to be a necessary condition of forgiveness, namely, the case of self-forgiveness: I cannot rightly forgive myself for wrongdoing unless I truly repent for that wrong; otherwise, I would indeed be letting myself off the hook too easily and not taking my wrongdoing seriously enough. In the case of others' wrongdoing, though, matters are a bit more complicated. Recall that on the present model, the fact that we forgive others does not necessarily mean that we release them from punishment, nor that we let go of our indignation over being wronged; even if we do not require sincere penitence on their part, accordingly, this does not mean that we cannot hold wrongdoers accountable, nor that we are condoning their wrongdoing. Requiring penitence is not the only way of ensuring that we are not condoning wrongdoing, therefore, which obviously undercuts the chief motivation for maintaining such a requirement. Recall, too, that Christians are to entrust their desires for vengeance to God; hence, insofar as a requirement of repentance is an expression of such a desire, as it sometimes seems to be—as if we were saying, "I won't forgive you for this until I know that you feel bad enough about it," and thus as if we were willing to forgive wrongdoers only when they had exacted our vengeance upon themselves—then, in imposing this as a condition of forgiveness, we would precisely *not* be entrusting our vengefulness to God. Taking these points together, then, it would appear that Christians may forgive others even in the absence of sincere repentance, for in so doing, they are not necessarily condoning wrongdoing.

The trickier question of when we *must* forgive arises, in part, because the New Testament seems pretty clear that Christians are obligated to forgive others, yet there are cases where it seems wrong to insist that someone is obligated to do so. To take the most troubling sort of example, consider a case where children have been abused by a trusted adult: do the children have an obligation to forgive the abuser? Do they have an obligation to do so immediately after being abused—or, perversely, even as they are being abused? Should they feel guilty if they are unable to forgive their abuser? If they are obligated to forgive, is there any reason that even the abuser cannot hold them to this obligation? These are difficult questions, to say the least, and they should help us see some of the problems that may arise if we were to treat forgiveness as if it were always obligatory. In order to address these issues, it might be best if we were to think of forgiveness as an obligation, but an obligation of the sort that allows for exceptions—which would be to say that Christians may have a general, but not exceptionless, obligation to forgive others. In that case, we could treat our obligation to forgive in much the same way that Jesus treated the obligation to keep the Sabbath: just as keeping the Sabbath allows for exceptions when these are required for the sake of loving others or taking care of one's own needs, so our duty to forgive might allow for exceptions in similar circumstances.[71] ("The duty of forgiveness was made for humans," Jesus might thus say, "not humans for the duty of forgiveness.") In exceptional circumstances, then, exceptions may be warranted: hence in extreme cases—cases of trauma and severe mistreatment, for instance, particularly when people are liable to internalize the demeaning message implicit in that mistreatment—it might actually be wrong to suggest that persons have an obligation to forgive, since feelings of vengefulness might then be their only means of holding on to their moral worth. In such cases, it seems better to focus not on forgiveness but on helping people acquire the resources they would need in order, eventually, to be able to let go of this defense mechanism—it would be better, in other words, to help them see God's love for them as that which is fundamentally true, help them experience that love as proof and guarantee of their worth, help them know that they should not have been treated as they were, recognize that God is utterly opposed to their mistreatment, trust that God will therefore vindicate them, and work with them to make sure that the wrongdoer is appropriately punished. Once they could experience these things as true, their vengeful feelings would not be their only means of holding on to and asserting their moral worth, at which point they could set those feelings aside without thereby condoning their mistreatment.

Exceptional cases like these thus help us to see more clearly what is going on in ordinary cases of (Christian) forgiveness. In such cases, to forgive is to set aside our desire for vengeance, and to do so for the sake of loving others as God does while trusting God for vindication. In forgiving others, accordingly, we do not condone their wrongdoing, since our sense of moral worth is rooted in God's recognition of that worth, just as our desire for justice is entrusted to God. By forgiving them, we can now desire good things for wrongdoers rather than bad things—or, perhaps more precisely, we can want good things for them *more* than we want bad things for them— and we can thereby return to having a benevolent attitude toward them.[72]

With that, we return to the place where we began. Christians are to love others as themselves, and thus to care about them, appreciate them, and want good things for them. This is often easier said than done, however, which is one reason Christianity includes several practices that are designed to cultivate such love. By practicing beneficence, we can become increasingly invested in others' well-being and, so, eventually grow to care about them in their own right. By looking for the image of God in others, we can prime ourselves to see others as such and thus to see them in the best possible light. And by forgiving others, we can set aside our vengeful desires—our desire for bad things to happen to others—so that we can once again desire good things for them. By doing these things, then, the hope is that, over time, we will grow in our disposition and ability to love others. That brings us to one additional set of considerations: if Christians are called to love others as ourselves, does this mean that we must work for justice? And if we are called to work for justice, is there a Christian way of doing so? To these considerations I now turn.

Love and Justice

Some theologians have maintained that Christian love is incompatible with justice. We hear something along these lines from Anders Nygren, who claims that "where spontaneous love and generosity are found, there the order of justice is obsolete and invalidated."[73] Emil Brunner likewise char- acterizes Christian love as "the incomprehensible gift, bound to no law of retributive justice and standing in absolute contrast to what we must call just in the things of this world"; from this, Brunner draws the conclusion that the rule of the Gospel "consists precisely in the cessation of all de- serving, in the denial of all lawful claims, and is hence the antithesis of the law of worldly justice."[74] Not to be outdone, the subtitle of one of Stanley Hauerwas's books describes justice as, simply, "a bad idea."[75] The train of thought here seems to go something like this: Christian love is marked by the offering of pure, unmerited grace; unmerited grace is obviously un- deserved; hence Christian love utterly transcends the order of desert and thus the order of justice.[76]

It is not at all clear, however, why *going beyond* the requirements of justice would necessarily be at odds with those requirements. To be sure, there are some cases where this may be true: as we have just discussed, to forgive people may mean that I set aside my desire to see deservedly bad things happen to them; in a case like this, accordingly, Christian love may not only go beyond justice but actually be incompatible with it, assuming that forgiveness is not usually something that wrongdoers deserve. It is not clear, however, why one would think that love would always have this character. Suppose I see a boy and a girl at our neighborhood playground, and the boy is demeaning and hurting the girl. If I love the girl who is being demeaned and hurt, I will surely step in to help. My so doing would hardly count as going beyond justice, much less as antithetical to it, for the simple reason that, in this case, love would consist in trying to make sure the girl was treated as she deserved to be treated. Indeed, we can go one step further: it would be perverse to try to understand a case like this by analogy with the case of forgiving a wrongdoer, for the simple reason that it would be perverse to suggest that, in trying to prevent the girl's mistreatment, I would be going beyond justice or beyond what she deserves. Hence, although there may be instances where Christian love could be said to go beyond justice, this hardly entails that the two are incompatible or antithetical. Small wonder, then, that the Christian tradition includes several voices that disagree with Nygren, Brunner, and Hauerwas; Basil of Caesarea thus maintains, for instance, that "it is necessary to give to each what is due in fairness" and that "apportioning to each what he is due is a trait of a noble mind unfettered in any way by human necessity," just as Gustavo Gutierrez claims that "to preach the universal love of the Father is inevitably to go against all injustice, privilege, oppression, or narrow nationalism."[77] Loving others may thus require us to give them more than they deserve, but it will never require anything less than that.

Obviously, this raises the question of what, from a Christian perspective, people deserve or have a right to, and just as obviously, we cannot offer anything approaching a complete answer to this question here.[78] But we can supply at least one crucial piece of the answer: humans have a right not to be treated as if they were of less value than they actually are, or, in sum, they have a right not to be demeaned; positively stated, humans have a right to be treated in accordance with their worth, which is to say that they are wronged insofar as they are not so treated.[79] "Demeanment," here, would thus include any way of treating others as "lowly": taking up a dehumanizing attitude toward people, for instance, or humiliating them, insulting them, being cruel to them, silencing them, or even being oblivious to their experience because they do not "count." To demean people in any of these ways is to wrong them, to treat them otherwise than they deserve, and thus to perpetrate an injustice against them. The idea here, accordingly, is that the concept "demeanment" picks out an especially important class of injustices and, indeed, that such demeanment is always unjust, even if not every injustice is an instance of demeanment.

To be sure, not everything that is *experienced* as demeaning is *actually* demeaning. Some privileged persons think that manual labor is demeaning, for instance, and would thus experience it as demeaning if, say, they had to clean their own toilets. There is nothing inherently demeaning about such work, though there are circumstances in which toilet cleaning could be used to demean someone. By the same token, not everything that is actually demeaning is experienced as such: hence, if people have internalized the idea that they are worth less than they actually are, they may not experience demeanment *as* demeanment. For our purposes, then, the point is simply that all actual demeanments are unjust, not that everything that is experienced as such is demeaning, nor that everything not experienced as such is not.

That brings us to the distinctively Christian element of this account: the fundamental reason all humans have dignity and worth and, so, why they deserve to be treated accordingly, is because each of us bears the image of God. James Cone thus insists that "it is the biblical concept of the image of God that makes black rebellion in America human. . . . In a world in which persons are oppressed, the image is human nature in rebellion against the structures of oppression."[80] We hear something similar from Gustavo Gutierrez: "If humanity, each person, is the living temple of God," he writes, then "we meet God in our encounter with others. . . . This explains why 'a man who sneers at the poor insults their maker.'"[81] We hear the same thing from earlier theologians such as Calvin, who draws several important implications from the idea that we bear God's image: "This doctrine, however, is to be carefully observed, that no one can be injurious to his brother without wounding God himself. Were this doctrine deeply fixed in our minds, we should be much more reluctant than we are to inflict injuries. Should any one object, that this divine image has been obliterated, the solution is easy; first, there yet exists some remnant of it, so that man is possessed of no small dignity; and, secondly, the celestial Creator himself, however corrupted man may be, still keeps in view the end of his original creation; and according to his example, we ought to consider for what end he created men, and what excellence he bestowed upon them above the rest of living things."[82] We could cite countless precedents, but the point is simple: if humans bear the image of God, it follows that we have immeasurable worth and that we deserve to be treated accordingly.

We can elaborate this notion by recalling some claims from the previous section. On the one hand, each human being bears God's image in the sense of *representing* God, which is to say that we are God's representatives or stand-ins; to violate a human being's dignity is thus to violate the dignity of God's emissary and thus to violate God's own dignity. On the other hand, we also bear God's image in the sense that we are meant to *resemble* God: each of us is meant to express God's infinite goodness in our own way, and each of these expressions is immeasurably precious; to prevent that goodness from coming to expression, therefore, or to devalue any of these expressions, is to treat that which is immeasurably precious as if it were not and, just so, in a way that does not befit its worth. As Simone Weil puts it, "Even in my worst moments I would not destroy a Greek statue or a fresco by Giotto. Why anything else then?"[83] If all humans bear God's image, accordingly, then they have inestimable dignity and worth; hence, if justice means that persons have a right to be treated in a way that befits their worth (and that they are wronged insofar as they are not treated that way), then it follows that every human being has a right to be treated in a way that befits their inestimable worth as God's image bearers.

Again, this is not the place to develop a complete theology of justice, but we can at least highlight two broad principles that follow from these claims. First, and most obviously, if all human beings bear the image of God, it follows that they bear an inviolable dignity; call this *the inviolability principle*. It is always and everywhere wrong, accordingly, to treat them otherwise—to torment them, to abuse them, to torture them, to rape them, to harass them, or, in short, to treat them "like dirt." Second, if every human being is of inestimable worth, then it follows that no human being is of less worth than any other; it is wrong, therefore, to treat them as if they were. Call this *the equality principle*. It is wrong, on this principle, to treat one class of people as if they were worth more than or less than other classes, and thus to value a person's contributions to group deliberations more or less depending on the class to which they belong, to pay them more or less depending on the class to which they belong, to respect them more or less depending on the class to which they belong, to give them more or fewer opportunities depending on the class to which they belong, to give them more or fewer second chances depending on the class to which they belong, and so on. Again, the principle here is simply that all humans are of inestimable, and so equal, worth, and that they have a right to be treated accordingly. It is easy to see why justice would require both the inviolability principle and the equality principle; otherwise, a society could plausibly allow for the violation of every person's dignity (and thus maintain the principle of equality), just as a society could insist upon the inviolability of individual dignity but permit all sorts of gross inequalities among them. Justice thus requires both principles. Elaborations aside, the point, for now, is that if we bear God's image, then we all bear an immeasurable worth and are wronged insofar as we are treated otherwise.

If justice is a matter of being treated as befits one's worth, then it turns out that injustice is fairly ubiquitous. Needless to say, that is a problem; it is also, for this reason, overwhelming: I should be opposed to every injustice I see and so have reason to do something about it—but because injustice is ubiquitous, I cannot do something about every injustice I see, much less about all the injustices I do not see. Thankfully, some cases of injustice are insignificant enough that they do not call for much of a response, and some are already being suitably addressed by others. An overwhelming number of cases remain, however, which brings us back to a crucial issue: when should we do something about the injustices all around us? More to the point, when do we have an *obligation* to do something?

One answer to these questions is straightforward enough: to whatever extent we are involved in the perpetration of an injustice, we have an obligation to do something about it. If I am disrespectful toward a particular group of people, for instance, or if I am cruel to one of my subordinates, then I am obligated to repent of my behavior and make things right with those whom I have wronged. Likewise if I am an authority-bearing member of a group that perpetrates injustices. I may also be involved in an injustice and so be obligated to do something about it insofar as I derive some benefit from it. The connection here is a bit less straightforward, but it seems safe to say that if I derive some benefit from an injustice, then I am obligated to do something about it if the injustice is a necessary condition of the benefit and I am in a position to do something about it. To say that the injustice must be a necessary condition is just a way of spelling out what it would mean for a benefit to be derived from an injustice, so that should be uncontroversial. Nor is it controversial to say that we are obligated to do something in such cases if we are in a position to do so, though the implication—that persons not in such a position may not be so obligated—might be. With that in mind, it may be helpful to consider a case such as the following. Suppose one of the shift managers at a factory is especially mean-spirited and, as such, "makes an example" of one worker during each shift—he humiliates and disrespects the worker. If the owners of the factory catch wind of this, they are certainly obligated to do something about the manager's behavior, especially (but not only) if they derive a benefit from the manager's use of these tactics. But what about ordinary shift workers? Are they likewise obligated to do something? Suppose the workers know that, if challenged, the mean-spirited manager will only be more severe in mistreating their coworker; do the shift workers have an obligation to do something even if it is likely to make things worse? Suppose, too, that some of the shift workers' existence is fairly precarious, that they simply cannot afford to lose this job, and that they likely would lose their job if they stood up to their manager. In that case, even if these shift workers derive a benefit from someone else being mistreated (since the other person's mistreatment means that, at least on that day, they themselves will not be mistreated), do they have an obligation to do something about it? Perhaps the answer to these questions is yes; if so, then it would follow that if persons derive a benefit from an injustice, they are obligated to do something about it—that is, that deriving a benefit from an injustice is a sufficient condition of acquiring such an obligation. To my mind, however, this way of putting it would lay too heavy a burden on persons who are in precarious circumstances, which is why I added the condition mentioned above: one is obligated to do something about such an injustice *if one is in position to do something about it.*

Some readers will also have noticed that the question of which injustices we have an obligation to do something about is relevantly similar to questions raised, in the last chapter, concerning vocation. Some of our claims about vocation can thus shed some light on these issues. Vocation, recall, involves one's being called to a particular sphere, as well as being called to care about certain goods; these dimensions of one's calling can likewise impose an obligation upon one to do something about injustice. Simply stated, if my vocation renders me responsible for certain persons or goods, then I am defeasibly obligated to do something about whatever injustices may befall them, at least insofar as those injustices fall within the sphere to which I am called. Consider a fairly straightforward example: suppose that a player on a Little League baseball team is belittling another player. If I am that player's coach, I am obligated to do something about this: at the very least, I am obligated to tell the former player that this is inappropriate and that they need to knock it off, but depending upon the seriousness of the belittlement and its impact on the other player, I may also be obligated to punish the offending player (by not letting them play, for instance) and to restore the offended player's standing. I would likewise have some such obligation if I were the umpire or if either of these players were my child, for in that case, too, I would have a vocation-specific responsibility for the players. It seems less likely that parents of other children on the team would have such an obligation, still less likely that a random passerby would have one, and even less likely that a distant stranger who somehow caught wind of the belittling on social media would have an obligation to do something about it. The injustice itself thus remains constant in each case, but our obligation to do something about it differs depending upon our role-specific responsibilities.

We can come at the same point from a different angle: if the injustice in question were more severe—if, say, one player was savagely beating up another one—then everyone in the immediate vicinity would have an obligation to do something about it, whether by actively intervening or calling for help. The implication here is that as the severity of an injustice rises, it triggers an obligation to do something upon a widening circle of onlookers. ("Severity" here includes both the gravity of the injustice itself as well as the vulnerability of the one upon whom it is inflicted. It may include more than these two factors, but it surely includes at least these.) To illustrate the point, picture several variously flammable materials: tissue paper, a chunk of dry wood, and a rubber tire. The slightest exposure to fire would be sufficient to ignite the tissue, whereas it would take a much more intense and prolonged exposure to ignite the wood, and more intense exposure still to ignite the tire. In the same way, I am suggesting that when people have a vocation-specific responsibility for a given person, even the slightest injustice can be enough to trigger their obligation to act, whereas it would take a much more severe injustice to trigger such an obligation in the case of someone who simply happens to be in the area. This raises the possibility, in turn, that some injustices could be so severe, so horrific, that simply hearing about them would suffice to impose upon us an obligation to do something (even if that "something" is merely to call for help); the Holocaust would surely be an example of such a horror.[84] Again, the point is simply that our vocation-specific responsibilities, along with the severity of an injustice, can suffice to obligate us to do something about an injustice.

The concept of vocation can also help us understand the sense of obligation some persons feel toward others with whom they would otherwise have no direct connection. Nicholas Wolterstorff thus explains how he experienced encounters with South Africans and Palestinians as calling him

to care, first-personally, about the injustices they endured, and therefore
as calling him to do what he could to rectify those injustices. In particular,
Wolterstorff cites a meeting in South Africa in which Black persons "described the daily indignities heaped upon them and the many ways in which
they were demeaned; they spoke of being expelled from their homes and
herded off into Bantustans. With great passion they cried out for justice.
Not only was I profoundly moved by this cry for justice, I felt convinced
that I had been issued a call from God. . . . Fidelity to God required that I
speak up for these victims of injustice in whatever way might prove appropriate."[85] In light of this calling, Wolterstorff now had an obligation to do
something about those injustices, whether that meant amplifying the voices
of its victims, organizing opposition to these injustices, or explaining why
charity work is an insufficient response to them. This is an extraordinary
calling, to be sure, but it fits within the framework we have been considering, since that framework insists that when we are called to care about certain persons or goods, we thereby acquire responsibility for their well-being
and, so, an obligation to do something about injustices they may face—
irrespective of our physical or relational proximity to them.

Vocation can also help us see a crucial reason why we cannot try to do
something about every injustice: caring for particular goods and persons
takes time and energy, and since we have these in limited supply, it follows
that we cannot care for every good and person that is worthy of our care.
In order to care well about certain persons and goods, accordingly, and thus
to try to right certain wrongs, we must resist the urge to do something
about every wrong that deserves to be righted. We see an example of this
in Thurgood Marshall's leadership of the NAACP's Legal Defense team:
Marshall recognized that his team could not take on every case that deserved an appeal; if their work against injustice was going to be effective,
the members of the team needed to focus on cases that would help them
build toward far-reaching decisions like *Brown v. Board of Education*.[86] Again,
the point is straightforward enough: if we have vocation-specific obligations
to particular persons and goods, then we likewise have vocation-specific
obligations to make sure that they are treated justly; in order to meet the
latter obligations, we must not scatter our time and energy among all the
goods and persons who deserve to be treated justly, for then we would fail
to care well for any of them.

Putting these points together, then, the basic guidance is simple: the
more serious an injustice, and the closer we are to it (where "closeness"
can be established by our culpability for the injustice, by our benefiting

from it, or by our vocations), the more we have an obligation to do something about it.

That brings us to another pressing question: even if we have an obligation to do something about a particular injustice, what, exactly, should we do? In other words, how should Christians respond to injustice—or, perhaps better, what would it mean to respond Christianly to injustice? In some cases, the answer to these questions is relatively simple. If I am the one perpetrating an injustice, for instance, then the proper response is obviously to repent and try to right whatever wrongs I have committed. Matters become considerably more complicated from here, however. To see why, consider an apparently straightforward case where someone does something unjust within a sphere where I wield power: suppose one of my male students publicly states that a woman was admitted to our Ph.D. program only because she is a woman. Statements like these are both unjust in their own right and can have an undermining effect on women. If I overhear this statement, accordingly, I not only have a responsibility to do something about it but as a teacher have some power to rectify the injustice. Now consider the range of options available to me. Should I give the male student a disapproving look? Should I tell everyone within earshot that the statement is, in fact, incorrect? Should I talk privately with the offending and the offended parties? File an official complaint against the offending student with our administration? Knock the offending student down a few pegs, as it were, both in his own eyes and in the eyes of others? Insist that he make a public apology and go through an antibias training program? Refuse to recommend him for any future opportunities? Try to get him thrown out of our school? Which of these responses, if any, is Christian?

In trying to sort through these options, we find some guidance from the idea that any such response must be an expression of devotion to God.[87] This means, on the one hand, that one's response must be an act of faith in God, which is to say that it must be an act of trusting God and of treating God alone as ultimate. To respond rightly to injustice, accordingly, we must not treat the powers that be as if they were ultimate, yet we must also resist the supposition that our justice-making efforts are ultimate. With respect to the latter, Marilyn McCord Adams insists that "what is pernicious from a Christian point of view is not active opposition to evil and the promotion of reform, but the notion that 'everything depends on us' with its correlative zeal for success that outruns human wisdom and power to insure it."[88] When someone has been wronged, it can seem incumbent upon us to make sure that justice is served and so, perhaps, to take justice completely into our own hands; instead of entrusting our efforts to God, then, we will do whatever it takes to achieve certain visible results. If our justice work is an expression of faith, by contrast, we will put our ultimate trust in God's might rather than our own, which means that we will resist the urge to do whatever it takes to make things right. With respect to the former, Christians must likewise resist the impression that the powers of the present age (and its attendant injustices) are ultimate and must therefore resist the temptation to resign ourselves to these injustices. James Cone cites the importance of just such faith among enslaved Black persons: "It was because of his [that is, the enslaved person's] vision into the future," Cone writes, "that he could never reconcile himself to the present evil of slavery. . . . If there is no vision of the future, we can easily reconcile ourselves with the *present*—the evil, the suffering and death."[89] Hence, even if we may need to accept the fact that we may not be able to rectify every injustice, we must not accept these injustices themselves—we must not reconcile ourselves to them, become acclimated to them, or otherwise treat them as if they had the final word. By treating God alone as ultimate, accordingly, we can resist the temptation to accept injustices, while also resisting the idea that we must do whatever it takes to ensure that justice prevails. (Needless to say, treating God alone as ultimate can also help us resist the temptation to see ourselves as ultimately righteous vis-à-vis others or as their ultimate judge.)

That brings us already to a second bit of guidance: if justice work is an act of devotion, then it should also be an expression of God's love for all involved. We must love those who are victims of injustice, accordingly, and must therefore seek to protect them, defend them, stand up for them, support them, console them, advocate for them, and, in sum, become first-personally invested in their plight. At the same time, we must also love even those who are responsible for these injustices. So Dr. King: "*Agape* means nothing sentimental or basically affectionate," he explains; "it means understanding, redeeming good will for all men, an overflowing love which seeks nothing in return. It is the love of God working in the lives of men. When we love on the *agape* level we love men not because we like them, not because their attitudes and ways appeal to us, but because God loves them. Here we rise to the position of loving the person who does the evil deed while hating the deed he does."[90] Christians are thus called to love wrongdoers as well as the wronged, though love will look different in each case. This means, among other things, that we must not be vindictive toward wrongdoers and that we must therefore be on guard against lashing out at them or seeking bad things for them.

Some Christians insist that this sort of love requires nonviolence and thus insist that a Christian response to injustice will therefore be characterized, centrally and necessarily, by nonviolence. The underlying assumption here seems to be that violence is necessarily an expression of hatred or enmity toward others; we hear something along these lines from Dr. King, who cautions us against an "anger-motivated drive to strike back violently, to inflict damage . . . to cause injury to retaliate for wrongful suffering," and we hear the same from Bernard Häring, who maintains that "violence . . . is always an undisciplined outburst, an expression of rancor."[91] If violence is necessarily an enactment of ill will toward others, then it cannot be an expression of Christian love; from this, it would follow that Christian love is incompatible with violence. In the vast majority of cases, this is surely true. It is not clear, however, whether violence is always retaliatory, nor whether nonviolence is always not. I can boycott a store out of a vindictive desire to hurt it, after all, which seems to indicate that nonviolence does not, by itself, mean that I am not acting out of a retaliatory spirit. There are also cases where a person can use violence for non-retaliatory reasons, and there may even be rare cases where a person uses violence precisely for the sake of love.[92] Suppose I am a high-school teacher (as, indeed, I used to be) and there is a man actively brandishing a rifle in my school (as, thankfully, there never was). If I had the chance, I might violently tackle the shooter and do what I could to stop him from endangering others; doing so could certainly be an act of love for my students, and it could also be an act of love for the shooter, since preventing someone from committing a great evil can certainly be a loving thing to do. I might also feel compassion for the shooter, especially if I had had him as a student or knew something about what brought him to this point; in that case, I would feel deeply upset not only about what he was doing but also about what I needed to do in order to stop him. I would not be acting in a hateful, retaliatory spirit, in other words. If so, then it would appear that violence is not necessarily incompatible with Christian love, though, again, in the vast majority of cases it surely is. Arguably, at least, what is more fundamental than nonviolence, for Christians, is a commitment to non-vindictive, non-retaliatory love; this is what Reinhold Niebuhr has in mind when he claims that "nonhatred is a much more important sign and symbol of Christian faith than nonviolence."[93]

Supposing, then, that Christians should respond to injustice, when called, in a way that reflects their faith and love, where would this leave us with regard to my male student's sexist remark to the effect that a female student was admitted to the doctoral program only because she was a woman? If I see the situation in light of God's justice, I should certainly try to support the students who were wronged by the remark, just as I should try to help the offending student understand why his remark was wrong and potentially hurtful. This is part of what it looks like to love the offended as well as the offending parties. Beyond that, I should also take steps to ensure that this sort of thing does not happen again, yet in so doing, I must resist the urge to ruin the offending student's life, just as I must resist the assumption that I should do whatever it takes to rectify the situation and make sure it never happens again, for in that case I would not be entrusting the situation to God. To be sure, I should undoubtedly do more than this; the point, for now, is simply that a Christian response must be an expression of devotion to God and, so, recognizable as an act of faith and love.

Naturally, not every injustice occurs in a sphere where we are in a position of power. We may have no direct power over corporations that exploit workers, for instance, or over governments that are corrupt or that discriminate against the powerless, or over churches that support abusive leaders. Supposing that we are nevertheless called to do something about these injustices, what would it mean to do so Christianly?

That brings us to the idea of Christian activism. To count as *activism*, our actions must be aimed at bringing about change, particularly at the righting of wrongs, and must have a plausible chance of actually doing so. If it is not so aimed, then our activity might be many things—symbolic protest, for instance, or a compelling performance—but it is not activism. In situations where we do not have direct power to bring about change, activists tend to rely on two broad, complementary strategies for trying to do so.[94] On the one hand, activists try to shift the prevailing circumstances in such a way that perpetrating or allowing injustice is now contrary to the interests of the powerful. If corporations were regularly subjected to lawsuits and penalties when they mistreated their workers, the cost of these penalties would soon outweigh whatever profit they could squeeze out of workers by mistreating them, and it would therefore no longer be in their interest to do so. Changing the interests of the powerful can thus induce them to change the way they treat people and can thus be a powerful lever in fighting against injustice. On the other hand, activists often try to loosen an unjust power's grip on us, both by helping us see the ways that it is, in fact, unjust, and by making us less beholden to it. With respect to making injustice visible, think of cases where persons have internalized their oppression and thus experience their oppression as understandable or even as just; in such cases, simply coming to see injustice *as* injustice can loosen its power over one.[95] With respect to making us less beholden to unjust powers, consider a case where banks discriminate against persons of color, and where persons of color respond by pooling their money in order to create a money-lending service of their own; by developing an alternative to an unjust power, they thereby loosen that power's hold over them and, just so, loosen the grip of an injustice. By changing what is in a powerful entity's interests, accordingly, and loosening that power's grip, activists can plausibly hope to bring about change.

There are other strategies that activists might pursue, but these are two of the most important. Again, the key point is that a given action can count as *activism* just insofar as it aims to bring about change. It can count as *Christian* activism, in turn, just insofar as the changes it aims to bring about reflect God's calling, and the manner in which it aims to bring them about, are an expression of devotion to God. For one thing, then, our activism must reflect the sort of faith and love we have already discussed. Beyond that, though, it should aim to bring about change precisely by bearing witness to another power—namely, God—and by living according to that power. (To be sure, Christians can also fight against injustices by joining non-Christian organizations; so long as these organizations pursue justice in a way that is not contrary to Christian devotion, this might be a perfectly faithful thing for a Christian to do—but in that case, it is more an instance of a Christian engaging in activism than of Christian activism per se.)

So what does such witnessing and living-according-to look like, and how would these loosen the grip of injustice and change the interests of the powers that be? In order to address these questions, it will be helpful to consider a handful of paradigmatic approaches to Christian activism, each of which played a vital role in the American Civil Rights movement. The first approach is *prophetic critique*, in which Christians amplify the cries of the oppressed, announce clearly that something is wrong, and hold the powerful accountable for their role in perpetrating or perpetuating injustice.[96] This is what Emilie Townes has in mind when she insists that "*the prophetic voice must be an agent of admonition*—pointing out the wrongdoing in society and stressing the need to have human action (and inaction) conform to God's will," what James Cone has in mind when he maintains that "the Church should be the voice of those who have no one," and Gustavo Gutierrez when he contends that the church "must make the prophetic *denunciation* of every dehumanizing situation, which is contrary to fellowship, justice, and liberty."[97] Simply by identifying injustice as such and denouncing it, prophetic critique may loosen its grip on those who are dominated and oppressed. Beyond that, however, prophetic critique can also bring about change insofar as it holds the powerful accountable to standards of justice. The powerful often justify their power by appeal to certain ideals; insofar as these ideals are consonant with those to which Christians are committed, we can hold the powerful to these ideals and, just so, pressure them to change. In such a case, even if we ourselves have no direct power over them, the powerful have given us a lever that we can use to change their behavior: if they have an interest in living up to their stated ideals (or at least in not looking as though they are not), then, by holding them accountable to those ideals, we can incentivize them to change. Then again, unjust powers may not profess any ideals, or their professed ideals may actually support injustice. (An example: "The only purpose of a business is to make money.") In that case, prophetic critique can hold the powerful accountable to a set of standards by which they will be judged, whether they know it or not, namely, God's standards of justice. To take one famous example, this is what Dr. King was doing in his "Letter from Birmingham Jail": "A just law is a man-made code," he writes, "that squares with the moral law or the law of God. An unjust law is a code that is out of harmony with the moral law. . . . Any law that uplifts human personality is just. Any law that degrades human personality is unjust. All segregation distorts the soul and damages the personality. . . . Hence segregation is not only politically, economically, and sociologically unsound, it is morally wrong and sinful."[98] King thus insists that human laws are appropriately judged by the standards of God's law and, on this basis, contends that segregation is unjust. If those in power care about whether they live up to God's standards, then this critique might give them a reason to change what they are doing. But even if they do not care, others may, and the latter may thus exert some pressure on them to change their practices.

Naturally, taken by itself, prophetic critique can seem like a cheap sort of activism. It is easy enough, after all, to call attention to others' injustices. The credibility of these critiques, if not their validity, thus depends upon the extent to which Christians embody the standards to which they are holding others accountable. (Their validity does not depend upon this, for if Christians fail to live up to their own standards, that calls into question their behavior rather than their standards. To suggest otherwise would commit the tu quoque fallacy.) As Cone puts it, "The Church must be in its own community what it preaches and what it seeks to accomplish in the world."[99] We hear something similar from Gutierrez: "It has been pointed out, and rightly so, that this critical function of the Church runs the risk of remaining on a purely verbal and external level and that it should be backed up with clear actions and commitments. Prophetic denunciation can be made validly and truly only from within the heart of the struggle for a more human world."[100] Taken by itself, accordingly, prophetic critique can seem fairly empty; for this reason, Christians generally insist that it be coupled with other forms of activism, to which I now turn.

On the negative side, prophetic critique is thus often joined with a strategy of *noncooperation with evil*. The name of this strategy is taken directly from Dr. King, who regularly characterized his own movement in these terms, and who often reminded people that "it is as much a moral obligation to refuse to cooperate with evil as it is to cooperate with good."[101] The idea here is fairly straightforward. If my superior tells me to wrong certain persons by, say, pressuring them not to let anyone know that they are being abused, it is obvious that I should refuse to go along with my superior. In the same way, if a system or institution or social pattern is set up in such a way that certain persons are wronged by it—if it discriminates against Black people, for instance, or keeps women "in their place"—I should likewise refuse to go along with it, and I should certainly refuse to play a role in carrying out these wrongs. We could say something similar in cases where I am the target of an injustice: whether it is an individual who wants me to subject myself to degrading treatment—a bully who tries to make me admit that I am a loser, for instance—or a system, institution, or social pattern that does so, I should not go along with that treatment. Again, the point is simply that we should not cooperate with evil, which is precisely why many churches divested themselves from South Africa during apartheid and why many Black people, galvanized by Rosa Parks and led by Dr. King, boycotted the segregated buses in Montgomery, Alabama. Refusing to cooperate with injustice is often simply the right thing to do, and it can also be an effective means of bringing about change since, on the one hand, boycotts, divestments, and the like can make injustice more costly and, just so, change the interests of those who might otherwise benefit from the injustice, and, on the other, it can loosen the grip of injustice, for the obvious reason that, by not cooperating with it, one no longer experiences injustice as fate, as a fact of nature, or as right. Noncooperation can thus be an effective form of activism, and if we do it because we are walking according to God's standards and in order to bear witness to those standards, it can be an effective form of Christian activism. (Given that noncooperation can be risky and costly for those who engage in it, it may also require the sort of faith that Christians profess to have.)

Prophetic critique and noncooperation are often coupled, on the positive side, with the strategy of *embodying an alternative* to unjust powers: if we live according to the reign of God rather than the powers that be, we should be living with one another in ways that approximate the justice of that reign, which is to say that Christians, in their life together, should be instantiating more just social arrangements. Insofar as we do so, our life together is, as Gutierrez puts it, "an annunciation of what is not yet, but will be; it is the forecast of a different order of things, a new society."[102] By offering a glimpse of the ultimate order of things, Christians can thus provide people with an inhabitable vision of a more just future; this is vital, for again, as Cone argues, "If there is no vision of the future, we can easily reconcile ourselves with the *present*—the evil, the suffering and death."[103] Think here of churches that affirm the "somebodiness" of Black people in the midst of a society that would tell them otherwise, or communities like L'Arche that treat disabled persons as God's image bearers, or Christians who have formed co-ops as an alternative to exploitative health insurance companies. Christians thereby create options beyond those provided by the powers that be, and they can thus enable persons to experience a foretaste of a more just future while challenging the seeming "naturalness" of the status quo. In so doing, they may compete with the prevailing powers and, just so, generate in them an interest in justice, but they may also generate change more directly, for insofar as they develop more just, inhabitable alternatives, they have already changed the situation of persons who enter into those alternatives. In turn, those who participate in these new ways of being will be less beholden to unjust powers and, crucially, will be better equipped to resist the latter's treatment of them.

Christian activism may thus take many forms, but prophetic critique, noncooperation, and the creation of alternatives are among the most common and, often, the most effective. By doing these things, Christians can reasonably hope to loosen injustice's grip on people and to bring about change by changing what is in the interests of the powerful.

So then: Christian love may do more than justice requires, but it should never do less—and sometimes doing justice is precisely what love requires. Christians have an obligation to do something about these injustices if we are perpetrating them or directly benefiting from them, or if our vocation lays such obligations upon us. When we tackle an injustice, in turn, we must do so as an act of devotion and, so, as an act of faith and love; such faith and love can be expressed through prophetic critique, non-cooperation, and creating alternatives, all of which can, one hopes, loosen the grip of unjust powers and shift their interests in such a way that certain injustices are no longer in their interests.

Conclusion

To be reoriented to God, we need to reorient the way we relate to others; we thus need to love them, which is to say that we must care about them, want good things for them, and appreciate that which is good about them. It is not always easy to love others, however, which is one reason Christianity includes several practices designed to cultivate such love in us. One such practice is beneficence: by doing things for the benefit of others, we make an investment in their well-being, and such investments can eventually dispose us to care about them in their own right. Another practice is looking for the image of God in others: if we are primed to see God's image in others, then we should be able to see them in the best possible light and be on the lookout for that which God made them to be; this should help us to appreciate that which is good about them and resist the urge to see only that which is bad about them. Even if we see others in this way, however, we may still have a hard time loving them insofar as they have wronged us. A third practice, then, is forgiveness: by entrusting our desire for vengeance to God, we can set aside that desire and thus clear the way to wanting good things even for a wrongdoer. That is not the only way that Christians will address wrongdoers, of course; they will also seek justice. Their so seeking should likewise be an act of faith and love, often expressed through prophetic critique, noncooperation, and the creation of alternative ways of being in the world. These strategies are a plausible means of effecting change, but no matter how successful these may be, Christians aim at a fulfillment that transcends anything that we can hope to bring about. That brings us to the topic of the final chapter.

CHAPTER SEVEN

The End

P REVIOUS CHAPTERS HAVE considered some of the key components of a Christian way of life. This chapter adds an important
dimension to that way of life, namely, an account of the telos at
which it aims: *eternal fulfillment*. Then, with this account on board, I
look back on some of the book's earlier claims, with an eye on a question
raised in chapter 1: is there *wisdom* in this way of life?

Eternal Fulfillment

I sometimes tell students that the best way to handle the doctrine of last
things is to follow the example of Thomas Aquinas and Karl Barth, and *perform* the doctrine (by dying before completing one's system), rather than
write about it. In this section I ignore that advice. The attempt is framed as
a response to a problem facing such doctrines, which we might understand
in terms of a dilemma: if eternal life is portrayed as standing in *continuity*
with current conditions, it does not seem that it would be a consummate
fulfillment of humanity's—and especially Christianity's—hopes; whereas
if it is portrayed as standing in *discontinuity*, it is not clear how the present-
day persons who hold such hopes could experience eternal life as fulfilling
those hopes.

This problem is an old one, though not one that has received much
theological attention. It is treated most extensively, as far as I know, in the
Glaubenslehre of Friedrich Schleiermacher, but almost no one reads that

far into the *Glaubenslehre*, and those who do tend not to take his eschatological deferrals seriously. (Perhaps for good reason, since Schleiermacher raises this dilemma precisely for the sake of not having to advance any doctrines about last things.)

Nevertheless, I think there are good reasons theologians should address this problem. For one thing, several preeminent philosophers have recently raised versions of the problem in order to argue against the very desirability—if not the very idea—of eternal life. I will say more about their arguments in due course, but I think they deserve to be taken seriously. Another reason is that addressing this objection can press theologians to think more carefully about eternal life and, one hopes, arrive at a more satisfying understanding of it. In particular, considering it in terms of this problem can push us to think more precisely about eternal life's relationship to the present, which may help us, in turn, to see certain implications for how we should live in and otherwise relate to the present.

In this section, then, I lay out two recent arguments raised against the desirability of eternal life and try to address these arguments by talking about two possible features of eternal life, namely, communion with God and what I call "abundant life."

Before proceeding, a few clarifications are in order. First, I am fully aware that what I am offering is neither the only nor even the most highly warranted way of understanding eternal life, nor the only one that might address the continuity/discontinuity problem. In addition to theologians, several philosophers have responded to this problem, and I find some of their responses helpful. (I consider one such response, that of John Martin Fischer, in a moment.) Yet even the best philosophical responses strike me as working with a fairly abstract, threadbare understanding of eternal life, such that it is not surprising that they would regard such a life as tedious or, at best, minimally fulfilling. Theologians, by contrast, tend to work with a much more robust, maximally fulfilling conception, and just so may have something worthwhile to contribute to the broader conversation.

Second, it may be worth noting that, for reasons discussed in chapter 1, I generally tend to favor continuity over discontinuity (except, crucially, on the issue of grace). I tend in this direction because continuity often goes hand in hand with a highly valuable epistemic good, namely, understandability, and because it seems to me that much of the pressure toward *dis*continuity stems from preconceived notions of what divinity must be like, such that if we could justifiably call these notions into question, we would be freed from the sense that God must be kept at a distance from, and so seen as discontinuous with, creation. I follow a version of that strategy in this section's argument, to which I now turn.

Let us begin with objections to the desirability of eternal life—objections to the effect that an eternal life could not, in principle, fulfill our desires or values, such that we have no reason to desire or value it. There are two especially influential recent formulations of this objection, one due to Bernard Williams, the other to Samuel Scheffler, and I consider them here in turn.

Williams's argument begins with a claim about the desirability of eternal life. His claim, simply stated, is that persons have reason to desire life beyond death only if they have what he terms "categorical desires," by contrast with what he terms "conditional desires."[1] Williams's explanation of the distinction is not entirely clear—the only example to which he appeals is the sort of desire that would render suicide rational—but I think we can make sense of it in terms of a more basic distinction between "lasting" and "passing" desires. As a rough way of thinking about the former, consider instances where we might say of someone who has died, "I wish he could have been here for this; he always wanted to see the Cubs win a World Series"; or "If only she had lived to see this day; she always wanted all of her children to graduate from college." In cases like these, the desires that persons had during their lifetime are such that we can reasonably imagine that they would want to be around for fulfillments of those desires that occurred after they died, from which it follows that these desires would give them a defeasible reason to want *not* to die. Not all desires are like this, of course; some desires—the desire to get over a cold, for instance, or to finish folding the laundry—seem insufficient to give us reason to want not to die, insofar as they are either too unimportant to us or not pinned to a fulfillment beyond our death; hence we can call these "passing" desires. Terminological differences notwithstanding, Williams's first argument is that insofar as we have reason to want to live on—forever or otherwise—it is because *lasting* or *categorical* desires give us such reason.

Williams next argues that such desires necessarily delimit what would count as fulfilling them, in the sense that a desire for Cubs' victories can be fulfilled only by Cubs' victories, a desire for children's flourishing can be fulfilled only by their flourishing, and so on. Hence, if I desire not to die on the basis of certain lasting desires, these specify what would make the ensuing life fulfilling for me. From this, it obviously follows that if we knew ahead of time that our lasting desires would *not* be fulfilled in an ongoing life, then these desires would not give us reason to want to go on living;

hence, it is not the desires themselves but the possibility of their fulfillment that gives us reason to want not to die. (To see why, suppose a genie
is willing to grant me an additional fifty years on earth, and that my only
reason for wanting an additional fifty years is to see Esperanto finally become the world's official language; if the genie informs me that Esperanto
will not become the world's language during that time, then I would no
longer have any reason to want those additional years.)

This brings us to the third step in Williams's argument, which is to
claim that there are only so many fulfillments to which a particular desire
is susceptible, such that people who lived an endless life would necessarily
run out of ways to fulfill their desires and would, accordingly, become
nauseatingly bored. That is to say, desires imply a delimited range of possible fulfillments, which means that the very desires that give us reason to
want not to die would also, in an eternal life, eventually be fulfilled in every
possible way, such that we would no longer have reason to want not to die.
On Williams's account, then, precisely the things that give us reason to
desire eternal life—namely, lasting or categorical desires—would end up
rendering eternal life *un*desirable.

I consider some objections to this account in a moment, but before
doing so I want to turn to another influential statement of the problem,
namely, that of Samuel Scheffler.[2] Scheffler accepts much of Williams's
argument but claims that the real problem with eternal life is not that
we would run out of fulfillments and so become bored but that we—the
present-day version thereof—could not *experience* these fulfillments as such,
for an eternal life would lack a fundamental structure of human valuing,
namely, "temporal scarcity." The idea here, simply stated, is (a) that valuing takes time, (b) that we have only so much of it, and (c) that the resulting scarcity structures our very experience of value, in the sense that to
value something, for us, necessarily involves tough choices. If we had an
endless supply of time, on the other hand, we would not have to make such
choices and could thus value everything that is worthy of valuing, such that
our valuing would thereby lose its forced-choice, prioritization-imposing
quality. But without that quality, Scheffler claims, it would not be recognizable *as* human valuing. He argues, accordingly, that if eternal life eliminates temporal scarcity, it likewise eliminates one of the basic structures
of human valuing, such that we—the here-and-now version of us—could
not experience it as fulfilling and would therefore have no reason to desire
it. This, too, is a variation on the continuity/discontinuity problem, for
if eternal life were to lack certain features of present life—here, temporal

scarcity—it would not be fulfilling, but if it had these features, it would not be eternal.

Before we proceed, it will be useful to bring the Williams and Scheffler objections into somewhat closer proximity. This is easy to do, fortunately. To be sure, desire and value are distinct—I can value something that I do not desire (knowledge of ancient horticultural practices, for instance, or, in a case where I deserve punishment, justice), just as I can desire something that I do not value (I may want something trivial, for instance, like seeing what is on my social media feed, or my desire may have been formed by a value that I have since renounced). But it would appear that we cannot categorically desire something without valuing it, such that Scheffler's worries about the structure of value would apply to categorical desires, too.

The objection, therefore, would be that categorical desires may give us reason to want to live beyond death, but they equally entail that such a life would not be fulfilling for the present-day persons whose desires they are, for (a) if eternal life fulfilled those desires as we now have them, we would eventually tire of it, whereas if it did not, it would not satisfy our reason for desiring it, and (b) an *eternal* life would lack a structural feature of human valuing, namely, temporal scarcity, which means that we—the present-day we—could not experience it as fulfilling, such that, again, *we* would have no reason to desire it.

Briefly stated, then, that is the problem I want to address here. Before turning to my argument, though, we need to consider two objections to which Williams's account seems liable. First, Williams's argument seems unable to handle a case like that of the young Schleiermacher, whose stated desire was to become a microcosm of the infinite and thus to experience literally everything. It is hard to see how someone with a categorical desire of this sort would ever run out of fulfillments, even in an endless life; if so, then we might argue that the problem is not with endless life per se, as Williams has suggested, but with categorical desires that are incapable of endless fulfillment and, so, of rendering eternal life endlessly desirable. This is related to a second, more important objection, to the effect that Williams's conclusions about immortal life follow only if we limit our attention, as he does, to an unduly narrow range of desires and fulfillments. This is the line taken by John Martin Fischer, who contends (a) that we must distinguish between *self-exhausting pleasures* (pleasures, that is, that we might want to experience only once or that will be experienceable as pleasures only a certain number of times) and *repeatable pleasures* (pleasures that we can enjoy again and again, such as hearing a favorite symphony or

spending time with a close friend); (b) that Williams's conclusions about
the tedium of immortality seem to have been derived from cases in which
we categorically desire only the former sort of pleasures, which would
mean that the tedium problem applies not to eternal life per se but only
to eternal life as it would be experienced by those whose desire is for self-
exhausting pleasures; and (c) that an eternal life with a sufficient mix of repeatable pleasures would *not* be unbearably tedious.[3] Fischer thus concludes
that if eternal life contained such a mix, it would meet a kind of minimum
threshold for desirability, and that immortality would then be at least bearable. (Fischer's minimalism is nicely reflected in the title of one of his essays: "Why Immortality Is Not So Bad.") This is an important argument,
and one that I take on board in what follows, even as I try to sketch a more
maximally fulfilling picture of eternal life.

To address the problems raised by Williams and Scheffler, let me now
outline a vision of eternal life that might endlessly fulfill one categorical
desire, namely, the desire for communion with God. Within the Christian
traditions, there is widespread agreement that such communion is that in
which eternal fulfillment consists. There is considerably less agreement,
however, on what such communion looks like; one prominent strand in
the tradition—we might call it the *mystical* or *beatific-vision* strand—understands such communion in terms of our seeing or beholding God with
God's own eyes, as it were, and understands this beholding as akin to seeing an overwhelmingly beautiful, blinding light—a light in which everything but God is washed out.[4] Another strand—call it the *abundant-life*
strand—understands communion with God in terms of an ever-increasing
plenitude of life shared with God and others and understands such life in
terms of an ever-enriching circulation of gifts given and received. To oversimplify a bit, we might say that the mystical or beatific-vision approach
portrays union with God as a kind of *identity* with God and thus as dissolv-
ing or at least greatly de-emphasizing particularity, whereas the abundant-
life approach sees particularity as a necessary ingredient in union with God,
since union with God is continually constituted by an endless multiplica-
tion of particular instantiations of such union. In what follows, I elaborate
a version of the latter understanding, though I do not mean thereby to
suggest that one would be unwarranted in pursuing the former, nor that,
in so doing, one could not address the continuity/discontinuity problem.[5]

My strategy here, then, is to build a model in three stages: first, I outline an account of Christ's own communion with the Father in terms of
their mutual devotion to each other and to a shared "cause," namely, such

communion as the highest good (for themselves as well as others); second, I use this understanding to think about the way in which others might be included in that communion; and, third, I explain the content of this communion in terms of an ever-enriching cultivation and circulation of gifts.[6] (I am unduly fond of numbering my points, not to mention lettering them, so in what follows, to reduce confusion, I refer to these three as my *major* points.)

I begin with a brief account of Jesus' own communion with God, not least because starting on this side of eternal life, so to speak, should help us establish continuity between this life and that. Toward that end, it will be useful to borrow some insights from earlier chapters, beginning with the idea of "devotion." Insofar as persons are devoted to something, recall, their beliefs, intentions, feelings, and the like will all be integrated into, and an expression of, that devotion, to such an extent that their life becomes, increasingly, a single thing—a single life plan or "whole," as Albrecht Ritschl puts it.

Importantly for present purposes, this whole can also include other persons. There are several ways that this could happen, but one is crucial here, namely, the inclusion in one's life plan of another person who is oriented toward a similar plan, such that inclusion of that person would itself be wholly oriented toward, and so seamlessly integrated into, one's life plan. To see how this might work, consider an instance in which two persons are wholly devoted to the welfare of nonhuman animals. By itself, this would not mean that the two were included in each other's life plans— except, perhaps, in the bare-minimal sense that a person who is devoted to a cause will to some extent care about and even identify with whatever contributes to its flourishing—since it is not hard to imagine that their lives would never actually intersect. Sharing a cause may thus be a necessary, but not sufficient, condition of another person's being included in one's life plan. A further condition—which I am inclined to say is likewise necessary and, in combination with the shared-plans condition, sufficient—is that we must *love* the other person. There is another, more troubling possibility, of course, in which we integrate others into our life plan by enslaving them or otherwise treating them as nothing but an instrument in the achievement of our intentions. In such a case, the other person *as a person* would not be integrated into our plans. This is not the only way in which someone can be so integrated, however, for if (a) a person's life were so wholly devoted to a particular cause that their life could be identified with that devotion, (b) another person were similarly devoted to that same cause, and (c) the first person were to love the second—to care about that person for their own sake and therefore take their well-being as the first's own end—then (d) loving the other person for their own sake would be fully consonant with the person's devotion to their own cause, since the other person identifies their well-being with the well-being of the cause to which the first person is devoted; moreover, (e) if the first person's love were reciprocated by the second, then the first person would be included as themselves, for their own sake, in that other person's life plan, such that in loving them, the first person would be "returned to themselves," in Hegel's nice phrase.[7] In a case like this, accordingly, another person could be integrated into one's life plan without being *reduced* to their role in that plan—without being treated as a mere instrument toward its achievement—for in this case, to love the person for their own sake and to include that person in the life plan to which one is devoted would come to the same thing.[8]

With that, we can now turn to some Christological claims. As we saw in chapter 3, Christians insist that all of Jesus' beliefs, actions, emotions, and the like must be understood in terms of the end he set for himself, or, in sum, in terms of his life plan or "vocation," since Jesus' entire life, including even the things that happened to him, is oriented toward that vocation, such that his entire life is organized around, and contributes to, its achievement. The end to which Jesus is devoted, in turn, is communion with God, but given who God is, such devotion necessarily entails that Jesus aims to bring others into this communion, who would in turn aim to bring others into it, and so on, such that in taking this as his end, Jesus also aims at establishing a loving communion among persons. Jesus' devotion to God thus means, by a sort of transitive property, that he is simultaneously devoted to seeing others share that devotion and, by this same transitive property, that these persons will be devoted not only to God but also to seeing others share that devotion, and so on.

Two aspects of this claim require elaboration. First, if the end to which Jesus is devoted is likewise that to which God is devoted, then Jesus' life, as oriented toward that end, reveals God's *own* life plan, as it were. (This is a fairly complicated idea, so I elaborate it here only as it applies to the Father-Son relationship; given our earlier claims, it should not be difficult to see how it would be extended to include the Spirit.) On the present account, Jesus' commitment to the establishment of a loving communion corresponds to, and means to enact, the Father's own commitment, such that Jesus thus reveals the Father's intention or "end." And if this intention is essential to who the Father is, as I argued in chapter 3, then it follows that the Father, too, is fundamentally committed to the establishment of such communion, or that the Father is as wholly devoted to it as Jesus is. Second, the Father is not only devoted to that to which Jesus is devoted—that is, the love of others—but also loves Jesus for his own sake, for if the Father and Jesus love others and are thus committed to drawing them into the communion that they share with one another, it follows that each sees that communion as an end in itself, from which it follows that the Father loves Jesus for his own sake, and vice versa. For comparison's sake, suppose that I know someone who is going through an especially lonely time, that I therefore want them to enjoy the sort of fellowship that I feel with certain friends, and that my friends want the same thing. In that case, my friends and I are all committed to someone else's good, and we see our relationship to one another as that which would be good for that person; from this, it follows that we see our relationship as good not only for the sake of some external purpose but for its own sake as well. As with my friends, so with God: if the Father wants what is good for us, and what is good for us, from his perspective, is to participate in the communion that the Father shares with Jesus, it follows that the Father takes that communion to be good for its own sake.

These claims provide us, in turn, with a way of understanding this communion itself. On this account, Jesus is wholly devoted to his vocation of bringing persons into loving communion with God and one another, to such an extent that he takes all his experiences, including his sufferings, up into that vocation, and his entire life is thus included in and oriented toward it. In that sense, Jesus' life is marked by a kind of simplicity or "partlessness," since, by hypothesis, there is nothing in Jesus—his intentions, actions, sufferings, perceptions, emotions, and so forth—that is not included in, and an expression of, his vocation. Jesus' relation to the Father is also included in this simplicity, since that to which Jesus is wholly devoted—namely, including us in the loving communion that he shares with the Father—is that to which the Father is wholly devoted, and, crucially, is equally included in and an expression of their love for each other. As I argued earlier, if two persons are each wholly devoted to a particular cause, then if they also love each other for their own sake, their love for each other would be seamlessly included in their devotion to that cause, and vice versa. This is precisely what we see in Jesus' relationship to the Father: each is wholly devoted to including us in their loving communion, and each loves the other for his own sake, such that there is no actual difference between the former and the latter. From this, it follows (a) that Jesus' life, as wholly devoted to God the Father, is characterized by a kind of simplicity, (b) that the Father's life is characterized by this same simplicity, and (c) that their relation to each other is itself simple, which is to say that they enjoy a kind of perfect communion with each other.

From here it is a short step to the claim that this communion is equally that in which God eternally subsists, which is also a point we considered back in chapter 3. The basic idea, recall, is that if God need not, and indeed does not, change in order to enjoy such communion and to include us in it, then it follows that God has always enjoyed this communion, that God has always willed to include us in it, that this communion has always been characterized by simplicity, and so on. This would mean, in turn, that we can move fairly easily from this model of God's *economic* communion to God's immanent or *eternal* communion—God's communion, that is, ad intra, apart from any determination to include us in it.[9] To make this move, we would need to posit (a) an intra-divine end to which Father, Son, and Spirit could be devoted and in which their love for one another could be seamlessly included; and (b) this end would have to be such that God's economic devotion to us would be an expression or repetition of this same intra-divine devotion. There are several candidates for such an end—God's glory, for instance, or God's self-enjoyment.[10] Based on the preceding, however, a different candidate recommends itself, namely, the loving communion of Father, Son, and Spirit as an end in itself. If that were their end, then (a) Father, Son, and Spirit would be devoted to the same end, and their love for one another could obviously be included in such devotion; (b) to devote themselves to including others in that communion—including others, that is, in their end—would be for them to persist in their eternal devotion to communion; and (c) if Father, Son, and Spirit have eternally (but not necessarily) determined so to include us, it would follow that they have always been devoted not only to loving communion with one another but to including us in that communion, too, such that their eternal communion would not have to change in order to accommodate or be expressed in their economic communion. God would subsist in utterly simple communion, accordingly, in eternity as well as in relation to us.

To enjoy communion with God, accordingly, would be to enjoy precisely *this* sort of communion—the sort of communion that the Son eternally shares with the Father and Spirit, which is equally the fulfillment of that to which his earthly life was devoted. We might even say that such communion was Jesus' categorical desire and thus already begin to see some continuity between his earthly life and its eternal fulfillment.

That brings us to my second major point, which is that insofar as others share this same devotion, and, so, categorically desire communion with God, they are already included in that communion, and eternal life, as the consummate enjoyment of such communion, would thus fulfill the desire that gives them reason to want to live beyond death.

My argument on behalf of this claim will have to be a bit oversimplified, but the main steps are as follows. (We already encountered these points in earlier chapters, so the oversimplification should be excusable.) First, insofar as persons share Christ's devotion—insofar, that is, as they are devoted to God and thus categorically desire communion with God—they already have a share in that communion and, indeed, in the very communion that Jesus shares with the Father and Spirit. With respect to the former, insofar as (a) we love God and God loves us and (b) we are committed to the "cause" to which God is committed—namely, communion with God as the highest good—then it follows (c) that we are in communion with God. The logic behind this claim should be familiar, since it simply adds a step to our earlier argument: if two persons love each other and are devoted to the same cause, then their love and devotion establish a special sort of self-returning relationship or, in short, communion between them. If someone else then comes to be devoted to that cause and to love and be loved by the first two, then the communion enjoyed by the former would now extend to the latter. So think here of a married couple, each of whom loves the other and is equally devoted to, say, fostering rescue dogs; if this couple has a child whom they love and who grows up to love them and share their devotion to fostering dogs, then that child will likewise participate in the communion that they experience with one another, and the parents will now experience that same communion in relation to their child. In the same way, insofar as persons love God and are devoted to that to which God is devoted, they share the communion that Jesus enjoys with God. Indeed, we would then have a properly internal or intimate share in that communion, for if (a) Christ is his devotion to God—if this is his "person" and not just his "work"—and (b) a person's devotion to God is itself not only due to Christ's work but is Christ himself living in the person through his Spirit, then (c) a person so devoted is united to or "in" Christ, which means (d) that that person has an internal share in Christ's relation to God.[11]

The first step of the argument, then, is to claim that insofar as persons love God and are devoted to communion with God, they already enjoy such communion. A key word thus far, obviously, is "insofar": *insofar* as we love God, *insofar* as we are so devoted, and so forth. That brings us to a second step: unlike Christ, our devotion is neither simple nor all-inclusive, which is why we long to be freed not only from external obstacles to our communion with God but from internal ones, too. So, according to claims rehearsed in chapter 2, all humans are oriented by and toward that to which Christian devotion is opposed: we set our hearts on earthly rewards like money and public esteem, such that we value these things as we ought to value God alone; we likewise put our trust not in God alone but in our own rectitude, or in earthly power, or in the world's reliability; and we treat worldly standards, rather than God's, as if they were ultimate. From this, it follows that, in this life, devotion has a peculiar shape, that of opposition to that which opposes such devotion, or, in short, of "repentance." In repentance, we turn against our old ways, and just so *stand behind* or *take sides with* one element of our evaluative perspective—namely, our devotion to God—against other elements. Persons who so stand are truly, but not at all wholly, devoted to God, which means that even though they already enjoy communion with God, they still long to be simply and wholly devoted to and so included in that communion, which is to say that they long for—they *categorically desire*—a fulfillment in which they would no longer face external or internal obstacles to enjoying communion with God.

The third step, then, is to point out the obvious: if (a) our here-and-now categorical desire is for unfettered communion with God, (b) eternal life includes (and maybe just consists in) such communion, and (c) in eternal life we would be freed from all internal as well as external obstacles to enjoying such communion, then (d) eternal life would fulfill our categorical desire. This is the sort of fulfillment that leads Augustine, for one, to exclaim, "How wonderful will the condition of a person's spirit be then, when it no longer has any vice at all: when it is neither subject to any nor yields to any, and when it no longer has to strive against any, however laudably, but is perfected in unalloyed peace and virtue!"[12] We hear something similar from Teresa of Avila: "Oh," she muses, "when will that happy day arrive when you will see yourself drowned in the infinite sea of supreme truth, where you will no longer be free to sin?"[13] In eternal life we would no longer experience any opposition to our devotion to God, such that we would be simply and wholly so devoted—in that case, our devotion would be fully conformed to Christ's, which would mean, in turn, not only that we would participate in the communion in which God eternally subsists but also that there would now no longer be anything of ourselves that remained outside this communion. (It would not be hyperbolic, at this point, to say that a person is thereby deified, but I will not develop that suggestion here.) From all of this, it follows that eternal life, as a sharing of communion with God to the highest possible degree, would represent a consummate fulfillment for those who categorically desire such communion.

So far, so good, but eternal life still might not sound very fulfilling—it might even sound tedious, in Williams's sense—especially because the account thus far lacks one crucial dimension of a fulfilling life: namely, *content*.[14] That brings us to my third major point, which is to suggest that the material content of this communion, what it *looks* like, as it were, is *abundant life*. In explicating this point, I verge into highly speculative, possibly mythological territory (if I haven't done so already), but for the sake of explaining what I have in mind, that is a risk I am prepared to take.[15]

There are three key moves involved in developing a model for understanding such abundance, each of which I can develop here only briefly. The first move is to claim that, in eternal life, each person loves God in their own way, where this includes caring about certain goods in order to receive them as God's gifts, to put one's characteristic stamp on them, and thus to present them as a sort of offering to God and others; this is a kind of vocation, even in eternal life.[16] Some might thus dedicate themselves to music, others to building things, still others to cooking or conversation or reading or countless other things, where in each case one takes God's gifts as raw material, as it were, and not only gives thanks for these gifts but *does* something with them as well—one cultivates their goodness, does something of one's own with them, and expresses one's gratitude precisely through such cultivation. By way of analogy, think here of getting a thank-you note from a niece to whom one has given some Legos, where she not only says that she is grateful for them but also includes a picture of what she has done with those Legos. The picture is a creative act of gratitude, which is just the sort of thing I am talking about here in terms of vocation: in eternal life, persons cultivate certain goods in a vocationally expressive manner and can thereby express gratitude for God's gifts in ever-new ways, each of which would thus represent a new fulfillment of their desire for communion with God.

The second move is to see these novel expressions in relationship to those of others who likewise love God in their own way, such that we would thus be part of a community in which each not only cultivates God's gifts but also appreciates the goods cultivated by others (as well as the way each person characteristically loves God),[17] and in which these newly cultivated goods open up new possibilities for still other cultivations.[18] In relating to others who are doing their own thing with God's gifts, accordingly, the possibilities for new fulfillments would be constantly and exponentially increased. To see what I have in mind here, think of a jazz combo in which all the musicians "do their thing" with a common melody: each contributes novel riffs and improvisations on that melody, and these riffs take that melody in new directions, thereby opening up new possibilities for the improvisations of others, and so on, such that each continually opens up new possibilities for the others, and vice versa. And then think of jazz as itself one among many ways of "doing one's thing" with God's gifts, where each such way is appreciated by and contributes to the possibilities of others—so the person who hears the jazz combo might write a poem about the experience of listening to the combo's music, or be inspired to write a computer program that can change its algorithms based on the input of other programs (and vice versa); likewise, the members of the combo might find musical inspiration in those who cultivate novel forms of conversational virtuosity, for instance, or those who work out new mathematical formulas for dealing with complexity. Specific examples aside, because each is in community with others who love God in their own way, endless possibilities for expressing that love are constantly being opened up—both within and across vocations—which means, in turn, that endlessly new ways of communing with God are constantly being opened up, too.

Nor is this all, for we can also imagine persons changing vocations over time: so persons who had devoted themselves to the telling of stories might eventually become devoted to musical expression or beadwork or swimming or literally any number of other preoccupations. (Then again, they might simply rest for a while.) Seeing others devoted to such vocations would surely provide a sense of endless possibility here, too—one would see not only ever-new goods, after all, but ever-new ways of loving God in one's own way—such that, again, eternal life would present ever-new possibilities of fulfillment and, because each of these is appreciated by others, ever-new *experiences* of fulfillment.[19]

This might be a good place to pause in order to address a potential misunderstanding, since my claims to this point might seem to imply that eternal life can contain no "repeatable pleasures," in John Martin Fischer's sense, or that, if it did, eternal life would no longer be fulfilling. To be clear, that is not what I am saying; rather, what matters for my account is not that there is no repetition in eternal life but that, if there is, such repetition must serve as an ingredient in an *abundant* life (by contrast with the minimal, "not so bad" sort of life envisioned by Fischer). To see what this might look like, consider two sorts of people. On the one hand, some persons seem to enjoy doing the same things over and over, and there is no reason, on my account, to insist that they cannot continue to do so in eternal life, so long as we bear in mind (a) that such repetition is not simply imposed upon them by the logic of eternity and (b) that even these repetitions must take place in communion with God and others. On the other hand, for those who prefer more variety, eternal life still need not be free of repetition, since, for them, such repetitions could be fewer and further between, and, more important, they need not be *mere* repetitions, especially insofar as the person experiencing them will have grown and changed in the interim. With respect to such growth, my colleague David Tracy has sometimes remarked that he rereads Proust every few years in order to see how he—Tracy, not Proust—has changed. Likewise in eternal life it is not hard to imagine someone repeating a particular pleasure—singing a favorite song, playing a favorite game, spending time with favorite persons—but nevertheless experiencing it as newly fulfilling, since the changes a person has undergone in the meantime (including, perhaps especially, what the person has learned from the experiences of others) can be counted on to open up new facets of that experience.[20] Either way, repetition can contribute to an abundantly fulfilling life, from which it follows that eternal life need not be free from such repetitions. Quite the contrary.

That brings us to one final move, which is to point out that, through such ever-new cultivation of goods, the infinite goodness of God would be infinitely expressed in infinitely many ways.[21] And since each expression takes up previous expressions as its raw material, each is itself a microcosm of that infinite goodness, such that we could then see God's infinite goodness in each as well as in all.[22] This might provide us, in turn, with a different way of thinking about beatific vision, a seeing of God not as a kind of blinding light but as an endlessly overflowing fountain of goodness endlessly manifesting itself and being appreciated in particular ways. God would finally be all in all, then, not in the sense that God absorbs or dissolves everything other than God but in that God is communion, and in eternal life each particular person, along with their cultivation and enjoyment of goods, shares fully in that communion, such that each person is not outside God in *this* sense, and the very communion that one shares with God is itself ever enriched by the abundant life to which each contributes.

Putting everything together, then, we can say that if we are devoted to

God, then we categorically desire communion with God, from which it follows that if eternal life consists in such communion, it would fulfill that desire—and if that communion were endlessly enjoyable in endlessly new ways, then, contra Williams, such fulfillment would never become tedious. Quite the opposite.

That brings us back to Scheffler's objection, to the effect that one of the conditions of valuing—namely, temporal scarcity—would be absent in eternal life, such that we could not humanly value anything in such a life or, then, humanly experience it as fulfilling. To respond to this objection, it is important to distinguish between two kinds of temporal scarcity: on the one hand, there is the kind of scarcity involved in being able to value only so many things in the limited time we have; we might think of this as the bucket-list variety of temporal scarcity. On the other hand, there is the kind of scarcity involved in being able to value only so many things at any given time, irrespective of the sum total of time allotted to us; this is the kind of scarcity by which to-do lists, by contrast with bucket lists, are constrained. With its appeal to vocation, my model makes a place for the to-do-list variety of scarcity—there is only so much that a person can value at any given time—but not for bucket-list scarcity. I would argue that the former is sufficient for human valuing, since what matters here, as far as I can tell, is the connection between valuing and *prioritizing:* if I could value everything all at once, Scheffler seems to be saying, I would not have to prioritize among values, but since such prioritization is a key feature of human valuing, it is hard to imagine how a valuing that lacked this feature would be recognizably human. If we get only so much time, all told, then we will certainly have to prioritize what we do with it, what we value, and so forth. But there are other ways of meeting this condition, including the one laid out here: if there are only so many things that we can value at any given time, then once again we will have to prioritize what we do with our time (even if we have an endless supply of it). If so, then the scarcity and prioritization structure of human valuing could remain intact even in eternal life, which would mean that the model just sketched can address Scheffler's principal objection as well as Williams's.

Before concluding, I should probably say something about a related objection raised by Scheffler and, before him, by Martha Nussbaum.[23] The objection is that human valuing is indexed to particular stages of life, including birth, aging, and death, such that if eternal life does not include such stages, it would, again, not be recognizable as human valuing. In response to this objection, I might point out that although some valuing is indeed indexed to a particular life stage, not all is: the commitment to serving others, for instance, may look different at different stages of life, but the value itself can remain the same throughout. The same could be said for a person's commitment to God. Or we might respond instead by pointing out that one salient feature of "the prime of life," as a life stage, is that it is not indexed to the beginning or end of life, which is precisely what eternal life would be like; hence, we might think of eternal life not as lacking such indices but as being indexed to one of the stages in which present life consists, and, so, as sufficiently continuous with present life. Or, finally, we might point out that in the case of wholehearted devotion, the importance of life stages themselves (along with bodily existence more generally) is relativized in relation to that devotion, such that what would matter about eternal life, for one so devoted, is not life stages, per se, but their fitness as expressions of such devotion. It would appear, then, that there are several ways that we might respond to this objection, and that any one of them would do the trick.

So then: if we think of eternal life as abundant life in communion with God and think of the present life in terms of devotion to and categorical desire for such communion, then we can see how eternal life would be recognizable as the fulfillment of present life, thereby addressing the problems raised by Williams and Scheffler. In response to their objections, I have argued, first, that communion with God can be understood in terms of Jesus' own communion with God; second, that insofar as we share Jesus' devotion to God, we enjoy that communion, too, but not yet fully, such that we categorically desire a consummate enjoyment of it; from this, it follows that if eternal life consists in such enjoyment, we would experience it as a fulfillment of our categorical desire; and, third, I argued that we can understand such communion in terms of an ever-enriching cultivation and circulation of God's gifts, such that communion with God would be endlessly new and endlessly fulfilling. Hence, it seems to me there is at least one categorical desire, namely, desire for such communion, that could be endlessly fulfilled in endlessly new ways and be experienceable by us *as* fulfilling, which means that it would not be unreasonable to desire an eternal life of this sort.

With that, one leg of this book is complete. I set out to render Christianity a bit more understandable, and to do so by providing a host of examples and models that relate Christianity to other phenomena and thus help us see it in terms of familiar patterns. These examples and models, in turn, were all connected with a single model, namely, an understanding of

Christianity as a way of life. Now that I have sketched the telos of this way of life, that part of the argument is complete. The book itself is not yet complete, however; one important task remains.

Wisdom

Back in chapter 1, I mentioned that this book aimed to contribute to the achievement of two epistemic goods: understanding and wisdom. Over the course of the past several chapters, I have provided quite a few frameworks, models, and examples to help us understand Christianity; insofar as these have been successful, I have made good on one of my aims. That brings us back to the other major aim, which is to help us see that Christianity, so understood, has some wisdom to offer us. Previous chapters have supplied us with plenty of resources with which to make this case, so the task of the present section is simply to gather some of these up in order to exhibit this wisdom a bit more explicitly. The argument of this section is thus twofold, to the effect that there is wisdom in each of Christianity's spiritual practices and that there is wisdom in the Christian way of life taken as a whole. As we will see, and as I promised in chapter 1, this wisdom should be recognizable as such even to those who do not share Christian beliefs about God or Jesus.

To see what I have in mind here, let us begin by considering how Christianity shapes our way of being with others. If it is good to become the sort of person who cares about others, who is benevolent toward them, and who appreciates that which is good about them, then there is obviously something good about practices that help us become such persons. (Assuming, that is, that these practices are also good in their own right, or at least not bad, for a bad practice that moves us in a good direction is still bad: think here of using torture to get someone to care about others.) Such practices would teach us to conduct our lives well, in other words, which would entail that there is practical wisdom implicit in them. It would be practically wise, accordingly, if we had a practice that trained us to see others in the best possible light and to be on the lookout for that which is good about them; this is precisely what looking for the image of God does. It would also be wise if we had a practice that helped us become invested in persons and things that we might not otherwise be; this is what beneficence does. And it would be wise to have a practice that enabled us to set aside our desires for vengeance, but in such a way that we did not thereby set aside our felt sense of worth and integrity; this is what forgiveness does.

Beyond that, it would also be good to know how to go about righting wrongs, in such a way that we would not thereby absolutize our efforts or demonize wrongdoers; this is what justice work, as an act of faith and love, is meant to accomplish. These practices are each designed to transform us into the sort of persons who love others; hence, if this would be a good way to conduct oneself in relation to others, and if these practices are themselves good, then it follows that there is practical wisdom implicit in them.

We see something similar in practices that reorient our way of being in the world. Prayer teaches us how to entrust our concerns to God and thus to receive all goods with gratitude; this helps us, in turn, to resist becoming too caught up in the world's goods, even as it helps us to experience more of the world's goodness *as* goodness. Wonder trains us to appreciate created goods in their otherness and thus to notice more and more of the richness and particularity of the world around us. Laughter provides us with a way of resisting the oh-so-seriousness with which the world can take itself and can thus help us withstand the temptation to treat the world (or ourselves) as if it (or we) were ultimate. Lament can render suffering more bearable precisely by bringing it into our relationship with God and others and, so, giving us some reassurance that it will not speak the final word about us. And vocation can enable us to experience the goodness of the particular lives, and the particular goods, to which we have been called, just as it can enable us to experience our life as a coherent and valuable whole. Each of these practices can thus transform our experience of the world, and taken together they can help us fashion a different way of being in the world—taken together they enable us to fashion a life in which we can perceive more and more of the good in the world, can better bear the bad in it, and can weave these together into a single fabric. There is wisdom in such a way of being in the world.

There can also be wisdom in reorienting ourselves toward something that transcends us, though this depends entirely upon how good that thing is. (Popular fascist groups may reorient people toward something transcendent, after all, but we would be unwise to let ourselves be shaped by such groups.) To take the simplest case, it is good to become more like good people, which is why there is wisdom in mimicking and emulating that which makes such people good. It is also good to have one's identity formed by and anchored in a good place, which means that there is wisdom in homemaking practices that create a fit between oneself and such a place. Insofar as others are devoted to something good, it can also be good for us to become like-minded and form a plural subject with them, for then the devotion of each will reinforce the devotion of all. Again, though, the wisdom of such practices is conditional: they reorient us, and if that to which they reorient us is good and the practices themselves are good, then they are wise. (This is a bit too simple: if the good to which they reorient us is trivial or if it is a penultimate good masquerading as ultimate, then it would be unwise to let ourselves be reoriented by them.) That brings us back to a fundamental question: is the God of Christianity a good thing to reorient one's life to?

We can address this question by considering whether the Christian way of life, as a whole, is wise, for if it is, and if it orients us to God, then we have a reason to consider God a good thing to reorient our lives to. So then: is this way of life itself wise? One way of answering this question is to consider the extent to which these practices reinforce one another. If there is wisdom in each of these practices, as I have already suggested, and if these practices are mutually supportive, then it follows that we will reap more wisdom from each practice insofar as we do it in combination with the others. If so, then there is wisdom not only in undertaking each of these practices but also in undertaking them together. We have already seen countless examples of these practices reinforcing one another: so, for instance, developing our sense of wonder will help us spot God's image in others (and vice versa); a sense of vocation can provide us with some clear guidance about which wrongs we are obligated to right; imitation and "becoming one" will themselves train us to pray, to love others, to laugh, to lament, to wonder, and the like, insofar as we are surrounded by others who do these things; by entrusting our concerns to God, we will be better able to love others more unselfishly, to pursue our vocation more single-mindedly, to resist the urge to absolutize our justice work, and so on; if I am at home with God and my identity is thus formed and anchored there, then I will be able to forgive without compromising my sense of worth. I could go on, but the overall point is simply that these practices reinforce one another in such a way that practicing one will often help us practice others. If there is wisdom in each of these practices, therefore, and the practices work together to help us practice them, then there is wisdom in their sum and not just the parts—there is wisdom in the way of life as a whole, in other words, and not just in the individual practices.

A different way of answering this question would be to consider the end toward which this way of life would orient us: if these practices work together to orient us toward an end that is itself good, and if the practices are good in their own right, then we can see this way of life as a whole as providing us with practical wisdom about how to conduct our lives. Hence, insofar as readers find the previous section's vision of eternal fulfillment compelling, they have reason to see wisdom in Christianity as a way of life. (Consider: if I am trying to decide whether to adopt a training regimen—a high-intensity interval program, for instance—then I might consider whether that regimen is reliably connected to certain results: if it is, and if those are results that I want, then I have good reason to adopt the regimen.) By the same token, if a way of life can free us from things that are bad, then we have reason to see it as wise; insofar, then, as these practices work to free us from our orientation by and to the "world"—and insofar as one sees that orientation as bad—we can likewise perceive the wisdom in adopting them. Taking these points together, we can understand Christianity as a way of life that is stretched between two poles, as it were, moving us away from a life oriented by and to the world, and toward an eternal fulfillment. If this vision of life resonates with us, then, again, we should be able to perceive wisdom in the Christian way of life.

That brings us to one last way of answering this question: if these practices orient us to God, and if they teach us to conduct our lives well, then we have reason to think that the God to whom they orient us is good. (If I never knew my mother but she left me a journal filled with all sorts of sound advice about how to live well, then I would probably assume that she was indeed a good person. And if her good advice taught me not only how to live well but also to become like her, then I would have dispositive evidence to this effect.) Moreover, although I have offered no arguments here in defense of the claim that God exists, I have provided something like a practical approach to such a claim, for insofar as persons are shaped by practices of the sort outlined in this book, they will find that devoting themselves to God fits with the shape of their lives and should thus increasingly seem like a reasonable thing to do. For those who want to become increasingly devoted to God, this should serve as the best evidence of all that there is wisdom to be found in these practices.

My hope, then, is that this book offers people some wisdom about how to conduct a life, just as I hope it helps them understand a significant number of things that a significant number of Christians are committed to—and, so, understand "Christianity"—irrespective of whether they are Christian. There are important limitations to the approach I have taken here, of course, not least of which is that I am trying to make sense of what Christianity is *supposed* to look like—by the lights of its own adherents—rather than what it *actually* looks like. A fuller picture would obviously have to include an account of the latter. But there is reason to think that a project like mine has something to offer even to those who are interested in a more empirical approach. To see what I have in mind, think of a coach who is sent to scout a rival football team and, in particular, to track the routes that the wide receivers run on each play. Notice that the scout is not being asked to record how many steps each receiver took on each play and in what direction; the scout is being asked, rather, to identify the routes that the receivers are running, which is to say, to identify what the receivers are supposed to be doing rather than what they are actually doing. Naturally, the scout may also identify sloppy route running, broken routes, and other mistakes, but crucially for our purposes, a scout can identify these things only if they have an idea of how such outcomes diverge from what the player was supposed to be doing; absent this, the scout will be able to describe only what actually happened, not to spot errors, slipups, and the like. As Max Weber observes, we can see persons or groups *as* falling short only if we know what they are falling short *of*; he claims, accordingly, that "in analyzing a political or military campaign," for instance, "it is convenient to determine in the first place what would have been a rational course, given the ends of the participants and adequate knowledge of all the circumstances. Only in this way," he continues, "is it possible to assess the causal significance of irrational factors as accounting for the deviations from this type."[24] I would say the same of Christianity: Christians regularly fail to embody the ideals to which they are committed, but we can recognize these failures as such only if we have a pretty clear picture of what those ideals are. By shedding light on the way of life to which Christians are committed, then, I hope not only to have shed light on Christianity itself but also, in so doing, to have helped us discern the difference between what Christians are committed to and what they are actually doing.

I hope the book also provides us with another sort of discernment. Just as a proofreader cannot help but spot errors and musicians a discordant note, so the practices discussed here are meant to make us the sort of people who cannot help but see all goods as God's gifts, cannot help but wonder at their particular goodness, cannot help but see the best in others, and so on. These practices thus aim to transform the way we see ourselves, our surroundings, and our neighbors. They should train us not only to see these things differently, moreover, but in some fundamental sense to see them more truthfully as well. At the beginning of this book, I mentioned that discernment is a crucial ingredient in practical wisdom. If the preceding arguments are on the right track, we should now be in a better position to see why that would be the case: if we are constantly tempted to see others simply in terms of our own interests and preconceptions, and if we are therefore tempted either to see them in a distorted way or not to see them at all, then we will likewise be tempted to treat them in a way that does not befit their worth. If conducting our lives well means, among other things, that we must conduct ourselves justly, then we must likewise learn to see others in a way that helps us resist these temptations. It seems all too evident that this is something we urgently need right now. My hope is that this book gives us an idea of how Christianity could help us meet this need.

Notes

Preface

1. Harding argues this point in several places; see, for instance, "Rethinking Standpoint Epistemology: What is 'Strong Objectivity?'" *Centennial Review* 36:3 (1992), 437–70; Harding's arguments are anticipated, in theology, by Valerie Saiving's influential essay "The Human Situation: A Feminine View," *Journal of Religion* 40:2 (1960), 100–112.
2. This is what Samuel Scheffler has in mind when he characterizes games as "self-contained bubbles of significance" (*Death and the Afterlife* [Oxford: Oxford University Press, 2013], 56).

Chapter One. The Good of Theology

1. Here I focus on intrinsic, as opposed to instrumental, valuing. The latter sort of valuing is connected to the former in all sorts of interesting ways—one necessarily values the necessary conditions of whatever one values for its own sake, for instance—but for present purposes, I need focus only on the intrinsic variety.
2. My account of valuing draws some insight from Samuel Scheffler, "Valuing," *Equality and Tradition* (Oxford: Oxford University Press, 2010) and *Death and the Afterlife* (Oxford: Oxford University Press, 2013); Harry Frankfurt, *The Importance of What We Care About* (Cambridge: Cambridge University Press, 1988) and *Necessity, Volition, and Love* (Cambridge: Cambridge University Press, 1999); Susan Wolf, *Meaning in Life and Why It Matters* (Princeton: Princeton University Press, 2010); and T. M. Scanlon, *What We Owe to Each Other* (Cambridge, MA: Harvard University Press, 1998).
3. "Significant portion" is a maddeningly imprecise qualifier, to be sure. But the boundary between devotion and non-devotion can be a blurry one; hence, as with other cases of vagueness, the best approach, it seems to me, is to focus

not on the blurry boundaries but on clear examples and non-examples of the phenomenon in question. That is what I am doing here.

4. Hadot, *Philosophy as a Way of Life*, ed. Arnold I. Davidson, trans. Michael Chase (Oxford: Blackwell, 1995), 102, cf. 58–59, 83.

5. Michael Fishbane, *Sacred Attunement: A Jewish Theology* (Chicago: University of Chicago Press, 2008).

6. Stephen Batchelor, *Alone with Others: An Existential Approach to Buddhism* (New York: Grove Press, 1983).

7. Friedrich Schleiermacher, *Christian Faith*, trans. H. R. Mackintosh and J. S. Stewart (Edinburgh: T and T Clark, 1928 [1830]), §19 Thesis; §15 Thesis; §19.3 (hereafter "CF").

8. Kathryn Tanner, *Theories of Culture: A New Agenda for Theology* (Minneapolis: Fortress, 1997), p. 73. Notwithstanding her usual association with postliberalism, note well that Tanner raises important objections to this construal of theology.

9. This raises for me a thorny question about the pronouns I use throughout the book. I had initially decided to use only impersonal pronouns—"one," "one's," "oneself"—so as to respect the fact that many of my readers may not identify with Christianity. When I read through the manuscript, however, it struck me that too many "ones" made the text seem fussy and certainly made it harder to read. In the interest of readability, accordingly, I traded out most of my impersonal pronouns for first-person-plural pronouns. To be very clear, I am *not* presuming that everyone who reads this book would identify with this "we"; I am simply trying to make the book more readable.

10. I elaborate and defend these points in chapter 3 of *Theology without Metaphysics* (Cambridge: Cambridge University Press, 2011).

11. The phrase "actually explain" may sound a bit fuzzy; if so, it might be helpful to observe that the sorts of pattern discussed above—causality, logical connection, narrativity, similarity, and so on—serve as sufficient conditions of understanding, whereas patterns of mere coincidence or association do not.

12. Athanasius, *On the Incarnation of the Word*, trans. Archibald Robinson, in *Christology of the Later Fathers*, ed. Edward Hardy (Louisville: Westminster John Knox, 1954), 2.10, cf. 3.13.

13. Anselm develops this model in *Cur Deus Homo*.

14. James Cone, *God of the Oppressed*, revised ed. (Maryknoll, NY: Orbis, 1975, 1997), 232–33n38; see also Kelly Brown Douglas, who makes a similar claim about her own theology: "What womanist theologians say about Jesus Christ," she writes, "must make sense, 'ring true,' to these women" (*The Black Christ* [Maryknoll, NY: Orbis, 1994], 114). For a nice example of this approach in sociology, see Arlie Hochschild, *Strangers in Their Own Land* (New York: New Press, 2016).

15. I am here drawing on insights from Linda Zagzebski, *On Epistemology* (Belmont, CA: Wadsworth, 2009); and Jonathan Kvanvig, *The Value of Knowledge*

and the Pursuit of Understanding (Cambridge: Cambridge University Press, 2003).

16. Barth, *Der Römerbrief*, second ed. (Zollikon-Zürich: Evangelischer, 1940 [1922]), 315.

17. This is one of the fundamental claims of my *Theology without Metaphysics*.

18. See Robert Nozick's nice formulation of this point: "Wisdom is not simply knowing how to steer one's way through life, cope with difficulties, etc. It also is knowing the *deepest* story, being able to see and appreciate the deepest significance of whatever occurs; this includes appreciating the ramifications of each thing or event for the various dimensions of reality, knowing and understanding not merely the proximate goods but the ultimate ones, and seeing the world in this light" (*The Examined Life: Philosophical Meditations* [New York: Simon and Schuster, 1989], 276).

19. I am hardly the only theologian who has tried to exhibit the wisdom implicit in Christianity; excellent recent examples include Howard Thurman, *Jesus and the Disinherited;* Ellen Charry, *God and the Art of Happiness* and *By the Renewing of Your Minds;* Miroslav Volf, *Flourishing, The Life of the World* (with Matthew Croasmun), and *Practicing Theology* (edited with Dorothy Bass).

20. A further worry might arise, for some Christians, from Paul's contention that the wisdom of God is foolishness to the world, and vice versa (1 Cor. 1:18–25, cf. 3:18–19). It seems clear from his other writings, however, that Paul does not think that nonbelievers are entirely foolish or entirely unable to recognize the wisdom of God *as* wisdom; see, for instance, Rom. 1:19–20, 1 Cor. 15:33, and, more generally, Paul's allusions to and use of the Greek philosophers and rhetoricians in whose works he was educated (for which see, for instance, Hans Dieter Betz, *Galatians* [Minneapolis: Fortress, 1989) and Margaret M. Mitchell, *Paul, the Corinthians, and the Birth of Christian Hermeneutics* [Cambridge: Cambridge University Press, 2010]).

Chapter Two. The Way of the World

1. Teresa of Avila, "Spiritual Testimonies," in *The Collected Works of Saint Teresa of Avila*, vol. 1, trans. Kieran Kavanaugh and Otilio Rodriguez (Washington, DC: ICS Publications, 1987), Testimony 32, p. 403.

2. For a handy example of this, see Paul Tillich, *Systematic Theology*, three volumes (Chicago: University of Chicago Press, 1951–1963), 2:48–49.

3. To take just two prominent examples, see the excellent work along these lines by Cornelius Plantinga, *Not the Way It's Supposed to Be: A Breviary of Sin* (Grand Rapids, MI: Eerdmans, 1996); and Alistair McFadyen, *Bound to Sin: Abuse, Holocaust, and the Christian Doctrine of Sin* (Cambridge: Cambridge University Press, 2000).

4. Day, *The Long Loneliness* (New York: Harper and Row, 1952), 149; Oscar

Romero had something similar in mind when he claimed, simply, that "Sin is slavery to the world" (Second Pastoral Letter, in *Voices of the Voiceless: The Four Pastoral Letters and Other Statements*, trans. Michael Walsh [Maryknoll, NY: Orbis, 2020 (1985)], 74). My use of the concept "world" is thus reminiscent of Albrecht Ritschl's: "This whole web of sinful action and reaction, which presupposes and yet again increases the selfish bias in every man, is entitled 'the world,' which in this aspect of it is not of God, but opposed to him" (*The Christian Doctrine of Justification and Reconciliation*, vol. 3, trans. H. R. Mackintosh and H. R. Macaulay [Edinburgh: T and T Clark, 1902 (1874)], §41); see also Augustine, *Confessions*, XIII.xxi.30.

5. Thomas Aquinas, *Summa Theologica*, trans. Fathers of the English Dominican Province (New York: Benziger Brothers, 1948 [1266–1273]), Ia IIae, q. 72, art. 2 (hereafter "STh"); see Augustine, *Confessions*, II.v.10.

6. Or perhaps I should say that the word "inordinate" tends to *connote* excessiveness, even if, strictly speaking, it does not *mean* excessiveness. But the connotation is a strong one, at least to my ear; hence, if I heard someone say, "She spent an inordinate amount of time studying for the quiz," "He drank an inordinate amount of water yesterday," or "We prepared an inordinate amount of food for the party," I would take it that the amount in question was *too much*. Insofar as English speakers hear the phrase "inordinate desire" in this way, accordingly, they will take it to refer to excessive desire, which is what I am discussing in this paragraph.

7. Augustine, *Teaching Christianity* [*De doctrina christiana*], trans. Edmund Hill (New York: New City Press, 1996 [397/426]), 1.4.4. For an excellent recent treatment of this approach to sin, see Jesse Couenhoven, *Stricken by Sin, Cured by Christ: Agency, Necessity, and Culpability in Augustinian Theology* (Oxford: Oxford University Press, 2013).

8. Augustine, *Teaching Christianity*, 1.4.4.

9. A person can have more than one end, of course. But unless the person's end is God, it follows that all these ends are, in some relevant sense, oriented to the "world" and therefore are a single end. For a nice example of the relationship between road trips and orientation, see Rachel Joyce, *The Unlikely Pilgrimage of Harold Fry* (New York: Random House, 2012).

10. A worry along these lines was famously raised by Hannah Arendt; for discussion of this issue, see Eric Gregory, "Augustine and Arendt on Love: New Dimensions in the Religion and Liberalism Debates," *Annual of the Society of Christian Ethics* 21 (2001), 155–72.

11. Martin Luther, Large Catechism [1529], in *The Book of Concord*, ed. Theodore Tappert (Philadelphia: Fortress, 1959).

12. It might be worth noting that even if the passes were not actually provided by my friend but I thought that they were, I would still count as *subjectively* trusting my friend. But since the passes were not provided by the one I was trusting, it would appear that my trust has no objective referent (just as the

phrase "the present king of France" has no referent), rather than that I am actually trusting whoever did provide them.

13. James Cone, *A Black Theology of Liberation*, Fortieth Anniversary Edition (Maryknoll, NY: Orbis Books, 2010 [1970, 1986, 1990]), 114–15. In addition to Cone and Ruether, see the influential arguments of Valerie Saiving, "The Human Situation: A Feminine View," *Journal of Religion* 40:2 (April 1960), 100–112; Judith Plaskow, *Sex, Sin, and Grace: Women's Experience and the Theologies of Reinhold Niebuhr and Paul Tillich* (Washington, DC: University Press of America, 1980); Susan Nelson Dunfee, "The Sin of Hiding: A Feminist Critique of Reinhold Niebuhr's Account of the Sin of Pride," *Soundings* 65:3 (Fall 1982), 316–27; Daphne Hampson, *Theology and Feminism* (Oxford: Blackwell, 1990), and "Reinhold Niebuhr on Sin: A Critique," in *Reinhold Niebuhr and the Issues of Our Time*, ed. Richard Harries (London: Mowbray, 1986), 46–60.

14. Cone, *Black Theology of Liberation*, 115.

15. Rosemary Radford Ruether, *Sexism and God-Talk: Toward a Feminist Theology* (Boston: Beacon Press, 1993 [1983]), 164; emphasis mine.

16. Ruether, *Sexism and God-Talk*, 162.

17. For a handy summary of the psychological research on this subject, see Daniel Kahneman, *Thinking, Fast and Slow* (New York: Farrar, Straus and Giroux, 2011).

18. My views in these paragraphs have been influenced by George Yancy, *Black Bodies, White Gazes: The Continuing Significance of Race* (New York: Rowman and Littlefield, 2008); Miranda Fricker, *Epistemic Injustice: Power and the Ethics of Knowing* (Oxford: Oxford University Press, 2007), especially 1–59, and various essays in *Implicit Bias and Philosophy*, vol. 1, *Metaphysics and Epistemology*, ed. Michael Brownstein and Jennifer Saul (Oxford: Oxford University Press, 2016).

19. For a classic treatment of this phenomenon, see Frantz Fanon, *Black Skin, White Masks* (New York: Grove Press, 1967 [1952]).

20. I am not considering here the potential harmfulness of associating negative traits with, say, certain breeds of dog or certain species of plant—not because such associations are not actually harmful, nor even because they are not potentially sinful, but simply because they raise several additional, complicated questions that I lack the space to address here.

21. Here I am indebted to the analysis of Kate Manne, *Down Girl: The Logic of Misogyny* (Oxford: Oxford University Press, 2018).

22. For an especially clear analysis of these interrelationships, see Sally Haslanger, "Ideology, Generics, and Common Ground," in *Feminist Metaphysics: Explorations in the Ontology of Sex, Gender, and the Self*, ed. Charlotte Witt (Dordrecht: Springer, 2011), 179–208.

23. Romero, Second Pastoral Letter, 75.

24. Teresa of Avila, "Spiritual Testimonies," Testimony 20, p. 395; see also Lu-

ther, *On the Bondage of the Will*, and Augustine, *Against Two Letters of the Pelagians.*

25. This point is sometimes summarized in terms of the Augustinian slogan *non posse non peccare:* it is not possible for us not to sin. It is worth noting that this phrase is Augustinian but not exactly Augustine's: although Augustine does use phrases like "posse peccare" and "non posse peccare," he only mentions the phrase "non posse non peccare" in a quotation from Pelagius (for which see *De natura et gratia*). I am grateful for Willemien Otten's help in tracking down this detail. As it happens, the fourfold typology often ascribed to Augustine (posse peccare, non posse non peccare, posse non peccare, non posse peccare) finds its origin in Hugh of St. Victor and Peter Lombard; on this point, see Ernst Kutsch, "Das posse non peccare und verwandte Formulierungen als Aussagen biblischer Theologie," *Zeitschrift für Theologie und Kirche* 84:3 (July 1987), 268ff. It is also worth noting that, in my hands, the slogan does not mean that we can only ever sin; it means, rather, that we are all sinful—it is a statement about our character, in other words, rather than our deeds.

26. Augustine, *Confessions*, trans. Henry Chadwick (Oxford: Oxford University Press, 1991 [397–400]), VIII.v.12; for his description of habit as the weight of the past, see VIII.ix.21; as holding one in the grip of the past, see VIII. xii.28; and as a chain, see VIII.v.10. See also Ritschl, *Justification and Reconciliation*, §41, 336–37, 349, and Karl Rahner, *Foundations of Christian Faith*, trans. William Dych (New York: Crossroad, 1978 [1976]), 95.

27. Augustine, *Confessions*, VIII.x.22.

28. Augustine, *Confessions*, VIII.xi.25–26. My reading of Augustine here is greatly indebted to that of James Wetzel, for which see his brilliant *Augustine and the Limits of Virtue* (Cambridge: Cambridge University Press, 1992).

29. Augustine thus describes his internal resistance to conversion: "Vain trifles and the triviality of the empty-headed, my old loves, held me back. . . . I hesitated to detach myself, to be rid of them, to make the leap to where I was being called" (*Confessions*, VIII.xi.26).

30. Teresa of Avila offers a good example of this: "If we tell a rich person living in luxury that it is God's will that he be careful and use moderation at table so that others might at least have bread to eat, for they are dying of hunger, he will bring up a thousand reasons for not understanding this save in accordance with his own selfish purposes" ("The Way of Perfection," in *The Collected Works of Saint Teresa of Avila*, trans. Kavanaugh and Rodriguez [Washington, DC: ICS Publications, 1980], 33.1). I am reminded, here, of Upton Sinclair's famous line: "It is difficult to get a man to understand something when his salary depends upon his not understanding it." In the same way, it is difficult to get people to change their habits when their sense of security depends upon those very habits.

31. Here I am drawing on Harry Frankfurt's notion "volitional necessity," for

which see *Necessity, Volition, and Love* (Cambridge: Cambridge University Press, 1998).

32. Schleiermacher defends a version of this claim in CF § 68.1.

33. Ritschl, *Justification and Reconciliation*, §41, 338; see also Ritschl, *Instruction in the Christian Religion*, §30; Schleiermacher, CF, §71.1, §71.2, and §72.6; Calvin, *Institutes*, II.iii.5 (citing Bernard); Rahner, *Foundations*, 107.

34. Schleiermacher, CF, §67.2.

35. The following paragraphs are indebted to a wide range of scholarship concerning Christian apocalyptic; relevant figures include Johannes Weiss, William Wrede, Albert Schweitzer, Rudolf Bultmann, Ernst Käsemann, Gustaf Aulén, G. Louis Martyn, and Beverly Gaventa.

36. The best recent treatment of this theme is Matthew Croasman, *The Emergence of Sin: The Cosmic Tyrant in Romans* (Oxford: Oxford University Press, 2017).

37. Justo L. Gonzalez, *Mañana: Christian Theology from a Hispanic Perspective* (Nashville: Abingdon, 1990), 154.

38. Luther, *Lectures on Galatians*, vol. 26 of *Luther's Works*, ed. Jaroslav Pelikan (St. Louis: Concordia, 1963 [1535]), 3:13; see Aulén's discussion of this passage in *Christus Victor*.

39. Basil, Homily on Psalm 115, §5 (in *On Christian Doctrine and Practice*, trans. Mark DelCogliano [Yonkers: St. Vladimir's Seminary Press, 2012]); James Cone, *Black Theology and Black Power* (New York: Harper and Row, 1969), 40. Note well that Cone uses this analysis of "alien powers" to provide the category with which to make sense of racism. This is a point to which we will return.

40. See examples of "household conversions" in Acts 10:1–11:18; 16:11–15, 25–34; 18:1–11. Commenting on one of these, Calvin writes that "Luke doth again commend the godly zeal of the keeper, that he did consecrate all his whole house to the Lord; wherein doth appear the grace of God, in that he brought all his whole family unto a godly consent" (*The Acts of the Apostles*, trans. Henry Beveridge [Edinburgh: Calvin Translation Society, 1844], 16:33). See also the analogy Watchman Nee draws between Adam and Abraham: just as Abraham is "the head of the family of faith, includ[ing] the whole family in himself," so Adam is "the head of the family of humanity" (*The Normal Christian Life* [Bombay: Gospel Literature Service, 1957]).

41. Gregory of Nyssa, *Catechetical Discourse*, trans. Ignatius Green (Yonkers, NY: St. Vladimir's Seminary Press, 2019 [c. 381]), §22.

42. Here as elsewhere, biblical translations are taken from the New Revised Standard Version (though I have sometimes seen fit to revise these translations, as too translations of other texts).

43. My understanding of Paul here is deeply indebted to recent biblical scholars, including E. P. Sanders (*Paul and Palestinian Judaism; Paul, the Law, and the Jewish People;* and *Paul*); J. Louis Martyn (*Galatians* and *Theological Issues in the Letters of Paul*); J. Christiaan Beker (*Paul the Apostle* and *The Triumph of*

God); Martinus de Boer (*Galatians* and *Paul, Theologian of God's Apocalypse*; and Beverly Gaventa (*Apocalyptic Paul*). For the individual passages that follow, I have likewise consulted the commentaries of Augustine, Thomas Aquinas, and Calvin.

44. Augustine, *Confessions*, IV.vi.11. To be sure, Augustine is recollecting this experience as part of a larger point to the effect that it is folly to set our hearts fully on anything other than God; this supports the point I am making about experiences of brokenness.

45. For further discussion of this concept, as well as relevant literature, see my *Theology without Metaphysics*, especially chapters 2 and 6.

46. *Gaudium et Spes*, in *Vatican II: Essential Texts*, ed. Norman Tanner (New York: Crown, 2012 [1965]), §27.

47. Mary Daly, *Beyond God the Father* (Boston: Beacon, 1973), 43.

48. See Jeffrie Murphy, "Two Cheers for Vindictiveness," *Punishment and Society* 2:2 (2000), 131–43.

49. I can also feel guilty about things that simply happen to me: if I was the only member of my platoon to survive an ambush or the only member of my graduating class to secure a job, then I might experience survivor's guilt. The peculiar thing about survivor's guilt, it seems, is that one ends up feeling *as if* one has done something wrong, even though one has not. In most cases, survivor's guilt arises in feelings one has about one's feelings: I feel guilt about feeling glad that I got a job, for example, because I cannot help but think of others who weren't so lucky. However that may be, survivor's guilt is best dealt with under the rubric of guilt that one should not feel, which is a topic to which I turn later.

   I can likewise feel guilty about things that others have done, insofar as I identify with them to such an extent that *their* doing it feels as though *I* have done it. People are often liable to such feelings when it comes to the wrongdoings of their children, for instance, or with a collective to which they belong. Contrary to some theorists, I see no reason to classify such secondhand guilt as shame; the only reason to do so, as far as I can see, is because theorists have decided, a priori, that guilt can only be first-personal, such that any second-personal feelings of this sort must be classified as something else. Better, I think, simply to revise our understanding of guilt.

50. Ritschl, *Justification and Reconciliation*, §12, pp. 57–58; Ritschl elsewhere remarks that guilt is a "judgment of condemnation" (*Instruction in the Christian Religion*, in *Three Essays*, trans. Philip Hefner [Philadelphia: Fortress Press, 1972 [1886], §31).

51. See here Reinhold Niebuhr on self-deception in *The Nature and Destiny of Man* (New York: Charles Scribner's Sons, 1941), 1:203ff.

52. My account of shame owes much to Gabrielle Taylor, *Pride, Shame, and Guilt* (Oxford: Oxford University Press, 1985), as well as the literature that interacts with her work.

53. Bonhoeffer, *Creation and Fall*, trans. Douglas Bax (Minneapolis: Fortress, 1997 [1937]), 124.

54. Lucy Grealy, *Autobiography of a Face* (New York: Harcourt Mifflin Harcourt, 1994), xv.

55. Rooney, *Normal People* (New York: Crown, 2018), 246–47.

56. I am inclined to read David's famous self-description—"Surely I was sinful from the womb"—as an expression of this sort of shame, too—expressing the sense that his badness goes all the way down.

Chapter Three. Deliverance from Sin

1. For a dispositive argument to this effect, see Johannes Weiss's objections to the theology of Albrecht Ritschl in *Die Predigt Jesu vom Reiche Gottes.*

2. My accounts of Jesus' life, teachings, and significance are informed by accounts by several theologians and biblical scholars, including especially Hegel, Schleiermacher, Ritschl, Weiss, Schweitzer, Bultmann, Bornkamm, Tillich, Barth, Jeremias, Kümmel, Sanders, Frederiksen, Kasper, Pannenberg, Frei, Cone, Ruether, Elizabeth Johnson, and Sobrino.

3. Lk. 12:35–40 (see also Lk. 12:43–47, Mt. 24:42–46); Mt. 24:42–44.

4. Some might wonder whether I have illicitly conflated what Jesus says about following him with what he says about entering the kingdom. (Sanders raises a version of this concern.) As the Gospels portray him, at least, Jesus seems to identify the two: hence, when Peter says, "Look, we have left our homes and followed you," Jesus responds, "There is no one who has left house or wife or brothers or parents or children, for the sake of the kingdom of God, who will not get back very much more in this age, and in the age to come eternal life" (Lk. 18:28–30). Leaving everything to follow Jesus is thus equated, here, with leaving everything for the sake of the kingdom of God, both of which are equated with what it takes to "be saved," "to enter the kingdom," and the like.

5. On this point, see James Cone: "The Kingdom is for the poor and not the rich because the former has nothing to expect from the world while the latter's entire existence is grounded in his commitment to worldly things. . . . It is not that poverty is a precondition for entrance into the Kingdom. But those who recognize their utter dependence on God and wait on him despite the miserable absurdity of life are typically the poor, according to Jesus" (*Black Theology and Black Power*, 36–37). Or, in the pithy formulation of Dorothy Day, "The main thing is not to hold on to anything" (*Selected Writings*, ed. Robert Ellsburg [Maryknoll, NY: Orbis, 1992 (1983)], 107).

6. Kazoh Kitamori, *Theology of the Pain of God* (Richmond, VA: John Knox Press, 1965 [1958]), 93.

7. Mother Teresa exemplifies such love: "We act under the conviction that every time we feed the poor, we are offering food to Christ himself. When-

ever we clothe a naked human being, we are clothing Christ himself. Whenever we offer shelter to the dying, we are sheltering Christ himself" (*No Greater Love*, ed. Becky Benenate and Joseph Durepos [Novato, CA: New World Library, 2001 (1997)], 168–69).

8. Teresa of Avila, "Interior Castle," in *The Collected Works*, vol. 2, V.3.8.

9. On this point, see, among many others, Gustavo Gutierrez, *Theology of Liberation*, trans. Sister Caridad Inda and John Eagleson (Maryknoll, NY: Orbis, 1973), xxvii, 160.

10. Rahner, *Foundations*, 303; see also Karl Barth, *Church Dogmatics*, in fourteen part volumes, trans. G. W. Bromiley and T. F. Torrance (Edinburgh: T and T Clark, 1936–1969 [1932–1967]), III/2, 63 (hereafter "CD").

11. Ritschl thus claims that "the suffering of Christ, through the patience with which it was borne, becomes a kind of doing" (*Justification and Reconciliation*, §48); see also Schleiermacher, CF, §104.4.

12. Julian of Norwich, *Showings*, trans. Edmund Colledge and James Walsh (Mahwah, NJ: Paulist Press, 1978), Long Text, chap. 22.

13. We see a nice example of this idea in von Balthasar's claims about Jesus' "mission-consciousness" (in *Theo-Drama*, vol. 3) and in Hans Frei's claims about Jesus' identity (in *Identity of Jesus Christ*); see also Barth, CD III/2, 61–70.

14. Here I am drawing a few sentences from my *Theology without Metaphysics*, 35.

15. Hegel, *Phänomenologie des Geistes* (Hamburg: Felix Meiner, 1988), 130–31. Rahner makes a similar point about such "radical and uncompromising decisions" (*Foundations*, 272). Kant makes a parallel point in the second *Critique*, 5:30.

16. Jon Sobrino, *Christology at the Crossroads*, trans. John Drury (Maryknoll, NY: Orbis, 1978 [1976]), 357; Kitamori, *Theology of the Pain of God*, 146.

17. See Schleiermacher: "There is only one eternal and universal decree justifying men for Christ's sake. This decree, moreover, is the same as that which sent Christ on his mission . . . and once more, the decree that sent Christ forth is one with the decree creating the human race, for in Christ first human nature is brought to perfection. Indeed, since thought and will, will and action are not to be sundered in God, all this is one divine act designed to alter our relation to God" (CF §109.3).

18. "Every moment of his existence, so far as it can be isolated, presents just such a new incarnation and incarnatedness of God, because always and everywhere all that is human in him springs from the divine" (Schleiermacher, CF, §96.3).

19. I trace some of these ideas at greater length in my "Immutability, Necessity, and Triunity," *Scottish Journal of Theology* 65:1 (January 2012), 64–81.

20. So Julian: "For I saw that God never began to love mankind; for just as mankind will be in endless bliss, fulfilling God's joy with regard to his works, just so has that same mankind been known and loved in God's prescience from without beginning in his righteous intent" (*Showings*, Long Text, chap. 53);

see also Ritschl: "We recognize God's eternity in the fact that amid all the changes of things, which also indicate variation in his working, he himself remains the same and maintains the same purpose and plan by which he creates and directs the world" (*Instruction*, §14).

21. In order to avoid unnecessary ambiguity, I here use the traditional term "Father" to refer to the first person of the Trinity. I recognize that some Christians have significant reservations about this usage—given voice, most famously, by Mary Daly—but this is still the customary reference. In my defense, then, I would ask readers to recall that this is an interpretive rather than a strictly normative project.

22. For an admirably clear statement of this view, see John of Damascus, *The Orthodox Faith*, III.iii.

23. For one famous example of such an approach, see Cyril of Alexandria, *On the Unity of Christ*, trans. John McGuckin (Crestwood, NY: St. Vladimir's Seminary Press, 1995), 130.

24. For two important examples of this sort of approach, see *Gaudium et Spes*, §22.2, and Barth, CD IV/1, 179 ff., and IV/2, 51ff.

25. Sobrino, for one, defends just such an approach against the start-with-two-natures approach: "They presuppose knowledge of who God is and what humanity is at the start, when they should start at the other end" (*Crossroads*, 386).

26. To take just one handy example, Thomas Aquinas claims that the Spirit "enlightens our mind, because whatever we know, it is through the Holy Spirit that we know it"; "makes us love God and cease to love the world"; and "unites us to God by love, for he is himself God's love" (*Expositio in Symbolum Apostolorum*, art. 8, in *The Aquinas Catechism* [Manchester, NH: Sophia Institute Press, 2000]).

27. See Thomas Aquinas, STh I, q. 37, art. 1, ad 3.

28. Teresa of Avila, "Soliloquies," in *The Collected Works*, vol. 1, 7.2, p. 449.

29. This account of the Trinity bears important resemblance to that of Karl Rahner (for which see especially *The Trinity*), Karl Barth (CD I/1, especially "The Root" and "The Meaning of the Doctrine of the Trinity"), and Eberhard Jüngel (see *God's Being Is in Becoming*).

30. The locus classicus of this model, naturally, is Irenaeus's *Adversus Haereses*; for a brilliant contemporary example, see Kathryn Tanner, *Jesus, Humanity, and the Trinity*.

31. Cone, *Black Theology and Black Power*, 35, see also 40, and *Black Theology of Liberation*, 122–25.

32. For a celebrated example of this approach, see Gregory of Nyssa, *Catechetical Discourse*, §24.

33. Here again, I am drawing on recent Paul scholarship, including especially the work of Albert Schweitzer, Rudolf Bultmann, Ernst Käsemann, E. P. Sanders, Christiaan Beker, J. Louis Martyn, and Beverly Gaventa.

34. So Paul: "Christ redeemed us from the curse of the law by becoming a curse for us—for it is written, 'Cursed is everyone who is hanged on a tree'" (Gal. 3:13); "But when the fullness of time had come, God sent forth his Son, born of woman, born under the law, to redeem those who were under the law, so that we might receive adoption as sons" (Gal. 4:4–5); "God has done what the law, weakened by the flesh, could not do: by sending his own Son in the likeness of sinful flesh, and to deal with sin, he condemned sin in the flesh, so that the just requirement of the law might be fulfilled in us, who walk not according to the flesh but according to the Spirit" (Rom. 8:3).

35. A fourth model of the atonement—the moral exemplar approach—is much less influential within mainstream Christian thought, at least as a primary way of understanding how Jesus delivered us from sin. Kant is one of the lone, clear defenders of this approach; for this, see the Christology laid out in his *Religion within the Boundaries of Mere Reason*, 6:61ff.

36. For these concerns, see Williams, *Sisters in the Wilderness*, especially the section "Doctrine: Surrogacy and Redemption"; Rita Nakashima Brock, *Journeys by Heart*, especially the chapter on "The Feminist Redemption of Christ"; Mary Daly, *Beyond God the Father*, especially the chapter "Beyond Christolatry"; Rosemary Radford Ruether, *Sexism and God-Talk*, especially the chapter "Christology: Can a Male Savior Save Women?"; and J. Denny Weaver, *The Nonviolent Atonement*, especially the introduction.

37. The literature on contemporaneous Jewish eschatology is vast and, indeed, it has become de rigueur for biblical scholars to engage with this material; two fairly early, influential examples include Rudolf Bultmann, *Primitive Christianity in Its Contemporary Setting*, and E. P. Sanders, *Paul and Palestinian Judaism* and *Jesus and Judaism*.

38. Augustine, "The Spirit and the Letter," 42, p. xxv.

39. Hans Küng, *The Church*, trans. Ray and Rosaleen Ockenden (New York: Burns and Oates, 1968 [1967]), 235, 356; see also Rahner, *Foundations*, 333, 343.

40. Calvin, *Institutes of the Christian Religion*, trans. Ford Lewis Battles (Philadelphia: Westminster, 1960 [1559]), IV.i.5; see also Barth, CD IV/1, 719; Dietrich Bonhoeffer, *Discipleship*, trans. Barbara Green and Reinhard Krauss (Minneapolis: Fortress, 2001 [1937]), 199/188, and *Act and Being*, trans. H. Martin Rumscheidt (Minneapolis: Fortress, 1996 [1931]), 109/113; Rudolf Bultmann, *Theology of the New Testament*, two volumes, trans. Kendrick Grobel (London: SCM Press, 1952–1955), 1:306–7.

41. 1 Thess. 2:13; 2 Cor. 5:20; 2 Thess. 2:14; emphases mine.

42. John 20:21; John 13:20; Lk. 10:16, see Mt. 10:40.

43. Here I am following some insights from Nicholas Wolterstorff, *Divine Discourse* (Cambridge: Cambridge University Press, 1995). (I am also reworking some ideas I first developed in my "Recognition of Baptism," *Koinonia Journal* 29 [2007], 13–38).

44. Letty Russell, *Human Liberation in a Feminist Perspective—A Theology* (Philadelphia: Fortress, 1974), 77.

45. This point is given memorable formulation in Barth's reflections on Grünewald's Isenheim altarpiece (CD I/1, 131).

46. And because that's true, our words have the power of God behind them; this would explain the sort of claims we find in such passages as Rom. 1:16 and 10:17, as well as 1 Cor. 1:18 and Gal. 3:2–5.

47. James Cone thus claims that "the kingdom demands the surrender of one's whole life" (*Black Theology of Liberation*, 123); Kosuke Koyama, that "The Word says to us today, 'Your identity is to be understood only in relation to the crucified Lord'" (*Water Buffalo Theology* [Maryknoll, NY: Orbis, 1999], 161); Jon Sobrino, that "In preaching the coming of God's kingdom Jesus brings people into serious crisis. Things cannot go on as before because the end is now at hand" (*Crossroads*, 355); and Kazoh Kitamori, that "the Gospel is not only a fact that stands outside us, but a fact which *enfolds* us" (*Theology of the Pain of God*, 33).

48. Justo L. Gonzalez, *Mañana: Christian Theology from a Hispanic Perspective* (Nashville: Abingdon Press, 1990), 159.

49. Dorothy Day writes perceptively about what it means to try to make sense of one's conversion after one's "whole perspective has changed" (*From Union Square to Rome* [Maryknoll, NY: Orbis, 2006 (1938)], 4–5).

50. Kathryn Tanner thus famously characterizes such relations as "non-competitive" or "non-contrastive"; see here *God and Creation in Christian Theology* (Minneapolis: Fortress, 1988).

51. Luther, "95 Theses," in *Career of the Reformer*, in *Luther's Works*, 31:26; "Explanations of the 95 Theses," in *Luther's Works*, 31:84. See also Calvin, *Institutes*, III.iii.5 and III.iii.10; Ritschl, *Instruction*, §49, Thomas, STh Supplement q. 4, art. 1; and Weiss, *Jesus' Proclamation of the Kingdom of God* (Philadelphia: Fortress, 1971), 105.

52. Barth, CD IV/2, 570, 538.

53. Bonhoeffer, *Discipleship*, 165/160, 46/58.

54. This seems to be what Teresa of Avila has in mind here: "I said to myself, 'Why, Lord, do you desire my works?' He answered: 'In order to see your will, daughter'" ("Spiritual Testimonies," Testimony 47, p. 412).

55. This is the key move in both versions of the Transcendental Deduction, a point that I elaborate in *The Theological Project of Modernism* (Oxford: Oxford University Press, 2015), 50ff.

56. Here I am borrowing some material from my *Theological Project of Modernism*, 66.

57. Barth, CD IV/2, 574; see also Bonhoeffer, *Discipleship*, 80–81/87; Luther, "Babylonian Captivity of the Church," in *Luther's Works*, 36:68. Because the old self is constituted by its orientation by and to the world, it follows that the death of one's old self is simultaneously one's death to the world (and

vice versa). This might help us understand what Paul has in mind, for instance, when he says that "the world has been crucified to me, and I to the world" (Gal. 6:14).

58. I am focusing here on so-called believers' baptism; those who baptize infants could apply this same model to confirmation; given the close connection usually drawn between baptism and confirmation, this should not be a problem (for which see, for instance, the Catholic Catechism, §§1285ff., and Alexander Schmemann, *For the Life of the World* [Crestwood, NY: St. Vladimir's Seminary Press, 1973 (1963)], 75ff.).

59. Luther, Large Catechism, 440/33 (see also "Babylonian Captivity," 36:64); CF §137.1.

60. Calvin, *Institutes*, IV.xv.13.

61. Luther, Large Catechism, 436/2; Calvin, *Institutes*, IV.xv.1; Schleiermacher, CF, §136.1; Rahner, *The Church and the Sacraments*, trans. W. J. O'Hara (New York: Herder and Herder, 1963), 87; Küng, *The Church*, 206.

62. Luther, "Babylonian Captivity," 36:62; see also Large Catechism 437/10; Calvin, *Institutes*, IV.xv.14 and 16.

63. See Calvin, *Institutes*, IV.xiv.3, 5–6, 13; Bultmann, *Theology of the New Testament*, 1:312.

64. Here especially I am trying to do justice to some features of the ecumenical consensus on baptism, as expressed in the important ecumenical document "Baptism, Eucharist, and Ministry," Faith and Order Paper no. 111 (Geneva: World Council of Churches, 1982) (hereafter "BEM").

65. So Bonhoeffer: "Sin no longer has any claim on those who are dead; with death the claim has been met and has ceased to exist" (*Discipleship*, 223/209).

66. So Luther: "To appreciate and use baptism aright, we must draw strength and comfort from it when our sins or conscience oppress us, and we must retort, 'but I am baptized!'" (Large Catechism, 442/44).

67. Think here of a scene in *Return of the Jedi*, in which Yoda informs Luke, "No more training do you require. Already know you that which you need." To this, Luke responds, "Then I am a Jedi," but Yoda rains on his parade: "Not yet." As the example makes clear, Yoda is in position to judge something that Luke is not, namely, when Luke has achieved the status of Jedi.

68. We can make this point more emphatically in view of some claims made elsewhere about the connection between one's devotion and one's unity with Christ: very briefly, one is devoted to God and thus raised to new life just insofar as the Spirit of Christ lives in one, such that in recognizing one as such a new self, God is likewise recognizing Christ—God's Child—in one. On this point, see Letty Russell, *Church in the Round* (Louisville: Westminster John Knox, 1993), 140ff.

69. Here I am obviously borrowing some ideas from J. L. Austin and, once again, borrowing some material from my "Recognition of Baptism." I depart from the latter account in one crucial respect: I would now say that baptism rec-

ognizes repentance, not a person's knowing how to go on in the same way as Christ.

70. We might draw support for this view from the words spoken at Jesus' baptism, but doing so would require me to defend exegetical and Christological positions that I cannot do justice to here.

71. Calvin, *Institutes*, IV.xvii.1, see also IV.xv.1; Schleiermacher, CF, §136.3.

72. On this point, see Barth, CD III/4, 99.

73. Luther, Small Catechism, in *The Book of Concord*, V.16, pp. 349–50; see also Large Catechism V.15, 22.

74. Teresa of Avila, "Spiritual Testimonies," Testimony 63, p. 434.

75. Bultmann, "Paul," in *Existence and Faith* (New York: Meridien, 1960), 138; see also Bultmann's claim that "deep friendship and love"—consummately that of God—"transforms man and gives him a new being. My friend, in holding me to be not the person I am in visible reality with my weaknesses and defects, but as the man I am meant to be and would like to be, makes me such; he frees me from myself, and bestows on me a new being" ("Grace and Freedom," in *Essays* [Macmillan, 1955], 179).

76. Bultmann, "Church and Teaching in the New Testament," in *Faith and Understanding* (New York: Harper and Row, 1969), 200; emphasis added.

77. Ambrose of Milan, *De Officiis*, III:132 (Oxford: Oxford University Press, 2002), 200; see also III:136, where Ambrose argues that such friendship follows the pattern of Christ.

78. Aelred of Rievaulx, *Spiritual Friendship*, trans. Lawrence C. Braceland, ed. Marsha L. Dutton (Collegeville, MN: Liturgical Press, 2010 [c. 1164]), 3:6.

79. Aelred, *Spiritual Friendship*, 1.20, 3.61; see also 3:28.

80. Aelred, *Spiritual Friendship*, 3:103.

81. Marilynne Robinson, *Lila* (New York: Picador, 2014), 86.

82. Robinson, *Lila*, 90.

83. Robinson, *Lila*, 67.

84. Robinson, *Lila*, 67. For the washing-off of baptism, see 103, 237.

85. Robinson, *Lila*, 259.

86. Robinson, *Lila*, 260.

87. For two paradigmatic examples of such renarration, see Augustine's *Confessions* and Teresa of Avila's *Book of Her Life*.

Chapter Four. Being Reoriented

1. Iris Marion Young, "House and Home: Feminist Variations on a Theme," in *On Female Bodily Experience: "Throwing Like a Girl" and Other Essays* (Oxford: Oxford University Press, 2005), 140.

2. Consider a lovely example from Marilynne Robinson, whose character Glory reflects movingly on just such an instance of meaning sedimentation: "His little boy touching that tree, just to touch it. The tree that sounded like the

ocean. Dear Lord in heaven, she could never change anything. How could she know what he had sanctified to that child's mind with his stories, sad stories that had made them laugh. I used to wish I lived here, he said. That I could just walk in the door like the rest of you did" (*Home* [New York: Farrar, Straus, and Giroux, 2008], 323).

3. bell hooks, "Homeplace: A Site of Resistance," in *Available Means: An Anthology of Women's Rhetoric(s)*, ed. Joy Ritchie and Kate Ronald (Pittsburgh: University of Pittsburgh Press, 2001), 387. Jacqueline Grant talks similarly of the "theology of somebodiness" that defined her grandparents' home, by means of which they "conveyed to their children that inspite of the world's denial of you, Jesus (God) affirms you" (*White Women's Christ and Black Women's Jesus* [Atlanta: Scholars Press, 1989], ix).

4. On this point, see, for instance, the case studies in *Religion and the New Immigrants*, ed. Helen Rose Ebaugh and Janet Saltzman Chafetz (Walnut Creek, CA: Altamira, 2000), and *Gatherings in Diaspora*, ed. R. Stephen Warner and Judith G. Wittner (Philadelphia: Temple University Press, 1998).

5. Soong-Chan Rah, *The Next Evangelicalism: Releasing the Church from Western Cultural Captivity* (Downers Grove, IL: InterVarsity, 2009), 168–69. Compare the similar remarks of James Cone: "Home was that eschatological reality where the oppressed would 'lay down that heavy load,' singing and shouting because 'there would be nobody there to turn [them] out.' Every Sunday the black brothers and sisters of Macedonia experienced a foretaste of their 'home in glory'" (*God of the Oppressed*, 1).

6. Basil, Homily Delivered in Lakizois, §8; First Homily on Psalm 14, §1 (in *On Christian Doctrine and Practice*). See also Barth, *Ethics*, trans. G. W. Bromiley (New York: Seabury Press, 1981), 487–88; Augustine to Proba, Letter 130, 2.5 (widely available; see, for instance, *Letters 100–155*, trans. Roland Teske [Hyde Park, NY: New City Press, 2003]).

7. Calvin, *Institutes*, II.viii.28.

8. Augustine, *Confessions*, X.xxxiii.49; Thomas, STh IIa IIae, q. 91, art. 1.

9. Augustine, *Confessions*, X.xxxiii.49; Thomas, STh IIa IIae, q. 91, art. 2.

10. Jenefer Robinson, *Deeper Than Reason: Emotion and Its Role in Literature, Music, and Art* (Oxford: Oxford University Press, 2005); and Peter Kivy, *Sound Sentiment: An Essay on the Musical Emotions* (Philadelphia: Temple University Press, 1989).

11. Cone, *The Spirituals and the Blues* (Maryknoll, NY: Orbis, 1991 [1972]), 31.

12. Thomas, STh IIa IIae, q. 91, art. 1; Calvin, *Institutes*, III.xx.31.

13. Howard Thurman talks, in this regard, of "a clear sharing by the members of the group with each other of the comfort and strength each found in his religious commitment" (*Deep River* [Richmond, IN: Friends United Press, 1975], 27).

14. Calvin, *Institutes*, III.xx.31.

15. Dietrich Bonhoeffer, *Life Together*, trans. Daniel Bloesch and James Burtness

(Minneapolis: Fortress, 1996 [1939]), 50/66; see also Isaak Dorner, *System of Christian Ethics*, trans. C. M. Mead and R. T. Cunningham (New York: Scribner and Welford, 1887 [1885]), §81.1, p. 594.

16. Thurman, *The Negro Spiritual Speaks of Life and Death* (Richmond, IN: Friends United, 1975), 32; see also Cone, *Spirituals*, 30; Augustine, *Confessions*, X.xxxiii.49.

17. Augustine, *Tractates on the Gospel of John*, trans. John W. Rettig (Washington, DC: Catholic University of America Press, 1988), Tractate 26; Thomas, STh IIIa, q. 83, art. 2, ad 3; Bonhoeffer, *Life Together*, 102/118; BEM, §19. There is a lovely rhyme in Augustine's original: "O sacramentum pietatis! O signum unitatis! O vinculum caritatis!"

18. Woolley and Fishbach, "Recipe for Friendship: Similar Food Consumption Promotes Trust and Cooperation," *Journal of Consumer Psychology* 27:1 (2017), 1–10. See also Claude Fischler, "Commensality, Society, and Culture," *Social Science Information* 50:3–4 (2011), 528–48; Hirschman, "Melding the Public and Private Spheres: Taking Commensality Seriously," *Critical Review* 10:4 (1996), 533–50.

19. Wu, Bischof, and Kingstone, "Looking While Eating: The Importance of Social Context to Social Attention," *Scientific Reports* 3:2356 (2013), 1–5.

20. Hillard Kaplan et al., "The Natural History of Human Food Sharing and Cooperation," in *Moral Sentiments and Material Interests*, ed. Gintis, Bowles, Boyd, and Fehr (Cambridge, MA: MIT Press, 2005), 75–113.

21. Rahner, *Foundations*, 29; Hegel, "The Spirit of Christianity and Its Fate," in *Early Theological Writings*, trans. T. M. Knox (Chicago: University of Chicago Press, 1948), 297/248.

22. BEM, §6 and §29. See also Dorner, for instance, who refers to it as "a meal prepared by the Lord himself" (*System of Christian Doctrine*, vol. 4, trans. J. S. Banks [Edinburgh: T and T Clark, 1890], §143, p. 306).

23. Augustine, *Answer to Faustus, a Manichaean*, trans. Roland Teske (Hyde Park, NY: New City Press, 2007), 19:11; Hegel, "Spirit of Christianity," 298–99/ 249–51. See again BEM, §19.

24. BEM, Eucharist, §1.

25. For an elaboration of this claim, see, for instance, Jeremias, *The Eucharistic Words of Jesus*, as well as the first volume of his *New Testament Theology*.

26. Needless to say, there is a sense in which a taste of home is a very tangible sign of an invisible grace.

27. Gregory of Nyssa, "On Virginity," in *Ascetical Works*, trans. Virginia Woods Callahan (Washington, DC: Catholic University of America Press, 1967), §23.

28. Kelly Brown Douglas, *The Black Christ* (Maryknoll, NY: Orbis, 1994), 1–2. We hear something strikingly similar in Delores Williams, *Sisters in the Wilderness*, ix–x.

29. Linda Zagzebski, *Exemplarist Moral Theory* (Oxford: Oxford University Press, 2017), 138.

30. Quoted in Dave McMenamin, "LeBron James Sad Kobe Bryant Retiring, Wishes They'd Met in Finals," https://www.espn.com/nba/story/_/id/14266468 /lebron-james-truly-sad-kobe-bryant-retiring (accessed January 25, 2022).

31. Here I am borrowing some material from my *Theology without Metaphysics*, 79–80.

32. Schleiermacher elaborates this model in CF, §6.2.

33. On this point, see CF, §6, Thesis, and §60.2.

34. CF, §60.2; §6.4.

35. For a nice summary of this research, see Alvin Goldman, *Joint Ventures: Mind-reading, Mirroring, and Embodied Cognition* (Oxford: Oxford University Press, 2013).

36. Schleiermacher, CF, §122.1.

37. Schleiermacher, CF, §122.1.

38. Schleiermacher, CF, §122.1.

39. Schleiermacher, CF, §6.2.

40. Schleiermacher, CF, §88.2.

41. Calvin, *Commentaries on the Epistles of Paul the Apostle to the Corinthians*, trans. John Pringle (Edinburgh: Calvin Translation Society, 1848), commenting on 1 Cor. 11:1.

42. We hear something along these lines from Karl Barth, who claims that the proper theological procedure is one in which "now this, now that article [of faith] figures as the unknown x, for which the investigation solves by means of the articles of faith a, b, c, d, etc., which are presupposed as known (without presupposing knowledge of x and, in this respect, *sola ratione*). . . . These are the a, b, c, d, etc., on the basis of which the x . . . is thus shown to be 'reasonable' or 'necessary'!" (*Fides Quaerens Intellectum*, 54–55, 55–56, in *Gesamtausgabe* II.13, ed. Eberhard Jüngel (Zürich: Theologischer Verlag Zürich, 2002). I discuss this approach in "Theological Method," in *The Wiley Blackwell Companion to Karl Barth*, ed. George Hunsinger and Keith Johnson (Oxford: Wiley Blackwell, 2020), from which I have borrowed a few sentences.

43. Wilfrid Sellars, *Empiricism and the Philosophy of Mind* (Cambridge, MA: Harvard University Press, 1997).

44. My understanding here is informed by Margaret Gilbert (*On Social Facts*, *Sociality and Responsibility*, and *Joint Commitment*), Raimo Tuomela (*Social Ontology* and *The Philosophy of Sociality*), Philip Pettit (*Group Agency*), and Deborah Tollefsen (*Groups as Agents*).

45. Dietrich Bonhoeffer, *Sanctorum Communio: A Theological Study of the Sociology of the Church*, trans. Reinhard Krauss and Nancy Lukens (Minneapolis: Fortress, 1998 [1930]), 62/98; 66/103.

46. For an example of claims along these lines, see Eberhard Arnold, *God's Revolution*, and Gerhard Lohfink, *Jesus and Community* and *Does God Need the Church?*

47. Peter Phan, *Christianity with an Asian Face* (Maryknoll, NY: Orbis, 2003), 178.

48. Schleiermacher, CF, §121.2.

49. Augustine, *Tractates on the Gospel of John*, Tractate 21.8.

50. Moralia in Job, praef. 14; STh III, q. 48, art. 2; Acts of the Trial of Joan of Arc (all cited from *Catechism of the Catholic Church* [New York: Doubleday, 1995], §795); Elizabeth Johnson, *She Who Is* (New York: Crossroad, 1992), 72); CD IV/3, 790.

51. Schleiermacher, CF, §122.3; see also Oscar Romero: "Christ founded the church so that he himself could go on being present in the history of humanity precisely through the group of Christians who make up his church. The church is the flesh in which Christ makes present down the ages his own life and his personal mission" (Second Pastoral Letter, in *Voice of the Voiceless*, 76).

52. Barth, CD IV/3, 790; See also Bonhoeffer, *Act and Being*, 109/112–13.

53. I am well aware that relationships between coaches and players are not usually as top-down as this analogy might make them seem.

54. For a strong recent statement of this objection, see Lauren Winner, *The Dangers of Christian Practice* (New Haven: Yale University Press, 2018). I return to this objection in chapter 7.

55. Bonhoeffer, *Sanctorum Communio*, 133/199; see also 127/190, 142/211.

56. Bonhoeffer captures both of these points: "All that we mean by human nature, individuality, and talent is part of the other person's freedom—as are the other's weaknesses and peculiarities that so sorely try our patience, and everything that produces the plethora of clashes, differences, and arguments between me and the other. Here, bearing the burden of the other means tolerating the reality of the other's creation by God—affirming it, and in bearing with it, breaking through to delight in it" (*Life Together*, 86/101).

57. I borrow the phrase "place of appearing"—and much of the inspiration for this paragraph—from Mary McClintock Fulkerson, *Places of Redemption* (Oxford: Oxford University Press, 2007).

58. Wittgenstein, *Philosophical Investigations*, trans. G. E. M. Anscombe (Malden, MA: Blackwell, 1953), §258.

59. See Korie Edwards, *The Elusive Dream* (Oxford: Oxford University Press, 2008), especially pp. 88–89, and Fulkerson, *Places of Redemption*.

60. "Each successive epoch of theology found its thoughts in Jesus . . . and it was not only each epoch that found itself in him: each individual created him according to their own personality" (*Quest of the Historical Jesus* [Tübingen: Mohr/Siebeck, 1906/1984], 48).

61. On this point, see, for instance, the literature on epistemic peers (e.g., Adam Elga, "Reflection and Disagreement," *Nous* 41:3 [2007], 478–502) and on feminist-standpoint epistemology (e.g., "Rethinking Standpoint Epistemology: What Is 'Strong Objectivity'?" *Centennial Review* 36:3 [1992], 437–70).

62. *Beyond the Pale: Reading Ethics from the Margins*, ed. Stacey Floyd-Thomas

and Miguel De La Torre (Louisville: Westminster John Knox, 2011), xxv. Letty Russell defends a similar perspective in *Church in the Round* (Louisville: Westminster John Knox, 1993), 25.

63. Aelred, *Spiritual Friendship*, 3:132.

64. Aelred, *Spiritual Friendship*, 1:46, see also 3:131, 3:88, 3:124, and Ambrose, *De Officiis*, III:133.

65. Adams, *Finite and Infinite Goods* (Oxford: Oxford University Press, 1999), 196.

66. So Thomas: "Yet neither does well-wishing suffice for friendship, for a certain mutual love is requisite, since friendship is between friend and friend: and this well-wishing is founded on some kind of communication" (STh IIa IIae, q. 23, art. 1).

67. For this point, see Aelred, *Spiritual Friendship*, 2:12 and 3:101.

68. Aelred, *Spiritual Friendship*, 1:32; see also 1:20, 2:11, 3:62, 3:83, 3:125; Ambrose, *De Officiis*, III:129, 132, 136.

69. So Aelred: "The friend's counsel has great authority" (*Spiritual Friendship*, 3:103; see also 3:17, 61, and 107).

Chapter Five. Being in the World

1. Volf, "The Crown of the Good life," in *Joy and Human Flourishing: Essays on Theology, Culture, and the Good Life*, ed. Miroslav Volf and Justin E. Crisp (Minneapolis: Fortress, 2015), 129, 130, and 132.

2. This is close to Robert Roberts's "defining proposition" for joy, according to which one's feeling of joy could be explicated in the following terms: "*It is important that X be in condition Y; and X is in condition Y*" (Roberts, *Emotions: An Essay in Aid of Moral Psychology* [Cambridge: Cambridge University Press, 2003], 279).

3. To be clear, I am not here arguing that prayer is *nothing but* such a practice, which is to say that my arguments should not be thought either to assume or to entail that, say, prayer plays no role in God's government of the world.

4. Coakley, *God, Sexuality, and the Self: An Essay "On the Trinity"* (Cambridge: Cambridge University Press, 2013), 6. Like Coakley, I am here arguing for an account in which prayer serves as a kind of ascetic discipline through which one's heart can be transformed. By contrast with Coakley, my account focuses on petitionary (rather than contemplative) prayer, and I am more interested than she is in the mechanisms, as it were, by which prayer might do the work ascribed to it.

5. Thomas, STh q. 83, art. 9, 2.

6. Rahner, *The Need and the Blessing of Prayer*, trans. Bruce Gillette (Collegeville, MN: Liturgical Press, 1997), p. 57; see also Luther, Large Catechism III.8, 421; Calvin, *Institutes*, III.xx.28; and Ritschl, *Justification and Reconciliation*, §66, p. 640.

7. Augustine to Proba, in *Letters 100–155*, trans. Roland Teske (Hyde Park, NY: New City Press, 2003), Letter 130, 11.21, see also 12:23; Thomas, STh q. 83, art. 9; Calvin, *Institutes*, III.xx.3; and Dorner, *System of Christian Ethics* §53.2, p. 425.

8. Calvin, *Institutes*, III.xx.28, III.xx.3; see also Thomas, STh, q. 83 art. 17; Barth, CD III/4, 99.

9. Julian of Norwich, *Showings*, Long Text, chap. 42.

10. Here my account draws from, among others, Aaron Ben-Ze'ev, *The Subtlety of Emotions* (Cambridge, MA: MIT Press, 2000); Ronald de Sousa, *The Rationality of Emotion* (Cambridge, MA: MIT Press, 1987); Peter Goldie, *The Emotions: A Philosophical Exploration* (Oxford: Oxford University Press, 2000); Bennett W. Helm, *Emotional Reason: Deliberation, Motivation and the Nature of Value* (Cambridge: Cambridge University Press, 2001); Martha Nussbaum, *Upheavals of Thought: The Intelligence of Emotions* (Cambridge: Cambridge University Press, 2001); Jesse Prinz, *Gut Reactions: A Perceptual Theory of Emotion* (Oxford: Oxford University Press, 2004); Robert C. Roberts, *Emotions: An Essay in Aid of Moral Psychology* (Cambridge: Cambridge University Press, 2003); and Christine Tappolet, *Emotions et valeurs* (Paris: Presses Universitaires de France, 2000).

11. This is what Isaak Dorner has in mind, apparently, when he asserts that "prayer"—explicitly uttered on particular occasions—"is the specific means of growth in the inner life," and, so, that prayer "is a *means* of virtue in quite a special sense, and not merely a *manifestation* of the life already possessed" (Dorner, *System of Christian Ethics*, §53.1, p. 423 [emphases mine]). See also Barth, CD III/4, 89, and Brunner, *The Divine Imperative*, trans. Olive Wyon (Cambridge: Lutterworth, 1941), 313.

12. STh q. 83, art. 2, ad 3; see also Luther, *Devotional Writings*, in *Luther's Works*, 42:87; Augustine to Proba, 8.17; Rahner, *Need and Blessing*, 46–47, Calvin, *Institutes*, III.xx.3, 28, and 44; Barth, CD III/4, 95–96.

13. So Julian: "It pleases him that we seek him and honor him through intermediaries, understanding and knowing that he is the goodness of everything" (*Showings*, Long Text, chap. 6).

14. Think here, paradigmatically, of the prayer traditionally recited before meals by Catholics: "Bless us, O Lord, and these thy gifts, which we are about to receive, from thy bounty, through Christ our Lord."

15. Michael Fishbane, *Sacred Attunement* (Chicago: University of Chicago Press, 2008), 122. See also the Catholic Catechism (New York: Doubleday, 1995): in blessing, "God's gift and man's acceptance of it are united in dialogue with each other. The prayer of blessing is man's response to God's gifts: because God blesses, the human heart can in return bless the One who is the source of every blessing," §2626.

16. Thomas, STh Ia, q. 83, art. 7 and 8.

17. Kitamori, *Theology of the Pain of God*, 97.

18. My usage is not completely idiosyncratic, for, to take just one example, this is how Kant uses the term in the "Transcendental Aesthetic" section of his *Critique*, and it is close to the way the term is used when we talk about "anaesthetics."

19. Weil, "Reflections on the Right Use of School Studies with a View to the Love of God," in *Waiting for God*, trans. Emma Crawford (New York: Routledge, 1951), 62.

20. For this, see Schleiermacher, *Hermeneutics and Criticism*, ed. Andrew Bowie (Cambridge: Cambridge University Press, 1998), 20.1, p. 24.

21. Weil had no familiarity with Moore, as far as I know, but Weil does see poetry as exemplifying the sort of attention she has in mind; she thus claims, for instance, that "the poet produces the beautiful by fixing his attention on something real" (*Gravity and Grace*, trans. Emma Crawford and Mario van der Ruhr [London: Routledge, 2002 (1952)], 119). Moore's poetry neatly instantiates exactly this sort of attention.

22. William Carlos Williams, "Marianne Moore," in *Selected Essays* (New York: Random House, 1954), 294.

23. Marianne Moore, "A Jelly-Fish," *Lantern* 17 (Spring 1909), 110. Note that this is the longer version of Moore's poem; a shorter version was published as "A Jellyfish" in *O to Be a Dragon* (New York: Viking, 1959).

24. Toyoda quotes this passage on her website, Super Ordinary Life (superordinarylife.com/blog-1, accessed June 24, 2021).

25. So Bultmann: "In my everyday work, in the use of my time, etc., I regard the world as at my own disposal. The world and my action in it are godless throughout. . . . But the concept of wonder radically negates the character of the world as the manageable world of everyday work" ("The Question of Wonder," in *Faith and Understanding* [New York: Harper and Row, 1969], 251, 255).

26. Barth thus claims that "wonder occurs when someone encounters a spiritual or natural phenomenon that he has never met before. It is for the moment something uncommon, strange, and novel to him. He cannot even provisionally assign it a place in the previous circle of his ideas about the possible" (*Evangelical Theology* [Grand Rapids, MI: Eerdmans, 1979 (1963)], 64).

27. Augustine, Tractate 24 (on John 6:1–14), *Tractates on the Gospel of John, 11–27*, trans. John Rettig (Washington, DC: Catholic University of America Press, 1988), 1.1, p. 231.

28. Calvin puts this nicely: "There is no doubt," he insists, "that the Lord would have us uninterruptedly occupied in this holy meditation; that, while we contemplate in all creatures, as in mirrors, those immense riches of his wisdom, justice, goodness, and power, we should not merely run over them cursorily, so to speak, with a fleeting glance; but we should ponder them at length, turn them over in our minds seriously and faithfully, and recollect them repeatedly. . . . Therefore, to be brief, let all readers know that they

have with true faith apprehended what it is for God to be Creator of heaven and earth, if they first of all follow the universal rule, not to pass over in ungrateful thoughtlessness or forgetfulness those conspicuous powers which God shows forth in his creatures, and then learn so to apply it to themselves that their very hearts are touched" (*Institutes*, I.xiv.21).

29. Weil, "Right Use," 105.

30. The logic here echoes that of Spinoza (*Ethics*, Part I, especially Definition VI and Proposition XVI) as reworked by Schleiermacher (especially in his second *Speech*).

31. Julian of Norwich, *Showings*, Long Text, chap. 35.

32. I defend such an account in chapter 4 of *Theology without Metaphysics*.

33. Perkins, *A Treatise of the Vocations* (London: John Haviland, 1631), 750; Brunner, *The Divine Imperative*, trans. Olive Wyon (Cambridge: Lutterworth, 1941), 198; See also Ritschl, *Justification and Reconciliation*, §48, p. 445; Barth, CD III/4, 595, 599–600; Merton, *No Man Is an Island* (New York: Houghton Mifflin, 1955), 131. My grasp of the relevant literature here owes much to William Placher's *Callings: Twenty Centuries of Christian Wisdom on Vocation* (Grand Rapids, MI: Eerdmans, 2005).

34. Mother Teresa, *No Greater Love*, 147.

35. Barth, CD III/4, 630. See also Ritschl, *Justification and Reconciliation*, §68, p. 666; Bonhoeffer, *Ethics*, trans. Reinhard Krauss, Charles West, and Douglas Stott (Minneapolis: Fortress, 2005), 293/292–93.

36. Adams, *Finite and Infinite Goods* (Oxford: Oxford University Press, 1999), 302; see also Merton, *No Man Is an Island*, 153.

37. I am here following some clues from Ritschl, who equates "vocation" with a "consciously pursued personal end" and with a "personal self-end" that gives orientation to whatever other ends one might pursue; for this, see especially *Justification and Reconciliation*, §48.

38. Ritschl, *Justification and Reconciliation*, §68, p. 667; see also Calvin, *Institutes*, III.x.6; Merton, *No Man Is an Island*, 147.

39. Bushnell, "Every Man's Life a Plan of God," in *Sermons for the New Life* (New York: Charles Scribner, 1860), 10.

40. Adams, *Finite and Infinite Goods*, 292; see also Calvin, *Institutes*, III.x.6, and Teresa of Avila, "Spiritual Testimonies," Testimony 10, p. 388.

41. Law, *A Serious Call to a Devout and Holy Life* (London: J. M. Dent, 1906), 36.

42. For a more elaborate critique of such approaches, see Adams, "Vocation," in *Finite and Infinite Goods*, 306ff.

43. Barth, CD III/4, 619; Dorner, *System of Christian Ethics*, §68.3, p. 502; Brunner, *Divine Imperative*, XX.3, 200; see also Adams, "Vocation," 308–9.

44. Perkins, *A Treatise of the Vocations*, 758; see also Dorner, *System of Christian Ethics*, §68.3, pp. 502–3.

45. Barth, CD III/4, 596; see also Brunner, *Divine Imperative*, XX.3, pp. 200–201.

46. Bushnell, "Every Man's Life a Plan of God," 22.

47. Baxter, "Directions about Our Labor and Callings," in *A Christian Directory, or, A Body of Practical Divinity and Cases of Conscience*, vol. 2 (London: Richard Edwards, 1825), Direction XI, pp. 586–87.

48. For an apt example of this, see James Cone's description of a pivotal meeting in which Benjamin Mays told Cone that he had the makings of an excellent scholar; for this, see Cone, *Said I Wasn't Gonna Tell Nobody* (Maryknoll, NY: Orbis, 2018), 38ff.

49. Here I am borrowing some insights from John Morreall, *Comic Relief: A Comprehensive Philosophy of Humor* (Malden, MA: Blackwell, 2009).

50. Niebuhr, "Humor and Faith," in *Discerning the Signs of the Times* (New York: Charles Scribner's Sons, 1946), 112.

51. Barth, CD IV/1, 446.

52. Niebuhr, "Humor and Faith," 119; Bonhoeffer, *Letters and Papers*, August 3, 1944, p. 495 (p. 551 of *Widerstand und Ergebung: Briefe und Aufzeichnungen aus der Haft*, in *Dietrich Bonhoeffer Werke*, vol. 8 [Gütersloher, 1998]).

53. Niebuhr, "Humor and Faith," 120.

54. Thurman, *Deep River* (Richmond, IN: Friends United, 1975), 57, 59; see also Kierkegaard, *Concluding Unscientific Postscript*, trans. Howard and Edna Hong (Princeton: Princeton University Press, 1992), 513–14; VII:447, VII:450–51.

55. Joseph Heller, *Catch-22* (New York: Simon and Schuster, 1961), 16.

56. Augustine, *Confessions*, IV.iv.9.

57. Cassell, *The Nature of Suffering and the Goals of Medicine* (Oxford: Oxford University Press, 1991), 33.

58. Calvin, *Commentaries on the Catholic Epistles*, trans. John Owen (Edinburgh: Calvin Translation Society, 1855), commenting on 1 Pet. 1:6.

59. Thurman, *The Negro Spiritual Speaks of Life and Death* (Richmond, IN: Friends United, 1975), 4, see also 37–8, 56; Cone, *Spirituals*, 58; *God of the Oppressed*, 132.

60. I am here borrowing a few sentences from my *Theological Project of Modernism*, 200–201.

61. Ritschl, *Justification and Reconciliation*, §48, p. 423; see also §§49–50, §58; *Instruction*, §23. Hence Ritschl's claim that "the suffering of Christ, through the patience with which it was borne, becomes a kind of doing" and that, "by his patience, the suffering inflicted on him is as such made his own" (*Justification and Reconciliation*, §48, p. 419).

62. In support of this point, see Crystal L. Park's review of the empirical literature: "Making Sense of the Meaning Literature," *Psychological Bulletin* 136 (2010), 257–301; for compelling anecdotal support, see Viktor Frankl, *Man's Search for Meaning* (Boston: Beacon, 1959), 76, 103–4.

63. Tillich, *Systematic Theology*, 1:268. The characterization of such faith as faith "in spite of" can be found on this same page.

64. Wolterstorff, *Lament for a Son* (Grand Rapids, MI: Eerdmans, 1987), 68.

65. On this point, see Calvin on Psalm 13:1: "When he saw not a single ray of

good hope to whatever quarter he turned, so far as human reason could judge, constrained by grief, he cries out that God did not regard him; and yet by this very complaint he gives evidence that faith enabled him to rise higher, and to conclude, contrary to the judgment of the flesh, that his welfare was secure in the hand of God. Had it been otherwise, how could he direct his groanings and prayers to him?" (*Commentary on the Book of Psalms*, trans. James Anderson [Edinburgh: Calvin Translation Society, 1845], 182).

66. Thurman, *Deep River*, 27.

67. On this, see Thomas, STh Ia IIae, q. 32, art. 5.

68. Hilde Lindemann, *Holding and Letting Go: The Social Practice of Personal Identities* (Oxford: Oxford University Press, 2014).

69. Thomas, STh, Ia IIae, q. 36, art. 4; see also Soong-Chan Rah, *Prophetic Lament* (Downers Grove, IL: InterVarsity, 2015).

Chapter Six. Being with Others

1. Thomas Aquinas, STh, Ia IIae q. 28, art. 2. My understanding of this point is informed by Harry Frankfurt, *Necessity, Volition, and Love* (Cambridge: Cambridge University Press, 1999).

2. Butler, *Fifteen Sermons* (Oxford: Oxford University Press, 2017), sermon 12, §7, p. 104. We hear something similar from Kazoh Kitamori, who claims that we need to "feel a love toward a suffering neighbor as intense as the love of a parent for his child" (*Theology of the Pain of God*, 88).

3. Butler, *Fifteen Sermons*, sermon 12, §7, p. 104.

4. Thomas, STh Ia q. 28, art. 1; see also Teresa of Avila, "The Way of Perfection," 7.1, p. 66; Søren Kierkegaard, *Works of Love*, trans. Howard Hong and Edna Hong (Princeton: Princeton University Press, 1995 [1847]), IX.98; Calvin, *Institutes*, III.vii.4.

5. My understanding of "pride" here relies on that of Margaret Taylor, for which see her *Pride, Shame, and Guilt: Emotions of Self-Assessment* (Oxford: Oxford University Press, 1985).

6. Calvin, *Institutes*, III.vii.4; see also Kierkegaard, *Works of Love*, 271/IX.259.

7. Barbara Hilkert Andolsen, "Agape in Feminist Ethics," *Journal of Religious Ethics* 9:1 (Spring 1981), 77. See also Dorothy Day: "When you love people, you see all the good in them, all the Christ in them" (*On Pilgrimage* [Grand Rapids, MI: Eerdmans, 1999], April 10, 1948, p. 124).

8. Appreciation is thus a way of repeating God's own judgment, concerning all that God has made: it is very good (Gen. 1:31).

9. Kierkegaard, *Works of Love*, 274/IX.261.

10. Kierkegaard, *Works of Love*, 376/IX.357; 121; IX.117; see 377/IX.357.

11. Anders Nygren, *Agape and Eros*, trans. Philip Watson (Philadelphia: Westminster Press, 1953), 66–67.

12. Thomas, STh IIa IIae, q. 23, art. 1, ad 2.

13. Kierkegaard, *Works of Love*, 160/IX.153.
14. Gutierrez, *Theology of Liberation*, 114–15.
15. Cone, *Black Theology and Black Power*, 52.
16. Kierkegaard, *Works of Love*, 49/IX.52; see also 19/IX.23.
17. Kitamori, *Theology of the Pain of God*, 89.
18. Butler, *Fifteen Sermons*, sermon 12, §3, p. 103.
19. Notice that what is basic for a Christian account of love is not universality, per se, but devotion to God. It stands to reason, then, that vocation will play a vital role in directing and delimiting the scope of one's love, though the resulting "special relations" do not exempt one from wider obligations. I return to these points later in the chapter. On the relationship between Christian love and special relations, see Gene Outka, *Agape* (New Haven: Yale University Press, 1972), 268ff., as well as the perceptive discussion in William Werpehowski, "'Agape' and Special Relations," in *The Love Commandments*, ed. Edmund Santurri and William Werpehowski (Washington, DC: Georgetown University Press, 1992).
20. There is an obvious connection here with the parable of the lost sheep: precisely because the good shepherd loves all the sheep, he will leave the ninety-nine to find the one.
21. Gutierrez, *Theology of Liberation*, 160, 135.
22. Luther, "Freedom of a Christian," in *Luther's Works*, 31:364.
23. Kierkegaard, *Works of Love*, 264/IX.252; see also 56/IX.58.
24. Nygren, *Agape and Eros*, 118; see Andolsen's discussion of this passage in the context of her broader critique of Nygren ("Agape in Feminist Ethics," 70).
25. Saiving thus claims that many women lack "center" ("Human Situation," 109); Andolsen talks about "excessive selflessness" and "destructive self-abnegation" and the tendency for "many women [to] live for others to a damaging degree" ("Agape," 74). Mary Daly points out that such idealizations of selflessness fortify discrimination and unjust treatment toward women; this is what she has in mind when she claims that women have "hardly been helped by an ethic which reinforces the abject female situation" (*Beyond God the Father* [Boston: Beacon, 1973], 100). Andolsen thus speaks for many when she insists that "*Agape* defined exclusively as other-regard or self-sacrifice is not an appropriate virtue for women who are prone to excessive selflessness" ("Agape," 74).
26. In this connection, Andolsen points out that Anna Howard Shaw, for instance, "did not necessarily disapprove of women making sacrifices on behalf of others. What Shaw criticized was an ethic shaped by men for women in which self-sacrifice was always the paramount virtue" ("Agape," 76).
27. For a compelling defense of this point, see Sarah Coakley, "Kenosis and Subversion," in *Powers and Submissions* (Malden, MA: Blackwell, 2002).
28. Here I am quoting Delores Williams's invocation of Alice Walker's well-known dictum; see *Sisters in the Wilderness*, xix. See also Karen Baker-Fletcher,

Sisters of Dust, Sisters of Spirit, 81ff. For the original, see Alice Walker, *In Search of Our Mothers' Gardens: Womanist Prose* (San Diego: Harcourt Brace Jovanovich, 1983), xi.

29. Kant, *Kritik der praktischen Vernunft* (Berlin: Walter de Gruyter, 1968 [1788]), V:83, see also Freud, *Civilization and Its Discontents,* trans. James Strachey (New York: W. W. Norton, 1961), 62ff., 109; Joseph Fletcher, *Situation Ethics* (Louisville: Westminster John Knox, 1966), 106.

30. Agnes Callard, *Aspiration* (Oxford: Oxford University Press, 2018). Callard does not apply her framework to love, but the application seems natural enough, and one about which, in personal correspondence, she seems enthusiastic.

31. For an especially perceptive account of the way this works, see Carl Wilson, *Let's Talk about Love: Why Other People Have Such Bad Taste* (New York: Bloomsbury, 2014).

32. *Autobiography of a Saint,* 211—quoted in Jean Vanier, *Community and Growth,* revised ed. (New York: Paulist Press, 1989 [1979]), 40; see also Bonhoeffer, *Life Together,* 73/90.

33. Calvin, *Institutes,* III.vii.6—emphasis mine.

34. Basil, "Homily Delivered in Lakizois," §9 (in *On Christian Doctrine and Practice*).

35. Gutierrez, *Theology of Liberation,* 114–15; see also Kitamori: "We do not love God with half our heart and our neighbor with the other half; we love God with all our heart and our neighbor with all our heart. This is what hitting two targets with one arrow means. If the two targets, God and our neighbor, were set up side by side, we could not do it. However, if God, the large target, and our neighbor, the small target, stand one in front of the other, with the same center, we can hit both targets with one arrow" (*Theology of the Pain of God,* 99). The idea of "representing God" that we are considering here is one way of explaining how these two targets could be lined up.

36. Kierkegaard, *Works of Love,* 164; IX.156.

37. Basil, "Homily on Envy," §1 (in *On Christian Doctrine and Practice*).

38. Thurman, *Jesus and the Disinherited* (Nashville: Abingdon, 1949), 67; see also Kierkegaard, *Works of Love,* 270/IX.257–58.

39. Jean Hampton, "The Retributive Idea," in Jeffrie Murphy and Jean Hampton, *Forgiveness and Mercy* (Cambridge University Press, 1988), 146.

40. Gustavo Gutierrez is right to insist, accordingly, that if we are to love others, "we have to break with our mental categories, with the way we relate to others, with our way of identifying with the Lord, with our cultural milieu, with our social class, in other words, with all that can stand in the way of a real, profound solidarity with those who suffer, in the first place, from misery and injustice" (*Theology of Liberation,* 118).

41. Kierkegaard, *Works of Love,* 88; IX.87.

42. On this point, see also the famous M and D passage in Iris Murdoch, *Sovereignty of Good* (New York: Routledge, 1970), 17–22.

43. On this, see, for instance, Calvin, *Institutes*, I.xv.4.

44. For further elaboration of Schleiermacher's account, see chapter 3 of my *Theological Project of Modernism*. On this point, see Balthasar, who insists that "infinite richness is rich in freedom and can [therefore] enrich others (and hence itself) in ways that are ever new" (Hans Urs von Balthasar, *Theo-Drama*, vol. 5, *The Last Act*, trans. Graham Harrison [San Francisco: Ignatius, 1998], 509). Gregory of Nyssa makes a similar point in *De hominis opificio*, XVI.10.

45. David Velleman provides a helpful, empirically informed account of how such self-fulfilling prophecies work; see his "From Self Psychology to Moral Philosophy," in *Self to Self* (Cambridge: Cambridge University Press, 2006).

46. Teresa of Avila, "The Way of Perfection," 6.8.

47. Stevenson, *Just Mercy* (Spiegel and Grau, 2014), 17–18. See also Mother Teresa: "Do not be surprised or become preoccupied at each other's failure; rather see and find the good in each other, for each one of us is created in the image of God" (*No Greater Love*, 45).

48. Kierkegaard, *Works of Love*, 291–92/IX.278; see also Basil, "Homily on Humility," §5 (in *On Christian Doctrine and Practice*).

49. For a helpful overview of the literature on priming, see Daniel C. Molden, "Understanding Priming Effects in Social Psychology: What Is 'Social Priming' and How Does It Occur?" *Social Cognition* 32 (special issue, 2014), 1–11.

50. So C. S. Song: "Human beings—whether Christian or not—have stories to tell. . . . We may also in those stories encounter God, catch a glimpse of God's secrets for humankind, and experience wonder at God's vision for the future of creation" (*Theology from the Womb of Asia* [Maryknoll, NY: Orbis, 1986], 126; see also Kierkegaard, *Works of Love*, 293/IX.279).

51. Kierkegaard, *Works of Love*, 292/IX.279.

52. Karen Baker-Fletcher, *Sisters of Dust, Sisters of Spirit: Womanist Wordings on God and Creation* (Minneapolis: Fortress, 1998), 113–14. For another example of what it looks like to come to see oneself as bearing God's image, see Olivia Bustion, "Autism and Christianity: An Ethnographic Intervention," *Journal of the American Academy of Religion* 85:3 (September 2017), 653–81.

53. On this point, see Dorothy Day: "I often think in relation to my love for little Becky, Susie, and Eric [her grandchildren]: 'That is the way I must love every child and want to serve them, cherish them, and protect them'" (*On Pilgrimage*, April 10, 1948, p. 123); see also Vanier, *Community and Growth*, 17 and 272.

54. On this point, see Basil, "Ethics," §49.3, in *On Christian Ethics*, trans. Jacob van Sickle (Yonkers: St. Vladimir's Seminary Press, 2014).

55. Thurman, *Jesus and the Disinherited*, 70–71; see also Cone, *Black Theology and Black Power*, 113; Marilyn McCord Adams, "Forgiveness: A Christian Model," in *Faith and Philosophy* 8:3 (1991), 297.

56. The importance of this condition is forcefully elaborated in Aurel Kolnai, "Forgiveness," *Proceedings of the Aristotelian Society* 74:1 (1974), 91–106.

57. Here I am disagreeing with an influential claim of Nicholas Wolterstorff, for which see his *Justice in Love* (Grand Rapids, MI: Eerdmans, 2011), 161ff.

58. Thomas Aquinas, *Commentary on the Letters of Saint Paul to the Philippians, Colossians, Thessalonians, Timothy, Titus, and Philemon*, trans. F. R. Larcher (Lander, WY: Aquinas Institute, 2012).

59. For further theological analysis of their act of forgiveness, see Cone, *Said I Wasn't Gonna Tell Nobody*, 138ff.

60. On the expressive function of punishment, see the celebrated essay of Joel Feinberg, "The Expressive Function of Punishment," *Monist* 49:3 (1965), 397–423.

61. My way of distinguishing these emotions differs from that of many philosophers; whether or not "resentment" and "indignation" are the right words to use to refer to them, my point is simply that one can respond to wrongdoing *as* wrongdoing by focusing on the wrongdoer or on the wrongdoing.

62. "Cum dilectione hominum et odio vitiorum" (Augustine, *Letters*, vol. 4, nos. 211–70, ed. Boniface Ramsey [Hyde Park, NY: New City Press, 2005], Letter 211, section 11); see also Julian of Norwich: "We must unreservedly hate sin and endlessly love the soul as God loves it" (*Showings*, Long Text, chap. 40).

63. "Acting for a reason" is far more complicated than I am here letting on; for some of the relevant discussion, see Elizabeth Anscombe, *Intention;* Donald Davidson, *Essays on Actions and Events;* and Michael Thompson, *Life and Action.*

64. Adams, "Forgiveness," 292, see also 300.

65. Bonhoeffer, *Life Together,* 21/33–34; see also Calvin's comment on Colossians 3:13 (Edinburgh: Calvin Translation Society, 1851).

66. Martin Luther King, Jr., *Stride toward Freedom* (Boston: Beacon Press, 1958), 149.

67. Cone, *Spirituals*, 82.

68. Adams, "Forgiveness," 291.

69. Thomas, STh IIa IIae, q. 108, art. 1.

70. For one forceful statement of this view, see Stacey Patton, "Black America Should Stop Forgiving White Racists," *Washington Post,* June 22, 2015.

71. This by contrast with exceptionless obligations, such as the obligation not to act cruelly toward another person.

72. C. S. Song puts the point beautifully: "Love," he writes, "if it is genuine, is not imprisoned in the past. Love imprisoned in the past contradicts its own nature. . . . Love is the power to break out of the past, to create the present, and to envision the future. For love to be love, it always has to create a new life from old life, a new world out of the ruins of the old world" (*Jesus in the Power of the Spirit* [Minneapolis: Fortress, 1994], 303). Needless to say, forgiveness is specifically designed to help us do this.

73. Nygren, *Agape and Eros*, 90.

74. Brunner, *Justice and the Social Order*, trans. Mary Hottinger (Cambridge: Lutterworth, 1945), 111.

75. Hauerwas, *After Christendom? How the Church Is to Behave If Freedom, Justice, and a Christian Nation Are Bad Ideas* (Nashville: Abingdon, 1991).

76. For a fuller discussion of this idea, see Wolterstorff, *Justice in Love*, 41ff.

77. Basil, "First Homily on Psalm 14," §5 (in *On Christian Doctrine and Practice*); "Ethics," §32.1; Gutierrez, *Theology of Liberation*, 135.

78. One important omission deserves mention: if justice is a matter of treating others in a way that befits their worth, it stands to reason that justice extends far beyond humanity. After all, if nonhuman creation has worth, too, then it, too, deserves to be treated in a way that befits that worth.

79. My thinking here is indebted to Nicholas Wolterstorff, especially his *Justice: Rights and Wrongs; Justice in Love;* and *Journey toward Justice*.

80. Cone, *Black Theology of Liberation*, 99–100.

81. Gutierrez, *Theology of Liberation*, 110; this explains what Gutierrez has in mind when he talks about the "sacrament of the neighbor" (115).

82. Calvin, *Commentaries on the Book of Genesis*, vol. 1, trans. John King (Grand Rapids: Eerdmans, 1948), commenting on Genesis 9:6.

83. Weil, *Gravity and Grace*, trans. Emma Crawford and Marion von der Ruhr (New York: Routledge, 2002 [1952]), 5.

84. For several illustrations of this point, see the stories collected in Marek Halter, *Stories of Deliverance* (Chicago: Open Court, 1998).

85. Wolterstorff, *Journey toward Justice: Personal Encounters in the Global South* (Grand Rapids, MI: Baker, 2013), 4.

86. For a popular account of this, see Gilbert King, *Devil in the Grove: Thurgood Marshall, the Groveland Boys, and the Dawn of a New America* (New York: HarperCollins, 2012).

87. On this point, see King, "Love, Law, and Civil Disobedience" in *A Testament of Hope*, ed. James Washington (New York: HarperCollins, 1986), 45; and Thomas Merton, "Blessed Are the Meek," *Sign of Peace* 8:1 (2009), 15–20.

88. Adams, "Forgiveness," 299; see also Merton, "Blessed Are the Meek," 18.

89. Cone, *Black Theology and Black Power*, 101–2; see also *Black Theology of Liberation*, 139; King, "Nonviolence and Racial Justice," in *Testament*, 9; "The Power of Nonviolence," in *Testament*, 13; and "Love, Law, and Civil Disobedience," 52; Athenagoras, "Plea for the Christians," 12; Ellul, *Violence: Reflections from a Christian Perspective* (New York: Seabury, 1969), 128–29.

90. King, "Nonviolence and Racial Justice," 8–9; see also 19; see also Townes, "Ethics as an Art of Doing the Work Our Souls Must Have," in *Womanist Theological Ethics*, ed. Katie Geneva Cannon, Emilie M. Townes, and Angela D. Sims (Louisville: Westminster John Knox, 2011), 47.

91. King, "The Social Organization of Nonviolence," in *Testament*, 32; Häring, *A Theology of Protest* (New York: Farrar, Straus, and Giroux, 1970), 33.

92. On this point, see Niebuhr, "Love Your Enemies," in *Love and Justice*, ed. D. B. Robertson (Louisville: Westminster John Knox, 1957), 219, 221.

93. Niebuhr, "Why I Leave the F.O.R.," in *Love and Justice*, 258. On the theme of non-retaliation, see Lactantius, *Divine Institutes*, VI.19; on the exceptional permissibility of violence, see Cone, *Black Theology and Black Power*, 143.

94. This is one of the persistent themes in Jeffrey Stout, *Blessed Are the Organized* (Princeton: Princeton University Press, 2010), and Wolterstorff, *Journey toward Justice*, 183–90.

95. I offer an account of how this works in *Theology without Metaphysics*, 275ff.

96. Note well that although prophetic critique is often spoken, it can also be enacted: by drawing injustice into the open, activists can make it visible as injustice and can thus draw attention to the ways in which people are being wronged. Dr. King characterized this sort of approach as *dramatization;* see King, "Nonviolence: The Only Road to Freedom," in *Testament*, 57–58.

97. Townes, "Ethics as an Art," 45–46; Cone, *Black Theology of Liberation*, 62; Gutierrez, *Theology of Liberation*, 152.

98. King, "Letter from Birmingham City Jail," in *Testament*, 293.

99. Cone, *Black Theology and Black Power*, 70; see also *Black Theology of Liberation*, 139–40.

100. Gutierrez, *Theology of Liberation*, 152; see also Gonzalez, *Mañana*, 166.

101. King, "Love, Law, and Civil Disobedience," 48; see also "The Power of Nonviolence," 14; "The Social Organization of Nonviolence," 33.

102. Gutierrez, *Theology of Liberation*, 136.

103. Cone, *Black Theology and Black Power*, 101–2; see also Merton, "Blessed Are the Meek," 15–16; Eberhard Arnold, *God's Revolution* (Walden, NY: Plough, 1997 [1984]), 32, 67.

Chapter Seven. The End

1. For Williams's arguments to this effect, see Bernard Williams, "The Makropulos Case: Reflections on the Tedium of Immortality," in *Problems of the Self* (Cambridge: Cambridge University Press, 1973).

2. I am here focusing on an argument from "Fear, Death, and Confidence," the third lecture in Samuel Scheffler, *Death and the Afterlife*, ed. Niko Kolodny (Oxford: Oxford University Press, 2013).

3. Fischer has argued along these lines in several places, the best known of which is John Martin Fischer, "Why Immortality Is Not So Bad," in *Our Stories: Essays on Life, Death, and Free Will* (Oxford: Oxford University Press, 2009); this essay originally appeared in *International Journal of Philosophical Studies* 2:2 (1994).

4. We find an example of this approach in the young Hegel, who likens such vision to the experience of seeing a blinding light; he writes, accordingly,

that "a person wholly immersed in seeing the sun would be only a feeling of light, would be light-feeling become an entity, so that the opposition of seer and seen, i.e. of subject and object, disappears in the seeing itself" ("Spirit of Christianity and Its Fate," in *Early Theological Writings*, 270).

5. I am obviously not trying to offer an exhaustive description of eternal life, nor do I take myself to be obligated here to do so. There are all sorts of interesting, important questions, therefore, that I am not going to address here—issues having to do, say, with the physics and even the metaphysics of eternal life (what an eternal body might be like, for instance), as well as issues concerning the place of certain particular goods in eternal life (such as sexual desire)—but, again, the claim I am defending does not obligate me to do so.

6. Again, for reasons discussed in chapter 3, I use the term "Father" to refer to the first triune hypostasis.

7. Here I am bending Hegel in the direction of Victorine Trinitarianism.

8. This account thus provides us with a way of cashing out the metaphors in a lovely passage from Teresa of Avila: "Since *my beloved is for me and I for my beloved*," she writes, "who will be able to separate and extinguish two fires so enkindled? It would amount to laboring in vain, for the two fires have become one" ("Soliloquies," 16.4, p. 461).

9. This is important, for as I have argued elsewhere, God could have been God without determining to be God with us, but God could not be God otherwise than as a perfect, loving, triune communion; on this, see my "Immutability, Necessity, and Triunity."

10. Recall here that, within the theological tradition, these ends have themselves been appropriated to the Spirit, which would explain why the Spirit is sometimes identified as the telos or "perfection" of God's triune life.

11. One may reasonably wonder at this point whether or to what extent persons might experience such communion in this life. This is an important question, in response to which I would say that although some persons may directly experience such communion, especially in connection with prayer, what I have said thus far may help us see a more common way of experiencing communion with God: one should be able to experience such communion precisely in the communion one enjoys with others, for if others are devoted to God and thus united with Christ, then in experiencing communion with them, one is experiencing communion with Christ himself and, so, experiencing the communion one will have with God.

12. Augustine, *The City of God against the Pagans*, trans. R. W. Dyson (Cambridge: Cambridge University Press, 1998 [413–426]), XXII.24. See also the much-loved refrain of Julian: "It is true that sin is the cause of all this pain," she writes, "but all will be well, and every kind of thing will be well" (*Showings*, Long Text, chap. 27, a theme echoed in chap. 31).

13. Teresa of Avila, "Soliloquies," 17.4, p. 463.

14. Schleiermacher raises a version of this problem; see Schleiermacher, CF, §163.1.

15. In addition to the figures cited below, my account of abundant life owes much to Mercy Amba Oduyoye, *Introducing African Women's Theology* (Sheffield: Sheffield Academic Press, 2001); Laurenti Magesa, *African Religion: The Moral Traditions of Abundant Life* (Maryknoll, NY: Orbis, 1997); and Kwame Gyekye, *Essay on African Philosophical Thought: The Akan Conceptual Scheme* (Philadelphia: Temple University Press, 1995).

16. For claims to this effect, see Hart, *The Beauty of the Infinite* (Grand Rapids, MI: Eerdmans, 2003), 401 (Hart is here citing Augustine's Letter 138 to Marcellinus); von Balthasar, *Theo-Drama*, vol. 5, trans. Graham Harrison (San Francisco: Ignatius Press, 1998), 485 and 521; and Joseph Ratzinger, *Eschatology: Death and Eternal Life*, trans. Michael Waldstein (Washington, DC, Catholic University of America Press, 1988), 235.

17. On this point, see Augustine, *City of God*, XXII.30.

18. See here Pannenberg, *Systematic Theology*, vol. 3, trans. G. W. Bromiley (Grand Rapids, MI: Eerdmans, 1998), 582–83; von Balthasar, *Theo-Drama*, vol. 5, 487; Moltmann, *The Coming of God*, trans. Margaret Kohl (Minneapolis: Fortress, 1996), 338–39; Ratzinger, *Eschatology*, 238.

19. With respect to God's place in all this, we might think of God as continually creating new gifts, even in eternity.

20. Eternal life could thus be seen as an outworking of Robert Nozick's claims about experiencing "more reality," for which see his *Examined Life: Philosophical Meditations* (New York: Simon and Schuster, 1989), or of Sandra Harding's claims about "strong objectivity," for which see *Whose Science? Whose Knowledge?* (Ithaca, NY: Cornell University Press, 1991).

21. On this point, see Adrienne von Speyr, *Angesicht des Vaters* (Freiburg: Johannes, 1955), 112; Calvin, *Institutes*, III.xxv.10; Hart, *Beauty*, 404–11; von Balthasar, *Theo-Drama*, vol. 5, 485–86, 509–11; Moltmann, *Coming*, 336.

22. For arguments to this effect, see Schleiermacher, CF, §163.2; Augustine, *City of God*, XXII.29.

23. For the latter, see Martha Nussbaum, *The Therapy of Desire: Theory and Practice in Hellenistic Ethics* (Princeton: Princeton University Press, 1994), especially 229.

24. Weber, *Economy and Society: An Outline of Interpretive Sociology*, ed. Guenther Roth and Claus Wittich, vol. 1 (Berkeley: University of California Press, 1978 [1968]), 6.

Index

Index of Biblical Passages

3 John
11; 134

Revelation
21:3, 124

Index of Names and Subjects